11-1.27

LIFE ON THE
ENGLISH MANOR

LIFE ON THE
ENGLISH MANOR

A Study of Peasant Conditions

1150—1400

by

H. S. BENNETT, F.B.A.

Fellow of Emmanuel College, Cambridge

CAMBRIDGE

AT THE UNIVERSITY PRESS

1969

PUBLISHED BY
THE SYNDICS OF THE CAMBRIDGE UNIVERSITY PRESS

Bentley House, 200 Euston Road, London, N.W. 1
American Branch: 32 East 57th Street, New York 22, N.Y.

First edition	*1937*
Reprinted	*1938*
	1948
	1956
	1960
	1962
	1965
	1967
	1969

Printed in the U.S.A.

PREFACE

THIS essay aims at building a little further upon the foundations laid by Maitland and Vinogradoff. Both, being lawyers and philosophers, naturally stressed the legal and abstract point of view. They pierced through the differences to get at the similarities; they were often forced to ignore the actual in order to establish the theoretical. Again and again they ask, "Is this man free, or is he not free?"—a most important question, and we owe them an incalculable debt for their pioneer labours in clearing away much rubbish which the centuries had accumulated about the discussions of peasant status. Yet their preoccupation with this capital question necessarily involved a rigid adherence to strictly legal considerations, and hence the obvious economic differences often involved were frequently outside their investigations. They knew, of course, that a free man with but a few acres of his own was considerably worse off in everything but status than an unfree man, holding his thirty acres or more; but, in general, the bias of their studies caused them to insist on the man's legal freedom, and to ignore his possible economic slavery.

And this, I believe, has had a great influence on the study of medieval peasant life. It has seemed to allow less acute observers to concentrate on legal status, and the natural balance has been disturbed. Our present knowledge of the legal position far outweighs our vaguer conception of the economic and social life in those thousands of English villages and hamlets scattered up and down the countryside. This is the disproportion which I am striving to reduce in the following pages. But, it must be remembered, that vast as are the accumulated records of the Middle Ages in England, they are not particularly favourable to the social historian—more especially to the historian of the illiterate masses who formed some eighty to ninety per cent. of the population of England between 1150 and 1400. "The short and simple annals of the poor" are wellnigh non-existent, and we are forced to piece together our picture from materials that were never meant to serve such a purpose. A modern enquirer, confined to the documents in a big country solicitor's office, would gain a very one-sided view of contemporary English countryside life. And so with the Middle Ages: we have, it is true, a mass of documentary material but how much of it we would willingly abandon for the letters of a thirteenth-century family, who had kept their correspondence as carefully as did the Pastons two centuries later? How many cartularies, or assize rolls, or *compoti* or Manor rolls would we not barter for one brief diary of a peasant of the fourteenth century set down as faithfully as the seventeenth-century diarists recorded their adventures in life and affairs?

Deprived of these, our task is infinitely more difficult, and we can only proceed by the examination of innumerable documents of the most various descriptions, from which we may hope to pick out a phrase or incident, here and there, which will help to lighten some dark corner of the medieval scene. The comparatively safe waters of legal status and the like, so well charted for us by Maitland, Vinogradoff, and others, must be left for the open seas, where the bald legal phrases of court roll and terrier on the one hand, and snatches of ballads, or biased *fabliaux*, or *ex parte* pleas on the other, represent our poor sailing directions.

And even such directions as these would have been infinitely harder to come by had I not been able to rely on the aid of others to help me in my search. The Bibliography will sufficiently indicate the main sources from which my evidence has been drawn. Manuscript materials abound: the only difficulty is how to use them. The masses of documents available at the Public Record Office, for example, have yielded up but a fraction of their secrets: a lifetime spent among them would only scratch the surface. Both there, and at the British Museum, expert help, so generously given by the officials, enabled me to do much that would otherwise have been impossible. Here, in Cambridge, my indebtedness is overwhelming: the staff of the University Library (and in particular Mr H. L. Pink, in charge of the Anderson Room); many College Librarians (especially Mr H. M. Adams of Trinity); the Secretary of the University Press, the University Printer and their assistants, as well as many friends and scholars, have all come to my aid on many occasions. Among them I must mention Mrs G. G. Coulton, Miss H. M. Cam, Dr F. M. Page, Professor Eileen Power, Mr W. S. Mansfield, Mr R. H. Robbins, Professor A. Hamilton Thompson and Mr E. Welbourne. Nor must I neglect to thank the Council of Trinity College for very kindly allowing me to reproduce pictures from several manuscripts in the possession of the College, nor the Master and Fellows of Sidney Sussex College for depositing their Abbots Langley rolls in the University Library for my use.

My greatest debts, however, have still to be recorded. In the Preface to *The Pastons and their England*, published in 1921, I wrote: "Finally, two names remain. Dr G. G. Coulton, the general editor of the series, has given of his time, his thought and his learning unstintingly to this study. In other directions I am almost equally indebted to my wife. To both I owe more than I can express here." The years between have immeasurably deepened my indebtedness to both. To one of them I owe the suggestion from which this study originated: to the other, as a token of my manifold indebtedness, I have dedicated this book.

H. S. BENNETT

August 1937

NOTE ON THE THIRD IMPRESSION

I have taken the opportunity which a reprint affords to make a few minor corrections in the text. In addition, one or two longer comments, which could not easily be inserted into the body of the book, are printed here:

p. 5, *line* 10. The statement that "no hedges or fences were to be seen" is too sweeping. The grass crops, of course, needed to be fenced off from the cattle, and there were several months when protection for the recently sown or young crops, as well as for the full-grown crops, was needed.

p. 44, *line* 10. The presence of "raised balks of unploughed land" is disputed by many scholars. They were not a regular feature of the French common fields, and I am now inclined to think that our knowledge of their presence in England is not sufficient to justify what is said in line 10.

p. 81, line 6. From the end of the thirteenth century peas were often sown like other field crops, and not dibbled.

p. 130, *line* 23. The free man also, if he held any land by villein tenure, owed suit of mill to the lord. Again, he might rent land under the condition, specified by the lord, of doing suit to the mill, but here it would be the special contract that bound him, not manorial custom.

January, 1947   H. S. B.

CONTENTS

CONTENTS

Chapter XII   The Church   319-336

Importance of the Church in medieval life—Peasant's attitude to religion—
The village church—The services—Art and symbolism—"Dumb dogs"—
Status of clergy—Their education—Their stipends—Limited capabilities of
the ordinary peasant-priest—Worldly occupations of the clergy—Tithe—
Visitation records and the parish clergy—The good priest and his influence—
"The Mother of us all"

ILLUSTRATIONS

With one exception, the illustrations (including those re-cut in wood) have been selected from the magnificent collection of illuminated manuscripts in the Library of Trinity College, Cambridge, and are here reproduced by the permission of the College Council.

PLATES

WOODCUTS

DEDICATORY LETTER

TO

G. G. COULTON

My dear Coulton,

It is now almost nineteen years since I was thrown up at Cambridge as a part of the refuse of war, and first entered your lecture-room. There, during that memorable autumn, while our troops were steadily advancing, I heard you speak of the Middle Ages, and realised what they could reveal to a mind and imagination worthy of understanding them. Under your inspiring guidance I turned to study one part of the medieval scene in detail, and *The Pastons and their England* was the result; and from that, in due time, I began the investigations which are the subject of the present study.

But you do not need to be told that a busy University lecturer and teacher has no longer the freedom of an ardent research student, nor that my task has been interrupted again and again since then. Indeed, I doubt if it would ever have been finished, but for your constant inspiration and encouragement—an encouragement not limited to my special studies alone. You will remember how Lord Bryce speaks of J. R. Green's inspection of some new town, "darting hither and thither through the streets like a dog following a scent". That phrase of his has frequently come to my mind, in our many travels together, as I have watched you making a first survey of some new town. How many times we have hastily dropped our bags at the first hotel; and then, despite the call of the dinner-bell, at once you have led us at a rapid pace through the streets, and with a quick glance here and there, and at times a halt, have thrust aside the modern additions, and have revealed the essentials of the medieval town! Wherever we have been together, you have always interpreted the medieval world for me as no one else can do, and have encouraged me to see the past in the present, even in Alpine châlet or French hamlet.

Hence almost every page in this book speaks of some experience shared together: our talks of the medieval church on the hills above Ballaigues and looking across to Mont Blanc; our pilgrimages to churches and villages in Normandy, Provence and the Morvan; our daily labours, side by side, at La Forclaz (while the June snows and biting winds raged without); and, most constantly, of course, our innumerable walks and talks by the side of the Cam.

So I dedicate to you what is in every valuable respect your own; well knowing that you will welcome what is good in it as a little step forward in the studies which we both have at heart; and, above all, hoping that you will regard it as a token of abiding gratitude and affection from your pupil and friend.

H. S. B.

August 1937

PROLOGUE

A faire felde ful of folke

A FAIRE FELDE FUL OF FOLKE

THE writing of a book on medieval life necessitates the scrutiny, assembly, and arrangement of innumerable documents and pieces of evidence, from which, by slow degrees, some coherent pictures emerge. In this way a writer is enabled to build up a series of studies, each revealing some facet of his subject. But, while this enables him to put these various aspects into focus the more clearly, it is apt to divert him from what many will hold to be his chief duty—to see life steadily and see it whole, and to present this vision to his readers. Such a vision, however, is even more difficult to communicate than it is to receive. It is comparatively easy to assemble detailed accounts of various sides of the peasant's life, but each of these accounts must deal with the mass, so that the individual tends to recede into the background. Yet it is as an individual human being, living his normal life, that he is of interest.

Thomas Hardy's poem, *In Time of " The Breaking of Nations "*, tells us of his fundamental place in the scheme of things:

> Only a man harrowing clods
> In a slow silent walk
> With an old horse that stumbles and nods
> Half asleep as they stalk.
> Only thin smoke without flame
> From the heaps of couch-grass;
> Yet this will go onward the same
> Though Dynasties pass.

This is the man our ideal picture would show us. Short of this, in an attempt to show what I believe to have been his normal life, I make bold at the outset of this book to draw an imaginary picture of one such man during a few days of the year. In doing so, I have not chosen one of the most well-to-do of the manorial peasants, nor do I forget that many lacked even the rudimentary comforts and the limited possessions which this man had. And although my picture is frankly imaginary, it is based on a wealth of definite evidence and backed up by an almost equal wealth of suggestions and hints, none of them in themselves clear or weighty enough, perhaps, to be vouched as evidence, but, nevertheless, possessed of a cumulative power which could not be denied.

The sun rose early, for it was late June, but not much earlier than the peasants of the little village of Belcombe, in the year 1320. As the light strengthened, bit by bit the village became visible, and the confused medley, in which here a roof and there a bit of wall stood out, began to arrange itself as a narrow street with flimsy houses dotted about in little groups. In the centre of it all the stone-built church loomed up high and very new-looking above everything about it, and made the peasants' houses appear small and insignificant. On closer view, the village was seen to radiate from the church and down each of the winding ways that led up to it the peasants had built their homes. There they stood, some neat and trim, with their thatched roofs and roughly finished walls in good repair, while others were dilapidated and showed evident signs of neglect and decay. The larger houses stood a little back from the lane, so that the ground in front of each of them was roughly enclosed and set with young cabbage, onions and parsley, and here and there a few herbs were growing along the sides of the pathway to the house. Most of them had a rudely constructed shed or lean-to at the back of the house, and running away from this stretched another enclosed piece of ground. This was mainly broken up and planted with vegetables, and both here and in the rough grass beyond there were a few apple and cherry trees. At the bottom of the garden where it ran down to the stream the pigs had their styes, and any villager fortunate enough to own a cow tethered it there in among the rankly growing grass. Smaller houses had meagre plots about them, with sparse room for cabbage or onion, and only rarely a pig or a few fowls.

Within most of these houses men were stirring, and before long began to appear at their cottage doors, taking a look at the sky before they ate a brief meal (if such it might be called) of a lump of bread and a draught of ale. Then they came out again, fetched their scythes and rakes from the sheds, and started off down the street, so that for a few minutes the noisy chatter and greetings of neighbours broke the silence. They soon passed by the church and came out into open country, for no hedges or fences were to be seen. One large tract, however, had clearly been cultivated recently, for as they passed they saw how it was divided into narrow plots, each with grassy raised strips dividing it from its neighbours. Now, however, this field was fallow, and, early as it was, one of their fellows was there before them, and was guarding the sheep which were quietly feeding on such sparse vegetation as was to be found, for the first ploughing had already taken place, and next month any weeds the sheep might leave would all be ploughed in.

A little farther on they passed a stone cross. Almost unconsciously (some even in perfunctory fashion) they crossed themselves, and a moment later turned from the main path to follow a track which led to a piece of meadow land. This, unlike the fallow, was enclosed on three sides with a hedge, whilst a little stream formed its other boundary. On entering the field the peasants broke up in little groups, some going to one and some to another part of the meadow, for amongst the long grass there were little pegs and twigs marking off one portion of the field from another. By this time the sun was well up and the dew was drying rapidly as they prepared for work. The wide blade of the scythe was sharpened with the whetstone, and then they turned, and with rhythmic movement began to mow the grass in wide sweeping swathes.

In one corner of the field John Wilde and his two sons, Richard and Roger, kept to their task for some time without pause. The younger son moved steadily across the strip, turning the hay which had been cut on the previous morning, while his brother Richard worked on side by side with his father at the mowing. Save for a pause when the scythes were re-sharpened they worked without resting and with but little to say, for there was much to do and time was short, since this was Sunday, and ere long they would have to leave their work for Mass. Indeed, they were fortunate to be on the field at all on such a day, but Sir William, their vicar, had always been lenient in times of harvest; and, although he looked with concern at such work, he did not absolutely forbid it, so long as the Mass itself were not neglected. So all three continued until the sun was getting well up in the heavens, when they stopped their work and left the field together with many others. As they passed the church John glanced at the Mass clock on its wall near the door, and saw by the shadow of its style that they had good time before the service, as it was not yet eight.

During their absence the house had not been untended, and after a while the good wife Agnes and her daughter Alice appeared from a room which led out of the main living room. Alice ran out in the garden close, and soon the clucking of the hens was heard, and a little later she returned and set down on the wooden bench inside the door a rough earthenware jar of milk which she had just taken from the cow. Meanwhile, her mother had brushed up the embers and had piled together the kindling and a few logs, and already a fire was burning cleanly, and over it hung a large metal pot of water. Then she and her daughter went into the small inner room, which was cleaner and less sooty than its neighbour, and pulled back the thick coverlets and remade the only two beds that stood there. Once this was done, the rough earthen floors of both rooms were swept out with a brush of large twigs, and then the trestle-table was put in its place near the side of the room. Some bread and a little ale satisfied Agnes' hunger, while Alice took a drink of the milk she had just brought in. All being done, they turned to prepare for

Mass. A large wooden tub on the trestle-table served for a wash-bowl, and after a little washing they occupied themselves for some time in plaiting and arranging their hair, before they drew out of a wooden chest, that stood at the foot of the bed, the bright coloured dresses which they wore only on Sundays and festivals. There were other childish garments in the chest, but they had not been worn these many days, for they were those of the two little girls, both dead now for ten years and more, one of the plague, and one lost by what the coroner called "misadventure". What this was exactly her mother never knew; for, while she was at play, she had fallen from the bridge over the big river, but no one could be found to say what had taken her so far from home, or how the end had come. Other children there had been, but like so many others they had died at birth or very soon after, and were no more than distant memories.

The return of the men-folk threw the cottage into confusion, for there was little room, and they all tried to wash and dress themselves for Mass at the same time. It did not take them long, however—the old "tabard" or sleeveless smock with all its traces of weekday work ("baudy tabard" Chaucer called it) was discarded for that kept for Sundays and special occasions, and they were ready. The bell was already ringing, and they moved off and were soon joined by friends and neighbours as they made their short journey to the church. John noticed that the low wall which enclosed the church and the graveyard was rapidly breaking down in several places: for many months now it had been cracking and stones falling away from it here and there, but nothing had been done to repair it, in spite of the archdeacon's periodical warnings. On two or three occasions John had noticed that pigs and sheep had wandered into the graveyard itself and had started to graze among the tombs. But he had little time to reflect on this, for his neighbours were pressing into the church since the time for service had come, and even the men-folk, who habitually lingered outside in little groups till the last moment, had turned to go in.

So he entered with his wife through that selfsame door at which they had stood when the priest had married them over twenty-five years ago. They touched the holy water, and crossed themselves as they moved into the nave, and there they parted to take up their places on either side of the aisle. They remained standing, as there were not yet even rudimentary seats or pews for them, for this was not one of the richest village churches. Only behind the chancel-screen were there any seats, but these were reserved for the clergy, although the lord of Hemings Manor and his family, when they were at the manor house, were also privileged to seat themselves there. Hubert Longfellow, the parish clerk, was the only other parishioner who had his seat within the chancel, and that because he was a bachelor. His predecessor had been a married man, and therefore, although he was in Minor Orders, he was kept out and had to stand with the ordinary congregation in the nave.

While they were waiting an animated conversation was going on, but at last Sir William, the vicar, entered followed by the parish clerk, and for a moment the congregation was still. As the service began, however, many resumed their whisperings and mutterings, while some lounged by pillars and seemed to be taking but small notice of the service. The priest's voice droned on: here and there it was raised for a moment while he intoned a prayer, or while he and the clerk sang their versicles and brief responses. But, for the most part, even the keenest ear could catch little more than an unintelligible murmur, interspersed with a *Dominus vobiscum*, or *Oremus*, or *Amen*, which, by countless repetitions, had familiarised itself to the ear. Even in those churches where traditionally the priest read the service aloud, it was not audible even to a Latinist, and the village congregation rarely had any such lettered person among its number. So the service went on its way, and John meditated awhile. It was all very familiar to him, for ever since he was a child he had faithfully attended the Sunday Mass—now these fifty years and more—and, when his lord's service did not forbid it, he frequently came on holy-days as well. He understood little, but yet there was something about it all that was dear to him. He knew that in some mysterious way Christ's body was made anew at this service: the bell would ring while the priest prayed, and then, after a pause, Sir William would then hold up before them all the blessed bread and wine now made God. But that great moment had not yet come, and his thoughts wandered as he looked about him in the high-roofed church. For a moment his eyes fell on the painting of the Last Judgment which had recently been renewed on the wall over the chancel arch. It fascinated him to contemplate the calm and severe majesty of Christ, as He sat enthroned in glory and meting out doom. The ecstasy of the saved as they were caught up in the arms of the angels, or the three naked souls cosily nestling in Abraham's bosom, were so vividly portrayed that his eyes lingered on them, and only with reluctance turned to gaze on those damned souls, who stood on the left hand of the throne of grace, and in varying attitudes of pleading, fear and bewilderment expressed their horrible condition. Others, even more fearful to behold, were already enduring the tortures destined for them, as the devils savagely seized them with flesh-hooks and pitched them into the cauldron and the everlasting fire.

Other pictures painted on the walls also told their story, and recalled to him fragments of sermons and tales, especially some of those told in the vivid and understandable language of a passing friar. Their own priest had no such gift. Indeed, how should he have such powers? The marvel was that now, at this very minute, the Latin phrases were flowing from his lips and he was God's minister to them all. Yet he had been born in this self-same village, and was the youngest brother of John's own wife Agnes. He had always been about the church as a boy, and was taught how to read and to sing the service by their old priest Sir John Walters. Then, he had become the holy-water carrier, and, little by little, had learnt all Sir John could teach him, and had been sent away to school. And now, here he was, back in the parish, and living in the vicar's house with its garden and stone wall round it, hard by the church, and standing at the head of them all. As John looked at him he recalled some of his kindly actions: no parishioner was too distant for him to visit if need arose, and no one led a more model life than he. "If gold rust, what shall iron do?", was his watchword, and he taught his flock more by what he was than by anything he was able to say. All men knew him to be their friend, and yet there was something about him which forbade men to be too familiar. Even his sister regarded him with the awe born of more than one snibbing he had administered to her, and which her conscience admitted to be just.

By this time, however, the Creed had been said, and Sir William had come from the altar steps to the door of the rood-screen. He looked grave, for it was but seldom that he attempted to teach his flock in a set discourse, rather than by short explanations of the main points of the Faith. But the bishop was constantly urging upon the clergy the need for more sermons, and he must obey. As he waited, his people settled themselves down, most of them squatting in the rushes which covered the floor, while a few lounged against the pillars and seemed to care little for what was to come. When all were settled, he reminded them of earlier sermons he had preached at intervals on the seven deadly sins, and then turned to speak of the fourth of these, namely sloth. Slothfulness kept men from church, and encouraged them to be inattentive at Mass, and to put off the day of repentance till it was too late. All this, as he said, would inevitably have to be paid for in purgatory, unless they were truly penitent and shriven. Not only in church, but in ordinary worldly affairs, idleness was to be shunned, and young men and women should be made to work and serve their masters with love and cheerfulness. Therefore, parents must chastise naughty children, or they would grow up idle and disobedient as were the sons of Eli. The tale of the death of the prophet and his two sons followed, and Sir William concluded his short sermon by bidding his hearers to think on Eli

PLATE I

" The three naked souls "

Asking the way

and his sons, and to chastise their children, and to see they learnt to labour well and truly while there was yet time, and further to think how best to labour for their souls as well as their bodies. All this was listened to in comparative quiet, although a few took but little notice of the discourse, and kept up a desultory conversation among themselves; and throughout the nave there was more whispering and occasional chatter than Sir William liked to hear, but he was powerless to stop it, for no one could remember when a little talking or even joking in church had been forbidden. When the sermon was ended he went back to the altar, and the service continued. Ere long the ringing of the bell called even the most inattentive to their devotions, since the great moment of the Mass had now come. *Paternoster*, *Ave* and Creed were all that John could say, but these he repeated again and again; and later, when he heard the priest intoning the *Paternoster*, he joined in heartily. Then, while Sir William was rinsing his holy vessels, he prayed silently again until the service came to an end with its *Ite, missa est*, and after the priest had retired, he too rose to leave. Many "sons of Belial" had not waited so long, and had hurried off, as soon as the communion had been finished, as if they had seen not God but the Devil, for some wanted to get to their work again, while others were only concerned to cross the green to the ale-house where they might refresh themselves and gossip at their ease.

Once out in the churchyard again John stopped to talk with his neighbours. One group was looking with interest at the platform, which was as yet but half-erected, at the one end of the churchyard. Here, in a week's time, they would see the actors from the neighbouring town, as well as some of their own folk performing in the Miracle Plays. Hubert, the parish clerk, was particularly skilful, and all remembered his performance as Herod, "that moody King", two years before, and also how masterful it had been. Besides this, however, there had been much to amuse them in the rough boisterous performances of many of the actors. They hoped to see Cain bullying his boy at the plough and ranting at his brother Abel, or Pilate shouting and raging as he had done the last time the plays had come. On the other hand, John recalled the affecting scenes in which the players had presented to them many of the poignant moments of the Gospel story, and he and his mates discussed with zest the scenes they would like to see again.

When he left this group he was stopped by two neighbours who wanted him to join with them in some work waiting to be done on their strips which lay side by side in the great east field. This he promised to do towards the end of the week when he had carried his hay; and, with a parting look at the sundial, he moved from the churchyard, and caught up his wife and daughter near their home. Agnes was full of news she had gleaned from her gossips: Cicely Wode was to marry John Freman of the neighbouring town, and she and her old mother were to leave the manor as soon as the marriage could take place. Matilda, the reeve's daughter, was in trouble, and would be accused at the next Manor Court of incontinency. Agnes Atwater had scalded her legs badly by overturning a vat of boiling water in her brew-house—and so on.

They soon reached their cottage; and, while the women-folk went indoors to prepare the midday meal John went behind the house and down to the bottom of the close where the pig was kept. He emptied into the trough the remainder of a bucket containing some sour milk and scraps of household waste, and pulled up a few rank-growing weeds and threw them into the trough. Then he turned to his garden and worked at this and that, for he had a good conscience, and his brother-in-law, Sir William, took a reasonable view of the Fourth Commandment. At last Roger came to call him in to dinner. Meanwhile, Agnes and her daughter had been busy in the house. The fire had been made up, and the large pot, in which the soup of peas and beans had been prepared on the previous day, was hung over it and heated. The trestle-table was now standing in the middle of the room, and the beechen bowls and spoons arranged on it. A few

mugs and an earthen jug filled with good ale stood ready, for
John was not one of those landless labourers in whom it was
presumptuous to drink anything more than penny ale. They all
sat down, and soon were supping noisily the thick pottage and
eating with it large hunks of a dark coloured bread. A good lump
of home-made green[1] cheese followed, and with this and mugs
of the good ale they made their simple meal.

There was much to be done in the garden at this time of year,
and John and his sons spent part of the afternoon in weeding and
thinning out their cabbages. Some of their neighbours returned
to the meadows and continued their haymaking, but John knew
how much Sir William disliked this, and how often he had
spoken against Sunday work, unless it were absolutely necessary
to avoid spoiling the crop. Hence he stayed at home, and did a
little here and there to clear things up in his garden. In this way
the afternoon wore on, and when John went into the house he
found that his wife and daughter had gone off to Vespers at the
church. Sir William liked to see a good congregation at this
service, especially on Sundays, and most of the women, and a
considerable number of men, attended this short simple service
as the day began to close. John's sons, however, had but little
thought for this, for they were more interested in the pleasure
they hoped for a little later in the evening, and after a while
both left the house to forgather with their companions. When
Agnes returned, the evening meal was soon on the table, for
as it was Sunday they had already eaten the most substantial
meal of the day. Now they fared on a few eggs, a bit of oatcake
and some cheese. Both the women drank milk, but John refused
this, and said he preferred a mug of ale since some still remained
of his wife's last brewing.

As the shadows lengthened they left the house, and a short
walk brought them on to the green, which looked at its best in
the evening light, and already many of the villagers were there.
Soon, to the sound of a rebeck and pipe the dancing began, for

[1] Green=fresh, new.

here again Sir William's moderate and friendly rule did not prohibit the dance, although he had a sharp word for any whose behaviour on these occasions seemed to call for correction. The measures were simple, and were trodden with an unaffected grace which seemed to recall a happier and more innocent age—far removed from the toil and difficulties of everyday life. Young men and maidens with linked hands went through the evolutions of the dance and smiled one at the other, and "dallied with the innocence of love". Yet, even so, there were some matrons who looked on with but half-approving eye, as if underneath the seeming innocence there lurked who knew what dangers? Agnes, partly from native prudery and partly as Sir William's sister, would not let Alice join in the dances, although her friends called to her from time to time, and she darted envious eyes on Joan and Cicely as they moved in concert to the music. Even while they stood there the airs seemed to grow a little less restrained, and very soon Alice and her mother moved away towards home. The dances, however, went on, and as dusk fell and journeys to the ale-house on the edge of the green became more common, the shrill cries of the rebeck were answered by the shrill cries and laughter of the girls, and by the lower laughter and snatches of song of some of the men. John watched all this with an indulgent eye, and sat for a while with some of his cronies on the ale-house bench, and listened to the shouts and sounds of revelry coming from within the devil's chapel, as a friar had once called it, in a sermon which told of how three men, after drinking and dicing there, had set off to find Death so that they might slay him, and of what had befallen them. The noise within grew louder: "there was laughing and lowering, and 'let the cup go'", and at last Clement Cooke, notorious in the village for his inability to carry his liquor, got up to go

...like a gleeman's bitch,
Sometimes aside and sometimes backwards,
Like one who lays lures to lime wild-fowl.
As he drew to the door all dimmed before him,
He stumbled on the threshold and was thrown forwards.

John thought it was time for him also to get home, for there was a good day's work to do with the hay on the morrow, and with a "Good-night" to his friends set off quickly. He soon came to the church, which seemed very tall and new in the fast fading light, and then, in a few minutes, he was once again at his door. The house was dark, since for some time now their scanty stock of rush-lights had been spent, though this was of small moment for they were seldom to be found out of bed long after dusk. He turned to go in, when a glance down the street showed him Walter, the beadle, going from door to door. He knew well what that meant, and had half feared his coming, so that he waited only for a moment while Walter called out to him that the lord had asked for a "love-boon" on the morrow. His own hay, he reflected, would have to wait, and with a last look at the sky and a hope for a few fine days, he went in and closed the door.

The next morning saw another early start, for John knew well the Lord Prior's officers would be on the look-out for late-comers; and indeed, it was only a few years since they had tried to insist on every one appearing at dawn. Though that had been declared contrary to the custom of the manor when it had been discussed at the Manor Court, and therefore had been quietly dropped, nevertheless, it was still unwise to appear much later than the neighbours. So John roused up the two boys, and Alice as well, for on these days every one, save the housewife, had to appear, and help with the lord's hay. As they started they soon met many neighbours: it was a far larger party than that of yesterday, all making their way to the lord's great meadow (for on this manor all the Prior's pasture was in one immense field) which lay in the little valley to the west of the village, and through the midst of which the streamlet flowed so sweetly. Soon after they arrived they had been divided up into groups, and placed in different parts of the field by the reeve and the hayward, who bustled about from place to place to see that all was well and that work was beginning in good earnest.

So to the music of whetstone striking on scythe the work began, and the mowers bent to their task, sweeping down the grass in wide swathes, as they slowly moved from side to side of the piece allotted to them. John was glad to see old William Honiset already in the field. He could no longer use a scythe, but he was very crafty in the straightening and sharpening of obstinate blades, and the whole day long sat under a great beech tree in one corner of the field with hammer and stone and put a new edge on many a scythe before nightfall. As the sun rose higher and higher the blades swung to and fro, while up and down the field moved a man, with a stave in his hand, whose duty it was to oversee the workers. John looked at him as he passed, recalling his own early days, and how often he and the father of this man who now stood over him had worked together in this very meadow, for they had been partners, or "marrows", as the country people termed it, and so did whatever was possible to help one another. But, in his old age, his friend had bought his freedom at a great price, for he had paid to the Lord Prior six marks of silver, the savings of a lifetime, and as much as the yearly income of Sir William, the vicar, himself. Now, therefore, his son was free of everything except a few small services from time to time, of which this was one.

The workers paused to sharpen their scythes, or for a momentary rest, or better still to listen while some belated arrival poured his tale into the ear of an incredulous reeve, or while some careless fellow, who was working in lazy or incompetent fashion, was soundly berated by the hayward. At other moments, again, there was a most welcome respite, for this was fortunately a "wet boon", and old Alice atte Mere, who had only a tiny cot on the edge of the village, held it on the homely tenure of carrying ale to the workers at these boons. Hence, she was continuously going to and fro from the manor house for reinforcements of ale which the thirsty labourers seemed to consume almost as soon as it was doled out to them. Although this was only the drink rationed out to the manorial servants, and was not exactly the corny ale—the *melior cerevisia*—brewed for the brethren of the priory, yet, perhaps this *secunda cerevisia* was a more prudent drink for the labourers, and certainly it seemed doubly delicious in the heat of the day. Steadily the work went on till wellnigh noon, when at last the hayward's horn was heard. John straightened himself, and made for the shade with his companions. There they threw themselves down, and soon the manor servants appeared, some carrying great loaves and cheeses, while others brought the ever-welcome barrels of ale. John and his family were given four of the loaves for themselves, and as they cut them open they saw that these were the good wheaten loaves, which so seldom came their way. They ate ravenously of these and of the cheese after their six hours in the open air, and called again and again for ale, of which there was no stint, for this was one of the few days of the year on which the customal specified that they were to "drink at discretion".

After this meal there was a short welcome rest, and then they went back to the field once more. Steadily the work went on, and from time to time the now tiring mowers looked at the sky, and watched the slow course of the sun over the big trees which bordered the field. The girls and women busied themselves in raking and turning the first cut hay, while the officials were moving busily from place to place trying to keep the workers at their tasks. At last the long-awaited sound of the hayward's horn was heard, and in a few minutes the field was deserted, and old and young were making their way and chattering together as they went towards the manor house. The toil of the day was over, and all that remained was the good evening meal that the Lord Prior always gave them as a reward for their labours. As they reached the manor house they saw that one of the large outhouses had been made ready with trestle-tables down the centre and at the sides of the building, and platters and mugs were soon laid out ready for the repast. In the courtyard the great cauldrons were steaming, and the hungry people were busy carving into hunks the remainder of their midday loaves. Soon the manorial servants brought in the cauldrons, and a mess of thick pease pottage was served out, to which had been added a little meat for flavouring. This, and a draught of ale, took the sharp edge off their hunger, and they awaited with pleasurable anticipation the next course. The winter had been a hard one, and few of them had been able to buy flesh, or to expect more than a bit of boiled bacon from time to time. Some could afford to keep but few chickens or geese, and had to exist as best they might on their scanty produce, and on cheese and curds, with oatmeal cake or thick oatmeal pottage to satisfy their ever-hungry children. This and a sour bread of peas and beans had been the lot of many for several months, so that the entry of the servants with great dishes of roast meat caused a hum of satisfaction to go up around the room. Each group tackled the portion set down before them with eagerness, and with many a call to a friend here and a joke with a neighbour at another table, the meal wore on. Ale flowed liberally, and there was " cheese at call " for those who were still hungry. When some of the women showed signs of wishing to leave, the hayward blew his horn for silence, and the reeve announced that if the weather remained fine there would be two more boons on the Wednesday and the following Monday, and by then he hoped all the hay would be cut and carried into the great manor courtyard. Little by little the company dispersed, most of them ready enough to get home and do whatever was necessary about the house before they went to bed. John and his family walked back together, and saw as they passed their own meadow that Agnes had been at work during the day. The hay that was dry had been raked up into small cocks, and she had turned most of that which had only been cut the previous morning.

Much of their time in the next few days was spent by the peasants either on the lord's hayfield or on their own. John had but little more to cut on his allotted portion, and all was done by the Wednesday evening. The following Friday he and his boys spent the afternoon in loading it onto a wagon they borrowed from a friend, Roget the ox pulled it home, and they stored it away in the little shed behind the house.

What little time John and his sons had from the haymaking seemed to go all too rapidly in a variety of tasks. The work which he had promised to do in the east field with his neighbours took up the Thursday afternoon, and besides this they were hard at work on an "assart" or clearing they were making near the edge of the great wood. The prior had granted this to John only the previous autumn; and, although it was but three acres in extent, the work of grubbing up the furze and briars and cleaning the land so that they could sow it this coming autumn seemed endless. Richard spent all the time he could at this, for he hoped one day to make this plot the site of a home for himself, since he was now fully grown and eager to marry Johanna, the daughter of William Sutton, an old friend of his father.

The other two days of work on the lord's meadow passed much like the first, except that there was no ale provided at the second boon, for it was a "dry-reap", but they had to work only till midday. The last boon, however, surpassed all the rest, for not only was there ale again, but other pleasures as well. As the last load was carried from the field the hayward loosed a sheep in their midst. All watched this poor frightened beast with interest, for if it remained quietly grazing they could claim it for a feast of their own, but if it wandered out of the field they lost it, and it remained the lord's property. As they looked on, restraining the children from noise or sudden movement, the sheep gazed around and then began to eat what it could find. Little did it think how in lingering over this Esau's mess it had sealed its fate.

All was not yet over, however. Indeed, many thought the best was yet to come, and John and the other householders next moved off to a part of the field where the reeve stood by a very large cock of hay. Everyone knew what was to be done, and no one wished to be the first to start. At last the reeve called on Robert Day to begin, and with a sly look at some of his neighbours he gathered together a great mass of hay, and rapidly

bound it into a bundle. Then, carefully placing his scythe-head
under the bundle, he slowly raised it from the ground amidst the
encouraging cries of the onlookers. Others were not so fortunate,
and some through greed or lack of skill were unable to raise the
load without letting the scythe-handle touch the ground, or still
more unfortunate, without breaking the handle altogether. Accompanied by the laughter and rude criticisms of their fellows,
they retired in confusion. So the ceremony went on till all had
had a sporting chance. Once this was over the farm servants
rapidly forked the remainder into a small cart, and accompanied
by the reeve and hayward left the field. John and his friends,
bearing their trophies aloft in victory, started happily for home.
For them it was a moment for rejoicing: the three "boons" were
over, and they knew that there were no further calls to be made
on them beyond the weekly service that went on from year end
till year end. Not before the Gules of August would any extra
works be again demanded of them.

Their happiness, however, was a little dashed within a few
minutes, for as they rounded a corner a small cavalcade rapidly
drew towards them. As the riders came nearer, John and his
friends recognised them, and when the party reached them all
the peasants doffed their hats and louted low, for the imperious
looking man who rode at their head, clothed in flowing garments
of fine black cloth, was none other than the cellarer himself. Two
others of the brethren rode just behind him, followed by two
servants. A few moments later John overtook old Margery who
had been at work at the Manor Court all day strewing the rooms
with rushes, and making the beds with sheets and counterpanes
—for these great ones demanded every comfort. On the morrow
the Manor Court would be held, and much time would be lost,
so John and his friends hurried on to do what they could
overnight.

On the next morning John was up and about his close from an
early hour, and this kept him busy until it was time to go to the
Manor Court. He called his two sons, for it was no ordinary

court, but a Leet Court, at which all over twelve years of age were bound to attend. Thus they started out, and reached the manor house a little before eight, and waited about outside chatting aimlessly with their friends. At last the beadle came out, and summoned them all into the court room. They entered, and found themselves in a long panelled room with a fine timber roof which showed up well from the light that streamed in from the large east window, as well as from the smaller mullioned windows on either side. They took up their places on the rush-strewn floor, and chattered away until the reeve and hayward entered, followed by the beadle, whose command for silence was still echoing in the hall when the cellarer entered from a side door at the west end of the room. He took his seat on a raised dais with his clerk by his side, and after the clerk had unfolded the great parchment Court Roll, and had begun to write with his quill the day and year of the Court, the cellarer nodded, and the beadle cried out an "Oyez" thrice repeated, and ordered all who had business and owed service to the Lord Prior of Honiwell to draw near.

At once several men stepped forward: one asked for a neigh-bour to be excused attendance since he was sick in bed; another pleaded that his friend was absent in the King's wars, while others told the cellarer that their man was unable to attend for various reasons, and pledged themselves to produce him at the next Court. All these facts were noted by the clerk on his roll, and then the reeve was told to put forward his pleas. First, he presented Roger le Bacheler to the cellarer, and said that he asked permission to take over the land of Alice Tunstall since she was a widow with no children, and could not work the twenty acres which were her holding. The cellarer allowed this, and told Roger that he might hold the land at the same rent and services as had Alice's husband, and that he would have to pay 6s. 8d. as a fine for entry. Since he willingly agreed to this, he was called forward, and the cellarer formally admitted him to the holding, handing him, in token of the exchange, a white wand

This done, Roger fell on his knees, and placing his hands between those of the cellarer, swore "so help me God and all His Saints" that from this day forth he would be true and faithful to the Lord Prior, and should owe fealty for the land which he held of him in villeinage, and that he would be justified by him in body and goods, and would not take himself off the lord's manor.

Next, the reeve told a long tale of many dilapidations that had accrued since the last Court: some houses were falling into serious disrepair; the path outside certain cottages was continuously foul; many men had taken timber from the Lord Prior's wood without leave; three men.... So he droned on, and John paid but slight attention, for he was not conscious of having broken any of the manorial laws, and only noticed with dismay that the name of his brother Henry was constantly mentioned. All these matters took but a short time, for no one denied his guilt, and a fine of twopence or threepence was generally imposed by the cellarer. The reeve then told the cellarer of the misdemeanours of several men at the recent haymaking—of their late-coming, their laziness or their impudence. These received short shrift, and were fined twopence each, all except Richard Cook, who spoke opprobrious words to the cellarer, for which he was sternly rebuked and fined sixpence. Lastly, the reeve brought forward Thomas Attegate, who told the cellarer how his son was eager for book-learning, and how Sir William thought so well of him that he wanted to send him to the grammar school in the near-by town if this were allowed. After some questions the cellarer gave his consent, on the assurance that the boy wished to devote himself to learning in the hope of rising to the dignity of the priesthood in due course. His father thanked the cellarer in halting words, and paid the sixpence demanded of him for the permission, and then fell back among his fellows once more.

After this the beadle called for the tithing men to come forward and make their reports. Each in his turn told the steward of how matters stood in so far as he was responsible. William Sleford presented that Richard Tubbing and Johanna atte Grene were common brewers and had broken the prior's orders about the sale of ale, and they were each fined twelvepence. John Morgan presented that a stray horse had been found by one of his tithing and surrendered to the beadle and was now in the village pound. He also asked that William Bonesay might be enrolled in his tithing as he was now twelve years of age. William Cook complained that Richard Jamys had received one John Freeman into his house, and that John was not in any tithing and was suspected of being a night-walker and eavesdropper. Richard was ordered to produce John at the next Court and to be ready to answer for him. Lastly, John atte Hethe was removed from his office of tithing man, and in his place William Craft was elected and sworn.

So the proceedings came to an end; and, after the cellarer had reminded them that the next Court would be held on that day six weeks, he withdrew to his private chamber, and amid a general chattering the peasants began to disperse. John left the Court with his sons who soon joined their own friends and set off homewards. He, however, made a roundabout circuit so as to pass by the great west field, for he was anxious to see how things were coming on, for the whole week past had been so taken up with haymaking and work elsewhere that he had had no time even to do an hour's work there. As he came round by the field his eye rapidly moved from strip to strip and he saw there was much to be done. St John's Day was already past, so they must set to work at once at the weeding, he thought, and he determined to spend the rest of the day at this. For a few minutes before turning homeward to his midday meal he sat down and looked across the great field at the village as it straggled over the neighbouring slope—a familiar sight, but dearer to him than any other place on earth. There stood the church, clean and white in the midday sun, and there a few hundred yards to the right his own little house and its narrow close which, with his land in the common fields, represented all he had in the world.

It seemed little enough, yet, he reflected, things might be

worse. The last winter had been hard, and the death of his only cow had made life even harder. Now, however, his twenty-four half-acre pieces were all ploughed and planted with crops which promised well, but everyone knew that twelve acres was none too much, if more than the barest existence was hoped for. Last year the crops had been poor, and for several months food had been scarce, so that many of his neighbours had been half starved, and nearly everyone in the village was forced to live on victuals lacking in flavour or variety. The oats had been their salvation: with oatcake and porridge, and with the bread they had made from a mixed corn of barley and rye they had been able to hold off the worst pangs of hunger; but for weeks on end no meat or flesh, except an occasional chicken or something snared by night in the prior's woods, had come their way. Since then, however, the summer had come, and the hay crop had been a good one, and hope sprang up once again. At the next Court, he thought, he would ask for leave to build a little cot on the piece of new land they had been clearing near by the great wood. Then Richard and Johanna could be married and live there, and could grow something on the three acres to help them all to live. His wife would know how to make the best of everything that came into the house: no one could make a bushel of corn go farther than she. That was the root of his brother Harry's trouble. His wife had been careless and slatternly, and their home was always uncared for and the meals ill-prepared. And yet, despite it all, Harry had been heartbroken when she went off with Thomas Oxenden, a rising burgess of Thorpston near by. Since then, Harry had gone down hill fast: his holding was badly kept, his house a disgrace, while his time was mainly spent with bad friends snaring in the prior's woods, or in drinking and "Hi tooral hay" at the ale-house. John reflected sadly as to the end of all this, but what was to be done to stay it he could not tell. Life was so strange and in his fifty odd years he had seen ups and downs in the village. Some he had played with as a boy had stolen away by night, and had been heard of no more; some, like his wife's brother, had become priests, and were now important people; some, like his own brother, had lost their grip on life, and had become a byword in the village. But there it was, and each must abide his fate. As Sir William had often told them, they were in the hand of God, and He and His holy angels would protect them all their days. Then, as he rose to go, the sound of the midday bell rang out clear over the fields. He crossed himself, and after repeating an *Ave*, went quickly to his own home.

Such, in my imagination, might have been a week in the life of one of these peasants who will occupy our attention throughout this book. It is imaginary, and as such may be sternly set on one side by some. Nevertheless, there is little in it, I believe, that cannot be supported by documentary evidence, and even that little is sufficiently close to the documents to have a confident chance of satisfying the majority of readers if they had time to consider all the details which have gone to its making. It is true that it represents but a few days in the life of one man, and that at a particularly favourable moment of the year, and in a parish blessed with a priest as worthy as was Chaucer's parson. The remainder of this book will show clearly enough the difficult existence which was all that most peasants could hope for. Many such sketches would be necessary before any very clear and valuable picture of the medieval scene could be obtained. Yet a knowledge that medieval life was complex and infinitely various must not dismay us, and prevent our attempting some such synthesis. While medieval life had so many points at which it was at variance with our own, so much of it was very like. The life of the fields, in many particulars, has preserved its main characteristics from earliest times. The rhythm of the seasons carries with it all those whose lot it is to till the earth; and, despite the unfamiliar conditions in which they lived, the people seem as recognisable as does that countryside so vividly drawn for us by the unknown author of *Mum and the Sothsegger*,[1] a poem of

---

[1] Edited for the E.E.T.S. by M. Day and R. Steele, 1936.

the first few years of the fifteenth century.[1] In this the writer
tells us of how he climbed to the top of a hill, and there

> I tournyd me twyes and totid[2] aboute,
> Beholding heigges and holtʒ[3] so grene,
> The mansions and medues mowen al newe,
> For suche was þe saison of þe same yere.
> I lifte vp my eye-ledes and lokid ferther
> And sawe many swete sightʒ, so me God helpe,
> The wodes and þe waters and þe welle-springes
> And trees y-traylid fro toppe to þerthe,[4]
> Coriously y-courid[5] with curtelle of grene,
> The flours on feeldes flavryng[6] swete,
> The corne on þe croftes y-croppid ful faire,
> The rennyng riuyere russhing faste,
> Ful of fyssh and of frie of felefold[7] kinde,
> The breris[8] with þaire beries bent ouer þe wayes
> As honysoucles hongyng vpon eche half,
> Chesteynes[9] and chiries þat children desiren
> Were loigged vnder leues ful lusty to seen.
> The havthorne so holsum I beheulde eeke,
> And hough þe benes blowid and þe brome-floures;
> Peres and plummes and pesecoddes grene,
> That ladies lusty loken muche after,
> Were gadrid for gomnes[10] ere þay gunne ripe....
> The conyngʒ[11] fro couert courid þe bankes
> And raughte[12] oute a raundom and retournyd agaynes,
> Pleyed forthe on þe playne, and to þe pitte after,
> But any hovnd hente[13] þaym, or þe hay-nettes[14]....
> The shepe fro þe sunne shadued þaymself,
> While þe lambes laikid a-long by þe heigges.
> The cow with hire calfe and coltes ful faire
> And high hors[15] in haras hurtelid to-gedre,
> And priesid[16] þe pasture þat prime-saute[17] þaym made....
> I moued dovne fro þe mote to þe midwardʒ
> And so a-dovne to þe dale, dwelled I no longer,
> But suche a noise of nestlingʒ ne[18] so swete notʒ[19]
> I herde not þis halfe yere, ne so heuenely sounes
> As I dide on þat dale adovne among þe heigges.

---

[1] *Op. cit.* XXIV.	[2] peered.	[3] woods.
[4] the earth.	[5] covered.	[6] smelling.
[7] manifold.	[8] briars.	[9] chestnuts.
[10] men.	[11] rabbits.	[12] went.
[13] caught.	[14] hedge-nets.	[15] stallions.
[16] praised.	[17] spirited.	[18] nor.
[19] notes.		

The Church

CHAPTER I

THE CHURCH

IT is customary to set out on any survey of medieval peasant life by attempting a description of the manor and its occupants, and this we shall have to do, however briefly, although throughout our emphasis will be more on actualities than on legal distinctions. But, before we come to that, it is essential to realise that the peasant (in this respect like his betters) was part of a great organisation whose power, now light, now heavy, continuously pressed upon him. The Church meant more to medieval man than we are ever likely to understand, but a little imagination allows us to glimpse its force and its prestige. The building itself, standing commonly in the centre of the village, symbolised the place of the Church in medieval life. The great moments of man's story on earth—baptism, marriage, burial—centred in the sacred building. There, on Sundays at least, the villagers heard Mass, and perhaps mattins and evensong as well: there they learnt what little they were capable of retaining from staring at the pictures on the walls or in the windows, or from the infrequent and halting sermon of their village priest, or from the picturesque and dramatic outpourings of a preaching friar. And the village Church was the more important because medieval worship was still mainly a matter of congregational worship—the altar, the chantry, the shrine were the places the villager came to naturally when he wished to express his religious aspirations. Whatever part family devotions may have played (and we have little evidence of any such happenings) it was to their parish church and to the parish clergy that men turned for instruction, consolation and refreshment.

Nor must we think that religion was a thing for Sundays, hastily assumed as men approached the church. It is probable that the peasant was unable to attend except on Sundays or great Saints' days, but his life was not thereby divided into two compartments—religious and secular. Rather the shadow of the Church was about him in his fields or in his close; as he laboured on the edge of the forest or carried his load to the neighbouring mill. The Angelus, which J. F. Millet's nineteenth-century peasants heard at midday in their fields, was a post-Reformation practice, but the Mass-bell earlier in the day had sounded down the ages, and had summoned the fourteenth-century peasant in similar manner:

> And ȝef þow may not come to chyrche,
> Where euer þat þow do worche,
> When þow herest to masse knylle,
> Prey to God wyþ herte stylle.[1]

And there was much besides to remind him of his fellowship and of his duty to the Church. As he moved about the manor he would see the wayside crosses and the local shrines, where from time immemorial prayers had been said and offerings made. In most places he could see from the hillside the spires of many a church, and the walls of abbeys and priories enclosing great buildings which were bywords in the village for their opulent splendour and vast design. If we add to this the constant passage of wandering friars, of ecclesiastics on business, the occasional palmer and the more frequent groups of pilgrims, the daily meetings with the parish priests or his assistants and underlings, we begin to realise how omnipresent the Church of the Middle Ages must have seemed to the toilers of the fields.

Nor did it rest at this. The Church was not passive—a kindly mother waiting the coming of her children. The medieval Church was the Church militant in many ways, and her contacts with the peasant were not solely those of love and mansuetude. When her rights or privileges were in question no medieval lay-lord was more instantly in arms, or fiercer upon his quarrel. The tithe barn was an ever-present reminder of the power and needs of the Church; and many a man must have played the part of Cain in the Towneley play of *The Killing of Abel*, where we see him grudgingly looking over his sheaves, selecting the worst for his tithe, and grumbling all the time.[2] Again, at the death of any man the Church frequently stepped in and claimed his second-best beast as a mortuary. This was a severe tax, and was felt the more since the lord of the manor claimed the best beast as a

---

[1] Myrc, *Instructions for Parish Priests* (E.E.T.S.), ll. 1603 ff.
[2] *Towneley Plays* (E.E.T.S.), 15, and see p. 330.

heriot on these occasions.[1] Then there were the Mass pennies to
be paid, and the Peter's pence to be found from time to time,
while the light-scot and the church-scot recalled to the peasant
other of his obligations to Holy Church.

And, as if this were not sufficient, in the majority of villages
the priest strove with the serf to win a living from the products of
the earth. He was priest first, but agriculturist after; or, as an
early Parson Trulliber, he might even be primarily an agriculturist. His beasts fed side by side with those of his
parishioners on the commons, and he bargained at the neighbouring market against his fellows in the hope of making a good
purchase, or of effecting a profitable exchange.

So it was not easy for the peasant to forget his Church with
these things set visibly about him and backed up by even more
powerful, though invisible, forces constantly at work upon his
conscience and his imagination. It is scarcely too much to say
that medieval life was haunted by the all-important fact that it
was a man's last moments which mattered. "In the place where
the tree falleth, there shall it lie" (Ecclesiastes xi. 3); as he died,
so would he live again. Nothing could overcome the fact of
death and its concomitants—judgment and doom. Not only in
those fearful paintings which covered the walls of many a church,
but in those more permanent "Last Judgments", carved in
stone on the façade of cathedral and abbey church, were to be
seen the sufferings of the damned and the joys of the faithful.
And since the Church taught that a soul, even in the article of
death, could be saved or lost, the idea of death and of preparation
for death was constantly brought before men's minds by these
things. And all this was emphasised by sermons and exhortations such as were to find their later and more artistic counter-
parts in Sir Thomas More's *The Four Last Things*, or in the
sombre eloquence of Donne. Well indeed might medieval men
have forestalled Marvell's cry:

> Yet at my back I alwaies hear
> Times winged Charriot hurrying near:
> And yonder all before us lye
> Desarts of vast Eternity.

[1] See below, p. 143.

If we could imagine with any clarity the narrow warped minds of the mass of the medieval English peasantry, we should easily realise how much such men must have been influenced by the carvings and paintings they saw about them in the church, and by the legends of Saints and the Fathers, the main incidents of the Gospel story and by the insistence on death and the life to come. Even though it is probable that many men and women were not eager and convinced believers, yet even these were more prepared to believe than to disbelieve. They lacked an active conviction, but yet had nothing strong enough to hearten them in a denial of the accepted faith. So the insistence of the Church was too strong for them: *Timor mortis conturbat me* had been so often repeated that it beat its way into even the dullest brain in time. And as with this, so with other of the doctrines of the Church.

It is necessary to emphasise the part played by seeing and hearing, for they were the peasants' only means of communication. Few indeed could have read the Mass Book and Prymer, even had they been easily available, and the Church was, perforce, the Poor Man's Bible, though it was a meagre substitute for the book we know. Modern scholars have shown how little of the Bible was ever depicted on the walls of the church, and in how travestied a form it was often displayed. At the same time large parts of what is religiously richest and best in it were unsuitable and neglected as pictorial material. Symbolism (so far as it was to be found in the village church) no doubt tried to meet the needs of the illiterate, but symbolism was a very vague and unsettled method of communication, and gave rise to innumerable errors and rash speculations.

Since these things helped him so little, the peasant could only watch with dim comprehension "the blessed mutter of the Mass". The Church had done her best, and had turned her central service into a great mimetic rite. She had given this a ceremonial elaboration that made it immediately popular, but its very elaboration had excluded the simple from more than a distant participation. The author of the *Lay Folks' Mass Book* does explain the meaning of the symbolical acts of the Mass to those who can read, but all he can advise the unlettered to do is to say the *Pater* and the *Ave* over and over again during the course of the Mass.[1] So the services, the symbolism, the paintings and the rest were but dim imperfectly apprehended things which years of use had made part of their being, but which demanded some living touch to make their meaning clear to such simple folk.

This touch should have come from the priest, but there can be no doubt that the medieval priesthood was not fully prepared for such an undertaking. The cry of Archbishop Peckham, that heads his constitutions of 1281, "The ignorance of the priests casteth the people into the ditch of error", is re-echoed centuries later by Wolsey. Clerical ignorance was widespread throughout the parishes, and the villager oftentimes could not hope to learn very much from his priest. Langland's portrait of Sloth the parson, who knew neither *Beatus vir* nor *Beati omnes*, but who rejoiced in rhymes of Randolph of Chester and Robin Hood, would seem impossible but for the strictest evidence of the Bishop's Registers which confirm its main lines in a striking fashion. In many parishes the priest only stumbled through some homily or sermon (his own or another's) on the statutory four times a year, and "left his shepe encombred in the mire" for the rest. In a good many other instances the evidence suggests neglect even of these statutory four. With so feeble a guide the villager could not get far on his quest for Truth, and there is little wonder that his religion was frequently a thing of "use and wont"—part sincere, part convention, part pure magic.

Not only this, but, as we have seen, the priest was far from being the kindly cultured patron of the village such as he has often shown himself in the past two hundred years. He was more likely to be a hard-hearted man of business, and frequently was a stranger brought into the parish, by influence or by his ecclesiastical superiors, with little in common with his parishioners except his determination to overcome the difficulties incident upon medieval agriculture, and his eye for a bargain. As modern observers in France and Italy have pointed out, the coming of the priest into a house was often so rare an event that at his arrival the village at once feared the worst! "*E venuto il prete* sounds like a death-knell to the family."[2]

---

[1] Myrc, *op. cit.* ll. 60, 82, 152, etc.
[2] L. D. Gordon, *Home Life in Italy*, 231 ; cf. N. Sabord, *Le Buisson d'Épines*, 237, for modern examples, and the stories of J. de Vitry (ed. T. Wright), 77, 110, for medieval feeling on this matter.

But when we think we have begun to appreciate the villager's mind, thus encompassed by his hopes and fears of the Church, we have but half done. "The broad shadow of the Cross lay over the whole medieval world", Mr B. L. Manning writes;[1] and, while we heartily agree with this, we have still to remember that other—perhaps broader—shadow that darkened medieval life and thought—the shadow of "the Devil and all his works". This was no abstraction for the peasant, but every corner of his fields and every corner of his home were liable to harbour some agent of Hell who could harm him unless it were exorcised and overcome.

For we must remember how circumscribed was the world in which the majority of these people lived. Their village was their world; beyond, some ten or twenty miles led to the local shrine or the great fair, and there, perhaps, once or twice a year they made their way; but, for the most part, their lives were ground out in a perpetual round from one field to another, and so to the next. London seemed very far off—almost as far as Rome or Jerusalem itself. Hence, they were easily impressed by "the wonders of the world"—and fact and fiction were indistinguishable to them. Even the greatest minds were curiously limited (according to our modern conceptions of knowledge): Aquinas could talk of the power of miracles, and enforce his argument that "it may seem miraculous to him who hath no comprehension of that power; as to the ignorant it seemeth miraculous that the magnet draweth iron, or that a little fish holdeth back a ship".[2] Similarly, all the chroniclers mingle fact and fiction in a bewildering fashion, and vagueness and confusion are of the very stuff of their information. It is not surprising, therefore, that the uneducated peasant, who relied on gossip and the stories of passing travellers, should be credulous and superstitious.

Superstition, which feeds and grows on ignorance, was indeed encouraged by the most powerful of the peasant's teachers—the clergy. The Church consistently showed itself slow to acknowledge the claims of human reason, which it saw pressing for

[1] *The People's Faith in the Time of Wyclif*, 15.
[2] Quoted from *Summa Contra Gentiles*, Lib. III, cap. 102, by Dr Coulton in his *Social Britain*, 532, commenting on Trevisa's account of this fish "scarcely a foot long"!

recognition on all sides. The doctor of medicine was frequently suspect—*Ubi tres medici, duo athei*. And it must be admitted that medicine and magic had much in common, and the Church had reason to fear these men whose "study was but little on the Bible", and whom her own restrictions had roused to antagonism. At the same time the fear of reason was so great that wherever the Church could do so it stifled free enquiry: even so great and orginal a mind as that of Roger Bacon fought for wellnigh a lifetime against the opposition of his ecclesiastical superiors. Most men, possessed of a less robust and enquiring intellect, jogged along unreflectingly content, and scarcely aware of the cramping effects of Church discipline. With all the innocence in the world they tended their congregations, unaware of any breath of the advancing thought and knowledge which was to threaten their own existence. Their very teaching was pernicious in so far as it encouraged in the peasant those qualities of superstition and belief in magic that lurk in the background of all uneducated peoples.

From earliest times they had endeavoured to give a Christian interpretation to old pagan customs and legends rather than to stamp them out.[1] Thus wells once under the protection of pagan gods were placed under the care of the Saints. The setting of the Midsummer Watch, the May Day ceremonies, the innumerable rites associated with the various agricultural seasons all had their roots in the past, and had to be adapted to the Christian religion as best they could.

Then again, there was a wealth of legend, fable, lives of saints and myths, all of which were widely disseminated throughout the Middle Ages and did much to increase the ready acceptance of the supernatural. One example will serve: the fifteenth-century translation of the *Alphabetum Narrationum* contains a collection of stories such as were used by itinerant preachers to lard their sermons for their unlettered audiences. Almost every story is

[1] See the famous letter of Gregory the Great to Mellitus and St Augustine (June 601) instructing them to so order their actions that "the people will have no need to change their places of concourse, where of old they were wont to sacrifice cattle to demons, thither let them continue to resort on the day of the saint to whom the church is dedicated, and slay their beasts no longer as a sacrifice, but for a social meal in honour of Him whom they now worship". Bede, *Hist. Eccl.* I, 30.

concerned with the part played by magical agency: an angel saves a damsel from death; the *Ave Maria*, said with devotion, overcomes a devil; the crucifix makes a sign of anger and stops its ears; the power of St Dominic's prayers draws down the Virgin and two angels to anoint a sick man, and so on. The mere reminder of such compilations as those earliest *Lives of the Fathers* in the Desert; the *Dialogus Miraculorum* of Caesarius of Heisterbach, or the *Gesta Romanorum*, should be sufficient to satisfy us of the medieval belief in the widespread nature of supernatural powers working for and against mankind.

Not only the teaching but the services did much to inculcate the belief in magic. We have seen that the unlettered could but imperfectly follow the service of the Mass, and superstition was actively encouraged by the tales told of the wonders worked by the Host, and of the benefits which came to those who had recently received the Sacrament. Such tales reposed on the theological doctrine of the *opus operatum*—the virtue of Masses even apart from the disposition of the worshipper or recipient. Hence, there was no witchcraft which the Host could not perform, and thus arose a body of tales.

Because these stories glorified the Sacrament the layman was encouraged to believe that the saying of a Mass could remove iron fetters from a knight's body, or sustain a miner who had been buried in a pit; that a man whose sickness prevented him from receiving the bread in the usual way received it through his side near his heart; that blindness would not strike the fortunate eyes which saw the Host carried to the sick. To increase the offerings of the devout they were told that a penny offered at Mass would secure an increase of worldly wealth as well as freedom from their sins.[1]

What wonder if men went further for themselves, and regarded the Host as a charm and placed it among the beehives to prevent the death of the bees, or scattered it in fragments over the cabbages to keep off caterpillars.[2]

In addition to the kindly magic of the Saints and of the reformed pagan gods there was still the fearful and ever-present black magic of the Devil. He was all-powerful, and in lonely places, by the shores of lake and forest, and in the desolate

---

[1] Manning, *op. cit.* 79.
[2] Caesarius of Heisterbach, *Dist.* ix, §§ 8

wastes and high mountains, his agents roamed about seeking whom they might devour, and at times could be heard and sometimes even seen. A quotation from a modern work describing the feelings and beliefs of a French peasant of yesterday indicates something of the world in which—to an intenser degree—his English brother of five hundred years ago lived and believed.

Blandin était de ceux qui, le matin du premier mai, plantent dans leur fumier, pour le préserver des serpents qui voudraient y faire leur nid, un arbuste orné de rubans. Le dimanche suivant il allait à l'église pour y faire bénir, à l'issue de la messe de huit heures, des baguettes de noisetier attachées en faisceau. De retour aux Vernes il les plantait dans ses deux champs et dans son jardin pour les préserver de la grêle. Il savait que, s'il venait à tonner lorsqu'il coupait du bois, il devait tenir sa hache le tranchant en l'air : la foudre, si elle s'avisait de tomber sur lui, serait fendue. Ni la Blandine, ni la petite Jeannette n'eussent fait la lessive pendant les Quatre-Temps, ni les jours de vigile et de jeûne, ni entre Noël et la Chandeleur. Ils savaient tous que le cri du geai est bon signe, que la chouette et la pie sont des oiseaux de mauvais augure, qu'il ne faut pas se marier au mois de mai, sous peine qu'un des nouveaux époux meure bientôt après. La poule qui veut imiter le chant du coq annonce un malheur. Tout cela faisait partie des choses que l'on ne comprend pas. Ils n'étaient pas seulement au milieu de l'hiver et de la misère humaine ; ils vivaient entourés de mystères. Le monde était habité par des forces obscures qu'ils divinisaient. Faibles, ils les sentaient liguées contre eux. Ils tâchaient tantôt de se les rendre favorables par des invocations et des signes, tantôt de conjurer leur mauvais vouloir par d'humbles sacrifices, tantôt, enfin, de deviner leurs dispositions au moyen d'indices sûrs qu'ils tenaient de leurs ancêtres.[1]

Such then was the background of the peasant's life—a background full of terrors and haunting suggestions, as well as one bringing him comfort and hope of another world. We shall see more of this after we have studied the peasant's daily life and activities on the manor, but it was necessary at the outset to emphasise the presence of this all-important side of things—the more so because (quite naturally) our legal and economic historians, in writing about medieval life, do not often take it into account.

[1] H. Bachelin, *Le Village*, 36.

The Manor and its cultivation

CHAPTER II

THE MANOR AND ITS CULTIVATION

MEDIEVAL ENGLAND was almost exclusively rural England, and rural England congregated in small groups of people, here fifty, here a hundred, and (much less often) here several hundreds, living in rude houses which clustered together in some places, while in others they straggled endlessly down the village street. Agriculture and its allied occupations engaged the energies of everyone as they strove to win a living from the soil. These small groups, on closer examination, are often found to be sharing certain rights and privileges and to be discharging certain duties, under the protection and control of a lord. There were many thousands of these little groups throughout England, and they formed the manorial society which existed for some hundreds of years after the Conquest. The origin of the manor, however, and how, and to what extent, the countryside had become manorialised are not discussed here: it is not the origination of the manor, but how men lived and what happened to them under the manorial system that is the main concern of this study. At the same time much of it will also necessarily be concerned with those peasants who were not directly controlled by manorial organisations, but who won a living with their hands as best they could, for both they and the *villanus*, or serf of the manorial system, were primarily agriculturists.

Even when we confine ourselves to those men who were under manorial control we do not necessarily find them living under identical conditions because they are living in the same area. The manor and the village were by no means interchangeable terms. Sometimes, it is true, everybody in the village was the tenant of a single lord, but frequently one village was divided up among two or more manors. This is admirably shown, for example, by Professor Kosminsky's study of the Hundred Rolls, where he finds that "out of 650 vills described and investigated, 336 are not identical with manors"; and, he adds, "In Northumbria, the Danelegh and East Anglia the co-incidence is (we already know) extremely rare ".[1] As a result of this it was possible for two men to be living in the same village, and each holding the same amount of land; but, because they served different lords, they might find themselves very unevenly burdened with services and rents. Yet, heavy or light, they both led the same type of life; and therefore, in seeking to understand the medieval peasant, we need not place undue emphasis on these differences so long as we remember their existence, and are ready to consider what effects they finally encouraged.[2]

Our enquiry, then, will be mainly concerned with the effects of the manorial organisation roughly between the years 1200 and 1350—a period which saw it at the height of its powers and yet also certainly declining towards its fall. Only the conditions of peasant life as determined by the manorial system will be discussed here, and many problems connected with the rise of the manor and its relation to the vill will be left untouched.[3] In so doing we shall, no doubt, assume a uniformity of organisation and conditions that more detailed investigations of limited areas will challenge or even deny.[4] " To ask for a definition of the manor ", said Professor Maitland, "is to ask for the impossible", and more recent workers have given us reason to believe that considerable parts of England were never manorialised at all. Yet, even so, one of the most brilliant of recent disintegrators of the manorial system admits that, " although it is true that we can no longer regard the large estate with villeins and labour service as the 'constituting cell' of English society in the thirteenth century, such estates do, nevertheless, form an important section of economic life."[5] Again, we may take encouragement from the words of Professor Ashley when he writes:

The manorial system is no doubt often conceived of as more

---

[1] *Econ. Hist. Rev.*, vol. v, No. 2, p. 30. Cf. *Year Book*, 3/4 Ed. II, 15; F. G. Davenport, *op. cit.* 7.

[2] See chapter XI, where the question of the part played by unequal services in the desire for freedom is discussed.

[3] The standard books on this subject are still Vinogradoff's well-known monographs: *The Growth of the Manor; Villainage in England;* and *English Society in the XIth Century.* With these go Seebohm's masterpiece, *The English Village Community* and Maitland's *Domesday Book and Beyond.*

[4] See, for example, the excellent studies of F. M. Stenton on the Danelagh; those of D. C. Douglas on *Medieval East Anglia* and those of J. E. A. Jolliffe (*E.H.R.* 1926) on Northumbrian conditions.

[5] *Econ. Hist. Rev.*, vol. v, No. 2, p. 44.

symmetrical and universal than it ever was in fact. But was it not sufficiently similar over large stretches of time and space to make it the most useful preliminary framework round which to gather the new material, if only care be taken at once to lay stress on the multiformity of actual life?[1]

It is with this point of view in mind that this essay has been written.

Let us begin then with a single village and the lands surrounding it, assuming for the sake of simplicity that it is all held by one lord. Whatever shape the actual village took—a shape determined by many factors[2]—in nearly every village the peasants lived in small houses, placed side by side, each often having a little enclosure or plot of ground behind it. Around the village and stretching away lay the common fields—the arable land—which in many ways formed the most notable characteristic of the manorial organisation. The history of the origination of these field-systems, again, is not our subject:[3] our concern is with their cultivation and the part they played in the life of the peasant. Besides these common fields there were the meadows: almost as vital to the community as the arable. Then, again, there were the commons on which the villagers had grazing rights, and beyond them stretched the "waste", and the woods and forests.

Such was the enclosing framework, "the web", as Dr Coulton calls it, "within which the medieval peasant lives and moves and has his being"; and, he adds, "it is a very complicated tissue, which we must take into account before we can understand his daily life".[4] It is indeed a "complicated tissue", and one not easy to understand in all its details, but perhaps our best plan will be to start from the church in the centre of the village and so work out to the very edges of the manor. Imagine, then, a little village, with its groups of houses, each of them with its garden and here and there an enclosed stretch of meadow. Beyond them stretches the open country, and at a closer view it

---

[1] *Econ. Journ.*, June 1926, reviewing *The Medieval Village*, by G. G. Coulton.
[2] For discussion of this, see *Geographical Journal*, xxix, 45–52.
[3] The best monograph is that of H. L. Gray, *English Field Systems*. This investigates the geographical distribution of the two- and three-field system in England, and attempts to explain the way in which special conditions, such as those in Kent or East Anglia, are to be accounted for. His work must be corrected, however, by such special studies as those of Stenton, Douglas, etc. mentioned above.
[4] *Med. Village*, 37.

becomes clear that immediately in front of us is a large arable field. Unlike a modern farm it seems to have no boundaries—at least there are no hedges, dividing one part from another, and nothing to prevent us from walking across its length and out into the grazing lands beyond. A closer examination, however, will show us that this great field is, nevertheless, divided up into a number of compartments or large divisions. These go by many names—furlongs, shots, dells—and each of these compartments is again subdivided into a certain number of strips (or selions), each divided from the other by raised balks of unploughed land. The strips run parallel, one to the other, the whole length of the furlong or shot, and are generally found to contain half an acre or one acre of land. At right angles to them run the "headlands" —unploughed portions which give access to the strips in that furlong, and also to the other parts of the great field.

As we shall see, the peasant did not hold all his strips in one convenient block, but had them allocated to him in various parts of this, and of the other great fields of the manor. This was a principle of great antiquity: it is of the essence of these peasant holdings that they shall each be of comparatively small size and scattered over the whole of the common fields.

The very term, "the common fields", reminds us that much medieval farming was a co-operative affair. But we are by no means as clear as we should like to be as to how far this was so in actual practice. The generally accepted theory envisages the peasants carrying out all the principal occupations of agriculture in common. Reasons will be given later for thinking that there was more individual enterprise than has been imagined, but we may begin by admitting that the fields were cultivated according to a plan which had the sanction of time immemorial, or of general village consent, and that everyone had to fall in with this. Individual cultivation of any particular crop was almost impossible and had to be reserved for the little "closes" round the home, or for the "assart" land newly brought into cultivation by the peasant, and which lay outside the "common fields" and was generally on the outskirts of the manor. In the common fields, however, when oats were sowed by one they were, perforce, sown by all. The most considerable operation, of course, was ploughing, and how far this was a communal affair it is hard to tell. Clearly, the most economical way would have been to yoke the oxen of various peasants together in one plough-team, and to have worked over the whole field, furrow by furrow, just as the peasants were forced to plough the lord's demesne by communal labour. We imagine that this is what was done, but little definite evidence exists to support this view. On the other hand, Dr Coulton has drawn attention to a passage in *Piers Plowman* which, as he says, "seems to point clearly to a good deal of private ploughing and reaping".[1] The dishonest peasant in *Piers Plowman* confesses: "If I went to the plough I pinched so narrowly that I would steal a foot of land or a furrow, or gnaw the half-acre of my neighbour; and if I reaped, I would over-reap (i.e. reach over into my neighbour's ground), or gave counsel to them that reaped to seize for me with their sickles that which I never sowed."[2] We may emphasise this point by noticing another example of this kind of dishonesty which is mentioned in Robert Mannyng of Brunne's *Handlyng Synne*. Here we read of "false husbandmen who falsely plough away men's lands, [and] take and plough away a furrow of land through and through".[3] And when we turn from literature to the records we find some evidence of a similar nature. An instance occurs at Thorner, in 1365, which suggests that communal operations were unusual, and that private agreements were resorted to at times. We read that "John de Roch complains of Robert de Eltoft on a plea of agreement. John comes and says that on a certain day and year he made a pact with the said Robert that they should be partners for ploughing the land of the said John and Robert with equal animals going to the plough, which partnership is called *marrows*, for a year only; and concerning this Robert in no wise held to the pact, etc."[4] Now this phrase "which partnership is called *marrows*" is defined in the fifteenth-century *Promptorium Parvulorum* as "a felowe yn travayle (or mate)". A nineteenth-century glossary of Antrim and Down states that the term still exists, and means "to lend horses and men for labour to a neighbour, and to receive a similar loan when needed"—exactly the meaning

---

[1] *Med. Village*, 42.   [2] *Piers Plowman*, B. XIII, 371; C. VII, 267.
[3] *Op. cit.* ll. 2445–8. Cf. the original from which Mannyng was translating, "Ki autru teres unt arer, Ou en autru semail a tort entrer." In France those guilty of this offence were called *mangeurs de raies*. See M. Bloch, *op. cit.* 38.
[4] Thoresby Soc. xv, 168.

attaching to the term at Thorner in 1365.[1] The survival of this term centuries later, and in another part of the British Isles, strongly suggests that the practice was persistent and widespread. If this can be maintained, then we are forced to imagine that co-operation was often left to individuals, and was not so universally a village or manorial matter as has generally been believed. Such a belief received encouragement from the undoubted fact that the peasants were forced to yoke their animals side by side with those of their neighbours so as to make up the teams they had to supply when the lord's demesne lands required ploughing. This, and other activities, such as mowing the lord's hay, or reaping his corn, they discharged as a body, and because of this it was easy (though unjustifiable) to think of them doing likewise on their own acres. On the contrary, it would seem that individual enterprise was not at all uncommon. The fact that a man could encroach upon his neighbour's strips, or that he is at times found reaping another man's corn suggests individual labour, and encourages the belief that co-operation was local, sporadic and a matter for individual arrangement.

Perhaps the strongest argument against individual enterprise is its absurdly wasteful character. But medieval agriculture was absurdly wasteful, and there can be no doubt that the common-field system exacted a heavy toll from its workers. This is abundantly shown, both from contemporary records and from the more scientific and detailed accounts of common-field conditions given by investigators of more modern times who have inspected those areas where the old conditions have survived from the past. Waste of time and effort was caused by the piecemeal nature of the normal holding. A man with thirty acres would find these spread out in twice that number of strips which were distributed over the east, south and west fields of his village. As time went on, in some parts of England further subdivisions of these original holdings made matters more complicated, and increased the amount of time wasted.[2] Again, one or two careless or lazy

---

[1] In Germany the same practice was still observed in 1870. See *Land Tenure Reports*, 406.

[2] See, for example, the fields of Rampton (Cambs) where in a part of one of the fields the strips are held by the following: M, D, H, B, N, G, B, G, D, C, F, C, E, K, F, B, K, E, C, D, P, C, F, E, H, E, E, D, C, G, etc. The plan is reproduced on p. 8 of J. A. Venn's *Foundations of Agricultural Economics*. For evidence of subdivision, see also below, p. 50.

peasants, or the neglect incident on a holding being vacant for a time, caused much trouble. Weeds neglected, and ground left to go to waste, encouraged the broadcast dissemination of harmful seeds, and the growth of unwanted vegetation. Even to get onto the fields was not always easy. Unless a watchful eye were kept, a path or headway gradually got ploughed in, or some enclosure was made which separated the field from the village, save by a roundabout route. Thus we find a chaplain covenanting to give a right of droveway for ploughs, carts and beasts over his pasture to the land of Sparkeford.[1] Without such permission there was nothing for it but to trample over the holdings of others, as was complained of, for instance, at Halesowen, and the lord was appealed to for protection. In this, no doubt, the men of Halesowen were within their rights, but what of their unfortunate fellow whose holding seems to have been enisled amid those of his neighbours, and to which he had no way of entry save by walking across their holdings?[2] Then, again, as we are told, "much vagueness often resulted from the custom of scattered possessions: a tenant sometimes found he had, by mistake, sown the strip of a neighbour, or had lost one of his own strips".[3] We might think this impossible but for two facts. First, the immense number of subdivisions which took place, especially in the fourteenth century, and secondly, the definite evidence we have of the difficulty which men found in knowing exactly where their own strip ended and that of a neighbour began. Often there was nothing but an imaginary line between them, or at best a line of hazel twigs such as we still see in Alpine pastures, dividing one man's share from another's. In such conditions strips lost or gained in size (not always deliberately), or even disappeared altogether. The surveyors of the Dean and Chapter of St Paul's were quite unable in 1222 to trace a holding of three acres held by one of the tenants according to an earlier survey and they had to make a new entry: "tres acrae...inveniri non possunt".[4]

We cannot say, any more than could the men of 1222, what happened to the three acres, but we can certainly say that one of

[1] *Ancient Deeds*, III, 13.
[2] *Hales Rolls*, 468. Cf. *Wakefield Rolls*, III, 148, where a man expressly stipulates for "right of ingress and regress for his manure and corn".
[3] *V.C.H. Berks*, II, 170. [4] *D.S.P.* II.

the greatest difficulties of the common-field system was the problem of how to cope with one's neighbours who sat cheek by jowl on every side. Men had to take their chance: a neighbour might be a careless worker who allowed weeds to flourish unchecked, or a helpful and friendly partner with whom one could share the common labours. But the real difficulty arose much more from the man who could not keep to his own, but who, as we have seen in *Piers Plowman*, would "pinch" on his neighbour's holding in some way or another. Sometimes he would move the stones marking off one strip from another and thus gain a few feet more of land for himself,[1] or he would plough up a balk between himself and another man.[2] When the time came for gathering in the crops he would falsely reap some of his neighbour's oats, and pitch into his cart a few sheaves from a convenient stook.[3] In short, such was the system (or lack of system) that it was hard for anyone to know exactly what was his own; and, even if he knew this quite well, it was harder still to be constantly on the watch to protect it against other men's carelessness or worse.

Offences of this nature were common enough to be mentioned by the medieval moralists. Take, for example, the story from Caesarius of Heisterbach, translated in the fifteenth-century English *Alphabet of Tales*, which related how a man on his deathbed was terrified by visions of a great burning stone coming towards his mouth to scorch him. The priest was called, and told him to think whether he had harmed anyone with such a stone. And he thought awhile and then said, "Ah, sir! I have now a good mind of how I removed this stone in the field to the intent that I would enlarge my own ground and lessen other men's ground", etc.[4]

Difficulties such as these were, of course, well enough known to the peasants, and they did what they could to alleviate them, either as we have seen by private arrangement, or by appeal to their lord for protection, or else by common agreement. Common

---

[1] E.g. *Durham Halmote Rolls*, 26, 27, 142, 158.
[2] *Select Pleas in Manorial Courts* (Selden Soc.), 93, and see also *Ramsey Cart.* I, 344, where a peasant holding two virgates has, *inter alia*, got possession of thirteen strips formerly belonging to four other peasants.
[3] E.g. *Hales Rolls*, 305–6.
[4] *Alphabet of Tales* (E.E.T.S.), 31.

agreement often meant no more than the sanction given by old-established custom. Often a path ran from one point to another because it had always done so, or the occupant of one holding knew that for as long as the oldest memory could look back that particular holding could not be ploughed till every one else had finished, and passed with their ploughs and teams across his particular strip for the last time. Common sense and give and take were at the back of such arrangements, which led in the course of time to the more formal common agreements which were enacted by the peasants in concert, and enrolled at the lord's court so as to give them permanent and added prestige. Mr W. O. Ault has investigated these "village by-laws", one of which may serve as an example: "No-one", says the Halton (Bucks) by-law of 1329, "shall have egress from his close over another man's land; and if his egress be over his own land he shall save his neighbour harmless" (i.e. he shall do no harm to his neighbour's property). Or again, in the same list: "No one shall make paths to his neighbour's damage by walking or driving [his beasts] or by carrying grain, be it by night or by other time."[1] Offenders against these by-laws were brought before the Manor Court and fined.[2] Nevertheless, Mr Ault agrees that the more usual practice of the peasants was to rely on ancient custom, and that by-laws and the use of the manorial machinery are a late and comparatively rare occurrence.[3]

The most damning evidence of the inefficiency of the common-field method of agriculture comes from modern observers, for their accounts are of conditions still obtaining, despite much that has been done for the improvement of crops since the fourteenth century. Mr G. H. Fowler writes, "I once saw an open field at harvest-time: on the whole the foulest land under a crop which I ever saw",[4] and the accounts given by English investigators of the conditions of common-field farming in parts of Germany, in 1870, disclose a frightful state of affairs.[5]

Such a system was so patently difficult to work that every here and there we find men sufficiently wideawake to attempt reform, and this clearly could most easily—and most effectively—be

---

[1] *E.H.R.* XLV, 212 ff.   [2] *Ibid.* 220–1.
[3] Cf. Vinogradoff, *Growth of the Manor*, 184.
[4] *Catalogue of Maps (Bedford County MSS.)*, ed. G. H. Fowler, 7 n. 2.
[5] See, for example, *Land Tenure Reports*, 306, 386, 436, etc.

brought about by the consolidation of holdings. If a man could reduce his strips from sixty to thirty he had obviously saved himself considerable time and labour in getting from one place to another. This is what Maurice II, Lord Berkeley, attempted to bring about by exchanging strips whenever he could so as to consolidate his holdings, and to get them all closer to his manor houses. His biographer writes, "also other husbandry was laboured by this prudent lord, whereby he drew much profit to his tenants and increase of rents, etc., to himself, which was by making and procuring to be made exchange of lands mutually with one another, thereby casting convenient parcels together".[1] But we cannot fail to note that the whole tenour of this passage is to emphasise the unusual nature of Lord Berkeley's prudence; and indeed, far from consolidation of holdings becoming at all common, we have evidence to show that the contrary was often true, at least in the east of England, and that in the course of time, division and subdivision took place to an amazing extent. For instance, an inquisition of Edward I's time shows that there were no less than 35 joint tenures among the *villani* of Ashfield Magna, consisting of groups of from two to seven holders.[2] This was, no doubt, the result of division among the peasant's children and relatives that went on continuously, and the results of such a process on one manor have been worked out in great detail by Mr William Hudson, who showed that on the Norfolk manor of Martham the 68 tenants of Domesday time had increased by 1291 to 107—a not unnatural growth—but, quite unexpectedly, subdivision had progressed so enormously that the land formerly held by the 68 had been split up into no less than 935 holdings in some 2000 separate strips. A further extremely interesting piece of detective work on his part has enabled him to show how one six-acre block—once two tofts—had been split up among ten tenants, so that several of them had only a few perches which they could call their own, and there could have been "but one way of distribution. The total number of sheaves of (say) barley would be divided proportionally according to the size of each tenant's holding and the due number

---

[1] Smyth, *Lives of the Berkeleys*, I, 141, 160. Cf. *Ramsey Cart.* I, 344; Levett, *op. cit.* 52.
[2] Powell, *Suffolk Hundred in 1283*, 76.

handed to him or her ".[1] However doubtful we may feel of the practice of communal agricultural operations, such minute holdings as these force us to imagine some such method. Often the sharers were linked by marriage or other ties, so that the difficulties were minimised, but the division of labour and of proceeds inevitably led to friction and family feuds.

Besides his strips in the common fields the peasant had other land. About his house he usually had a small "close" (i.e. an enclosure) in which he grew such vegetables and fruits as were possible at that time. We shall see more of this in later chapters, and need do no more than to record it here. But, besides this close, many peasants had still other plots of ground they culti-vated as a private matter. These were usually on the outskirts of the manor and were originally rough uncultivated waste, or land often bordering on the forest edge. A small yearly rent gave permission to break in a patch of some few acres of such virgin soil, and many peasants eked out their scanty livelihood by such a holding, technically called an "assart". For a family burdened with more children than their shares in the common fields would warrant such assart land was a godsend. Here they could utilise their spare labour, and produce something to help fill the many hungry mouths at home. Furthermore, the land was cultivated in their own way. On the common fields, of necessity, the whole community acted in common. The animals which had pastured on the stubble throughout the winter were driven away upon a certain day, which was agreed upon by the peasants, or deter-mined by immemorial custom.[2] Then there followed the plough-ing, and the sowing of the crop for the year, and in all this there was but little room for any individual choice. The peasant was chained down to a routine that was, seemingly, unbreakable. On his assarted land, however, he was his own master, and could grow how and what he liked. Against this advantage we must set certain drawbacks: his "assart" was frequently at the edge of the manor, and was land not yet broken into cultivation, so that it required constant hard work to reclaim it from the forest or heath that was ever in wait to snatch it back again. Nor did

---

[1] *Hist. Teachers' Misc.* I, 165 ff.; *Norf. Arch.* xx, 179 ff. See also many examples of subdivision in Univ. Lib. Camb. MSS. Kk. v. 29.
[2] See *Durham Halmote Rolls*, 41.

the possession of an "assart" carry with it any communal privileges such as went with the strips in the common fields. It did not give a man the right to put any extra beasts on the common, nor was the yearly rent relaxed on it when its holder served as reeve and all his other manorial services and dues were relaxed or diminished. His assart was an extra, and had to bear its own burdens.[1]

We cannot expect to know much in detail about the piecemeal parcelling out of small portions of the waste for assarts.[2] Sometimes they were granted by the lord for a fixed rent; sometimes the land was just seized by the peasant and cultivated, and when he was found out he accepted the fine imposed on him as an additional charge for his new holding.[3] However it was done, assarting went on continuously: we read of "old assarts" and "new assarts", and every cartulary reminds us of their existence.[4] But we have nothing to tell us what persuaded lords of manors to allow of their cultivation. We may perhaps guess with some degree of certainty that assarting within limits was acceptable to the lord: it provided him with a yearly rent, and it broke up virgin soil that hitherto had been unremunerative. He naturally objected if land was taken without his knowledge and consent, but otherwise must often have found it a solution for those of his tenants whose families had grown too numerous for their original holding.[5]

Although, as we have seen, our information is mainly fragmentary, yet here and there a more connected account of what was happening is available, and may serve as an example of how assarts were being carved out of the waste of innumerable English manors. Let us take as an example what was happening in the great Forest of the Peak of Derbyshire. We must remember that the technical medieval term "forest" was not confined to a densely wooded domain, but included much open waste country suitable for agriculture. Throughout the centuries

[1] *V.C.H. Berks*, II, 183. The author of this article draws attention to the comparative lowness of assart rents. See also *Villainage*, 333.
[2] See *Growth of Manor*, 170–73.
[3] See, for example, *Wakefield Rolls*, I, 149; II, 53; III, 147, 152, 157.
[4] *D.S.P.* 8; *Ramsey Cart.* I, 342; II, 90, 296, 297; *Worc. Priory Reg.* 12 *a*; *Early Yorks Charters, passim*, etc.
[5] See p. 66.

after the Conquest, the dwellers on the fringes of the great area preserved for the King in Derbyshire were nibbling away acres here and there, and bringing them into cultivation. Since this was mainly without permission, whenever the Court of the Forest was held such offences had to be presented, and thus it is that we find out what was going on. The evidence fills many pages when extracted from the Rolls, and only a few examples can be given here. In one area (Hayfield) during the first twenty-six years of Henry III's reign some 140 acres in various small parcels had been taken into cultivation, while at Combes in the first eleven years 160 acres had been occupied by some twenty men. Or again, during a brief period the abbots of Basingwork, who had rights in the forest, had assarted no less than 291 acres in various places.[1] All these encroachments on the King's rights were presented to his officials, and we may well wonder what was happening on the manors of lesser lords when this could happen on the King's demesnes, and with the terrors of the Forest Law hanging over the wrongdoers.

Another form of forest encroachment was called "purpresture", a term difficult to define because it was somewhat differently applied to different forests. More usually, as was the case at this eyre (1251), it signified the building of a house or homestead within the forest bounds. Since the last pleas of 1216 one hundred and thirty-one persons had built new houses without warrant, and were therefore in mercy, and liable to fines. In almost a like number of cases, namely one hundred and twenty-seven, new houses had been raised in the King's demesnes with the license of the bailiff.[2]

If we turn from a forest area to a less highly protected part of the country we see much the same was happening there. The detailed researches of Mr H. J. Hewitt on medieval Cheshire have shown how much was being done there in the twelfth and thirteenth centuries. He writes:

An increasing population had already necessitated some enlargement of the bounds of cultivation, and throughout the period under consideration the work of reclamation was being gradually pushed forward. The work proceeded slowly and laboriously, and some of it

[1] J. P. Yeatman, *Feudal History of Derbyshire*, III, 237 ff.
[2] *V.C.H. Derby*, II, 403. For detailed evidence, see Yeatman, *op. cit.*

would, of course, escape mention in any document. Yet the "Forest Rolls and Rentals" of the period afford abundant evidence of assarting, new ploughing and enclosing in many parts of the county and especially in Wirral.[1]

Mr Hewitt goes on to show with a great deal of detail "how in all parts of the county the work of enlarging the cultivated area was making gradual progress". Again, the more recent work of Mr T. A. M. Bishop shows with beautiful clarity how parts of Yorkshire were brought into cultivation, and turned from waste into useful and integral parts of the near-by villages.[2]

While on the King's forest and in some places progress was comparatively slow, since it proceeded in defiance of the lord's rights, on many manors the lord was willing to allow assarting, and something like a considered scheme of development was possible. Miss Neilson, in her introduction to the *Bilsington Cartulary*,[3] has shown this in detail for the manors of the Archbishop of Canterbury and other ecclesiastical bodies which lay in Romney Marsh. Sometimes the tenant had to win back and protect the land he was assarting from the sea; sometimes the lord had already built a sea-wall, in which case heavier rents or services were demanded of the incoming tenant. But in either case there seems to have been a definite policy: "land grants permitting the inning [assarting] of land were made in gavelkind; the holds were often of uniform size in a given marsh, and were burdened with the defence of walls and waterways, according to the law and custom of the marsh. The tenements so gained were subject sometimes to strict regulations with regard to improvement, the tenant being required to build on them, unless he already had a house in the vill to which the marsh belonged."[4] Further research may show that other lords had similar schemes for developing their lands. We constantly hear, for example, of permission being given by the King to lords to include considerable areas within their domains. These, however, were not necessarily part of the manor since they formed part of the great empty wastes that lay between one village and another, but before we turn to them we must look nearer home at the peasant's other lands—the meadows and commons.

[1] *Mediaeval Cheshire*, 10.
[2] *E.H.R.* XLIX, 386, and the *Econ. Hist. Rev.* VI, 10.
[3] *Op. cit. passim.*　　　　　　　　　　[4] *Op. cit.* 53 ff.

First, the meadows. These lay near the village, and generally adjacent to the great open fields, but unlike them were fenced about or protected by a ditch. The Lammas lands, as they are often called, were a vital part of the village economy, and were carefully enclosed soon after Christmas until the crop had been taken off them in the summer.[1] They were under the special protection of the hayward, whose job it was to see the fences were not broken down, or that the villagers' cattle did not get into the growing grass, to impound straying animals and to present their owners as offenders at the Manor Court.[2] The meadows, like the other fields, were held in common, and each man had his portion allocated to him, either by a system of rotation or by the drawing of lots. Unfortunately, no early account of this custom appears to have survived, although we constantly read of the "lot-meadows", and hear of the sale of lands "lying at Middel dole as the lot geuyth", and so on.[3] The custom itself, however, survived to within living memory, and we have a number of detailed accounts of the way in which the meadows were divided. In most cases it was by lot: either small pieces of stick were drawn out of a pocket, as in Sussex,[4] or a number of apples with distinctive marks cut on them were distributed from a hat by a boy, as in Somerset,[5] or pieces of wood were cut from an arrow and marked to correspond with the landmarks in the field, as in Northamptonshire.[6]

Imagine that the crop has been gathered. At once the meadows become common land once again. Both here and in the arable this principle applied, and was of the greatest importance. Of course the occupier alone had any right to the crop (whether of grain or of hay), but once that had been lifted the fields reverted to the whole community. This was a wellnigh inevitable consequence of the whole common-field arrangements, for any other system would have been unworkable. On the one hand let us

[1] Generally this period was from Candlemas (2 Feb.) until Lammas (1 Aug.), but local custom varied these dates.
[2] The term hayward comes from the Middle English, "haye = a hedge". For details concerning the hayward and the court, see p. 178.
[3] See, for example, *Godstow Cart.* (E.E.T.S.), 220, 446, 447.
[4] Sussex Arch. Soc. Coll. IV, 307.
[5] Collinson, *History of the Antiquities of Somerset*, III, 586.
[6] Bridges, *History of Northants*, I, 219. See also Gomme, *The Village Community*, 268–71; Oxford Hist. Soc. XXIV, 308–11.

suppose each man had enclosed his own strip of arable, so that when the time came he could have put his own cattle to graze on its stubble, and could have excluded those of other men. At once great difficulties would have arisen: he could not have got his plough or carts on to his own strips because of his fences and those of others, nor could he have had room to turn his plough or harrow without wasting much of his land. On the other hand, in a field without any enclosures, to have kept one's own cattle strictly to one narrow strip, and to have prevented them from straying would have been almost beyond a man's power, and at best would have led to all kinds of disputes. "Right of common", therefore, as it was called, was one of the most valued of the peasant's rights, and allowed him to make use, not only of the uncultivated pastures which were specially assigned to that use—the "commons" of popular speech—and of the "wastes" which stretched away on every side, but also of the open arable fields and of the meadows as soon as they were cleared.

The value of the arable and the meadows to the peasant once they were thrown open was considerable. We are apt to think of the manorial flocks and herds as roaming only on the "commons" and the waste, but this is to disregard those lands more centrally placed in the village, and open, at the least, for several months of the year to all comers. The meadows, as we have seen, were available throughout the autumn and part of the winter, and must have afforded much welcome feeding for men's cattle. The arable also was not neglected. If the two-field system was in vogue there was always a considerable part of the arable available for the herds, and even under the three-field system a good deal of land was open for such purposes. And, although technically it was "empty", there was much feeding to be obtained, first from the stubble and afterwards from such small plants and weeds as rapidly spring up on any uncultivated plot of land. The "empty" lands were a considerable asset to the peasant throughout the year, for always some part of the open fields was at his disposal. In general, every one who had the right turned their beasts loose, with those of their neighbours, to crop what they could both here and in the meadows.

Closely connected with the manorial economy were the commons and open spaces—"the wastes" as they were frequently termed—of the vill. No completely satisfactory interpretation of their early history has yet been formulated; but, whatever may be the tangled legal theory that lies behind them, we may begin by noting that "right of common" was vital to the villager. He relied on pasture to keep his plough beasts in good condition, and therefore "common of pasture" was what he most tenaciously clung to. This was not an unlimited right, but was controlled by the number of acres he held in the common fields; and further, only those who had cattle *levant e couchant en le maner* could claim even this limited use. And since the whole object of common was to support and sustain the manorial agricultural routine only those animals thus directly engaged were "commonable", viz. horses and oxen for the plough, and sheep and cows for manuring. Other common rights, apparently of later date, treated by some writers as "common appurtenant", allowed the villager to pasture his goats, swine and geese on the waste, and were extended so as to include those who had no holding in the common fields, but had only a close or an assart which they held of the lord.

The gradual assarting of land, as we have seen, meant the enclosure of pieces of the waste for the individual use of some one person, and this obviously meant that there was that much land less for the common use of the vill. Now as long as the waste was large, and not overcharged by the number of cattle put on it, no difficulties or hardship arose. But as soon as the licences to assart became too numerous, then the tenants found themselves deprived of "sufficient pasture", and the lords' actions had to be restricted. The Statute of Merton (1235) laid it down that the lord was to leave "sufficient pasture" for his free tenants according to their holdings. But this was not satisfactory: it made no attempt to define what was "sufficient pasture"; it did not touch the question of rights of neighbours to intercommon, and it only legislated for free men, and therefore left the main body of villagers unprotected. A second statute (Westminster II, 1285) rectified this a little: it extended the privilege of "sufficient pasture" to neighbours who had hitherto inter-commoned, but did nothing else. There has been much controversy as to what were the exact implications of these two statutes, but "the better opinion of our books" suggests that once they were passed, the lord could enclose his common lands without any assent of the free tenants being necessary. This still left him "the custom of the manor" to deal with, and this was generally a powerful force.[1] The "common assent" of the whole vill determined the dates at which various parts of the common should be open, or the number of cattle which each member of the manor might pasture thereon. Any infringement of these arrangements caused instant trouble and litigation. Nevertheless, after these two statutes came into force, the lords gradually exercised more and more pressure, and the peasants were slowly deprived of their sometime powers and privileges.

Where the commons merged into the wastes would be difficult to say. Some manors had only a limited amount of common strictly reserved for its own members, but in many parts of the country there were large tracts of waste lying between one vill and another. They were no-man's-land, and frequently so vast in extent that no very clear delimitation of ownership had ever been made.[2] The vills surrounding them inter-commoned thereon at will. Such, for example, was the waste in the district of Whalley, where some 36,000 acres were used as pasture and woodland by various vills, and only 3500 acres were cultivated as arable.[3] The waste of the New Forest was calculated at about 60,000 acres and fringed upon some twenty-one vills; that of Ashdown contained nearly 14,000 acres, and being Crown land formed part of no manor. Epping Forest contained about 6000 acres and extended into seventeen manors, and so the list might be continued.[4]

These vast stretches of waste were utilised by all those vills which were near enough to do so and their rights run back into time immemorial. These vills inter-commoned in the waste in groups roughly determined by their geographical position. To take an example: Miss Neilson, in her introduction to *A Terrier of Fleet*, has analysed with great care the arrangements made in

[1] See, for example, *A Terrier of Fleet* (ed. N. Neilson), lxxviii, and also below, p. 100, for a discussion of the force of custom.

[2] See, for example, *Bracton's Note Book*, Case 1194, where the jury say a certain piece of waste "ampla est et magna, et nesciunt aliquas divisas quantum pertinet ad unam villam quantum ad aliam".

[3] Whitaker, *Whalley*, I, 233.

[4] Dartmoor Preservation Association, I, xxviii.

the Fens for inter-commoning, and has shown clearly how far back in time these arrangements had existed. Any attempt to partition the wastes, on the theory that the waste was the lord's, led to trouble, and to a claim that the vill had inter-commoned thereon from time out of mind, with the other vills of the group, and that the waste was held *pro indiviso* by them.[1]

One important fact should be emphasised. So far we have been mainly thinking of the wastes as an auxiliary means of helping to maintain their stock, but there is also the possibility that they were far more than that. It may well be that future detailed investigation will show that a considerable number of peasants were mainly dependent on these wastes for their means of livelihood. At Rossendale, in Lancashire, for example, we are told that "Facilities of common in this district were not so much the complement of a holding, as an extension of the chief means the tenement provided of earning a livelihood".[2] In neighbourhoods such as this, where the soil and climate were unfavourable to arable farming, a more pastoral type of farming was a necessity. Not only this: every manor had a number of inhabitants who had but little share in the common fields (and hence in the commons), and who were therefore forced to pasture their beasts in the adjoining wastes.[3]

The waste was much more than extra or even a main pasturage. To it the peasant looked for a hundred other things essential to his daily life. To begin with, it provided him with wood—a primary requisite. His house, his farm implements, and his household utensils were all mainly made of wood. He relied on it almost entirely for fuel. Hence his rights of hous-bote, and haye-bote and of fire-bote were of great importance to him. These varied in details from manor to manor, but commonly the peasant was allowed to take what wood he could get "by hook or by crook"—that is to say, such timber as he could knock off, or pull down from standing trees. Then again, he was often allowed to cut so many trees a year for repairs to his house, and implements and hedges, or to take undergrowth, or loppings, or

---

[1] *Terrier of Fleet*, p. 1.
[2] G. H. Tupling, *Econ. Hist. Rossendale*, 98.
[3] For a full discussion of the position and importance of such people, see p. 65.

any dead wood lying about on the ground.[1] In areas where the waste was large and under little control, he obviously had even greater opportunities to take what he would.

Many other things were available: for example, turves were cut in immense numbers. Some of these were used for roofing sheds or for making up balks; some were dried and used for fuel. Clay was dug for use in mill dams or for dikes; sand and gravel were excavated for building purposes. Bracken was cut and used for litter; the sedges of the fens and ponds were much sought after for thatching. Wild fruits and berries were gathered for the kitchen, and on every side the peasants found something of value which would help them in their struggle to live.

This, then, was the peasant's world. Naturally conditions varied throughout England. Some villagers had but little "waste" at their disposal, others had unlimited areas: in some parts the meadows were rich and provided ample crops, in others they yielded but poorly, and so on. The reader must constantly bear this in mind: it is one of the inevitable drawbacks of a general picture that it fails to show individual details and interesting variations. We must be on our guard against imagining too great a uniformity: on the other hand we need not let this reduce us to a pessimistic belief that no general account of the medieval manor and its occupants is possible. It is possible if only we will bear these conditioning factors clearly in mind.

[1] See, for example, *Yorks Inquis.* I, 28 (Pickering Forest, 1251); *Ramsey Cart.* I, 307 (1251); *Cust. Rents*, 83.

The Manorial Population

CHAPTER III

THE MANORIAL POPULATION

Now that we have considered the very complicated web within which the medieval peasant lived and moved and had his being we may turn to the man himself. And first, in thinking of the manorial population, we must be careful to differentiate between the many grades that even this humble society comprised. We are apt to rest content with the lawyer's easy division of free and serf; but, while this is an obvious difference which needs no labouring here, it is necessary to insist again that, if we pay overmuch attention to such a classification, we shall be ignoring equally important considerations of an economic rather than of a juridical nature. We must think of the manorial population as a body of people whose material circumstances were of the most varied nature. A man might well be a free man and yet possess only a mere two or three acres, and his only hope of keeping body and soul together was to find employment—probably on the holding of one of these despised villeins who had more land than he could work without help. True he could cease to work whenever it pleased him, with the knowledge that no one could compel him to return—until hunger drove him forth once again to seek his bread. But, in fact, it is clear that such men were no more free then than is the mill operative or the typist now: to throw down his tools may be the privilege of a free man, but it is one he but sparingly uses if he is prudent.

Even if we omit any question of free or serf, a glance at any cartulary shows us that there were many subdivisions, even among the servile population. First, we have the aristocracy, as it were, of the peasantry: men holding 30 or sometimes 60 acres in the common fields, followed by others holding only half this "full land" of 30 acres. Others again have to be content with "fardels" or "furlongs" of 10 or 15 acres, and below them come the cottars, and crofters, and "pytel-holders" who eke out an existence as best they can, for their land is only an acre or two, or sometimes only the bare croft or garden about their little house.[1] It is obvious that the 30-acre holder who owes his lord manifold rents and services is in a different category from the holder of some miserable pytel, who perhaps renders a couple of hens once a year, or does a day's work at harvest as the sole payment required of him for his holding. Yet, in the Manor Court, as in the King's Court, both are equal, and in certain circumstances, both are null: for both have the stain of serfdom upon them, and may be called upon by their lord "to answer for their villeinage as a villein ought".

The essential point to emphasise, however, is that so far as the manor is concerned there was considerable differentiation among the peasantry, and it is wrong to underestimate this. The lord certainly did not. In his Manor Court he constantly empanelled certain men to act as a jury, and we find that these generally included the large holders of the village. Again, it is the large holders who have to find a plough of their own to work on the lord's demesnes at certain seasons of the year: lesser holders are allowed to come with a team made up by two, three or more of them putting their resources together. Then again, at harvest, the greater tenants are forced to act as overseers to the rest of their fellows, and ride or walk about with white wands of office in their hands.[2] They provide carts and horses for carrying services, and generally are used by the lord in proportion to their holding and equipment. So with lesser men, according to their capacities, until we reach a level at which the agricultural tools the man has at his disposal are confined to spade, hoe, mallet and the like. This indeed is a dividing line in the village, for now we are dealing with the "poor labourers who live by their hands",[3]

[1] There seems to be little need to linger over the differences between cottars, crofters and other lesser holders. They were all of the same class: perhaps the cottars held rather larger pieces of land, and therefore were called on to render greater services. The medieval clerks did not discriminate very clearly. In the *Ramsey Cart.* (I, 397) some men are described as holding crofts, but a few lines later they are called cottars. Cf. I, 489 ("viginti quatuor cottarii, quorum quidam tenent croftas, quidam curtilagia", etc.); Vinogradoff, *Villainage*, 148: "The constant denomination for those who have no part in the common arable fields, but who only hold crofts, or small plots with their homesteads, is cotters"; and cf. p. 256. A special note, perhaps, should be made of the *Lundenarii*, men who are bound to work for the lord on one day a week (generally Monday) throughout the whole year.

[2] *Mon. Exon.* 352 *b*; *Ramsey Cart.* I, 309, 311; II, 47; *Eynsham Cart.* II, 8 and 129, etc.

[3] *Inquis. Nonarum*, 13 *a*.

and whose small holdings are quite insufficient to keep them, however intensively they are cultivated. These men are the "undermanni", the "crofters" and the like, and their history is as important as it is difficult to unravel.

Many years ago Vinogradoff drew attention to "the remarkable history of the small tenants", and added that this had "hardly been appreciated rightly by modern scholars". The years that have intervened since this was written have left the position but little changed. Mr Lipson in his *Economic History of England* has devoted some attention to the problem, but little else seems to have been done, although some writers in the *Victoria County Histories* have shown themselves aware of the importance of the small tenant in the manorial economy. Such neglect is the more surprising, for it seems clear that we shall not understand the daily life of the medieval village with any clarity all the while we ignore this section of its population. Naturally the number and importance of these small tenants varied from manor to manor, but everywhere they were to be found working as an essential part of the manorial organisation.

Modern scholars, however, may plead in justification that these men were equally neglected by their contemporaries. The clerks, who drew up the medieval extents and customals, spent but little time on such small fry. They held but small parcels of land—five acres seem to have been a common maximum, and often a beggarly two or three acres, or even a toft, is all the stake they have in a manor.[1] Hence the payments and services they were called upon to render were commensurately small, and the customals rapidly recite their meagre commitments in a few words after they have dealt with the greater tenants. All this is clear enough: small tenants, small services—but what is not so clear (because it was no business of the lord's clerks to make it so) is how these men managed to exist. Their holdings, in themselves, were insufficient to support them—even five acres, it is certain, could not do so—and they had to find other means of support. Hence their importance: they provided that pool of free or semi-free labour which was constantly available to all who could afford to pay for it by one means or another. The

---

[1] *Econ. Hist. Rev.* vol. v, No. 2, p. 37 n. 1, gives an excellent analysis of the average size of villein holdings in Cambridgeshire Manors.

virgater with no children, the widow left with a young family, the holder of land burdened with difficult or onerous services— all these, as well as the lord himself, whose demesne lands cried out for daily, as also for seasonal labour, were ready enough to make use of the small tenant; and without his presence life on the medieval manor would have been very much more difficult.[1]

These smaller tenants steadily grew in number as lords allowed more and more new land to be assarted, or as new-comers to the manor were given an odd corner here for a small money rent, or a pytel there in exchange for a few minor services.[2] Little by little we may imagine the growth of a body of men standing almost apart from the rigid compulsions of communal ploughings and other works,[3] as well as the presence in the countryside of those who had the fortune to live on manors where labour services were small or non-existent.[4] Their lack of shares in the common fields, which was part of their lot, also left them freer than many of their fellows, and this freedom they used in many ways. Some of them found a livelihood by supplying needs which their neighbours had but little time to fulfil for themselves: they became the village carpenters, or smiths, or weavers, or miller's assistants, and so on. For example, on the Bishop of Chichester's manor of Amberley, in Sussex, as well as the great tenants, who held virgates and the like, we find Benet Smith (*Faber*) who holds only "four acres belonging to the smithy", and in return for this his duties and obligations are as follows: "He shall mend with the lord's iron all the iron-gear belonging to two ploughs, but do nothing new. He shall shoe two horses, and the sergeant's horses with the lord's iron, and receive nothing....He shall grind all the scythes used in the lord's meadows, and all the shears while they shear the lord's sheep", etc.[5]

Another small tenant, Alexander Carpenter, held only a house and half an acre, and for this he paid but sixpence a year. His living was evidently made by means of his craft, for every village

---

[1] Lipson, *op. cit.* 44, 45; *Medieval East Anglia*, 121 n. 3; *V.C.H. Berks*, II, 182; *Herts*, IV, 184, 190; Page, *op. cit.* 39.
[2] See, for example, *V.C.H. Durham*, II, 209; *Hatfield's Survey* (Surtees Soc.), 32.
[3] Neilson, *Ramsey*, 27 ff.; Page, *op. cit.* 41.
[4] *Econ. Hist. Rev.* vol. v, No. 2, *passim*.
[5] Sussex Rec. Soc. XXXI, 48; cf. 37, 75, 82, 92.

found plenty of work for a skilled man who could repair and build the ploughs, carts, harrows and other agricultural implements, as well as oversee, and carry out the more difficult pieces of joinery needed for the medieval house. Contemporary account-rolls almost universally contain entries of payments made to both the smith and the carpenter for work of this kind.[1] Similarly, on these Sussex manors, we find many other small holders who were of some consequence to the easy working of the village. We have Robert of the Mill, holding three acres about the mill as well as one acre he has assarted, for which he makes an annual cash payment, but also has to attend the harvest boon work as one of the officials.[2] Such names among these smaller men as Robert Mason (*cementarius*), Adam Baker (*pistor*) or Geoffrey Weaver (*textor*) are indicative of the way in which these men found a living for themselves.[3]

These detailed accounts of the conditions on one or two manors are confirmed by a recent extensive examination of the *Hundred Rolls*.

Names and nicknames of the villagers suggest that they did not all live on the yield of the land (writes Professor Kosminsky). Crafts connected with the manufacture of textiles are indicated by such names as Draper, Comber, Fuller, Napper, Cissor, Parmentarius, Tailur, Tinclor, Textor, Textrix; with metal-work, by such names as Faber, Ironmonger, le Ferrour; with leatherwork, by such names as Tannur, Sulor, Corduanarius; with woodwork, building and carpentry, by such names as Carpentarius, Couper, Cementarius, Masun, Pictor; or with food-production, by names such as Cornificus, Cocus, Braciator, Baker, Pistor, Espicer.... Rural pursuits other than agricultural are indicated by such names as Bercarius, Gardiner, Grazier, Porker, Vaccarius, Piscator, Venator. Of course, not every Taylor engaged in tailoring, and not every Cooper made vats.[4]

Nevertheless these names are indicative of the occupations which

[1] Sussex Rec. Soc. XXXI, 100; Neilson, *Ramsey*, 79.
[2] *Ibid.* XXXI, 65; cf. 21, 38.
[3] *Ibid.* XXXI, 38, 97; cf. Knoop and Jones, *The Medieval Mason*, 107, 108. A great deal of evidence on these lines is available in any of the Cartularies or Rentals. See, for example, *Glastonbury Rentalia*, 34 (R. Carpentarius holds only two acres of assarted land); 93 (R. Taillur, J. Textor and W. Pistor all have small holdings and few duties). *Ramsey Cart.* I, 329 (Smith and Carpenter); 351 (Carpenter); 391 (Cooper and Carpenter) etc.
[4] Kosminsky, "The Hundred Rolls of 1279–80", *Econ. Hist. Rev.* vol. III, No. 1, p. 36. Or see for one occupation only the wide distribution of bakers in Worc. Hist. Soc. *Collectanea*, 1912.

were an inseparable part of country life, and which constantly absorbed a portion of the manorial surplus population.

Not only this: these men, as well as providing necessary services for their fellows within the village, were also among those who most easily got free from the manorial organisation. As we have seen, they were burdened with but small duties, and it was comparatively easy for them to get the lord to commute their work for a money payment.[1] This left them almost free, and we should be wrong not to consider the great if indirect effect this had in stimulating their neighbours to approximate to their status. The virgater with a multitude of claims upon him must frequently have sighed for the comparative freedom of the little man, who held only a few acres, it is true, but who could do what he wished in his own time and in his own way. We must not press this too far: the virgater frequently enough found his family could easily divide up among them the duties their holding imposed, and still leave plenty of time for their own strips and crofts; but, nevertheless, this was a freedom attaching to many of these small tenants that must have given some virgaters cause for reflection.

Their comparative freedom will be seen when it is realised that, once they had done the limited amount of work their little holding imposed upon them, they could turn their attention from one master or occupation to another more easily than could the greater tenants. They were able, therefore, to make experiments in crop production, or to cultivate their small holdings in ways impossible to the virgaters who were bound by age-long custom and the necessity for co-operative work at frequent intervals. Hence, we may with some justice think of this section of the medieval villagers as being far more important in several ways than at first sight might appear to be the case.

We must also note how the gradual spread of a desire to commute works for money payments increased the need for such men as these. The more the lord allowed his tenants to buy their freedom from week or boon works, the more necessary it was that he should be able to command a steady supply of labour for his various needs. This he would have found it very much more difficult to do unless there had already existed on his manor, or

---

[1] See e.g. Neilson, *Ramsey*, 26, 28.

near by, a number of men whose comparative freedom from the incessant cares of husbandry left them leisure to "live by their hands" in serving whosoever cared to employ them.[1]

On these manors where money rents were predominant, and services few or nil, much the same state of affairs prevailed. Small holders could not exist on their own few acres; they were forced to seek work wherever it could be found, and obviously it could be found on the acres of larger holders. Free or serf, the land had to be cultivated, and the labour came from the multitude of small tenants and their sons who formed part of every manor.

One further point must be considered. We must always remember that beneath the apparent fixed condition of affairs as revealed in the extents and customals there was a constant state of flux and change on the manor. The extent was concerned almost solely with the holding: the individual units of father, mother, children and other relatives which each holding might be supporting were of comparatively minor importance from this point of view. But, as we may easily imagine, a man who had only a small part in the common fields and yet was burdened with a large family was forced to do what he could to provide an outlet for them. Hence we find him purchasing assarts, or taking over extra cots and plots within the vill so as to accommodate his numerous progeny. In short, a constant movement was going on between the various sections of the manorial tenantry: some were leaving their father's home to start a life for themselves in some empty house and toft, or were prepared to build one on the assart clearing at the edge of the village. Others again were turning to seek a living by labour connected with the normal manorial arrangements: they engaged themselves as ploughmen, or carters, or shepherds who served the lord all the year round in return for a fixed wage, or they came to the aid of a fellow peasant unable, or unwilling, to discharge the duties incumbent upon his holding. The pressure of work at special seasons also called for a body of workmen who could be recruited at harvest or other times of stress, and who could aid the normal servants in a multiplicity of ways which varied according to the special and local needs of the many manors.

So far we have been stressing the differences between the

[1] *V.C.H. Berks*, II, 175, 182; *Herts*, IV, 184; *Dorset*, II, 233.

greater and the lesser tenants. It remains to note wherein their paths ran side by side. The lesser tenants, as we have seen, had little or nothing to do with the communal cultivation of the common fields. Nor had they any but the most insignificant of shares in the common meadows, and therefore they were not called on for plough and other services on the lord's demesne to the same extent as were their fellows. But some return they had to make for their holdings, and this return usually took the form of a day's work from time to time at the lord's will. Since they were not liable to perform the major works they were usually turned on to the many odd jobs always waiting to be done. They spread dung, or hedged, or ditched; they drove pigs and cattle to and from market; they helped to repair walls and thatches, to make new barns and pigstyes; to toss, and rake and collect the hay; to bundle and stook and load the sheaves on to the wagons; to winnow and thresh in the barns; to clear out the manor buildings before the coming of the lord; to gather reeds or rushes, or to plant potherbs or beans—these and a thousand other things were their usual lot.

If any one duty more than another attached to them it was the housing and guarding of thieves and prisoners awaiting judgment. Sometimes they are ordered to house them in their own homes for the time being as part of their duties, while at others they are responsible for them in the village lock-up.[1] They have to produce them for judgment and to take them to higher courts when required. When we recall how difficult it was for the king's officers to keep men from breaking gaol, we may imagine the troubles which beset a man charged with such a duty, with nothing better than a fragile structure of lath and plaster to keep his prisoner under arrest.

Another duty which commonly devolved on them was the carrying of letters and writs. They are made responsible for warning their fellows of the coming of the steward to hold a court, or they carry writs within limited areas (generally within the county).[2] They go from one manor to another carrying

[1] *Ramsey Cart.* I, 484; *Yorks Inquis.* I, 75; *Worc. Priory Reg.* 15 a, 66 b; Suff. Inst. Arch. III, 244; *Econ. Docs.* (Tawney) 61; *Banstead*, 54; *V.C.H. Surrey*, III, 29; *Cal. Inquis.* II, No. 443.
[2] *Econ. Docs.* (Tawney) 63; *Black Book St Augustine*, 27, 28; Sussex Rec. Soc. XXXI, 48, 114, 117, 120.

letters from the lord or his officials; and, indeed, so long as it was
something that could be conveniently *super dorsum* they were
commonly pressed into service. If the journey should be unusually long they received a small payment, but otherwise it
merely counted as one of the duties they owed to the lord.[1]

We see then that the manorial population was a complex social
group. The comparatively easy circumstances of the larger
holders have to be set against the struggles of the *undermanni*, and
every manor was a world of change, and rising and falling fortunes—not at all the ordered static affair we read of in the extents. And this state of things was common whatever else varied.
It is true that in different parts of the country certain conditions
varied a great deal. For example, the men on many Yorkshire
manors were principally occupied in driving and tending their
sheep, while their brethren on more southern manors were
mainly engaged with plough, harrow and reap-hook. The life of
the peasant on the Lincolnshire fens was very different in some
ways from that of his fellow on the edge of the great Wealden
forest. The prevailing occupation of any area—agricultural or
pastoral—naturally made a great deal of difference as to how a
man spent his day; but, nevertheless, for our purpose, it is
sufficient that there rested on all these men, in their degree, the
curse pronounced on Adam: "Cursed is the ground for thy
sake; in toil shalt thou eat of it all the days of thy life; thorns also
and thistles shall it bring forth to thee; and thou shalt eat of the
herb of the field; in the sweat of thy face shalt thou eat bread, till
thou return unto the ground."

It is with this in our minds that we may turn to study in some
detail the everyday life of the medieval peasant on whatever
manor he found himself, and in so doing we shall be deliberately
limiting ourselves to a certain extent, for we shall be forced to
ignore something of what was happening in many parts of
England where the manorial system had but partially and
sporadically obtained a hold. Recent investigations have considerably modified the views of Seebohm and Vinogradoff concerning the origin and development of the manor. They formed
their conclusions mainly from evidence taken from the centre of

---

[1] *Cust. Rents*, 66; *D.S.P.* **27**, 68; *Ramsey Cart.* **I**, 302; Sussex Rec. Soc.
XXXI, 20, 27, 36, 74, 82.

England, and from ecclesiastical estates, but were forced to see that the conditions of the north and west would not fit into their theory. As a result they propounded the view that commutation took place more easily and at an earlier date in these areas than in the south. They also are mainly responsible for the theory that the peasantry was considerably depressed in status after the Conquest, and that many who were free became serfs. We are no longer able to accept these views in their entirety, for the researches of Professor Stenton, Mr Jolliffe and Mr Douglas alone have made it clear that in large areas "the typical manor" never became at all common. Professor Kosminsky writes:[1]

Stenton's researches have shown that in the Northern Danelaw (East Yorkshire, Derbyshire, Nottinghamshire, Leicestershire, Lincolnshire and Rutland) the typical manor, with serfdom and labour dues, was never a predominating institution. Gray's well-known work, *English Field Systems* (1915), revealed the existence in medieval England of a whole variety of local field types, and thereby forces us to consider the possibility of local variations in the structure and organisation of rural institutions as well.... Jolliffe's article further subtracted from the area of the "typical" manor the extreme North of England—Northumbria, which includes Lancashire, the Lothians and the highlands of Yorkshire.

Then again there must be added the work done by Mr Douglas in East Anglia, and in view of all this we are forced to realise the truth of his contention that

the social history of this epoch must no longer concern itself with "English Society in the Eleventh Century", but rather with a number of diverse social structures varying greatly from district to district.... Research, therefore, is tending to become more localised in its scope, and the interest and importance of this period is that therein the Norman government is attempting to apply a uniform feudal theory to the whole of England. This affected materially the upper ranks of society throughout England, but, underneath, the peasant substructure in each district long remained substantially unchanged; and only slowly and imperfectly was it made to conform to the new order.[2]

Our knowledge, therefore, of conditions on the land between the time of the Conquest and the early thirteenth century is still very fragmentary, and it would be rash to venture any wide

[1] *Econ. Hist. Rev.* vol. v, No. 2, p. 28.
[2] *Feudal Documents*, xviii, and cf. clxviii.

generalisations, or to attempt to give any full-scale picture of what was happening to the peasant during that time. From the thirteenth century onwards, however, things are clearer. The Norman attempt to impose a feudal organisation has spent its force, and the manorial system is seen in its full flower. While we may no longer believe that the whole of England was manorialised almost completely—indeed we now know that some parts were never manorialised at all— yet the most recent studies, such as those of Professor Kosminsky, show that when all allowances are made, the manorial system had a very firm hold on large areas, especially in Central England.[1] It still remains true, therefore, that hundreds of thousands of men in twelfth- and thirteenth-century England were born to live and die in villages which were under the control of this or that lord, and that these men knew no other life than that conditioned by the enclosing web of the feudal manor.

Yet, while our main concern will be to follow the lives and fortunes of these manorial peasants, we shall in effect be describing the lives of many others as well. The serf had much in common with his free, or half-free brother. Both were engaged in agriculture and in the pastoral life, and both were subject to the routine such pursuits necessitate. Much of the time of both was spent in the fields and about their closes. Although we shall see how many things there were which separated them, we must never lose sight of the fact that, free or serf, they were engaged on similar tasks.

---

[1] *Econ. Hist. Rev.* vol. v, No. 2, p. 44: "Although it is true that we can no longer regard the large estate with villeins and labour services as the 'constituting cell' of English society in the thirteenth century, such estates do, nevertheless, form an important section of economic life."

The Peasant's Year

CHAPTER IV

THE PEASANT'S YEAR

L ET us now turn to the actual day-to-day operations which medieval agriculture made necessary, and let us consider for convenience the task confronting a manorial peasant, who, as we have seen, had his strips in the common fields. In those parts of England where the two-field system prevailed he found himself working on one field during one year while the other field lay fallow for most of the year, but was ploughed from time to time, and the next year vice versa. In those areas where the three-field system was in vogue, one field was planted in the autumn with wheat (and perhaps rye) as its main crop, another with oats, vetches, or barley in the following spring, while the third field was fallow. The next year the fallow field was used for wheat, the first for oats, etc., while the second field rested. The third year completed the cycle, and in this elementary fashion men sought to keep their land fertile. It was a wellnigh impossible task, for the number of species they had at their command was very limited: wheat, oats, rye, barley, vetches, beans and peas were the main crops; roots and artificial grasses were unknown, so that any serious rotation of crops which would give the ground a chance to recover was impossible.

The peasants were even worse off than their lords in this respect, for not only had the lord the unrestricted right to the manure of his own herds, but he had also a *jus faldae*—a right of folding all the manorial sheep (and sometimes all cattle) on his own lands. This privilege he sometimes was able to exercise for a limited period only, but on some manors he could exercise it throughout the year. The lord's shepherd, therefore, was expected to see to it that his master's fold was moved about from place to place on the demesne, and also to report any peasants who were so bold as to keep their sheep on their own holdings. The privilege to do this could be got only by a cash payment. Cattle markets and fairs were also a welcome aid in fertilising the ground, but here also the lord usually insisted that these were held on his land, and even that the dung in the streets of the vill should be reserved for his own use.[1]

All this evidence clearly indicates that medieval farmers understood quite well the need for constant manuring, and yet at the same time it was very difficult for the peasant to accomplish this on his own holding. When we recall the slender resources which were at his command the reasons for his constant defeat are obvious. First, as we have seen, the lord had the *jus faldae*. Secondly we must bear in mind that the peasant could not keep any large number of animals himself owing to the difficulty of feeding them throughout the winter. He had great difficulty in keeping the comparatively limited numbers he owned, and was forced to feed them on what would now be considered very scanty rations. The amount of manure, therefore, he could hope for from animals fed in this way was limited. The peasant was caught: he had neither the number of animals, the unrestricted use of them, nor adequate fodder to produce the quantity of manure that soil, cultivated under the medieval cropping system, required if it were not to lose its productive power. He did what he could: he worked to get his land manured, and even at times went to the great labour of carrying marl or lime and treating his land with this, but it was an uphill task.

Indeed, some writers have gone so far as to declare that the soil was becoming exhausted in the thirteenth and fourteenth centuries, and that the comparatively wretched crops which were then produced were mainly occasioned by this. So far, however, very little evidence of any value has been produced which would suggest that the yield per acre was falling decade by decade, and it is difficult to see on what grounds such a theory can be supported.[2] Exhaustion would probably have shown itself much earlier than this, for most of the common fields date back for several centuries; and, again, the experiments at Rothamsted seem to be strongly against the "exhaustion" theory. There for nearly 100 years a plot has been sown with wheat and left without manure. For the first 30 years the crop diminished rapidly, but then seemed to reach a stationary condition, and has re-

---

[1] Denton, *op. cit.* 152.
[2] The case against the "exhaustion" theory has been best argued by R. Lennard in the *Econ. Journ.*, March 1922, where the authorities for and against this view are quoted and discussed.

mained at an average of about $12\frac{1}{2}$ bushels for many years, "and will in the future diminish very slowly, if at all ".[1] Few medieval holdings could have been starved to a greater extent than this, and if the "exhaustion" theory is to be sustained it will require better evidence than has yet been produced in its support. The comparatively low yield of medieval cropping is sufficiently accounted for by the poor supply of manure, the lack of variety of crops and the inefficient methods of preparing the soil at the disposal of the medieval husbandman.

With these difficulties in mind let us assume that we are dealing with an energetic and reasonably successful peasant who has thirty acres under the three-field system, and follow him throughout the year as he works upon them. First, the ten acres of fallow. These present a comparatively simple problem. As we have seen, they form part of one of the common fields and are open to all to feed upon, and the peasants turn their cattle out upon them, in part to manure them, in part to graze upon the scanty vegetation that they supply, each acre of which should be sufficient to support two sheep at the very least.[2] From time to time, however, preparations for the coming crop have to be made, and the field is ploughed on three occasions. April is a good time for this first ploughing, Walter of Henley tells us, for then the earth breaks up well, and it is good to do it again in a couple of months' time, taking care not to plough too deeply, but just sufficiently to destroy the thistles.[3] After this it can be left until the autumn, and then in October it is ploughed for the last time before the winter corn is sown. This time the plough should go some two finger lengths deeper than before, "then the plough will find sure ground, and clear and free it from mud, and make fine and good ploughing".[4]

The other two fields, however, took up much of the peasant's time. In January he could do little upon them, save perhaps cart out manure or spread marl ready to be ploughed in as soon as the weather was suitable. These were his main means of

---

[1] A. D. Hall, *The Book of the Rothamsted Experiments* (1905), 37, as quoted by Lennard.
[2] *Walter of Henley*, 143.
[3] *Ibid.* 11, 13. Fitzherbert advises two "stirrings": one in June and a second early in September.
[4] *Ibid.* 15.

fertilising the soil and were most important. The straw of the previous year's harvest was carefully saved, and was used in the cowsheds and stables during the winter, and then piled up outside and mixed with earth, or even thrown in roads and paths for a time.[1] Before the drought of March it was carted on to the fields, and ploughed into the earth;[2] and so valuable was it considered that we are told that the straw kept for this purpose was worth half the price of the corn.[3] The peasant, therefore, did his best to have some of this precious manure ready for his fields, even though his lord had exercised his rights of folding his cattle for part of the year, and thus deprived him of part of this most valuable fertiliser. Marl was less commonly used, and it must have been an exceedingly laborious and slow business to cart the large quantities required on to the land, break it up sufficiently small and then spread it about.[4]

Ploughing in the early spring kept the peasant busy on his strips, and once this was done, harrowing and then the sowing of the spring corn (oats, barley) or the peas and beans followed. Something has already been said about the problem of co-operation among the peasants, but a few more words may be added. The plough was a comparatively light and simple affair, and in many types of soil did not require a large plough team. There is abundant evidence to show that it was possible to manage with only a yoke of oxen or pair of horses, and this, it is arguable (at the least) is what many men did do. They had, or could assemble, a plough with two beasts to pull it, and with this could quite well plough their strips. It is true that the ploughing was not very deep, but it was all the ploughs of those days could manage.

Once the ground was ready the seeds were sown. These were brought on to the field in a sack, and then a quantity from this was placed in a wooden basket or box slung round the sower's neck, or tied round the waist. This box was called a seed-lip, or hopper,[5] and from it the sower took seed and scattered it abroad

---

[1] *Walter of Henley*, 19, 20, 101.
[2] *Ibid.* 20.
[3] *Ibid.* 143. Cf. *Sixth Report Hist. MSS. Commission*, 598.
[4] "Marle mendeth all manner of grounde, but it is costly." Fitzherbert, *Surveyenge*, cap. 32.
[5] Cf. *Piers Plowman*, B. VI, 63:
    "And hang myn hoper at myn hals in stede of a scrippe;
    A busshel of bredcorne brynge me ther-inne."

with a rhythmic movement of the body: "when as thou walkest thy left foot be up, let thy right hand cast abroad—and when thy right foot be up then fling from thy left hand."[1] At other times a kind of apron was worn instead of the seed-lip, and the seed scattered from this. Peas and beans, on the other hand, were "dibbled": a small hole was made with a pointed stick, and the seeds at once dropped in[2]—a task which, as it seems, was usually performed by women.

After the sowing came the harrow—"or els crowes, doves, and other byrdes wyll eate and beare away the cornes"; else, as Walter of Henley says, "to pull the corn into the hollow" which is between the two ridges.[3] The harrow was much as we know it to-day, if we follow the illustration in the *Luttrell Psalter*. There is pictured a solid cross-barred wooden frame with teeth projecting on its under side.[4] It is drawn by a horse, and a boy follows, scaring off the birds by the use of a sling and stones.[5] No doubt many peasant farmers could not afford so expensive a thing, and made use of a rude bush-harrow, formed of blackthorn or whitethorn which was dragged across the ground at the tail of a horse, and served its purpose reasonably well.[6] Some-

---

[1] "But howe to sowe? Put thy pees in-to thy hopper, and take a brode thonge of ledder, or of garthe-webbe of an elle longe, and fasten it to both endes of the hopper, and put it over thy heed, lyke a leysshe; and stande in the myddes of the lande, where the sacke lyethe, the whiche is mooste conveniente for the fyllynge of thy hopper, and set thy lefte foote before, and take an handefull of pees: and whan thou takeste up thy ryghte foote, than caste thy pees fro the all abrode; and whan thy lefte foot ryseth, than cast them fro the." This extract from Fitzherbert's *Book of Husbandry* (1534 ed.), § 10, although some two centuries later than our period, no doubt embodies long-standing country custom.

[2] For illustrations see D. Hartley's *Thomas Tusser*, 57, 97, 130 and her *Life and Work of the People of England*, Fourteenth Century, 24e; *Luttrell Psalter*, Pl. 93.

[3] *Walter of Henley*, 15.   [4] *Ibid.*, Plate 94.

[5] Cf. Rogers, *Prices*, I, 540: "In 1334 a sling is bought, to drive away the birds, with which a boy is armed." In Joan Evans' *Medieval France*, 28, is reproduced an illumination of the late fourteenth century, showing the wooden harrow, and a man with bow and arrow dealing with the birds. For other pictures see Hartley, *Thomas Tusser* (1931), 57, 95.

[6] A. Neckham, *De Utensilibus*, 113; Rogers, *Prices*, I, 540. Thorold Rogers was quite mistaken in saying (p. 16) "I find no trace of harrowing or rolling," and again on p. 540: "We cannot conceive that an article like a harrow could have escaped entry in the accounts had it been in use." There is, for example, a *hersiarius* on the Glastonbury Manor of Longbridge (p. 139) and harrowing is one of the most common of duties. See pp. 81, 87, 91, 96, 100, etc. Cf. *Battle Customals*, 53.

times on hard clotted ground where the harrow could make but little impression it was necessary for the peasant to break up the clods with wooden mallets, as they are seen to be doing in the *Luttrell Psalter*.[1]

Once all this was finished the peasant's labours were not so pressing, and he could turn to the many other secondary jobs waiting to be done. If the land was heavy, draining operations were constantly necessary and worth while; ditches wanted digging out after the winter floods, and the good earth put on to the land again; hedges and enclosures round the little home or any private bit of enclosure required attention, and so on. Then, as we have seen, it was time for the first ploughing of the fallow field, and the busy activities in the garden where such vegetables and fruits as were then available were grown.[2]

So the days went by with plenty to occupy men till the end of May. The coming of June saw them making renewed efforts. The haymaking called for all their strength: first, there were the numerous compulsory days which they had to spend in getting in the lord's hay; and, as well as this, there was their own crop waiting in the enclosed meadows which had been carefully guarded and reserved for this purpose since Christmas. The mowers used a long scythe, not very different from that in present use, the blade almost at right angles to the handle, and perhaps a little shorter and broader than the modern scythe.[3] With this they appear to have mowed not more than one acre in a day.[4]

After the haymaking, the strips again called for much attention. Thistles had to be uprooted, but this was not done before St John's Day (June 24) as a country tradition asserted that thistles cut before this would but multiply threefold.[5] The fallow ground was also ploughed up again to destroy weed—the "second-stirring", or *rebinatium*, as it was called in the books. Hemp and flax were gathered by the good-wife, and dried before being spun into yarn for thread, rope or linen yarn. Both of these plants were pulled up by the roots, not cut like corn, and then

[1] *Ibid.*, Plate 94.
[2] For the peasant's garden, see below, p. 232.
[3] For illustrations see Joan Evans, *Medieval France*, 50, and Hartley, *Thomas Tusser*, 77.
[4] *Wilts Arch. Mag.* XXXII, 318.   [5] *Walter of Henley*, 17.

PLATE II

The peasant at work

laid out on the ground to dry a little before being put into a convenient stream to rot away the fleshy part. This was vigorously rubbed away, and the remainder dried thoroughly, and then beaten so as to get the fibres clean and separate. Then it was ready to hang up in "strikes" to finish drying, before it was combed out and ready for the spinning-wheel.[1] Meanwhile the men-folk were busy weeding in the two fields under cultivation; they used two long sticks, the one held in the left hand had a forked end, while the other had a small curved blade. With these they worked up and down their strips, cleaning the corn of dock and other weeds.[2]

With the coming of August the peasant's activities reached their climax. Once again the demands made upon him by his lord were often very heavy. He had to appear in person again and again to gather in the lord's crops—and, although he usually worked one or two days more a week from August to Michaelmas than at other times in the year, this was not enough, and he had to give several extra days of his time as a boon or gift to his lord. And further, he had to come with all his family: everyone able to work, save perhaps the housewife, was pressed into service for so many days. This made the getting-in of his own crops a more difficult and anxious matter, and work during these crucial weeks must have been wellnigh unending. The scythes were at work mowing down the barley, rye, oats, peas and beans, but the wheat was cut with a reap-hook or sickle as in recent times. The ear was cut off high up on the stalk leaving the straw standing. The author of *Seneschaucie* speaks of five people as making a team for this work, which suggests four to cut and one to bind. Men working thus, he says, can gather some two acres of corn a day.[3] The cocks and sheaves were small so that they could dry the more quickly, and be the more easily carried from the field.[4] The band tying the sheaf together is said to have been twice the

---

[1] For full details see Bartholomew Anglicus, *Medieval Lore*, ed. R. Steele, 106. Cf. Chaucer's Pardoner (*C.T. Prologue*, 676), whose yellow hair hung smoothly "as dooth a strike of flex".

[2] See illustration, *Luttrell Psalter*, Pl. 96. Here again Fitzherbert's *Husbandry*, § 20, has much to tell us of "wedes as thistyls, dockes, kedlokes, cocledrake, darnolde, gouldes, haudoddes, dogfenell, mather, ter, and dyvers other small wedes". Kedloke = charlock; cocledrake = cockle; mather = dog-fennel; ter = tares; gouldes = marigolds.

[3] *Op. cit.* 69.   [4] *Ibid.* 97; *Fleta*, Bk. II, cap. 81, § 2.

circumference of a man's head, or that of a cord stretching from his knee to the sole of his foot,[1] and the *Luttrell Psalter* shows us men walking in the fields each carrying two sheaves to put on to the great pile.[2] Gloves were worn to protect the hands while at work, and these were usually issued freely by the lord to his men.[3]

After the corn was cut and put into sheaves the Church's portion—the tithe—had to be selected.[4] We see this being done by Cain in the Towneley play of Cain and Abel, and may there glimpse something of the grudging spirit with which many men paid their dues to Holy Church.[5]

Now the heaviest part of the year's work was over, and the strips in the common fields all stood bare, and once again the cattle wandered over them to seek what they could. This they were allowed to do until the time came for the autumn ploughing. Then they were moved away from the field that had stood fallow for a twelvemonth and there a third and last ploughing preluded the planting of the wheat and other seed for the coming year. On the other fields manuring or marling were all that was necessary, and the peasant then turned towards home and to making provision for the coming winter. First, such fruits and nuts as were available were gathered and stored; then, the supply of winter fuel had to be assured. The right of taking timber from the nearby woods was jealously controlled, and it was only such dead wood or timber not exceeding a certain dimension that was at the peasant's disposal. The cutting down of oak or ash, without permission, meant a fine at the Manor Court; and, in general, the lord's officers were here, there and everywhere, on the look out for over-zealous appropriators of wood. Yet wood was essential, not only for fuel to help pass the long winter nights, but also for the thousand and one things about the medieval home.[6]

---

[1] Delisle, *op. cit.* 309. Cf. Gras, *Economic and Social History of an English Village*, 235.

[2] *Luttrell Psalter*, Pls. 97, 98.

[3] *Eynsham Cart.* ii, lxxxiv; *V.C.H. Berks*, 176.

[4] See Owst, *Literature and Pulpit*, 261. For a long discussion (with references) of the reasons for believing that tithe was normally deducted from the corn crop in sheaves and on the fields, see R. Lennard, *Econ. Journ.* (Supplement), Feb. 1936, 173. Tithe is here more fully discussed on p. 330.

[5] *Towneley Plays* (E.E.T.S.), 15.

[6] For further details and references, see p. 229.

Even when the wood-pile was large enough, and turves or peat had been stored wherever possible, much remained to be done. In some parts (especially in East Anglia) the sedge was cut, for this was well known to make the very best thatch; bracken was gathered in great quantities to be used as bedding for the cattle in the coming winter. The stubble, which had been left standing when the corn was cut, was now gathered, either for thatching or bedding, or to be cut and mixed with hay as fodder. If it was not thus wanted, it was often ploughed in and allowed to rot and thus nourish the soil.[1]

In wet weather there was always plenty to do in threshing the corn. The lord, of course, was able to have his done in his great barn, but the peasants probably made shift with the more cramped space under a lean-to against their house, or anywhere which was dry and sufficiently large to allow of the easy swinging of the flail. This was made of two pieces of wood (frequently thorn) tied one to the other by a leathern thong. The worker stood over a pile of corn and by a rhythmical circular motion brought one end of the flail down smartly on to the ears, thus dislodging the grains of corn. Once this had been done, it was necessary to separate the chaff and straw from the grain. This they did either by winnowing the whole with a fan so that the lighter husks of the chaff were blown away leaving the grain, or by tossing it up in the air near the door of the barn so that the breeze could catch and bear away the chaff, leaving the grains of corn to fall to the ground. The chaff itself was not wasted, but swept up and mixed with damaged corn and used as food for the beasts.

The advent of Christmas saw the bad weather bringing work in the fields to a standstill; and, once the peasant had made his preparations outlined above and threshed his corn, he could estimate what return he had received for all these exacting labours throughout the year. We, unfortunately, have no exact means of knowing this, for no kind of peasant's accounts have survived, or indeed, in all probability, ever existed. We can only make an estimate based on figures obtained by an analysis of the yield on the lord's demesne, and from what has already been said, it is unlikely that the peasant's land would yield equally well. Nevertheless, this is our only method of approach, and so

[1] See *Medieval Lore*, 105, 106.

long as we bear in mind that our figures are only approximations we can proceed safely. To begin with the theory laid down by Walter of Henley: he tells us that land which did not yield more than three times the seed sown gained its owner nothing unless the price of corn was high.[1] It is generally agreed that something like 2⅖ bushels of wheat were commonly used to sow an acre in medieval times, so that it is clear that nearly 8 bushels per acre had to be harvested in order that there should be no loss.

Turning from theory to fact we find that, as a result of his investigation of thousands of accounts, Thorold Rogers gave it as his opinion that "the rate of increase was not more than four times", i.e. (4 × 2⅖) bushels[2]—say between 9 and 10 bushels. A great deal of work has been done since then;[3] and, although even now the range of statistics is not sufficient to allow of certainty, the figures of Sir W. Beveridge (with certain small adjustments) may be taken as our most accurate modern evidence. By an examination of the account rolls of the Bishop of Winchester he obtained records of wheat yields per acre from eight manors in various counties—three in Hampshire and one each in Somerset, Wilts, Oxford, Bucks and Berks.[4] His investigations led him to the conclusion that the average yield for the period 1200 to 1250 was about 9·44 bushels.[5] These figures have since been examined by Mr M. K. Bennett who gives reasons for believing the Winchester figures to be rather low as an average for all England, and comes to the conclusion that "perhaps 10 bushels would not be too high; but a conservative guess would be 8 to 9 bushels".[6]

If, then, we reckon the yield of wheat on demesne lands to have been 8 to 9 bushels, we shall probably be over-estimating the

---

[1] *Walter of Henley*, 19.   [2] *Hist. of Agric.* I, 56.
[3] See especially Milton Whitney, "The Yield of Wheat in England during Seven Centuries", *Science*, Oct. 1923, p. 320; H. Bradley, *The Enclosures in England* (Columbia Univ. Studies in History, Economics and Public Law, LXXX, No. 2); R. Lennard, "The Alleged Exhaustion of the Soil in Medieval England", *Econ. Journ.* March 1922.
[4] *Econ. Journ.* (Supplement), May 1927, "The Yield and Price of Corn in the Middle Ages", 155.
[5] The modern 60 lb. bushel is 20 per cent. heavier than the medieval bushel, which would give us a figure of 7·5 bushels of 60 lb. The wheat sown would be correspondingly less.
[6] *Econ. Journ.* (Supplement), Feb. 1935, "British Wheat Yield for Seven Centuries", 12.

peasant's actual return if we put it at some 8 bushels per acre. But, of course, he did not sow the whole of his land with wheat, and Sir William Ashley[1] and others have argued very strongly that wheat was only a small part of his crop, and that we must envisage him as sowing rye, barley, oats, peas and beans, or mixtures of these, all bringing in a varying return. If we suppose, for the sake of argument, that these are all sown in equal proportions, then the yield according to the author of *Hosebonderie* would be sixfold,[2] or if we take Sir William Beveridge's figures for wheat, barley and oats only, we get a figure of 11·4 bushels per acre.[3]

From the above figures it is obvious that we shall be weighing the balance in the peasant's favour if we assume his holdings could be cultivated as successfully as could those of his lord, and that, at the maximum, his average yield from all kinds of seed was about 11½ bushels per acre. We can be a little more definite by saying that if he planted his 20 acres in equal areas of wheat, barley and oats his crop would yield him 68 bushels of wheat, 95 bushels of barley and 70 bushels of oats. We need not, in this connection, take any notice of the question of tithe, for, as Mr Lennard has recently shown in so convincing a manner, tithe was taken in the field, and before the sheaves ever reached the grange where it had to be accounted for by the manorial officers.[4] Two deductions, however, must be made from this total of 233 bushels. First we must deduct the amount required as seed corn. Again, using the Winchester figures, we find that approximately 2½ bushels of wheat, or 3¾ of barley or 4¼ of oats were required for each acre,[5] so that the 20 acres would use up 16⅔, 25 and 28⅓ bushels respectively, leaving 163 bushels to go to the miller. Now if we assume the miller took an average multure of one-sixteenth,[6] this left the peasant with approximately 48, 66 and 39 bushels—a total of about 153 bushels.

The problem now faces us—what could the peasant do with this 153 bushels of mixed corn? No answer of any great value

---

[1] See *Econ. Journ.* XXXI, 285, and *The Bread of Our Forefathers, passim.* For a rebuttal of Ashley's views see *Econ. Journ.* XXXII, 119.

[2] *Op. cit.* 71.

[3] *Op. cit.* 161. This would equal 9·12 modern bushels.

[4] *Econ. Journ.* (Supplement), Feb. 1936.

[5] Beveridge, *op. cit.* 158.   [6] See below, p. 133.

can be given, for we lack nearly all the information which would enable us to proceed with any certainty. But several lines of investigation give us some insight into the peasant's standards of living, and are worthy of consideration. We may first of all deal with the corn allowances made to manorial servants. On those manors where the lord employed a permanent staff of ploughmen, carters, shepherds, etc., they were paid, partly by a small yearly wage, partly by food provided at the hall, and partly by periodical gifts of corn. These, naturally, varied to some extent from manor to manor and from servant to servant; but, confining ourselves to the most highly rewarded servants—the ploughmen and carters—we find a constantly recurring figure asserting that they received one quarter of corn in ten weeks, or more usually in twelve weeks.[1] When this was so, it follows that they had some 36 bushels (or in modern reckoning some 29 bushels) at their disposal in the course of the year. What, precisely, they did with these 36 bushels we do not know; the frequency with which some such allowance occurs suggests that it was a normal living allowance—but whether for a single man or for a family is more difficult to say. In later times it would certainly have been considered a family allowance. Writers in the eighteenth century, and more scientific critics of recent times, seem to agree that something like one quarter of wheat was consumed annually by each person in eighteenth-century England;[2] so that, if we assume for the moment that the consumption of bread was the same in the thirteenth as in the eighteenth century, a medieval family of five (two adults and three children) would want between four and five quarters of grain a year. It may well be that the thirteenth-century peasant ate considerably more bread than his descendant, owing to the more limited variety of foodstuffs at his disposal. But even if so, our 20-acre holder had plenty of margin between his 151 bushels and the 36 bushels which are in question. All that we need to argue here is that

[1] The evidence for this figure comes from a large number of manorial accounts, printed and unprinted: see, for example, Davenport, *op. cit.* 24; *E.H.R.* IX, 422; Neilson, *Ramsey Econ. Conditions*, 83; Rogers, *Prices*, I, 288; II, 626; and *Ministers' Accounts*, 751/18–21 (Berks); 859/23 (Glos); 843/31 (Essex); 998/25 (Suffolk). It also corresponds with what we are told by the author of *Hosebonderie*, 75.

[2] See references and discussion in Elizabeth W. Gilboy, *Wages in Eighteenth-Century England* (Harvard Economic Studies, No. 45), 22 and n. 3.

15 1 bushels gave such a peasant much more than was sufficient for his needs.

Not all his corn was used for bread: indeed it is doubtful whether the peasant was so extravagant as to eat wheaten bread at all, save if and when it was provided for him by his lord.[1] We may well imagine that whenever possible he sold his wheat to give him a little ready money for such things as he could not make or get by exchange from a neighbour. Rogers gives the average price of a quarter of wheat between 1261 and 1400 as 5s. 10¾d., so that if we suppose that the peasant sold the whole of his 48 bushels, he would have got 35s. 4½d. in cash. The barley and oats he would be more likely to keep for domestic needs. Much of the barley doubtless went in the production of his home-brewed ale; while the remainder, and part of the oats, were used for bread-making, and the rest of the oatmeal provided the basis of that most common of the peasant's daily dishes—the pottage.

Thus we see that, taking a very favourable view of what the servile holder could produce on his 20 acres, and assuming a good year, it is clear that he could grow enough for his needs, and a good deal to spare for sale or exchange. But, of course, we cannot assume that all land would not yield anything like an average of 11½ bushels per acre, and that every year would not be a good year. And further, we are here dealing with the village aristocracy—the virgaters with their 30 acres of strips. When we remember that they were a minority on the manors, and that tens of thousands of men had something less than a quarter of this as their main source of livelihood, it becomes evident that life for them was always a struggle—a struggle in which they were bound to lose unless the seasons were propitious to them.[2]

But the resources of the peasant were not limited to his sacks of grain. He had other means of livelihood, and of these the most important was his stock of animals. These, as we have seen, were limited in number, both by manorial custom or by-law, which determined how many of each kind should feed on the commons or fallows, and further by the fact that the peasant

---

[1] See below, pp. 111, 235.

[2] In Germany in 1871, on lands where conditions were still medieval, it was officially stated that 20 acres in some parts (*Land Tenure Reports*, Part II, 131) and 10 acres in others were necessary to support a family of five or six.

could not afford to have an unlimited number of beasts to feed throughout the winter. For the average peasant, however, some stock was vital, but when we come to enquire as to the numbers of these kept by the peasantry we have no body of reliable information to help us. There are a few local Assessment Rolls for taxes on moveables between 1290 and 1334 which give the stock on which the villagers were assessed, but they are very few in number and their evidence is difficult to interpret.[1] It seems probable that the number of sheep, for example, kept by any one peasant depended on the nature of the country. Thus in pastoral districts such as Holderness, or the South Downs, or Wiltshire, peasants are found owning considerable numbers of sheep, while in agricultural districts they own comparatively few.[2]

Oxen and cows demand attention first, for they came into the peasant's everyday life in innumerable ways. The oxen, of course, were invaluable for all kinds of farm work and were widely used all over England. Horses, it is true, were more and more used from the Conquest onwards, but, nevertheless, conservative landowners, like Walter of Henley, still believed in oxen, and thought them more useful and more economical than horses. More than that, as he says, "When the horse is old and worn out then there is nothing but the skin; and when the ox is old, with ten pennyworth of grass he shall be fit for the larder."[3] Similarly the cow played a considerable part in all but the humblest households. It provided milk for most of the year, although the quantity fell off considerably after Michaelmas, owing to the lack of good feeding, and it was not till the following May that the cow came into full milk once again. The difference is estimated by the author of *Hosebonderie* to be such that the yield was worth 3s. 6d. during the summer months, but only 10d. for the rest of the year. After Christmas, indeed, the yield was so small that milk fetched three times its summer price.[4] At the worst, however, even two or three cows were a real asset to a struggling

---

[1] The best monograph is that of Willard, *Parliamentary Taxes and Personal Property.*

[2] By the kindness of Prof. Eileen Power I have had an opportunity of studying her transcripts of a number of the existing assessment rolls which show quite clearly the variations in stock in different parts of the country. It is to be hoped that she will be able to publish an account of her researches in this side of the pastoral economy before long.

[3] *Op. cit.* 13.   [4] *Op. cit.* 77.

family. If they wished they could make butter and cheese of the milk, or sell it in the neighbouring vill. Each cow was reckoned to produce seven stone of cheese and one stone of butter between May and Michaelmas.[1] If we take the average price of seven stone of cheese to have been about 5s. 0d. from 1260 to 1400, and that of a stone of butter at $9\frac{1}{2}d.$, it is clear that the cash value of a cow in full milk was considerable, and cows were hired out at from 5s. to 6s. 8d. a year.[2]

But, as Walter of Henley reminds us, both oxen and cows had their value as food, and the peasant salted down his ox at Martinmas, and it undoubtedly provided his main store of flesh for the winter. It was probably tough and stringy, and lacking in fat, but he had perforce to make the best of it. Then again the hides were of the greatest importance, and were probably tanned in the village, and afterwards used for innumerable purposes both domestic and agricultural. Further, these animals could always be sold for cash at the local market or elsewhere. Oxen were worth some 13s. 0d. as an average price in the thirteenth and fourteenth centuries, while cows and bulls fetched about 10s. per head.[3]

After his oxen and cows, the sheep probably gave the peasant most concern, for while they were not so easily managed nor so productive as the pig, nor so useful on the farm as the ox, they were almost a necessity. Their wool, their skins and their carcases were obviously all of prime importance to the peasant in many ways, and even their milk was used to eke out other supplies. Hence, although as we have seen, the villagers were not always allowed to get full value from their sheep, since they were from time to time folded on the lord's land, and also were not easily kept in some districts, yet, nevertheless, they were of sufficient value and importance to form part of almost every peasant's stock. We may, therefore, picture our imaginary peasant as striving, year by year, to preserve, or even to enlarge his small flock, despite the terrible incidence of murrain and the shortage of feed which were continuously warring against him, since he could provide but little food for them other than that

---

[1] *Op. cit.* 77. Cf. p. 27, where Walter of Henley says that 3 cows will only produce 14 stone (1 wey) of cheese between Easter and Michaelmas.
[2] Rogers, *Prices*, I, 397, 452.   [3] *Ibid.* I, 361.

they could obtain for themselves as they wandered over the open fallows and the waste surrounding the village.

Of all his animals, however, in some ways the pig (then as now) ranked highest in the peasant's eyes, for no animal was so easily fed, and no animal so easily put on flesh and was so soon prepared for the slaughter according to medieval standards. The village swineherd[1] was of the first importance in village life: he it was who gathered together the swine of his neighbours and led them off into the woods when these were thrown open to them, and the acorns were falling. At other times he drove them on to the waste or on the fallows to get what they could; for, unless they could obtain a great deal of food in this way, it was considered highly unprofitable to keep them. Only during the hardest months after Christmas was it thought economically sound to supply them with anything but waste and what they could pick up outside the house and on the manor. Thorold Rogers tells us that "it would seem that the medieval farmer reckoned on two to four bushels as necessary in order to bring what we should call marketable pigs into sufficient condition".[2] We may suspect, however, that those pigs which were not destined for the market seldom received such luxurious feeding, and that they were slaughtered in what we should consider to be a miserable condition.

These were their most valuable accessory food supplies after their corn, but to these we must add poultry of many kinds. Chickens were everywhere: we are constantly surprised at the large number of eggs a peasant has to produce at given seasons of the year, and the ideal of Henri IV that every peasant should have a chicken for his pot must have been a fairly widespread possibility in the thirteenth century. Walter of Henley tells us that a hen ought to lay 180 eggs a year, but the author of *Hosebonderie* is content with 115 eggs and 7 chicks. Besides these chickens, geese were fairly common, and sometimes numerous enough to demand the presence of a village gooseherd.[3]

---

[1] For the swineherd's duties see *Walter of Henley*, 113. For illustration, see *Luttrell Psalter*, Pl. 14.

[2] Rogers, *Prices*, I, 337: "Some idea of the condition of these pigs may be gathered from the note in vol. II, p. 383, in which we learn that 35 pigs gave 180 lb. of lard, that is, a little more than 5 lb. apiece."

[3] See picture of gooseherd in *Luttrell Psalter*, Pl. 91.

Further food supplies were at times and in places available, but are very much more difficult to assess. At the edge of every manor, where great woods or waste or fen began, the wild animal life was abundant—more abundant, perhaps, than we have any means of estimating. Certainly the vast extent of cover provided by these wild uncultivated stretches gave shelter to almost endless numbers of wild beasts and birds. The great stretches of thorn, for example, housed myriads of small birds, and the wily villager had little difficulty in trapping these by means of small nets, much in the same way as the bird-snarer worked within living memory on unwatched heaths and open places. These birds could be caught in great numbers and sold, or used as welcome additions to the housewife's pot. Such action may or may not have been tolerated by custom (depending to some extent on the local lord's rights); but, undoubtedly, much hunting and snaring went on that could by no means be thought of as lawful. Indeed, poaching seems to have been one of the most common of the pastimes of the peasant, and every manorial record is likely to bear evidence of the arrest or of the depredations of the village poacher.

All seem to have been implicated—the parson as well as the peasant, and it is clear that few men could resist the temptation offered to them by the sight of this " God's plenty "[1] which was all about them, and which (to be fair to them) fed on their corn and constituted a formidable nuisance at their very doors. Take rabbits for example. We learn that in certain parts of the country they were little short of a pest. The men of Ovingdean (Sussex) say that there are 100 acres of arable, lying annihilated by the destruction of the rabbits of the lord Earl Warenne, valued at £1. 5s. 0d.;[2] or, as another inquisition tells us, the holding "is of small value because the rabbits are beginning to burrow in that place".[3] In another part of England altogether, on the manor of Higham Ferrars, we are told that they abounded, and special enclosures were made by the lord for their protection.[4]

Another nuisance to the peasant was the dove or pigeon. The lord's dove-house was one of the most familiar of medieval

<hr>

[1] *Durham Halmote Rolls*, 91, 131, 178, 185; Davenport, *op. cit.* 75; *Wakefield Rolls*.
[2] Sussex Arch. Soc. Coll. 1, 62.　　　[3] C. Pullein, *Rotherfield*, 70.
[4] *A.A.S.R.* xxxiii, 135.

sights. No peasant was allowed to have one, or to kill these birds however numerous they were, and however harmful to his crops.[1] After a monotonous fare of salted fish or meat the dove was a great delicacy, and from Norman times onward the birds had been protected in the interests of the great. Large dove-houses, sometimes holding hundreds of birds, were built and from thence hordes of these voracious feeders descended on the unfortunate peasants' fields taking their fill and fattening themselves for the lord's table at his men's expense. Little wonder that the dove-house became one of the most hated landmarks of the lord's position and of the subjection of the villagers. Both doves and rabbits, however, found their way into the hands of others than their owners, and men were constantly presented at manorial courts for taking rabbits with snare or ferret, or for catching pigeons with nets or divers traps (*diversa ingenia*).[2]

Many kinds of wild animals were also abundant, but forbidden to the villager, for by the thirteenth century most manorial lords had got from the king a grant of free-warren[3] which prevented anyone entering their lands to hunt wild animals. The legal implications of such rights became very tangled in the course of time: no one might follow the hunt of a fox or a hare into warren land; but, on the other hand, to follow the hunt of a deer, in such circumstances, was no trespass, for deer were "beasts of the forest", and not "beasts of the warren". Further, the lack of any clearly marked boundaries delimiting a warren made matters more difficult. The forest had its "pale" or fence, but the warren lay open. Within its confines, however, the hare, rabbit, pheasant, and every kind of bird, as well as many kinds of vermin were all plentiful, and it was impossible to prevent the peasant, either out of sheer desperation or sheer devilment, from taking what he could get whenever the chance offered.

Yet another source of supply was at the peasant's very door. The rivers were full of fish—sometimes carefully preserved, but

---

[1] *Y.B.* 7 Ed. II, 183 n.
[2] For illustrations and much information, see A. O. Cooke's *Dovecotes*, and *A.A.S.R.* xxxiii, 138 and 368, and many references there.
[3] This is an excellent example of F. W. Maitland's dictum that when we read in medieval times of a man having a free this or that, in reality what was meant was that he was thereby free to oppress somebody else. So here: the lord's "free-warren" obviously was anything but free to the villager.

PLATE III

Country Sport

generally unwatched save for the sporadic care of one of the lord's servants. All great houses and large establishments also had their fishponds, and throughout the year fresh and salt fish from river as well as from the sea was a constant item in the diet of the upper classes. Here again the peasant could not be denied: in the north of England the salmon was a rich prize. If a man could be lucky enough by a bit of quiet night work to get a sizeable fish from the waters of his lord, then he and his family were well provided for during the next few days. Eels again were everywhere and were eagerly trapped, and so were the ordinary river fish as we know them to-day. Men were caught fishing with "Angleroddes", or setting eel traps, or using nets and other "engines" against the orders of their lord, and were fined in his court.[1]

Our rapid examination of the 30-acre holder's resources leaves the impression that, given reasonable harvests, he had no difficulty in producing enough corn and livestock to keep himself and his family, and to leave something over for sale or exchange. But we have constantly to be reminding ourselves that no manor was made up of the "typical" villein—the virgater or 30-acre holder. As we have seen, every manor had a number of *undermanni*— men holding anything from a little "close" of a rood or two to seven or eight acres, as well as others who held as much as half a virgate and so on. The manorial holdings were capable of in- numerable grades, and the resources of the lowest of these grades must have been slender. If we assume that some 36–40 bushels of corn were a minimum requirement for a normal family, it is clear that this required a holding of between five and ten acres— and probably nearer ten than five—on which it could be grown. Those who held less than this were forced to adopt a lower stan- dard of living, or to seek auxiliary means of augmenting their incomes by helping on wealthier men's holdings, or by working as manorial servants, or as communal shepherds or swineherds, or in one of the village trades.

But whatever means were employed, it seems that a consi-

---

[1] E.g. *Hales Rolls*, 135, 284. The men of the monks of Eynsham (*Eynsham Cart.* ii, 10) gave them 6d. a year for the right to fish in certain waters, while three men were fined 1s. 6d. at Carshalton for using too close a net in the common water "to the great destruction of the fish" (Surrey Record Soc. ii, 23). For further remarks, see also p. 269.

derable number of peasants in the medieval village lived very
near the border line of actual want.[1] For them, as for the poor
man in *Piers Plowman*, there was many a "winter time when they
suffered much hunger and woe".

[1] For an account of the foodstuffs available to them, see p. 234.

God spede ye plow, & sende us kvrne now

Rents and Services

CHAPTER V

RENTS AND SERVICES

DESPITE the fact that both free and serf spent much of their time at similar labour in the fields there was a profound gulf between them in other ways. Once the free man had paid his yearly rent it was not often that anything further except of a trifling nature was required of him by his lord. The serf, however, found things very much more oppressive. Not only had he to pay his rent, but a number of other small cash payments were exacted. Miss Neilson, in her *Customary Rents*, has given a full account of such payments, and it will suffice our purpose to note that they are all charges upon the serf for this or that small favour or privilege. Before he could touch even a piece of dead wood he had to pay his yearly "wood-penny"; he was forced to take a hen or some eggs at set seasons to the manor house as a payment for the privilege of keeping poultry about his own house; when he sold one of his beasts the lord frequently received a part of the purchase price. On all sides he found himself unable to do what his free neighbour could do. As is well known, his lord demanded a small payment when the serf wished to give one of his daughters in marriage; he could not let his boy go away from the manor to be taught by some friendly priest or at a nearby school without again putting his hand in his pocket —the restrictions under which he lived were many; and, although many of them were petty, yet in sum they bulked large, and influenced his whole life.

Some of them, however, were far from being petty even in themselves, and were a constant charge on his energies and his pocket, and a constant reminder to him of his servile condition. He was continuously forced to put his lord's affairs first and his own second, and to find pence and shillings for reasons he could not have understood, even if they had been explained to him.

Such a state of affairs had gradually evolved as a consequence of the introduction and development of the manorial system in England. Little by little, throughout those parts of England that became manorialised, a state of affairs between lord and serf had grown up which became known as "the custom of the Manor". Vinogradoff asserts that the lords "allowed" such a custom to grow up,[1] but this seems too simple a view of a very complex matter. The domestic staff of any household to-day have conditions of labour, and hours "off duty", which would have seemed impossible to our grandmothers. In a sense our mothers have "allowed" these conditions to grow up, but in fact it is only by making such allowances that they have been able to retain a staff at all. Even the most reactionary employer finds she must allow "Sundays off", and half-days every week, at whatever inconvenience to herself. So it was on the manor. Certainly, in theory, the will of the lord was all-compelling, and in that sense it may be said that any privilege or relaxation of strict legal theory was a result of the lord's indulgence. But, in actual fact, it is much more probable that the lord "allowed" what he found himself powerless to prevent. A strong steward or bailiff on the one hand, or a determined body of serfs on the other, could change things on any one manor in the course of a very few years, especially before "the custom of the Manor" became sufficiently established and fixed in men's minds to be of any very great importance, and also before lords had had it written down formally. For many decades after the Conquest, a continuous change was taking place: every manor was the scene of an endless contest in which lord and serf each struggled to obtain their own ends. On the one hand there was the lord (or his agents) exercising the power which his ownership of the manor gave him. This power was often very considerable—whether by right or by usurpation we need not now consider[2]—and naturally it was used to protect and to extend the lord's own ends. He may at times have been a beneficent patriarch and at times something considerably less than this; but, in any case, there he was, controlling the peasant's life to a very great extent. It is true that gradually there was created "the custom of the manor", and it is generally correct to say that this was determined by the verdict of the peasants from time to time. They gave the "dooms", and these were really determinations of the customs obtaining on the manor. Yet, even so, a powerful lord or a harsh steward could do much to force a decision favourable to

---

[1] *Econ. Journ.* x, 309.   [2] For this see below, Chapter VIII.

himself; and when, during the second half of the thirteenth century, lords began systematically to put their customs into writing, they at once arrested any hope of rapid change, and also protected themselves against the possibility of its being easy to convince the court of the wisdom or the necessity for any fresh interpretation of custom. Henceforward the custom of the manor is on record; it no longer exists merely in the memories of the "wiser and saner" peasants empanelled to give a "doom", but can be (and is) constantly turned up while the Court sits, and is quoted and used on the lord's behalf. Not only is it on record, but it is a record drawn up by lawyers eager to make all things clear, who tended to reduce any wavering and uncertain customs to a steady and clear-cut pattern, and to phrase in the lord's favour any equivocal or doubtful matters.

Against all this the peasant fought, and was continuously fighting. He probably found it difficult to realise the implications of much that happened in the Manor Court when he was called on for a decision. He knew that it was the custom to ask his opinion, and that his "dooms" were the result of his own personal knowledge and of his practical judgment, and had to leave it at that. Common sense urged him to interpret matters in his own favour as far as was possible, and the rigid cash basis on which manorial affairs were conducted encouraged him to buy himself freedom from this or that liability as he saw the chance. No general account of this slow process is worth much, for conditions varied enormously from manor to manor, but over several centuries the fight went on, and the immense variation of custom, as expressed in these rents and services, is evidence enough of this. Every variation, could we but read between the lines, has its own story to tell, for every variation came about only by pressure on one side or the other. Occasionally the veil is lifted, and we can see something of what must have happened again and again up and down the country throughout these centuries.

Take, for example, the quarrel over the payment of sheep as part of the heriot by the men of the Abbot of Vale Royal. The customal says: "And as to sheep, let them be divided like all other goods of the deceased which ought to be divided." The revealing sentences, however, follow, and are most illuminating:

This is inserted in this place, by itself, because when the convent first came to Darnhale, the bond-tenants said that no division ought to be made of the sheep, but that all the sheep ought to remain wholly to the wife of the deceased. Which is quite false, because we always used to divide them without gainsaying it at all, until Waren le Granteunour was bailiff of Darnhale; and while he was bailiff he was corrupted with presents, and did not exact the lord's share of all things in his time; and afterwards the bond-tenants endeavoured to make this a precedent and custom, which they by no means ought to do.[1]

But for this addendum we should have known nothing of the struggle which had been waged over the partition of the sheep, and by it we are also reminded of the extent to which the lord was dependent on his agents, and of the wisdom lying behind the careful drawing up of the written customals. Cases such as this, or the revolts at Dunstable,[2] or Burton,[3] or Meaux,[4] are evidence enough of the necessity for reading the bald statements of the customals with a wideawake attention. Only by so doing shall we sense the underlying agitation that was changing conditions on innumerable manors—an agitation, however, which was seldom violent enough to leave any very obvious traces, even to the diligent reader of customal and court roll.

With such general considerations in mind we may now turn to see the way in which the "power of the lord" had determined what services and what payments the serf should make, and how they are to be found in their essentials all over the country, despite local modifications and variations, due to "the custom of the Manor".

One of the most characteristic features of the manorial system was its insistence on manual labour as one important element in the return a man made to his lord for the privilege of holding land on the manor. He might, and generally did, make certain money payments, but his obligation to render a specified amount of work from time to time was all important. The lord depended to a greater or less degree upon the work thus exacted for the cultivation of his part of the manor, for the proper tending of his cattle and the upkeep of his manor house. Of course it is true

---

[1] *Vale Royal Ledger Book* (Lancashire and Cheshire Rec. Soc.), 119.
[2] *Ann. Dunst.* (R.S.), 122.
[3] (Wm. Salt Soc.) *Staff. Collections*, v, 82.
[4] *Melsa Chron.* (R.S.), III, 126.

that he often had a nucleus of servants who lived all the year at his house,[1] and also that sooner or later most lords allowed their serfs to make an additional money payment in place of some or all of their works. Nevertheless, for a long time, and over large areas of England, many hundred thousands of peasants were forced throughout the year to leave their own affairs from time to time in order to do work of various kinds for their lord.

We cannot generalise very exactly as to what such a demand meant. It varied on various manors, in various areas, and at various times. It was not even the same on all the manors held by any one lord. This we may say, however: in general it was a distinguishing mark between bond and free. A number of instances can be quoted which show free men rendering week-works, but they must be regarded as exceptional, and were so regarded by the lawyers of the thirteenth century, who more and more tended to consider the uncertainty which attached to week-works as one of the *stigmata* of the serf. Hence Bracton's famous definition: "For that is an absolute villainage, from which an uncertain and indeterminate service is rendered, where it cannot be known in the evening, what service is to be rendered in the morning."[2] Further, we may note that the work required by the lord was roughly commensurate with the size of the holding. Everything depended upon this, and the number of mouths to be fed, or of young sons eager for work who resided on each holding, was of no account to the lord. He was concerned only with the due render of what had been determined to be the burden of such a holding. Hence a virgate-holder's duties, which look so formidable at first sight, become far less onerous when we reflect that in all probability he was married, and had sons and daughters, and even servants of his own to help him. Thus he was able to plough his own acres and those of his lord, and to carry on a hundred and one other jobs without undue strain, by the simple method of sending one or more of his own family or helpers to the manor house, while the rest of the household carried on at home.

It is true, as we have already seen, that he was expected on a few

---

[1] See below, p. 182.
[2] Bracton, *op. cit.* I, 207. But see below, p. 139 n[1]., which shows this to be an undue simplification.

occasions to appear with all his family and servants; but, for the most part, the lord contented himself by exacting only such service as might be rendered by a single person in the course of a day's work. And even when we have said this we have not made clear what was meant by a day's work in the thirteenth-century cartularies. For example, a day's work is frequently defined as the threshing of two bushels of wheat or a quarter of oats, or the mowing of an acre or rather less of hay, or the cutting of a half acre of corn—or a multiplicity of other jobs[1]—all of which, however, have this in common: they represent only something like half a day's actual work.[2] Old farm labourers still speak of cutting two acres of wheat by hand between the hours of 4 a.m. and 10 p.m.; and, making allowances for then and now, this helps us to realise that (in the later Middle Ages, though it had doubtless been stricter in the past) the man who was called upon to work three days a week, as a matter of fact actually worked only for a portion of each of those days, and even then, as we have seen, this generally took but one member of the household away from the family holding.

We may emphasise this point (which is of great importance, and has not been fully appreciated in modern discussions of this question) by noting the terms used to define the hours of work demanded of the peasant, especially at the busiest times of year—the hay and corn harvests. The cartularies make it clear that it is an unusual thing to demand a man's work for the whole day, and when this is exceptionally required the cartulary says so quite clearly. Thus the men of Stoneley in Warwickshire are to be in the field during the harvest *at sunrise* and to work *till sunset*,[3] and the same hours are expressly required in many other instances.[4] Again at Forncett, for the greater part of the year the lord exacted manual works which lasted for half the day only: in the autumn, however, the works are stated to be *per diem*

---

[1] See any cartularies *passim* for this. E.g. *Ramsey Cart.* I, 288, 299, 310, 323, 335, 345, etc.

[2] Cf. *Norf. Arch.* XIV, 19, where Mr W. Hudson writes: "Work for a whole day on the land counted for 2 works".

[3] Dugdale, *Warwick*, 177 a.

[4] *Frideswide's, St. Cart.* II, 357; *Arch. Journ.* LVIII, 355; *Min. Acc.* 987/19, etc. The men of the monks of Eynsham come to their harvesting *ante pulsum campani missa beate Marie*, and are not allowed to sit to eat their breakfast or otherwise *ante collacionem*—presumably about noon. *Eynsham Cart.* II, 40.

integrum.[1] Even in the harvest season a day's work often means only till noon: a man may send two men to work till noon, or only one if he stays till evening (*usque vesperam*);[2] or again, work terminates at noon unless the lord gives a repast, in which case work is resumed until evening.[3]

If we bear these facts in mind we shall not be so overwhelmed when we read that at Waldon and Walpole in East Anglia (*c.* 1270) six days' work a week were performed throughout the year,[4] or that in the West of England, the monks of Gloucester in 1266-7 were exacting a minimum of four days' work most of the year and five days at harvest.[5] Even on manors as heavily burdened as these, it left a man with considerable time for his own work, except on a very few occasions. And he was protected from attempts to demand more of him by the exactness with which his services were usually defined. Years before the first accounts of such services were written down (and few written accounts exist earlier than 1225) custom had hardened and settled what was each tenant's burden, and any move to increase this was fiercely resisted by him and all his fellows.[6] It is true that they were not always able to withstand pressure from above, and no doubt services actually increased on some manors in the thirteenth century; but, generally speaking, services slowly dwindled as the peasants bought their freedom from such liabilities.[7]

The exactness with which services are defined, and the meticulous way they are accounted for in the annual accounts may lead us too far in a belief in medieval order and regularity. Although the lord had a right to the works, he did not always demand them as regularly or as completely as we may easily be led to believe. As regards regularity Mr Hudson writes:

It is often taken for granted that the obligation to do one work a week, or sometimes three or four, meant literally so many days' work regularly, in consecutive weeks. Whatever the original practice may

---

[1] Davenport, *op. cit.* xxxix.

[2] *Battle Cust.* 87: cf. *a mane usque nonam*, 63, 74, 76, 78, 94 and *Crondal Records*, 112, 113, 120.

[3] *Norf. Arch.* xx, 185; and cf. p. 189, where ploughing goes on till noon if dinner is provided, otherwise it ceases at tierce (9 a.m.).

[4] *Med. East Anglia* 81; cf. *Norf. Arch.* xx, 185; *Ramsey Cart.* I, 310.

[5] *Glouc. Cart.* III, 52, 53.

[6] Neilson, *Ramsey Econ. Conditions*, 29; *Cur. Reg. Rolls*, I, 4; Levett, *op. cit.* 65 n. 2.

[7] See below, p. 279.

have been, by the thirteenth century the week-works were, at least in many places, not regular, but largely occasional. They were, so to speak, kept in stock by the reeve, and demanded when and where most needful, a strict account being rendered at the end of the year.[1] This point of view is emphasised by Miss Levett from her intensive study of the Bishop of Winchester's manors, where she finds that

there was always a very considerable margin [of works] of which the lord may take advantage when crops are exceptionally heavy, when the weather was unfavourable, or the Saints' days fell unfortunately, or when some change of method, such as increased fencing or enclosing, caused an unprecedented demand for labour.[2]

If, as sometimes happened, the lord had no need to take advantage of this margin, the works were either excused or sold to the peasants. A common item in the manorial *compoti*, which gives a full account of "works sold" or "works acquitted",[3] is a reminder to us that many more works were often owed than were in fact ever demanded. Hence, here again, the seemingly heavy demand of the cartulary or extent needs some scrutiny before it can be taken at its face value.

With these considerations in mind we may turn to examine the various types of work exacted from the peasant. His obligations here fall into two main divisions, week-works, and "boon" works. Week-works, as the name implies, were rendered week by week throughout the year; "boon" works were only performed occasionally and as "extras". The working year was divided into two parts—from Michaelmas to the beginning of August, and from then on to Michaelmas again. During this latter period, on account of the corn harvest, rather more work was demanded from the serf, so that whereas for the greater part of the year he had to perform say two or three days' work a week, during this period he was called on for three to five days a week, as well as for a number of "boon" works in addition.

The week-works may be grouped conveniently about certain operations, and of these the most important was the ploughing. Whether the lord's land (the demesne) was a separate part of the

---

[1] Sussex Arch. Soc. LIII, 172.
[2] Levett, *op. cit.* 65; cf. 88, 180; *V.C.H. Berks*, 181.
[3] *E.H.R.* IX, 420 ff.; *Trans. Royal Hist. Soc.* XIV, 124; Levett, *op. cit.* 65; *Glouc. Cart.* III, 185, 194.

manor, or whether his strips lay side by side with those of his tenants, they had to be ploughed by the communal teams of the villagers. Every holding had a certain duty imposed upon it. Sometimes this was expressed in the number of acres to be ploughed, or in the number of days of ploughing to be given in the year; sometimes the customal exacted a certain quantity of work from a group of serfs and left it to them to make their own arrangements.

A few cases, taken from the manors of the Bishop of Chichester in the middle of the thirteenth century, will illustrate the incidence of these ploughing works. A virgater of Ferring is bound every other week to attend with one of his fellows, and to do whatever ploughing is needed,

unless a holy-day or rainy weather prevents. If the weather is rainy so that he cannot plough, in that week he shall do another work; but if he has ploughed two or three furrows, and then has to unyoke owing to rainy weather, he shall do no other work that day, unless the weather clears enough for him to plough.[1]

At Selsey, the virgater ploughs an acre and a half, if needed, every other week between Michaelmas and Lady Day, and aids with his plough team the ploughing and harrowing of the land before barley is sown.[2] At Sidlesham, the holder of two virgates ploughs and harrows twelve acres in winter, and twelve acres in Lent, and must do another acre in winter and Lent if so desired in place of other work.[3] And with this ploughing often went the associated works of sowing and harrowing. A man has to fetch the seed from the lord's granary, sometimes to be sown by the lord's sower, sometimes to be sown by himself,[4] or he may even be sent to fetch it from another manor,[5] either because of a shortage, or because of a common belief that seed from another manor would yield better than that produced and sown on the home land.[6]

Besides work in the fields, repairs to the manor house and the buildings around it were usually done by the peasants. Under the care of expert carpenters or masons "they tore down old

---

[1] Sussex Rec. Soc. XXXI, 71.
[2] *Op. cit.* 16.   [3] *Op. cit.* 23.
[4] *Op. cit.* 88.   [5] *Op. cit.* 89.
[6] *Walter of Henley*, 19: "Change your seed every year at Michaelmas, for seed grown on other ground will bring more profit than that which is grown on your own."

walls, dug the clay, and fetched water to 'temper' it; pulled
off the old thatch and cut and brought stubble for the new".[1]
A clear account of the sort of work demanded may be found in
the customal of Fure in Sussex (c. 1250), where men are ordered

to come with carpenter's tools to make a hay barn, if needed, or to
mend it, and they shall help the master carpenters to flaw the timber
and carry it at the precept of the carpenter, but shall make no holes
to put the posts in; they shall find the timber for the said barn from
their own wood, at the lord's will. They shall have the bark and the
top and lop, and the lord shall throw the timber. If the master
carpenter is not content with their work they shall make a fine at the
lord's will and depart home (et recedent); and [otherwise] they shall
stay until the barn is built.[2]

Once the land was ploughed and sown there was plenty for the
serf to do (during the lull before the harvest) in order to discharge his weekly obligation. Sometimes, the customals merely
say that he does "whatever the lord wills" on such days, but
often it is more explicit, and we may see exactly how he was
occupied. He carts dung from the stables and cowsheds and
spreads it about his lord's fields; then, after the ploughings he
comes to harrow and to weed from time to time; he tends and
plants in the lord's garden; in the summer cuts the hay, binds
and carries it to the lord's barns. Then in autumn, after cutting
and carrying the corn, he helps to clean, thresh and winnow the
grain, and to collect the best of the straw for use in roofing stacks
and houses. He scours ditches, trims hedges and makes fences;
he gathers reeds and rushes for thatching, or apples for cider.
There was also the care of the animals of the lord and of the vill:
the swineherd drove the pigs to feed in the woods; the shepherd
had the flock to wash and shear and to pasture on the commons
and in the meadows when they were thrown open, as well as to
move the lord's fold from place to place on the demesne; the
oxherd had to plough and work with the lord's oxen and clean
out the byre. Every customal has its variations, but all show us
the bulk of the manorial population performing all the innumerable services incident to agriculture as a part of the price they
had to pay for their own holdings.

[1] Davenport, op. cit. 22; cf. Sussex Rec. Soc. XXXI, 54.
[2] Sussex Rec. Soc. XXXI, 76. Fure is Highfure in Billingshurst.

Apart from all this, which was mainly work round about the village, the serf was liable to render carrying services both in or out of the manor if required. On many manors it was necessary to carry the corn and other produce either to the lord's residence (often in another manor or part of the county), or else to the nearest market town where it could be sold. This carriage was performed by the serfs—those with large holdings being obliged to lend their horses and carts for the purpose, while the smaller holders were forced to carry on their backs (*super dorsum*). In some surveys we find it stated clearly that so many days of such work are required, and also the distances or places are named. For example, on one Ramsey manor a man might be forced to carry to a distance of twenty leagues,[1] while on another Ramsey manor he could stop after going only twelve.[2] On yet another of these manors a serf was obliged to carry to Ramsey, London, Ware or Cambridge as required, but he was compensated by food and relaxation of other works for his journeys to London and Ramsey.[3] Again, the serf on some manors only carried when his turn came round,[4] or after he had had a day off to get his cart ready.[5]

On manors such as those of the Canons of St Paul's, or the monks of Battle, these carting services outside the manor were peculiarly heavy, since an old system still prevailed whereby each manor had the duty of sending its produce from time to time to the lord's residence. On the St Paul's manors, for example, this was carried by the peasants *secundum quantitatem tenementi*, and several times a year by cart, or sometimes by boat, they had to bring food to London.[6] Even the smaller holders were not exempt, for they were compelled to help load the boats, or drive the swine to London.[7] Similarly on the Battle manors, or those of the Bishop of Durham and elsewhere, the peasants were continually moving to and fro in order to provide food and corn for the use of their lords,[8] since these large households, with their

---

[1] *Ramsey Cart.* I, 50; cf. *Glas. Rentalia*, 165 (20 leagues).
[2] *Op. cit.* I, 56; cf. *Glas. Rentalia*, 136 (15 leagues).
[3] *Op. cit.* I, 46. [4] *Glas. Rentalia*, 161.
[5] *Op. cit.* 83. [6] *D.S.P.* 17, 34, 47, 68.
[7] *Op. cit.* 27, 68.
[8] *Battle Cust.* 122; *Hatfield's Survey*, 4, 8, 38, 99, etc. And cf. *Cust. Roff.* 2, 9.

masses of retainers, required the produce of many manors in the course of a year.

Even within the manor, as we have seen, a good deal of carrying service was exacted from the serfs. Anything the lord needed at the manor house was carried by them; building materials, wood for firing, corn, hay—all imposed a fairly heavy burden. Some details concerning the carriage of wood may serve as an example. At Amberley, in Sussex, the large holder had to link his team with that of one of his fellows, and their four oxen had to fetch five wainloads from the forest and bring them to the ferry. He had also to cart to the ferry the stakes and hurdles which had been made in the forest; and furthermore, with one of his fellows, he had to cart timber from the wood to the lord's barn whenever all his fellows were ordered so to do.[1] On the same manor the smaller holders had only to carry wood when the lord's pinfold required repair, or a new pigsty had to be built.[2] Similarly on other manors: men were required to go to the wood and haul out the timber and cart it to the lord's manor house; or, if the services were not performed, to pay a wood-penny or wood-silver.[3]

But even these constant exactions did not wholly meet the needs of the lord, and at harvest time he generally exacted more service from the peasants.[4] The getting in of the crops was the crucial operation of the year, and everything had to give way to this—even the peasants' own crops! Not content with this extra work during the harvest months of August and September, the lord usually claimed extra or "boon" services (*precariae*) at this period, and during the hay-making. These services were theoretically given freely by the tenants for love of the lord (and are sometimes called "love-boons"), but the freedom was more theoretical than real. Often these "boons" required the presence of the whole population of the manor—only the housewife and sometimes the marriageable daughters were excused.[5] A multiplicity of variations may be noted in the severity of the

---

[1] Sussex Rec. Soc. XXXI, 61; cf. *Ramsey Cart.* II, 37, 43.
[2] *Op. cit.* 59.
[3] *D.S.P.* 26, 62, 82, 85, etc.; cf. Neilson, *Rents*, 51, 53, 63.
[4] Neilson, *Ramsey*, 39 ff.
[5] Vinogradoff, *Villainage*, 174, 175; *Ramsey Cart.* I, 394; *Battle Cust.* 59, 89.

demands that were made: sometimes the lord demanded help only on every other day; sometimes only after the peasants had got in their own hay; sometimes the head of the house went only to the first boon, and so on:[1] but in general we may say confidently that these boons drew the majority of the able-bodied folk of the village from looking after their own crops at a vital time, and forced them to devote their attention to those of the lord.[2] He usually provided good meals and drink in order to help matters, but here again custom varied greatly. Generally, however, there were a number of "wet" boons, and a number of "dry" boons. At the "wet" boons, ale or cider, either in considerable quantities, or "at discretion", was provided; at the "dry" boons only water was given! The food was plentiful, generally consisting of a dish of flesh or fish, pottage (of peas or beans) with bread and cheese to conclude.[3] The Abbot of Battle's serfs, in order to placate them, had the right at the second and third "boons" to bring a comrade to the supper where they were to be, as they say, "solemniter depasti".[4]

Other "extras", besides meals and drink, were at times provided as an inducement. In connection with the boon services at hay-making there was a widespread custom whereby the lord released a sheep into the meadow. On some manors it became the property of the serfs only if they could catch it before it escaped out of the field;[5] on other manors it was handed over to them for their feast as part of their reward; while on others again a definite money payment was made to them by the lord, called *medsipe* or *madsheep*,[6] in lieu of the beast itself. As well as this they were frequently allowed to take some of the hay for their own use. On certain Ramsey manors the peasants were allowed to carry home so much hay or straw as they can bind in a single bundle and lift upon their sickle [or scythe] handle, so that the handle touch

[1] *Ramsey Cart.* I, 49, 354; II, 6.
[2] *V.C.H. Beds*, II, 80; *Glouc. Cart.* III, 119, 170; *Battle Cust.* p. 59.
[3] Univ. Lib. Camb. MSS. Kk. v, 29, ff. 29, 103, 104; *Battle Cust.* 87; *Court Rolls*, 998/21, 1030/3, 1030/6; and cf. *Glouc.* and *Ramsey Cart. passim.*
[4] *Battle Cust.* xxxix.
[5] *Ramsey Cart.* I, 298, 307, 476; *Glouc. Cart.* III, 64. Cf. *Pembroke Survey*, xcii; "the ram was brought to the centre of the field; if it remained quietly grazing then the customary tenants claimed it, but if it wandered out of the field they lost it and the abbess had it restored to her".
[6] Univ. Lib. Camb. MSS. Kk. v, 29, f. 69; *Eynsham Cart.* II, 24; Blomfield, *Norfolk*, I, 315; *Cal. Inquis.* II, 313; *Min. Accounts*, 859/23, etc.

not the ground. And, if perchance the handle break, then he shall lose his straw or grass, and be at the lord abbot's mercy, and pay a fine, coming to the best accord that he can with the abbot.[1]

Many other interesting variations might be quoted from the Ramsey manors, as for instance the custom which allowed the serf to take from the abbot's courtyard a bundle of as much straw as he could carry, "but, if the band break before he has passed through the yard door, he shall lose his straw, and compound by a fine as best he may".[2] In the West of England, on a manor of the Abbot of Glastonbury, the size of the sheaf taken by the peasant was measured in a strangely elaborate manner:

If any sheaf appears less than is right, it ought to be put in the mud, and the hayward should grasp his own hair above his ear, and the sheaf should be drawn midway through his arm; and if this can be done without defiling his garments or his hair, then it is adjudged to be less than is right; but otherwise it is judged sufficient.[3]

On other manors the serfs had the right to *medkniche* when they mowed the lord's meadow. This was as much hay as the hayward could lift with his little finger as high as his knees.[4]

Whatever else may be thought of conditions such as these, it is obvious that work demanded in this fashion and at such frequent intervals was often work grudgingly given, and often work badly done. We have only to glance through manorial documents to see that this was so. To take the first few pages of the Abbots Langley rolls: men were fined for not coming to the harvest, or for not producing a sufficient number of men; they came late, and when they did come performed their work badly or in an idle fashion.[5] Sometimes, not one, but a whole group of men failed to appear and so left the lord's crops ungarnered.[6] Others, even when they came, made themselves very unpleasant; Hugh le Waterleder, despite his name, cursed the lord's servants when they summoned him to carry water;[7] Roger Cook, when told to

---

[1] *Ramsey Cart.* I, 394; cf. 311, 324, 336, 399; *Worcester Priory Reg.* 14b; *Camb. Antiq. Soc. Proc.* XXVII, 165; *Glouc. Cart.* III, 64, 167, etc.; *Glas. Rentalia*, 10, 14, 53, 65, 71, 85, etc.
[2] *Ramsey Cart.* I, 415. For other interesting customs see I, 49.
[3] *Glas. Rentalia*, 135; cf. 68.   [4] *Ibid.* 85, 87, 88, 90, 91, 92.
[5] *Abbots Langley Rolls*, ff. 1, 2, 3, 4, 8, 9, 13, 14, 16 (all *c.* 1270). Cf. *Hales Rolls*, 168; *Tooting Bec Rolls*, 236, 240, 241, 246, 249, etc.
[6] *Abbots Langley Rolls*, ff. 20, 21, 34. Cf. *Cal. Pat. Rolls* (1299), 461; *V.C.H. Berks*, II, 184.   [7] *Chester Rolls*, 184.

carry wheat, at first would not come, and when he did, flung his first load on the tithe heap, and his second on the ground, so that all the sheaves were broken, and the carts had to pass over them to get into the grange.[1] On the other hand, we read of a lord who "wickedly slew William Bright with a dung fork, because he found him idling in his service!"[2] The mere enumeration of these few incidents of the harvesting will doubtless be sufficient to suggest to the reader the ever-present possibilities of drama which were part of the life of the fields.

Little wonder that Walter of Henley again and again insists on the necessity of watching over these workers:

Let the bailiff and the messor, be all the time with the ploughmen, to see that they do their work well and thoroughly, and at the end of the day see how much they have done....And because customary servants neglect their work it is necessary to guard against their fraud; further, it is necessary that they are overseen often; and besides the bailiff must oversee all, that they all work well, and if they do not well, let them be reproved.[3]

Such in brief were the various types of service which were commonly demanded by lords throughout England. They admitted of the utmost variation, and, no doubt, were enforced with very various degrees of severity: but there they were, an inseparable part of the peasant's life, and one of the most obvious signs of his serfdom. He could not avoid them; and since, as we have seen, it was the custom to exact work throughout the year, it was necessary to make arrangements for sickness or other causes of absence. This we find done in a variety of ways: sickness was generally considered a sufficient cause for absence, and a man was allowed a period of sick-leave varying on different manors and at different times of the year. On one of the Ramsey manors we find a man allowed three weeks' absence most of the year, but only fifteen days in autumn;[4] on others he can take a year and a day before he need attend;[5] on others again he has a year and a day but must plough.[6] On the manors of the Bishop of Chichester something between a fortnight and a month was

---

[1] *V.C.H. Middlesex*, II, 85.   [2] *Cal. Inquis. Misc.* II, 8.
[3] *Op. cit.* II; cf. 17, 21, 29, 33, 69, etc.
[4] *Op. cit.* I, 464; cf. Sussex Rec. Soc. XXXI, 83.
[5] *Op. cit.* I, 312, 325.
[6] *Op. cit.* I, 290, 300, 347, 370, 384, 395.

allowed the sick man, "but no more even though he is (still) sick!"[1] The test of sickness is sometimes stated: the man has to be so ill that he is unable to leave his house, or he is confined to his bed,[2] or even has to have the Sacrament before he can obtain relief.[3] These wide limits are evidence enough that no very clear rule can be laid down. Every manor had evolved its own custom in this matter; but common sense had realised that some consideration must be shown to the sick, and the arrangements in each manor were probably the result of common agreement between lord and serfs, and but seldom the autocratic decision of the lord. Hence, on the various manors of the Abbot of Ramsey, for example, we find the variety of arrangements outlined above.

Other causes such as bad weather, or attendance at some court in the lord's interests, also exempted men from work at times; but, in general, the custom seems to have operated more in favour of the lord than of his serf. Often the work is only postponed: he has to come at another time when summoned to do his share in the ploughing or reaping. As the customal on a manor of the Bishop of Winchester runs: "If they (the serfs) be hindered by rain, or in any other way, from doing their day's work, they shall come on the morrow; and if they be hindered on the morrow also, they shall come the day following, and so from day to day until they have fully completed one day's work."[4] It may be that this severity is only due to the urgency of getting in the crops, or of ensuring that the ploughing is done in good time, as there seems little clear evidence as to how the ordinary week-work at other times was regulated. On the whole it seems that the lord was far less strict outside the harvest season, as we may see by noting the general arrangements about attendance at courts and on holy-days.

Attendance at court, whether it was the ordinary manorial court or that of the sheriff, excused a man his day's work; but if the court day fell upon a holy-day some lords took advantage of the

---

[1] Sussex Rec. Soc. XXXI, 15; cf. 17, 23, 35, 83, 108. Cf. also *Camb. Antiq. Soc. Proc.* XXVII, 168 (15 days excused only), 171 (no excuse admitted).

[2] *Ramsey Cart.* I, 300, 457.

[3] Sussex Rec. Soc. XXXI, 53, 61, 65, 108; *Ramsey Cart.* I, 477.

[4] *Reg. Pontissara*, 659; cf. *Ramsey Cart.* I, 46, 312, 346, 393; *Battle Cust.* 29, where carting in autumn is discussed. If three loads had been carried before rain came on they could cease for the day: if less than three they were forced to thresh, or perform any other work.

coincidence and made no allowance.[1] It was in the main to holy-days that the serf had to look for any lightening of his burden,[2] and they are a real item to be reckoned with in our estimation of the burdens laid on him.

The Church, from time to time, had laid down rules concerning the due observance of holy-days, and these may be seen from a passage of *Piers Plowman*:

> holy churche hoteth alle manere puple
> Under obedience to bee and buxum to the lawe...
> Lewede men to labourie; and lordes to honte...
> And vpon Sonedayes to cesse godes servyce to huyre,
> Bothe matyns and messe and, after mete, in churches
> To huyre here euesong every man ouhte.
> Thus it by-longeth for lorde, for lered, and lewede,
> Eche halyday to huyre hollyche the seruice,
> Vigiles and fastyngdayes forthere-more to knowe,
> And fulfille tho fastynges.[3]

The man who tried to live up to such a standard would find himself ceasing work on fifty or more holy-days in the year, and certain modern writers have assumed that something like this did actually happen.[4] Dr Cunningham nowhere commits himself to a definite figure, but says that "the holidays were frequent", and "must have made a difference to the wage-earner",[5] while Mr Denton calculates that a man in the fifteenth century could reckon on being able to work only four and a half days a week.[6] They, however, are considering conditions in the late fourteenth and fifteenth centuries, and are mainly concerned with wage-earners. The position of such folk was controlled theoretically by an enactment of 1403, which forbade labourers to work for

---

[1] *V.C.H. Hants*, v, 414; *Ramsey Cart.* I, 47, 464; Suff. Inst. Arch. XI, 2, etc.

[2] *V.C.H. Sussex*, II, 183.

[3] C. x, 219 f.: "Holy Church orders all kinds of people to be obedient and to comply with the law. The uneducated have to work and the lords to hunt. And on Sundays this should cease in order that they may hear God's service: both matins and mass, and after meat each man ought to hear evensong in the church. And thus it behoves lords, as well as the learned and the ignorant, to hear the whole of the service every holy day, and also to know the vigils and days of fasting and to observe them."

[4] *Evolution English Farm*, 179, and 200, "The festivals averaged nearly one day a week."

[5] *Growth of Industry*, 390, 449.

[6] *England in the Fifteenth Century*, 219, 222.

hire on holy-days, or after noon on the vigils of holy-days.[1] The serf, however, did not come under any such act, for his work was not for hire but in return for his holding. The Church preached what we have seen Langland advocating, but it was a counsel of perfection, not one of common use. Even the ecclesiastical authorities themselves did not expect such devotion (and neglect of their own interests) from the peasant. Simon Meopham, Archbishop of Canterbury, in prohibiting any servile work inconsistent with the devout celebration of Good Friday, adds: "Nevertheless, we do not by this law mean to lay a burden on the poor, nor put any obstacle in the way of the rich to prevent them affording the customary assistance for charity's sake to help on the tillage of their poorer neighbours."[2] The canon lawyer Lyndwood in his gloss on this says that "the poor" are "those who have not animals and beasts to plough with, and who lack means to hire the assistance of others", and goes on to adopt the opinion of another canon lawyer, that though it would not be lawful to plough a poor man's holding on Sunday itself, or on the greater feasts, nevertheless this is permissible on the minor feasts wherever the relaxation is tolerated by the custom of the country.[3]

This is exactly the point of view expressed by the author of *Dives and Pauper*, who tells us that on the lesser feasts needful works like "erynge and sowynge, repyng, mowynge, cartyng" were not reckoned servile or a breach of the holy-day, if they were done in a right spirit and not for avarice; but Sundays and the great feasts must be observed more punctiliously; "suche workes shudde natt be done but ful grete nede compelle men thereto".[4]

Such, in brief, was the theory. What of the practice? A general survey of the evidence available can only lead to one conclusion: the law of the Church was violated on all sides, often by churchmen themselves. On the Bishop of Chichester's manors, for example, the Sunday itself was used as a day on which to hold

[1] *Statutes of the Realm*, 4 Henry IV, cap. 14.
[2] Lyndwood, *Provinciale* (Bk. 2, Tit. 3, De Feriis), 100.
[3] *Ibid.* 101.
[4] *Dives and Pauper*, III, 7, 3, as quoted by B. L. Manning in his *People's Faith in the Time of Wyclif*, 129. The whole of chapter IX of Mr Manning's book should be consulted on this subject.

the Manor Court;[1] to perform carrying duties;[2] to act as a letter bearer[3] or to do any kind of work required;[4] and similarly on two at least of the Ramsey manors Sunday carrying might be required.[5]

As for holy-days other than Sundays, on a great many manors the lord did not allow his serfs to take every holy-day off, as he should have done by strict canon law, but allowed them only one out of every two.[6] On some Ramsey manors they were given the day's holiday but had to make it up later on;[7] while on others, no allowance or excuse was contemplated, but the work went on, holy-day notwithstanding.[8] This seems to have been the view taken by Walter of Henley, for he reckons the lord can get forty-four working weeks in the year after taking away "eight weeks for holy-days and other hindrances".[9] Thus after deducting Sundays he only allows for four "other hindrances" in the shape of holy-days during the year!

It will be noticed that nearly all these examples are taken from manors owned by churchmen, and we may fairly argue that conditions on lay manors were no better and probably a little worse. We may, therefore, expect to find a widespread ignoring of holy-days, and an examination of the manorial accounts proves that this was so. The reeve, in making his annual reckoning, had to account for all the works owed and how they were discharged; and therefore his account generally included an item under the heading of holy-days, noting how many such days occurred in the year, and the number of works thereby excused. An examination of a large number of such accounts shows no clear-cut rule as to the observance of holy-days, but it does show clearly that few or no lords tried to live up to the requirements of canon law. In no instance has anything like fifty or more days' work relaxed been noticed: something between fifteen and twenty would be a generous estimate of the number of holy-days the

---

[1] Sussex Rec. Soc. XXXI, 15.   [2] Ibid. 17, 34, 71
[3] Ibid. 36.   [4] Ibid. 37.
[5] Ramsey Cart. I, 290, 310; cf. Eynsham Cart. II, 19.
[6] Worc. Priory Reg. 33b; D.S.P. 66; Rot. Hund. II, 630b; Ramsey Cart. I, 350, 384, 398, 463, 486, 492; Sussex Rec. Soc. XXXI, 15, 36, 42, 64 (but see page 7 which says that in total only eight such days are to be allowed).
[7] Ramsey Cart. I, 302, 366.
[8] Ibid. I, 369; Clutterbuck's Hertford, II, Appendix 10; III, 614; Camb. Antiq. Soc. Proc. XXVII, 170.   [9] Op. cit. 9; cf. Rogers, Wages, I, 256.

serf could count on.[1] But any figure is liable to mislead: we are only justified in asserting that there is no evidence to support the belief that the canon law was observed with any degree of strictness. In every diocese the practice varied to some extent, and every local area, as Lyndwood himself recognised, had its own peculiarities and time-hallowed practices "according to the custom of the country".[2]

Apart from these allowances for various reasons, the peasant got few chances of rest from his weekly labours on his lord's behalf. The only other relief he could expect was during the holidays round about Christmas, Easter and Whitsun.[3] At these festivals a brief respite was allowed him, sometimes amounting to as much as fifteen days at Christmas.[4] Then the Yule celebrations, and perhaps a special feast at the manor house, made that season a memorable one. An account of such feastings will be found in a later chapter,[5] and here we need only note the occurrence of these periods of rest in the otherwise unending toil demanded of the peasant, both by his lord and by the land itself.

One further service remains to be described, namely service in time of war. As we shall see, this only gradually came to concern the serf, but little by little the King demanded larger and larger armies and cast his net more widely, until in the end it caught even the peasant within its meshes. Unlike other services, however, this had nothing to do with his serfdom, so far as the King was concerned (although undoubtedly lords used their power over their serfs to compel them to serve), but was the result of the growing demand for man power. It was so insistent that in time the remotest village and its inhabitants were shaken from their secluded life, and forced to take note of a much greater world.

For it must be remembered that to the majority of English peasants their world was a very circumscribed affair. Their village and the immediate surroundings were their all, and within perhaps some fifteen or twenty miles of their cottages the great

---

[1] This figure is the result of the examination of a large number of manorial accounts before 1350, and is taken from different parts of England, both from lay and ecclesiastical manors.

[2] Lyndwood, op. cit. 101.

[3] D.S.P. xxvii; Cunningham, op. cit. 585; Hatfield's Survey, 172; Sussex Arch. Soc. LIII, 158; Levett, op. cit. 95.

[4] Camb. Antiq. Soc. Proc. xxvii, 165; Ramsey Cart. I, 344.

[5] See below, p. 263.

unknown began—a world of which they knew next to nothing by personal experience, and little more by repute. Yet from time to time echoes of this greater world came to the peasant in his fields: news of conflicts between great neighbouring lords, whom he might, perchance, have seen spurring through the village street, or riding upon the uplands hawk on wrist. At times news of the King's wars came to the village, brought by a passing soldier *en route* for his home once more. War, however, for many years after the Conquest, meant little or nothing to him: it was true that in times of great stress he could be summoned to join a mass levy, and then, armed with cudgel or knife, he formed one of an ill-disciplined rabble, led by untrained and ill-prepared leaders. It was such a body that was assembled to meet the Scottish invaders, and which won the Battle of the Standard in 1138. Here, two wild undisciplined bodies of troops met and fought out their quarrel more like wild beasts than soldiers. Except for such very unusual emergencies, however, the peasant knew little at first hand of war for some 150 years after the Conquest.

The coming of the thirteenth century saw the beginning of a change which was to have a marked influence on the peasant's life. From time to time the King had issued Assizes of Arms, which laid down the various categories of men liable for military service in certain circumstances. The first of these, the Assize of 1181, contemplated only the arming of freemen,[1] but in 1225, a writ for the collection of a tax of a fifteenth mentions among those to be exempted "quantum ad villanos armis ad quae jurati sunt".[2] From this it seems clear that villeins could be sworn to arms, and this power is extended by a writ of 1242 enforcing the Assize of Arms so that it includes not only citizens and burgesses, but adds "libere tenentes, villanos et alios",[3] from which it

---

[1] Stubbs, *Select Charters* (8th ed.), 154.   [2] *Ibid.* 356.

[3] *Lanc. Lay Subsidies*, I, 68, 69, and also a parallel writ for 1230. The date given in Stubbs (p. 371) is 1252, but this is an error. (Lancashire and Cheshire Rec. Soc.) The Rev. W. Hudson in his valuable and suggestive article on the "Norwich Militia in the XIVth Century", *Norf. Arch.* XIV, 263, interprets this phrase to refer to such "villeins and others as held lands above a certain value as sub-tenants (*i.e.* free tenants in villeinage)", but Pollock and Maitland, *History English Law*, I, 421 n. 4, accept the words at their face value to mean "the villani if rich enough should be armed". And see *Cal. Inquis. Misc.* I, 558, "as they were sworn to arms, both freemen and villeins".

further appears that all villeins "secundum quantitatem terrarum et catallorum suorum" were to bear arms. It was the force assembled by these means to which Edward I appealed when war broke out against the Welsh in 1276. The military resources of the nation at that time have been admirably summarised by Dr J. E. Morris in these words:

The arms were ready, and each man was equipped at his own expense, the country bore the expense of mobilisation, and the crown paid wages from the date of the outward march. In 1277 occasionally the sheriff led his contingent to the war, but as the reign wore on the King appointed special officers to take over the men from the sheriff. Writs were issued authorising them to raise a specified number of men; such writs became more common from the war of 1282 onwards, and the system was in full force in 1294. The Commissioners of Array, as they came to be called, were usually experienced officers, and being often sent, war after war, to the same counties, they doubtless knew the right men to choose.[1]

Edward I soon learnt that the measures taken by his ancestors were insufficient to provide the numbers of men which his growing knowledge of the technique of war and of the importance of infantry saw to be necessary. The Statute of Winchester in 1285 reorganised the military resources of the country, and brought the vast mass of peasants definitely within reach of the King's Commissioners of Array. From this time onwards, the continuous wars in France, Scotland and Wales became of considerable moment to the serf; and, more and more, he found himself caught up by great forces whose ultimate aims were far beyond his comprehension, but whose immediate needs absorbed him and his fellows in increasing numbers and threw them into the wars. At first it was the peasantry of the Welsh marches, together with the men of the neighbouring counties, who were forced to march at the word of command; then the battles in Scotland called for levies from all the counties north of the Trent, and finally the wars of Edward III necessitated the raising of promising recruits from the peasantry of all England.

How far this continuous demand was met by a willing response it is not possible to decide, but, as we might expect, the balance of evidence suggests that the Commissioners met with considerable difficulties in their recruiting marches. The peasant was

[1] J. E. Morris, *The Welsh Wars of Edward I*, 92.

untrained in war, and was slow to see that any advantage could come from leaving his fields and going to an unknown country, while travellers' tales of the wild and barbarous Scots and Welsh did not allay his fears. So the King was constantly calling for fresh forces, and the Commissioners were hard pressed to find even half or three-quarters of the men that were required. Although the King paid them twopence or threepence a day (as compared with a penny a day which was often given for hired field work), and although they were seldom kept on active service for more than three months at a time, the fear of the unknown and the reluctance to leave their homes held most men from the army, and it was only the more hardy and adventurous spirits who came forward willingly. The Commissioners had to find men, however, and were aided in their task by the Muster Rolls which were compiled in each county. From these they were able to see fairly exactly what men there were available for service in each village and town throughout the realm, and from such drew their levies. Thus from nine hundreds of the Rape of Hastings in 1335 there were returned the names of 751 men liable for service, and from the existing Muster Roll we can see how these names were arranged in military fashion in companies nominally 100 strong, each company divided into groups or sections of twenty men. The Commissioners drew from this Roll the 200 archers and the 200 armed men which they were ordered by King's writ to raise from the county. These lists, therefore, are of the greatest importance and interest, for not only do they show the number and names of those available, but also they give us information about their weapons, and we find these Sussex men were variously armed—some with bows and arrows, others with knives and cudgels, while others again are described as pikemen and billmen.[1]

There can be little doubt that men bearing arms such as these were of humble origin for the most part, and this view is supported by the clearest evidence when we look at the manorial records. For example, an entry in the Hales Court Rolls of 1295 shows that several suitors of the Court were elected to serve in the King's army in Wales,[2] or again from a document of 1307 we

[1] Dawson, *History of Hastings Castle*, I, 176; J. G. Nichols, *Collectanea Genealogical and Topographical*, VII, 118. Cf. *Norf. Arch.* XIV, 263; Hearne, *Textus Roffensis* (Oxford, 1720), 236.
[2] *Op. cit.* 318; cf. 324, 329; cf. *Select Coroner's Rolls*, p. 75.

see that the men of Pentirik, who were villeins, were bound to follow their lord to war when called upon.[1] Again, in 1325, John Beaucosin, the hayward of Littleport, was convicted by a jury in the Bishop of Ely's court of having taken a bribe of two shillings from one of the lord's villeins "by saying that he was elected to serve the King in the parts of Scotland, and that for the said sum he (John) would protect him against having to go there".[2] Many other cases could be quoted to uphold the view that the serf was never certain that it might not be his fate to go to the wars, although like most others he had little desire so to do.

But someone had to go: the King's needs were imperative, and compulsion, whether to a greater or lesser degree, was applied. In the first place it would have been very difficult for men to withstand the pressure which their lord could bring to bear on them if he so desired. We have seen how the custom of the manor forced the men of Pentirik to march at their lord's call, and, on many other manors, although this duty may not have been so clearly defined, it was doubtless operative. Smyth, in his *Lives of the Berkeley Family*, notes that the personal retinue of Lord Thomas Berkeley touched 200 foot archers, and adds, "at this time it is collected by the Musters that each great captain had for the most part their own tenants with themselves".[3] Again, the cry of the widows of Painswick in Gloucestershire is suggestive. They beseech their lord, Sir John Talbot, to hear their cry, for when "he had been beyond the sea in the King's wars he had sixteen men out of Painswick, of the which there were eleven slain".[4] As a result "since some of them were his bondmen they had not only lost their husbands, but also their holdings".

Apart from manorial compulsion there was always the possibility that the King's officers might insist on exercising the great powers which their Commission gave to them. It is true that on many occasions the King ordered his officers to explain his needs to possible recruits in the "most loving and courteous manner",[5] and at times he even offered to grant foot soldiers "such gratuity beyond their fixed wages when they come as shall content them in reason".[6] But behind all these fair words we constantly find

---

[1] *Inquis. Post Mortem*, IV, 295.   [2] Selden Soc. IV, 141.
[3] *Op. cit.* III, 22.
[4] S. Rudder, *History of Gloucestershire*, 594; cf. *History of Painswick*, 100.
[5] *Calendar of Close Rolls* (1296–1302), 79.   [6] *Ibid.* 372, 375.

more peremptory language. The same year that Edward I offered a gratuity to the men of Northumberland who would join him at Berwick, he had also ordered his Commissioners in several counties to select footmen and "to bring to justice and to punish as they think fit all those whom they find rebellious in this business"; while another writ of the same year threatened recalcitrant recruits with "seizure of their bodies and imprisonment".[1] The Commissioners were constantly ordered to select the "most powerful and fencible" men; and, with such powers at their back, and faced with the constant demands of their master for fresh levies, it is easy to imagine what was the position of the peasant.

But though the Commissioners or the lord might with some difficulty make him march to the wars, it was quite another matter to keep him there and to make him fight. Year after year the issue of the writs of summons is followed a few months later by another sheaf of writs ordering the sheriff to arrest and punish deserters. A few days on the march, or a taste of fighting seems to have satisfied the martial ardour of many of these peasant recruits, and they took the first opportunity of deserting. Thus we find a paymaster, in 1300, noting on his roll that certain commanders of hundreds were in camp, but without any men *quia repatriaverunt sine licencia*.[2] Even the device of giving the men an instalment of their pay in advance failed to hold them, for Edward I indignantly ordered his sheriffs to take action against men who had received his pay, and yet "afterwards returned home fraudulently with the money".

The trouble did not end here, for the careful investigations of Dr Morris have shown how little a medieval commander could depend on keeping his force at the wars, even if they had been got there by one means or another. His analysis of the pay-rolls of the Scottish campaign of 1300 shows that although 16,000 men were ordered to be at Carlisle on June 24, only some 3500 had arrived by July 1, and that the most the Commissioners could muster by the middle of the month was 7600. That was the crest of the wave, and daily after that the force began to dribble away, and by August little more than 3000 men remained with the

---

[1] *Calendar of Patent Rolls* (1292–1301), 491, 512.
[2] Morris, *op. cit.* 302.

King.[1] The rest had gone: some no doubt killed or taken away wounded; some having served their time; but, for the most part, these amateur soldiers had just faded away, and started on the long trudge back to their more peaceful fields. From their seat at the village ale-house we may well imagine them entertaining their fellows with stories of their adventures: some of them, perhaps like Langland's man,

> With a look like a lion and lordly in speaking;
> The boldest of beggars; a boaster who has nothing;
> A teller of tales in towns and in taverns;
> He says what he never saw and swears to his honesty;
> He devises deeds that were done by no man,
> Or is the witness of his well doing, and will say sometimes:
> "Look! If you believe me not, or think I lie basely,
> Ask him or ask him, and he can tell you
> What I suffered and saw."[2]

During the fourteenth century things became worse for the villein. Edward III made many and imperative demands for his services, going so far, at times, as to ask for the mustering of all able-bodied men between the ages of sixteen and sixty. However exaggerated we may estimate this to have been—a huge demand in the hope of a moderate response—there can be no doubt that the call for men must have affected every village in England. As we have seen, the Statute of Winchester had recognised the potentialities of a peasant force trained to arms, and the next fifty years saw the peasantry of England becoming more and more familiar with their weapons. The bowmen of Crécy were the men who had trained on the village greens throughout England, and side by side with them stood their sturdy companions of field and plough, now, however, armed with knife and cudgel.

It is at least doubtful whether these men were more willing recruits than their brothers had been in the time of Edward I. There are signs enough throughout the reign of Edward III that

---

[1] Morris, *op. cit.* 301. Cf. the army at Berwick in 1298: "16,000 foot on Feb. 9th; relays brought the figure up to 21,500, but soon it dropped to 18,000 and to 15,000 again, and in March to 10,000 and 5,000." Dr Morris calculates that in all 21,500 foot were engaged, "and though that high total was maintained only for a few days, 18,000 on an average served for over a month, and 10,000 for six weeks". *Op. cit.* 285–6.

[2] *Piers Plowman*, B. XIII, 302–10.

compulsion was constantly necessary. The King adopted an indenture system, whereby men undertook to provide a certain number of troops for a certain length of time, and such men were probably mainly volunteers. But, apart from these, we find the King ordering his officers to compel the men chosen by the ordinary methods to come forward, and giving them powers to punish the refractory and rebellious. Even so, he had the greatest difficulty in getting enough men into the ranks, and had to issue pardons to those criminals and outlaws who would come forward to serve him. We may well believe that the peasant was the first to feel the pressure of all such coercive measures. Where other men could buy themselves off with a bribe they had nothing but the barest household goods or stock to offer, and little power to withstand the officer who impressed them in place of a richer faint-heart. Here, as in many another situation, the serf had to suffer in silence, for he knew no one in the village sufficiently learned and powerful to voice his wrongs.

Servile Burdens

CHAPTER VI

SERVILE BURDENS

BUT when the peasant had performed all the ploughings and carryings demanded of him, and had sown and mown, and threshed and garnered for the lord, he was still under many obligations. His lack of freedom showed itself in a host of ways: he could neither brew nor bake where he would; he was not allowed to grind his own corn, to sell his own beasts, to give his own daughter in marriage, nor to do many other things without his lord's permission "prayed and obtained". The lord's power was about him on all sides: not only did he fear the occasional visit of the steward—armed with powers of life and death as it seemed—or the more frequent visits of the itinerant bailiff, whose authoritative commands every one learnt to respect, but he also came under the supervision of the local village officials—reeve, messor, beadle, etc. All these were constantly influencing his actions, and to some extent infringing on his freedom. If we look at some of the ways in which the peasants were controlled we shall quickly realise why they sought so passionately and constantly to buy their freedom.

Let us start with the village mill. We may safely assume that every village (and almost every manor) had one or more mills where all kinds of grain could be ground,[1] unless it were to the lord's interest to concentrate the grinding at one mill and thus to save working costs. These mills were either the property of the lord, or had been so at some earlier date, until he found it worth his while to accept a yearly rent for them, either from an individual tenant, or less frequently from his men as a whole. Here, as everywhere, we see the lord profiting from the needs of his

---

[1] Both water-mills and windmills were to be found in medieval England. The former were perhaps the more common throughout this period, for the windmill was a comparatively late invention, and does not seem to have appeared in Western Europe before the second half of the twelfth century. Abbot Samson pulled down the *molendinum ad ventum* of poor deacon Herbert in 1191, according to Jocelyn de Brakelond, and this is one of the earliest records of a windmill (if not the earliest) known in England. (*J. of Brakelond*, ed. Sir E. Clarke, 1907, p. 75.) For mention of a windmill earlier than 1191 see *Cal. Charter Rolls*, III, 319 for a charter dated by the editor 1163–81, which mentions "Unam toftam et unam Edvatum terre et vseliuncas ubi molendinum ad ventum situm fuerit."

manorial dependents: he seizes upon the fact that men must grind their corn in order to make bread, and so he insists on it being ground (at a price) at his mill.

The mill, therefore, became a valuable part of his income, and is frequently mentioned as a separate (and considerable) item when the value of a manor is being assessed. When, for example, in 1185, the Templars made a survey of all their lands in England, one of the seven headings of their enquiry concerned their mills, for, as the editor of the volume says:

These small and numerous manorial corn mills, mainly worked by water power, were not the least valuable part of the Templars' property. They ground the corn of a fairly extensive district and of a considerable population, and their close concentration in the hands of the lords of the manor, on demesne, shows that the Templars early appreciated the financial importance of seigneurial monopolies.[1]

Miss Lees is here actually referring only to the Essex properties of the Templars, but her remarks are a fair comment on their whole policy, and indeed on that of all medieval lords who had mills on their manors.

Since the mill was of such financial importance it was necessary for the lord to see that its business was ample and that it was not threatened by any rivals. This was achieved mainly by an insistence that the unfree must bring their corn to the manorial mill to be ground. This duty is constantly expressly stated, and as constantly the Court Rolls show men being fined for attempting to avoid their obligations. Thus the men on the Ramsey manors of Broughton, Wardeboys, Caldecot, Woodhurst and Waldhurst are all forced to bring their corn to Broughton[2] where the Abbot has a mill; or, as is said on another manor of this Abbey: "All the tenants owe suit to the mill, whereunto they shall send their corn.... If any tenant be convicted of having failed to render suit to the lord's mill, he shall give sixpence before judgment; or, if he have gone to judgment [i.e. if the matter has come before the Manor Court], he shall give twelvepence."[3]

[1] *Templars Records*, LXXIX. For comparative value of mill and total value of manor, see *Worc. Priory Reg.* xiv; *Yorks Inquis.* 1, 213, 222, 245; and Savine, *English Monasteries on the Eve of the Dissolution*, 126 ff.

[2] *Ramsey Cart.* 1, 333. Cf. *Worc. Priory Reg.* 32, where three vills have to mill at Bradewas.

[3] *Ibid.* 1, 473. Cf. 1, 302; *Durham Halmote Rolls*, 33, 40, 160, 184.

Despite all manorial injunctions men were constantly failing to bring their corn to the lord's mill, and in due time found themselves accused in the Manor Court. Here they usually received short shrift, and were fined, sometimes for grinding at another's mill, sometimes for grinding at home with a small hand-mill.[1] Men tried to avoid this liability, at times successfully, by pleading that they held the lord's license to grind wheresoever they liked, but this was not a privilege freely given.[2] At Hales, for example, on one occasion when the services of three applicants were relaxed, on payment of a fine, the lord insisted on their rendering suit of mill.[3] If men were caught on the way to a rival mill, the custom of the manor was often such that, if the offence was other than the first, the lord was entitled to seize the man's horse, while his miller took whatever corn or flour the wretched man was carrying.[4] The validity of such a custom seems to have been recognised in an action before the itinerant justices at Cirencester in 1302. Here the plaintiff admitted he was *en route* to another mill and off the manor when his horse and corn were confiscated by the Abbot—who kept the horse and passed on the corn to his miller. The plaintiff bases his claim only on the fact that the seizure took place off the manor, and does not dispute the recognised custom of seizure itself.[5]

Some lords recognised that often it was not wantonness but necessity that made men go elsewhere. They would arrive at the mill, only to find the miller overwhelmed with work, or with his mill out of repair, or his head of water weak, or the wind feeble and variable. With the best will in the world (and the miller was notoriously not overburdened with goodwill) much of the corn must wait many days before it could be ground. But at home the family could not wait, and so, perforce, the peasant went to the next mill or ground furtively at home with a hand-mill. Conditions similar to these are sometimes provided for, as on the Ramsey manor, where,

if they (the peasants) cannot on the first day grind the whole of the corn, the mill must grind as much as may keep their household in

---

[1] *Hales Rolls*, 118, 119, 136, 138, 152 etc.; *Court Rolls*, 176/130, and see below.

[2] *Hales Rolls*, 364, 366. [3] *Ibid.* 225; *Abbots Langley Rolls*, 44, 45.

[4] Bennett and Elton, *Hist. Corn Milling*, III, 220; IV, 66; *Worc. Priory Reg.* lxiii. [5] *Y.B.* Ed. II (R.S.).

bread for that day; and if the peasant cannot grind there that day, then he may take his corn elsewhere at his will.... From August 1 till Michaelmas each man may grind where he will, if he be unable to grind at my lord's mill on the day whereon he has sent the corn. Moreover, if it chance that my lord's mill be broken or his milldam burst, so that the tenant cannot grind there, then, as in the former case, he may take it elsewhere at his will.[1]

The greatest difficulty that faced the lord, however, was how to deal with the secret milling that went on in the peasant's own home. The hand-mill (or quern) was an object of the greatest antiquity, and its working was extremely simple and was known to all. One of these small machines set up in the house, if it remained undiscovered, could cope with the limited amount of grain many holdings provided. Hence they were a great temptation to the poor man and were in common use. The lord tried to prevent this, and wherever possible fined those found in possession of hand-mills. The Court Rolls are full of such matters: "It is presented that A. B. does not mill at his lord's mill, and further that he has a hand-mill at home. It is ordered that the mill be seized, and he is fined 6d."[2] At the next Court he still has the mill, but is made to come before the Court and find pledges not to use it in future, and it is to be taken from him.[3] An interesting case at Cirencester, in 1300, shows us the seizure being made. The bailiff of the Abbot was accused of entering several houses, and of seizing the millstones and taking them to the Abbey. The bailiff admitted that as bailiff of the manor he had gone to certain men's houses with a white rod in his hand, in the name of his bailiwick as was the custom, and had ordered the nuisance to be abated. When the men had utterly refused to obey, he had gone again at the Abbot's command and removed the stones. The justices upheld the Abbot's right, and it cost the men of Cirencester the large sum of 100 marks to make their peace with him. A side-note in the cartulary states that the Abbot could seize the mills, but ought not to destroy them.[4] It will, perhaps, be remembered that in the famous quarrel be-

[1] *Ramsey Cart.* I, 473. Cf. II, 313, where if a mill is out of action for two days serfs may go elsewhere.
[2] *Abbots Langley Rolls*, 20; *Wakefield Rolls*, II, 8, 164; Selden Soc. II, 47; IV, 123; Page, *op. cit.* 47 n. 2.
[3] *Abbots Langley Rolls*, 21 v.
[4] Bristol and Gloucester Arch. Soc. IX, 315.

tween the monks of St Albans and their tenants (graphically retold in Froude's *Short Studies*, "Annals of an English Abbey"), when the Abbot had successfully carried off the hand-mills, he used the stones from them to pave the floor of his private parlour.[1]

The lord took his profit in kind from all those coming to the mills. Every one had to contribute a certain proportion of his grain which was known as "multure". No clear figure can be given to express this proportion: it varied very considerably, and the *Statuta Pistorum*[2] (thirteenth century) assessed it at the twentieth or twenty-fourth part of the grain, but the details given in accounts and other documents show it to have averaged something more like a sixteenth part.[3] Now it must be remembered that the price of corn varied very considerably during these centuries, so that the value of this multure also varied very considerably. The serf, therefore, was not charged a fixed price for the mill's service, but found himself forced to yield up something considerably more precious in times of shortage than after a good harvest. Hence, no doubt, many of the charges of extortion so commonly levelled against the miller. Added to this was the galling knowledge that the lord paid no multure, neither did the parish priest, despite their comparative wealth.[4] Then again, the amount of multure taken varied as between free men and serfs: on Durham manors we find the free paying only one twenty-fourth, while the serf gave one thirteenth[5]—all incidents emphasising the differences between class and class, and inevitably leading to friction and bad blood.

The mill standing by the river bank was fed by water diverted along a watercourse and into a mill-pond. This was banked up with clay and turves, and the water was regulated by flood gates, and by sluices which allowed the miller to control his head of water. A very full account of the structure of the medieval Welsh mill may well serve to describe the innumerable water-mills throughout England at this period.

[1] *Gesta Abbatum* (R.S.), I, 410 ff; II, 149 ff.
[2] *Statutes of the Realm*, I, 202–3.
[3] *Guisborough Cart.* I, 278; *Whitby Cart.* II, 367, 370; *Yorks Inquis.* I, 76; Cumb. and West. Arch. Soc. Trans. I, 282; *Mamecestre*, 315; *Cust. Rents,* 98.
[4] *Mon. Exon.* 256; *Glouc. Cart.* III, 180, 193, 197.
[5] *Durham Halmote Rolls*, 134, 135. Cf. *Med. Village*, 57 n. 1.

The outer wheel consisted of a central oaken beam, into which was secured a double set of spokes or "arms", joined by "curves", strengthened by iron bands and stays to form a large double wheel. Between the outer rims, a series of trough-like "ladeles" were arranged to catch the current of the water. The axle extended into the mill, and on its other extremity was built an inner single wheel, also made of wood and banded. The inner wheel was cogged, the "cogges" secured by "keys", setting in motion a third small cogged wheel. This, in turn, was fitted on to an elevated and vertical spindle, itself revolving and with its lower extremity resting on a cup of brass. The opposite and squared end of the spindle passed into the upper storey of the mill, through the middle of a stationary millstone lying in its bed on the upper floor. Upon the squared end of the spindle an iron "trendel" or driver was fixed which clutched the iron stay or "rind" firmly secured across the perforated centre of the upper and moving millstone. This movable stone, thus balanced upon the spindle, could be adjusted by lowering or raising the spindle from below, and it could be made to revolve at a minute distance from the nether and fixed stone. The corn was then passed from the container, held on a framework, through the hole in the centre of the upper stone. The flow was regulated by a small mechanical contrivance, the "hopper", vibrated by means of a "jack" worked from below by the "rind" and spindle. The revolution of the stone forced out the meal, which was directed by the close-fitting framework to the spout where it was ejected into the holder. The full weight of the upper stone upon the spindle and the continual friction naturally proved a severe test for the soft iron of which the latter was made, and for the brass pivot at its base. Hence the very frequent references in medieval accounts to expenses incurred in "lengthening" and repairing the "neck" of the spindle and recasting the brass, both very expensive items. The purchase and haulage of the millstones were also costly and, probably on account of their poor quality, they required to be renewed periodically.[1]

The upkeep of the structure of the mill and its accessories was an expensive business, and in general was a charge on the lord. In making over a mill to the canons of St Agatha in 1190, Sir Gerald de Mansfield grants them also the right of taking stones for its repair wherever they may be found on his land,[2] and a little later another deed ensures the monks of Haughmond a little copse for wood, and resources for the repair of the mill-pool.[3]

[1] W. Rees, *South Wales and the March*, p. 137.
[2] *Corn Milling*, III, 51.
[3] Eyton, *Antiq. of Shrops.* VI, 54; and see X, 102; *Glas. Rentalia*, 87 (mill rented at 16s. but lord does the repairs); *Ramsey Cart.* III, 217.

The actual work when repairs were necessary was laid upon the serfs. They carried wood to the mill, or cleaned out and repaired the sluices, or helped in re-thatching: in short were called on for all the semi-skilled and unskilled labour required. Loss of time meant loss of money to the lord, and thus the tenants of the Bishop of Durham were fined for not coming in good time to help repair a broken mill bank.[1]

Lastly, a few words must be said about the miller himself.[1] "What is the boldest thing in the world?" asks the medieval riddle. "A miller's shirt, for it clasps a thief by the throat daily", is the answer, and serves to indicate the unenviable reputation of the miller during this period. The Coventry Leet Book,[2] and the Red Paper Book of Colchester[3] (both fifteenth-century documents it is true), tell us by inference of some of his tricks, in their injunctions forbidding the miller to water or change corn sent to him, and give worse for the better. Nor shall he keep hogs, nor more than three hens and a cock, and especially are gluttonous geese to be banished from his premises. But no great time need be spent on this matter, for Chaucer has dealt so faithfully with the Miller in the *Canterbury Tales* that, to use his own phrase, "there is namor to seyn".[4]

Just as the peasant was not allowed to grind his corn wherever he thought best, so he was forbidden to bake his bread at home or anywhere, save in a special oven constructed for the purpose, and belonging to the lord. Of course, it is clear that very many peasants had not the means of baking at home: the construction of an oven was a semi-skilled affair, and many houses could not have included one in their flimsy structures without grave risks and great difficulty. So the lord's oven must not be looked upon solely as a seigneurial oppression. Undoubtedly it provided a certain income for the lord, often at no trouble to himself, for he generally rented it to an individual or to the peasants as a body, and, save for repairs from time to time, had no further concern in the matter. Still, so long as the baker did not exact too large a fee for his work, the village oven or bakehouse was a communal convenience.

[1] *Durham Halmote Rolls*, 30, and cf. 39, 87, 103; *Ramsey Cart.* III, 243.
[2] *Cov. Leet Book* (E.E.T.S.), II, 397.
[3] Benham, *Red Paper Book*, 18.   [4] *C.T. Prologue* and A. 3120 ff.

The communal oven, however, never seems to have been so widespread in England as in France, and we have no very clear details as to its administration. We have a number of entries showing that it was often a valuable asset to the lord: sometimes in granting a charter to a vill the lord will forgo his rights of oven, but this is not invariable, and is in itself an indication of the value of such rights.[1] Again, we can find information respecting its hire to individuals, or to the members of the village as a body.[2] As we saw when considering the mill, the repairs were chargeable to the lord or to the tenant, according to the arrangement made at the time of drawing up the lease. And again, men are fined for not baking at the oven, and so on.[3] But we have no information of the detailed working of the system, of the method of payment, of the ease with which one could make use of the oven, of the way in which all those wishing to bake were dealt with, etc. As with many other of the commonest activities of the peasant's life, the very frequency and "matter of factness" of the operations have been our undoing. The medieval mind thought them not worth recording.

Nevertheless the widespread activities of the village bakers are vouched for by the way in which the name occurs everywhere under different forms. In a Worcester Subsidy roll, for example, we find the following names all denoting the presence of the baker: Bakare, Bachessor, Bagster, Baxter; Bollinger, Bullinger, Ballinger, Bellinger; Furnur', Furner, Furnage, Fernier; Pain, Pannier, Pottinger; Pistor, Pestour, Pasteler; Rybbare; Wastel, Wytbred; le Ovane, atte Novene.[4]

What we have lost because of the commonplace nature of the baker's activities may be seen by looking at an entry concerning the village oven printed by Maitland in a volume entitled *The Court Baron*. In this volume there occurs a detailed account of how to hold a court and pleas, in which the writer takes one by one the common types of offences the steward may have to deal with in holding the Manor Court, and sets out an imaginary case of each. Naturally only the most frequent causes of litigation are

[1] Ballard, *Brit. Borough Charters* (1042–1216), p. l.
[2] Selden Soc. II, 25; *Mamecestre*, 315; *Tatenhill*, II, 6, 12; *Kettering Comp.* 12.
[3] *Tatenhill*, II, 62; *A.A.S.R.* XXXIII, 330 ff.
[4] Worc. Hist. Soc., *Lay Subsidy Roll*, 1 Ed. III, p. x.

mentioned, and among these is the oven. The trouble which might arise over this is thus stated:

It fell out that on Monday next after S. Andrew that M. wife of the hayward and E. wife of a neighbour were baking at an oven, to wit that of N., and a dispute arose between them about the loss of a loaf taken from the oven, and the said old crones took to their fists and each other's hair and raised the hue; and their husbands hearing this ran up and made a great rout. Therefore by award of the court the said women who made the rout and raised the hue are in mercy. And so on with other cases as they arise.[1]

Both mill and oven, then, were common sights in the medieval village and we may perhaps sum up this section of our enquiry with Champion's verdict:

What rendered these monopolies so odious was not so much the fixed tariff or the prohibition against crushing one's own grain with a hand-mill or between two stones, and baking this meal at home, as the compulsion to carry the corn for long distances, over abominable roads, and then waiting two or even three days at the door of a mill where the pool had run dry; or, again, of accepting ill-ground meal, burned or half-baked bread, and of enduring all sorts of tricks and vexations from the millers or bakers.[2]

Let us turn from these obligations of mill and oven to other forms of oppression. In doing so we shall necessarily ignore a number of burdens, similar to those already described, which weighed upon the peasant. As we have already noted he could not indulge in many of the most common actions without first obtaining his lord's leave, and this was usually given only as the result of a money payment. The fish in the rivers and the game in the woods were not at his disposal; the doves, which ravaged his crops and lived safely in the great dovecot at the manor house, were things he might not touch. On all sides he saw rude plenty —yet on all sides the lord's *No* was generally overwhelming. It required famine or undue oppression to cause the ordinary peasant to cry out with John Ball, "We are men formed in Christ's likeness, and they treat us like beasts."

---

[1] Selden Soc. IV, 73.
[2] Champion, *La France d'après les cahiers de 1789*, 139, 142, quoted by Coulton, *Med. Village*, 58.

Not only did the peasant find his freedom to use the things he saw about him sadly circumscribed by the power of the lord, but he also found himself controlled in many other ways. He was subjected to a series of money payments, all of which emphasised his servile condition. Rent he paid, as did the freeman, and services he rendered in addition, as we have seen, but still more was demanded of him. He was forced to make payments from time to time to meet divers demands of his lord, and these were often of an uncertain nature, or came at times of stress. Of these the most onerous were tallage and heriot, and each of them deserves some detailed consideration.

Tallage is defined by Vinogradoff as "a rent on the border-line between personal subjection and political subordination",[1] and by the thirteenth century it had come to be looked upon as one of the tokens of serfdom. And this was not an unreasonable view, for the right of one man to exact from another whatever sum he thought desirable, and to do this at uncertain intervals, certainly established an *a priori* case of complete subjection. It had its justification in the theory slowly formulated by the law that the serf's all belonged to his lord, and therefore the lord could take what was his own when and to what extent it seemed best to him. Thus in the stricter customals we constantly read that the amount of tallage was fixed *ad voluntatem domini*, and the serfs had no redress if one, two or more calls were made on them, even in the same year. On the other hand, the serfs steadily worked to obtain some certainty in these things; and, from the twelfth century onward, we find the lord's rights modified and controlled. The peasants got the principle established of a yearly tallage *ad voluntatem domini quolibet anno*, or of tallage "according to the custom of the manor". Little by little the principle was established that both the amount and also the frequency of the charge became matters of certainty. Once this was achieved it was easy to regard tallage as an additional rent charge merely, and once its uncertainty was removed there was nothing in such a payment which marked it out specifically as a servile burden.

But this was a state of affairs won only after much travail. "Tallage at will", with all the uncertainty it entailed, became

[1] *Villainage*, 162.

one of the lawyer's tests of servitude.[1] The canonists also took this view. Dr Coulton writes:

Let us begin with an extract which has almost the value of a direct generalization. Richard Middleton (or de Media Villa) was an English Franciscan who became Professor of Divinity at Paris about 1285, and is reckoned among the masters of Duns Scotus. In the 27th question of his third quodlibet he discusses the question whether subjects are morally bound to obey a lord who imposes tallages which are justified neither by custom nor by public utility:

"I answer, that these subjects are either serfs [servi] or free. If they be serfs, I say that they are bound to pay the tallages newly imposed upon them, even though these tend to the profit of their lords alone; for serfs and their possessions are the property of their lords.... [In the case of freemen], if those tallages be in no way to the profit of the community, then I say that neither king nor prince can impose such tallages upon his free subjects. And the reason here is, that the possessions of free subjects are not the property of their lords."

When a doctor of this kind can thus decide against the moral right of the serf to resist new and arbitrary taxation, it is more significant even than the complaints of his fellow-moralists that the lords and their bailiffs commonly oppress the poor.[2]

There can be no doubt that "tallage at will" was oppressive, and was thought to be oppressive by the peasants. In 1299, the serfs of the monks of Dunstable, for example, asserted that "they would rather go down to hell than be beaten in this matter of tallage", and after much controversy they finally bought their freedom from this tax by the huge fine of £60.[3] This strong expression of opinion by the men of Dunstable was echoed by many other serfs, and we constantly meet with evidence showing how the lords were "destroying the peasants by exactions and tallages", or that they were "exacting tallage from them by force and oppression, some years taking 100 shillings, some years not".[4] The Ministers' Accounts show us in detail what was happening. For example, at Halvergate, in Norfolk, the tallage varied from £10 to £12 from one year to the next; then it rose to £13, and the following year was down to £8, where it remained for the next

---

[1] *Rot. Hund.* II, 530, 619, 623, 642, etc.; *Worc. Priory Reg.* 15 a, 43 b, 56 a, etc. For an important discussion of "uncertainty" and tallage, see Vinogradoff's article, *Econ. Journ.* x, 311–15.

[2] *Med. Village*, 482.   [3] *Ann. Dunst.* (R.S.), 122.

[4] *B.N.B.* Nos. 485, 574, 691; cf. *Bensington*, 24; *Cal. Inq. Misc.* I, 100 (No. 290).

ten years.[1] Again, on a neighbouring manor, after being stationary at £8 for years, it suddenly rose to £12.[2] Fluctuations such as these were hard to bear, and probably the cause of much bitterness on the manor, for it must be remembered that the serf had no understanding of why these sums were wrung out of him. The lord's needs may have been real or only fanciful: the peasant was but dimly aware that for some reason or other this year (possibly most inconveniently for him) he had to pay more tallage than usual.

Hence we should expect to find men endeavouring to fix the sum, and thus it is that the customals begin to state that the amount is fixed and may not be increased or diminished,[3] and the Ministers' Accounts show manors on which the tallage exacted remains constant over a long period of years.[4] We get a little further light from a Yorkshire inquisition of 1250 which states that "the tallage set in Newland, Kirkedrux, and Langerak is £10, to which all must give whose names are placed on the roll after those who only pay rent".[5] Clearly here the fixed amount had to be found by the peasants of the vills, possibly in proportion to their holdings, while those who paid rent—that is the freeholders—were quit of this tax. No doubt many wondered why the freeholders went quit while they were forced to pay, and a desire to be free as were these men undoubtedly rose in many breasts.

Although at first sight it would seem that a fixed tallage was much to be preferred to one which varied from year to year (and so undoubtedly it was for the majority), yet even a fixed tallage had its dangers, for its inelasticity made no allowance for bad seasons or for altering conditions in the neighbourhood. Whether all the holdings, or only half of them, were occupied, the full sum had to be found and this naturally created hardships. We have an excellent example of this in thirteenth-century Yorkshire. The men of Hedon, a jury of 1280 tells us, were "straitened and poor", and the inquisition asserted plainly that unless some change were soon made, men would move away "on account of

[1] *Min. Acc.* 936/4–16. Cf. 756/3–10.
[2] *Ibid.* 936/18–32. Cf. Davenport, *op. cit.* 46; *Villainage*, 293.
[3] *A.A.S.R.* xxxv, 7.
[4] See, for example, *Min. Acc.* 918/2– ; 987/15– ; 1004/1–
[5] *Yorks Inquis.* I, 127.

the yearly tallage and go to the good near-by towns of Raven-
sered and Hull, which have good harbours growing daily, and no
tallage".[1] Here we see a fixed sum being exacted, despite the
fact that towns like Hull, with great attractions to the serf, were
growing up and daily recruiting in part from dissatisfied men,
such as heavily tallaged Hedon could provide. Later on we shall
see how these burdens drove men to consider how they could
end such conditions.

Fixed or "at will", tallage was an important item in the
manorial income and had to be forthcoming. It was usually
exacted at Michaelmas,[2] sometimes from each individual, but
often assessed on the vill or manor as a whole.[3] The *Gloucester
Cartulary* gives us a great deal of information about the way in
which the tax was assessed. The serf pays "each according to
his land and the number of his animals", and these animals all
have their value;[4] or sometimes he is assessed on the number of
acres he holds,[5] or again the serfs are assessed "in communi",[6]
and probably left to work out the individual payments for
themselves.

Yet whatever method of collection was in force, tallage remained a hated sign of inferiority, and men tried to get rid of it
in the only way possible to them. They "bought their blood"
free of this, as they had to do of other servile incidents, and found
it to their advantage to commute the payment for an added general
charge on each holding.[7] Although this made little or no difference to their annual outgoings to the lord (assuming the
tallage to be steady) yet it meant that henceforth it formed but
one item in the rents of assize[8]—that lump sum each man paid
to his lord, and which hid within itself who knows what of ancient
rents, charges, personal fines and dues. Once the serf had seen

---

[1] *Yorks Inquis.* I, 216.
[2] *Eynsham Cart.* II, 7; *Glouc. Cart.* III, 88, 100, 103, 119, 121, etc., where
it is called "the aid of St Michael"; *Worc. Priory Reg.* xcviii n. 12a, 93a,
104a.
[3] Davenport, *op. cit.* 46.
[4] *Glouc. Cart.* III, 50, 53, 57, 180, 188, 206, etc. Cf. *Ramsey Cart.* II, 52.
[5] *Glouc. Cart.* III, 100, 110, 121, 129, etc.
[6] *Ibid.* III, 97, 191; *Eynsham Cart.* II, 129.
[7] E.g. *Worc. Priory Reg.* 19a, 61b, 66b, etc.
[8] For a discussion of the nature of *redditus assiza* see Levett, *Econ. Hist.
Rev.* I, 70–5, and Page, *Crowland Estates,* 91–9.

the hated tallage swallowed up in this annual fixed charge he could breathe the more easily, for another obvious sign of his servitude had dropped away from him.

We may, perhaps, note here a special tallage that was at times raised as part of the incoming—the *joyeux avènement*— of the new lord. It was a custom particularly associated with ecclesiastical manors: at Wynslowe 20 marks were exacted,[1] at Otterton 10 marks,[2] at Tooting 4 marks,[3] and on the manors of the monks of Worcester, and the Bishop of Chichester the sum is not stated,[4] but on one Worcester manor it is said to be "secundum quod ratio exigat".[5] The Prior of Norwich, in 1471, had only 86 tenants at Martham but they had to pay £20 on his incoming, and the same sum was exacted in 1504 on the election of another prior.

So far the actual account-rolls testify; but, on looking at Dugdale's *Monasticon* we find that three other priors have come between, in 1480, 1489 and 1504. If the rolls for these years existed and had been searched, it is practically certain that they would show us similar entries, and leave us to conclude that the Martham tenants had paid this tax five times in a single generation, at whatsoever irregular intervals it had pleased Providence to remove their former prior.[6]

The forced hospitality exacted from the manorial population (the *gîte*, so common in France) seems to have been rare in England. Vinogradoff quotes one example only, and gives no other references. His one case dates from the mid-thirteenth century and concerns the tenants of the Abbot of Osulveston in Donington and Byker, who were

bound to receive their lord during one night and one day when he comes to hold his court at their place. They find the necessary food for him and for his men, provender for his horses, and so forth. If the abbot does not come in person, the homage may settle about a commutation of the duties with the steward or the sergeant sent for the purpose. If he refuses to take money, they must bring everything in kind.[7]

---

[1] U.L.C. *Wynslowe Rolls*, 56b.
[2] *Mon. Exon.* 254a.
[3] *Tooting Bec Rolls*, 248.
[4] *Cal. Inquis. Misc.* I, 64.
[5] *Worc. Priory Reg.* cxvi n., 638a.
[6] *Med. Village*, 197. The years 1489, 1504 are corrected from those in Dugdale by the recent work of H. W. Saunders, *An Intro. to the Rolls of Norwich Cathedral Priory*, p. 190.
[7] *Villainage*, 303.

A remnant of this forced hospitality is seen on some manors at the coming of the steward to hold the Manor Court. The serfs of the Prior of Durham had to provide the steward's servants with beds, and were constantly failing to do so, and being admonished.[1] If house-room and beds were not required on a Sussex manor, then counterpanes and sheeting had to be sent for use at the manor house.[2] The Hundred Rolls, again, contain some evidence on this point. Food was requisitioned by officials—bailiffs, foresters, constables—as they rode from place to place on business. They demanded hay and corn, poultry "at the will of the giver", bread and beer—or in their place a money payment, and most of this came from the peasantry.[3] All this, however, is as nothing compared with the elaborate provisions made in continental customals for the annual entertainment of the lord, or even for such of his friends as he cared to send in his place.[4] In this, as in many other ways, the comparatively peaceful and settled state of England throughout the later Middle Ages made conditions so much more possible for the serf. His lord did not consistently wring the utmost out of him, in the fear that to-morrow he might be displaced by another—either by the fortune of war or by the loss of his protector's favour. Harsh as some of these exactions seem to us, they inevitably flowed from the feudal lawyer's theory that in strictness all the serf possessed was his lord's, and their harshness seems less outrageous when compared with the ruthless provisions of many continental customals.[5]

The lord's claims on his serf were not confined to the exaction of rents and services during life. Even after the peasant's death, the lord still had a claim on his property which was known as a heriot, and the Church had also another, known as a mortuary. The first of these was claimed by the lord of the manor on the death of one of his tenants. It arose from an old custom, whereby all—both free and bond—were bound to make a return on death of the *hergeat*, or war-gear, with which the lord had originally supplied them. This war-gear—consisting of horse, harness and

---

[1] *Durham Halmote Rolls*, I, 72, 101, 125, 140, 144, 146; Sussex Rec. Soc. XXXI, 53.
[2] Sussex Rec. Soc. XXXI, 53.
[3] *Rot. Hund.* II, 31, 40, 307. Cf. *Cust. Rents*, 148.
[4] Sée, *op. cit.* 362.
[5] See *Med. Village, passim*.

weapons—in strict theory remained the property of the lord, and it was but right that he should resume possession on his man's death. In the course of time, however, the conditions which had obtained earlier were seriously modified: a great number of free-men had managed to shake off this obligation, and were no longer either equipped by their lord, or liable to pay a heriot on their death. The serf, however, was not so fortunate. While he was liable to give military service only on infrequent occasions and in a very limited way, in theory he was still held to receive his *hergeat*; and, therefore, on his death, was forced to pay a heriot which generally took the form of his best beast or chattel.[1] As Pollock and Maitland say:

In this case the term "heriot" must in the eyes of the etymologist be inappropriate. We may guess that in the heriot of the later middle ages no less than four ancient elements have met: (1) the warrior who has received arms from his lord should on his death return them; (2) the peasant who has received the stock on his farm from his lord should return it, and if his representatives are allowed to keep it, they must recognise the lord's right to the whole by yielding up one article, and that the best; (3) all the chattels of a serf belong in strictness of law to his lord, and the lord takes the best of them to manifest his right; (4) in the infancy of testamentary power it has been prudent, if not necessary, that the would-be testator, however high his rank, should purchase from the king or some other lord that favour and warranty without which his bequests will hardly "stand". But at any rate in the course of time the heriot is separated from the relief.[2]

Side by side with this claim went one made by the Church called a mortuary. This was exacted by reason of the convenient theory that during his lifetime a man would be unlikely to pay in full all his tithes and other charges due to the Church, and there-fore it was necessary for the Church to make a final claim in exacting a mortuary. This was taken after the lord had first chosen the best beast or chattel as his heriot, and the Church had second choice.[3] Canon Law endeavoured to define what had

---

[1] See e.g. *Glouc. Cart.* III, 43, 46, 59, 87, 172, 204, 211; Sussex Rec. Soc. XXI, 90, 98, 102, 110. In the *Worc. Priory Reg.* 102 we find the virgater has to give three heriots: a horse, its harness, and two oxen. The military has com-pletely given place to the agricultural claim.

[2] *Hist. Eng. Law*, I, 317.

[3] See this fully set out, for example, in Oliver's *Mon. Exon.* 254 *b* (Otterton), where it is declared to be an obligation on free or serf. See also *Glouc. Cart.* III, 130, 170, 172.

originally been no more than a custom (though custom, so long as it is laudable, acquires the force of law to the canonists), and forbade the taking of a mortuary unless there were at least three beasts.[1] This, however, was rigorous enough, since after the lord had taken one, and the Church taken another, the widow or heir was often left with a solitary remainder. It is also to be remembered that often the manor was the property of the monks or of some cleric, so that they were certain of their heriot in any case![2]

So far the theory. In practice we find a diversity of customs, as we should expect; but, what is important to note, we find very frequently that a good deal more than the best beast or the best chattel is demanded. In some cases the heriot is as much as one-third of a man's total assets. In 1300 a Yorkshire free man holding four bovates of the Prior of St John of Jerusalem has to give one-third part of all his goods at his death,[3] and the accounts of Tatenhill about 1380 return the sum of £1. 7s. 11½d., "being the third part which belongs to the Lord" of the man's assets of £4. 3s. 11d.[4] A rental of the same manor, dated 1414, shows even harsher customs. The lord was entitled to the best animal, and also to all copper vessels, carts and iron-bound wagons, hives, colts, oxen, porkers, whole sides of bacon, all woollen cloth if uncut and any treasure the man might have![5] We may see from entries in the accounts of the previous century that this was no mere theory, but that such customs had actually been enforced. For example, in March 1347, on the death of a serf, the lord seized his horse, cart, sheep, and two pigs worth twelve shillings. The widow was allowed to buy them back for this sum, and given till August to find the cash.[6]

An extreme but illuminating case is that of the monks of Vale

---

[1] See Coulton, *Ten Medieval Studies*, 126 for a full discussion, with references to the Canon lawyers.

[2] *Glouc. Cart.* III, 88, 138, 159, 170, 182; Bristol and Glouc. Arch. Soc. IX, 304.

[3] *Yorks Inquis.* IV, 10.

[4] *Tatenhill*, II, 56; cf. *Trigg Minor*, III, 47 where it is declared that the lord is entitled to all the cattle of serfs, but only to the best of those of the free men.

[5] *Tatenhill*, II, 97; cf. Blount, *Tenures*, 45; Vinogradoff, *Villainage*, 160.

[6] *Tatenhill*, II, 34; cf. 58 where horse, two pigs and household pots and jars are seized to the value of 11s. 6d.

Royal, where both heriot and mortuary were exacted with the utmost rigour. The customal runs:

When any one of them [the bondmen] dieth, the lord shall have all the pigs of the deceased, all his goats, all his mares at grass, and his horse also, if he had one for his personal use (*si habuerit domesticum*), all his bees, all his bacon-pigs (*bacones integras*), all his cloth of wool and flax, and whatever can be found of gold and silver. The lord shall also have all his brass pots or pot, if he have one, because at their death the lord ought to have all things of metal. Abbot John granted them in full court that these metal goods should be divided equally between the lord and the wife on the death of every one of them, but on condition that they should buy themselves brass pots.

Also the lord shall have the best ox for a "hereghett" and holy church another. The lord shall choose the best ox by his bailiffs, before the "hereghett" be given to the church.[1]

The customal then goes on to discuss how the rest of the property is to be divided between the lord and the family, and it is clear that the widow and her children are left to begin anew with something over half their possessions taken from them.

One or two more examples will emphasise the severity with which this exaction weighed on the poor. The Bishop of Rochester as lord of the manor of Hedenham was entitled to his serf's best chattel, and if he had but one horse, the customal declared that it ought to be sold, and thirty pence given to the lord and the balance to the widow![2] Or again, in 1345, at Barchester, the lord claimed an ox worth 8s. and a cow worth 5s. as a heriot. It was found that after this the widow could not take her husband's holding on account of her poverty, and the reeve was ordered to take the land and house into the hands of the lord.[3]

Not all lords were so merciless. On the Ely manor of Melbourne if the serf had no beast then no heriot was claimed, and

---

[1] *Vale Royal,* 118. Dr Coulton (*Med. Village,* 175) writes: "I have not met with any lay manor in England or France on which the death-dues even approach these in severity."

[2] *Cust. Roff.* 11. Thirty pence, or thirty-two pence, seems to have been reckoned as a suitable sum in the thirteenth and fourteenth centuries. See e.g. Blount, *Tenures,* 382; *Camb. Antiq. Soc. Proc.* xxvii, 164; *Ramsey Cart.* 1, 416; Page, *Crowland,* 116; *Worc. Priory Reg.* xlii, etc. Cf. *Cust. Rents,* 89 and references given there.

[2] W. Kennett, *Paroch. Antiq.* 11, 85.

this was so on the manor of Bernehorn, belonging to the monks of Battle.[1] The charity of St Hugh of Lincoln became a matter of legend, and Giraldus Cambrensis tells of how he exercised it in this very matter on one occasion at least:

Hugh had such bowels of pity, and was so utterly uncovetous of earthly things, that when his servants had carried off the ox of a certain dead peasant of his lordship (as the dead man's best possession which the custom of the land gave to the lord), and the widow had come forthwith to the bishop, beseeching with tears that he should order the restoration of that ox, which alone was left to her for the sustentation of the miserable and orphaned family, then he granted her request. Hereupon the steward of this manor said unto him: "My lord, if you remit this and other similar lawful perquisites, you will never be able to keep your land." But Hugh, hearing this, leapt straight down from his horse to the ground, which in that spot was deep in mire; and, grasping both hands full of earth, he said: "Now I hold my land, and none the less do I remit to this poor woman her ox." Then, casting away the mire and looking upwards, he added: "For I seek not to cling to earth beneath but to heaven above. This woman had but two workfellows; death hath robbed her of the better and shall we rob her of the other? God forbid that we should be so covetous; for she doth more deserve our consolation in this moment of supreme affliction, than that we should vex her further."[2]

St Hugh's attitude was not generally shared, however. It will have been noticed that his own steward strongly disapproved of it, and Giraldus recounts the story as an example of the Saint's exceptional charity. Few lords were content to forego their heriots, as any series of accounts or court rolls will show. They formed an important item in the income year by year flowing into the lord's hands from his villeins.

Not only the serf's stock and household goods were subjected to a fine; but his land also, since in theory it belonged to his lord, was occasion for a payment whenever it changed hands through death or other cause. As we have seen this payment was not strictly a heriot, but medieval scribes (and often medieval lawyers) were not very certain of the exact meaning of the terms they used, and gradually the payment was called a heriot.

---

[1] *Worc. Priory Reg.* xlii; *Battle Cust.* 22.
[2] *Opera* (R.S.), vii, 96. For a layman's remission of heriot in perpetuity, see *Terrier of Fleet*, ed. N. Neilson, p. 18.

We may see how the confusion arose from the Hales court rolls. There in general we read that a heriot was paid, sometimes in the shape of an ox, or a cow, or sheaves of corn, sometimes in the form of a sum of money; and, on that being completed, and not till then, the new tenant was allowed to take up the holding. At other times, however, not only has the scribe recorded a payment of the heriot, but also of a fine or "relief" for entry on the holding. Thus in 1278 a son presented *nomine herieti patris* two oxen worth twenty shillings, a male horse worth half a mark (3*s*. 4*d*.) and two hogs worth two shillings. As well as this, he paid two and a half marks for being allowed to take over the holding.[1] From this it was an easy step to lump the two things—heriot and relief—together, and to regard the whole thing as a single transaction.

This became even more natural when the whole transaction was entirely expressed in money terms, and no animal or chattel, but only its monetary value, was mentioned. Thus, on the Ramsey manors, the virgater constantly paid five shillings for his heriot, and lesser holders paid smaller sums;[2] and on other manors the heriot was always valued in money.[3] Heriot, or relief, or fine on entry—whatever it was called—it seemed all the same to the man who had to pay; and the scribe, unless unusually intelligent, saw in the whole business only the passing of the holding from one serf to another, for which his lord naturally received a money payment.

The confusion surrounding the word was carried one stage further when the fine paid on the surrender of a holding from one man to another also began to be called a heriot. From the lord's point of view, whether the surrender was caused by death, or by a man's desire to acquire or relinquish his land, made little difference. The lord was entitled to his fee—the best animal or its value. Thus at Hales, in 1277, when a man surrendered his land into the hands of the lord he had also to pay a heriot of eight shillings.[4] Again, on the manors of the monks of Crowland, the custom was clearly established whereby "every holder of a *terra*

---

[1] *Op. cit.* 104, and cf. 215, where the terms *herietis* and *relevio* are used to describe a similar transaction.

[2] *Ramsey Cart.* I, 301, 303, 304, 337, 347, 359, 370, 384, 395.

[3] E.g. *Wakefield* and *Ingoldmells Rolls, passim.*

[4] *Op. cit.* 79.

nativa, shall owe the lord on his outgoing his best animal as heriot", and later it was declared that if he had no animal he was to pay 2s. 6d. "in the money of the King of England, by way of heriot".[1]

The tangled process which we have been trying to unravel is a reminder to us of the variety and confusion lurking everywhere in medieval terms. Even the lawyers cannot lay down a clear definition of heriot, but have to admit of exceptions and uncertainties. Britton tells us that they are generally paid by serfs rather than free men,[2] while Glanvill, on the other hand, tells us that it is the free man who ought to recognise his lord by leaving him the best thing he has.[3] Bracton, on the whole, agrees with Glanvill; but adds that local customs vary, and says that heriot comes to the lord by grace rather than by right.[4] When we look at the Court Rolls we see what a deal of variation can exist beneath the common formula of the extent: "and on his death he owes his best beast or chattel as a heriot". On the Tooting Bec manor, for example, the heriot is not forthcoming because the land is held conjointly with another;[5] because it is held for a period of years;[6] because only a part of the holding is surrendered;[7] because there is no tenement on the holding[8]—in short, there seem to be innumerable ways whereby custom has altered and deflected the straightforward operation of the old law.

Furthermore, innumerable questions arose which had to be settled by the decision of the suitors of the manorial court. The Hales tenants had to deliberate as to whether a heriot was due from a married woman;[9] or whether a man fortunate enough to own a male horse was entitled to keep it, or must pay it as heriot on his wife's death.[10] If a man holds two tenements does he pay one or two heriots? The Hales custom demands one, so does that of Crowland, but the manors of the Bishop of Hereford[11] and those of the monks of Ramsey[12] have customs which demand a heriot for each messuage or toft, or each virgate of the holding.

[1] Page, *Crowland Estates*, 115, 116.   [2] Britton, II, 51.
[3] Glanvill, VII, 5.   [4] Bracton, ff. 60, 86; cf. *Fleta*, 212.
[5] *Op. cit.* 16, 172, 184, 186.   [6] *Op. cit.* 28; cf. *Hales Rolls*, 281, 285.
[7] *Op. cit.* 108, 146; cf. *Hales Rolls*, 260.   [8] *Op. cit.* 198.
[9] *Op. cit.* III, 58.   [10] *Op. cit.* I, 298.
[11] *E.H.R.* April 1928.   [12] *Ramsey Cart.* I, 370.

Everywhere we turn we find local custom interpreting the way in which heriot is to be claimed. Sometimes, as at Vale Royal, it presses with intolerable harshness on the peasant: at other times, as at Melbourne, it is merciful and humane. But, looked at generally, it must be said that it was a heavy burden, and was the more grievous since it could but aggravate the keen sense of loss which the household had already sustained by the death of the head of the house. We must not easily allow ourselves to believe that "the power of the lord" was not a very real thing. True, in some fortunate manors it was softened and controlled to some extent by the "custom of the manor", but even so it remained a powerful force which could exhibit itself in such ways as this— ways repugnant, not only to our modern ideas, but, as we have seen, to such men as St Hugh, or to a moralist such as Jacques de Vitry, who characterised the lords who took heriots as "vultures that prey upon death—or more loathsome still, as worms feeding upon the corpse".

Manorial Administration

CHAPTER VII

MANORIAL ADMINISTRATION

FROM what has already been said about the rents and services which the lord demanded from the peasants it will be obvious that some organisation was required by which to collect these rents from time to time, and to arrange for the punctual and efficient rendering of the various services. Not only this: the lord had also to make provision for the farming of his own part of the manor—the demesne lands as they were called, on which, as we have seen, the unfree peasants laboured throughout the year. A large part—sometimes the whole—of a lord's livelihood came from these sources, and it was of vital consequence to him to arrange for their efficient exploitation.

When the lord himself resided in the manor house and could supervise the work of his men, it was, no doubt, a comparatively simple matter for him to see that his lands and stock were properly kept, and that everyone who owed him rent or service paid it whenever it was due. But for many lords the problem was not so simple. They frequently held more than one manor—sometimes they held many—and these might be scattered over a county, or perhaps over half England. Even had they no other affairs, it would have been wellnigh impossible for them to have overseen the whole of their manors efficiently; but, in many cases, they were busy servants of the King, or great soldiers engaged on foreign wars and crusades, or merely idle men of fashion who followed the Court and despised the country boors and the life of the fields, save as necessary adjuncts to the delights of the chase. For very different reasons the great ecclesiastical landowners, such as Cathedral chapters or the innumerable religious houses of monks and nuns, were equally unable to supervise their many manors. It was impossible for these people to be absent long from their homes, and here again, they had to employ others to look after their interests. Hence we find that a widespread system sprang up, whereby manors were controlled by paid agents of the lord, and a whole hierarchy of officials and minor servants was created.

In order to aid them in their work it was necessary for the lord to give the chief officials the clearest account possible of what were the lands and people they had to control, and what things they might expect from the manorial population, in money, in service and in kind. Two main classes of documents gave them this information: the rentals or extents, and the customals. The rental or extent set out in the greatest detail exactly what was to be demanded of every single landholder on the manor. It first dealt with the freeholders, and this was a comparatively brief matter, for once their rent was paid little but an occasional service, such as attendance at the Manor Court on special occasions, or coming to oversee the workers during harvest was expected of them. The unfree, however, were another matter: they had to render numerous rents and services, and often every detail of what was to be demanded of them was set out in the minutest fashion. And it did not follow that because one man did certain things his fellow would do likewise. Further, as we have seen, there were many groups in the manorial society, and the services of each of these groups demanded its own space in the extent. Once he had got this, however, the official knew what he might legitimately demand from everyone who held land of his lord.

We have already noted the way in which the customal came into being. It embodied the many by-laws, as we may call them, which had gradually been evolved, and which, henceforth, represented "the custom of the manor". Both official and serf knew full well what these customs were, and after he had grasped what were a man's services as laid down in the extent, the wise official was careful to see how far (if at all) it was modified by anything laid down in the customal before he took any action.

Our information concerning the manorial organisation comes from these two primary sources and also from the detailed accounts which the manorial officials were required to make yearly, and also from the Manor Court proceedings about which much will be said later.[1] In addition to this, we have a number of

---

[1] These detailed accounts or *compoti* are classed in the Public Record Office as *Ministers' Accounts*, i.e. accounts rendered by an official appointed to minister affairs on the lord's behalf. They are discussed in detail below on pp. 186 ff. The Manor Court and its proceedings are dealt with in chapter VIII, pp. 195 ff.

books of estate management which were written down in the late thirteenth century, such as *Fleta*, *Walter of Henley* and others. It is necessary, however, to add a word of caution at the outset concerning the use of these works. Léopold Delisle noted the wealth of early handbooks on estate management which have survived in England, and he lamented that no such records survived in France. But they have not been an unmixed blessing.

Many students of manorial documents written in the late thirteenth and fourteenth centuries will have noticed how difficult it is to find in Court Rolls or in Ministers' Accounts many examples which will bear out the statements of these contemporary manuals of estate management. *Walter of Henley* or *Fleta* can tell us with a wealth of confident detail the exact duties of, say, the sergeant (*serviens*), the bailiff and the reeve. The sergeant, they say, does this and this; the bailiff may do that and that; while the reeve is restricted to exercising his authority here and here. The documents, however, tell us quite another story, and show us the sergeant usurping the duties of bailiff or of reeve; and worse still, the underlings daring to act in ways in which only their superiors should do. The question at once arises: Which are we to accept as giving the more trustworthy witness—the treatises or the various types of manorial records? The question would seem to be easily answered *a priori* in favour of the documents, were it not for the fact that the influence of the treatises on modern scholars has been so great that almost all accounts of the working of the medieval manor are based on some such condition of affairs as is set forth in the pages of *Fleta*, etc. And this, no doubt, is the inevitable evolution of the study of these intricate matters: first, attention is paid to the general theory and contemporary exposition, and only later comes scrutiny of the *minutiae*.

Thus the late Dr Cunningham writes:

> The bailiff was appointed by the lord to look after the whole estate in detail; he was directly responsible to the lord for everything connected with the prosperity of the estate, and had to account in great detail for everything under his charge.... The (reeve) seems to have been the official representative of the villeins, who was responsible for them.[1]

---

[1] *Walter of Henley*, Intro. xii, xiii.

This view also seems to be accepted by Vinogradoff, who lends his great authority to the statement that "on every single manor we find two persons of authority—the bailiff or beadle...an officer appointed by the lord....By his side appears the reeve, nominated from among the peasants of a particular township and mostly chosen by them."[1] The statements of both of these authorities seem to be amply justified by reference to the treatises only, but there is surely much value in Sir William Ashley's caution:

> It may be doubted whether the description in *Fleta* actually corresponded with the general practice—whether there were in fact both reeve and bailiff on every manor. It is more likely that was a lawyer's generalisation, never really true, or that, if it ever had been true, it was already, by the time that book was written, ceasing to be so.[2]

Any careful study of manorial documents will show that the contemporary scribes who compiled the accounts and the Court Rolls could not differentiate clearly between the various manorial officers. Bailiff, bedell, reeve, sergeant—these titles are bandied about in a way which indicates how hazy the writer himself was of their precise meaning. A man is called Alan the reeve in one entry and in the next is given the title of sergeant: Henry the bailiff becomes the bedell lower on the same roll, and so on, though few scribes, it is to be hoped, were so muddled as the one who bracketed comprehensively the reeves, ale-tasters and foresters elected at the Hales Manor Court, and promoted them all by calling them bailiffs (*ballivi*).[3]

The truth is that the documents and treatises are complementary, but, even so, they require to be used with the greatest caution before any valid generalisations can be made. Two considerations at least must always be borne in mind: first, that the widest variations of procedure and customary use were possible on manors only a few miles apart, and therefore we cannot accept any clear-cut system such as that shown in *Fleta*; and, secondly, that the lax use of terms by the medieval scribe, as

---

[1] *Villainage*, 318.
[2] *Economic History*, I, 12.
[3] *Hales Rolls*, 430, 460. Cf. *Durham Halmote Rolls*, 46, 47; Davenport, *op. cit.* 50 n. 4; *Wakefield Rolls*, III, viii, etc.

illustrated above, makes it necessary for us to examine what the various manorial officers are actually found to do before we can accept the titles indiscriminately conferred on them by the writers of the documents.

So much it was necessary to say, for it is the overwhelming influence exerted by *Fleta* and other treatises which has confused our knowledge of the actual working arrangements of a medieval manor, giving us a Utopian rather than a real version. On some manors, doubtless, there was a hierarchy of servants such as is there laid down, but in very many manors a more primitive organisation sufficed, and about this *Fleta* and *Walter of Henley* are silent. We must bear in mind, therefore, that the full-scale organisation which must now be discussed was the exception rather than the rule, and yet it was sufficiently prevalent to make it important for us to understand its working, since it undoubtedly controlled the lives of tens of thousands of men centuries ago.

Let us consider this organisation at its fullest—say that required by a Bishop or one of the great nobles to administer his estates. The personnel may be divided into two groups: one, the administrators whose primary duty it was to see that every part of their lord's property was used to the best advantage. Secondly, there was a select band of manual workers, such as ploughmen, carters, shepherds, etc., whose activities were vital to the well-being of the manor. The higher ranks of the administrators were all free men, while those in the lower ranks, as well as the manual workers, were drawn from the lord's serfs. All these men came into contact with the ordinary peasant from time to time, and their various activities were of great importance to the everyday lives of the villagers.

At the head of the lord's officials stood the seneschal or steward. To the peasant he must oftentimes have seemed as all-powerful as the lord himself, and indeed he was frequently a man of rank and standing. The stewards of the manors of the Abbey of Ramsey may serve as examples. "About 1160 the steward was the brother of the abbot....About 1188 Sir Joscelin of Stukeley was steward....It is possible that he is the man of that name who is mentioned as the sheriff of Cambridgeshire about that time. Sir Joscelin's office of steward descended to his son Sir

Walter, etc.".[1] We may judge of his position by noting his emoluments as compared with those of the reeve—another manorial official: the steward of Berkhamsted in 1300 received a yearly fee of £15. 6s. 8d. and two robes with fur, as well as hay, litter, and firewood at all his lord's manors, with an additional 6s. 8d. for returning the King's writs. The reeve, on the other hand, got five shillings a year only and an allowance of four shillings for his food in the busy autumn harvesting season.[2] The steward's duties, however, were commensurate with his rewards: he was the voice and executive of the lord on the manors. To him was committed the management of the agricultural exploitation of the land; he appeared from time to time to preside over the Manor Courts and to hold the view of frankpledge. Every year he summoned before him those underlings whom he had charged with the day by day conduct of the manor, and extracted from them, in the presence of the auditors, a detailed account. He enquired into the use made of every animal on the estate, and the produce resulting therefrom down to the last egg, the results of the year's harvests, the amounts received in rents and fines and in every other way from the tenants, and generally conducted so searching an examination as must have terrified many of the humble rustics forced to account before him.[3]

The thirteenth-century manuals indulge in a wealth of detail. *Fleta* demands a paragon of virtues:

Let the Lord then procure a Seneschal; a man circumspect and faithful, discreet and gracious, humble and chaste and peaceful and modest, learned in the laws and customs of his province and of the duties of a Seneschal; one who will devote himself to guard his Lord's rights in all matter, and who knoweth how to teach and instruct his master's under-bailiffs in their doubts and their errors; merciful to the poor, turning aside from the path of justice neither for prayers nor for bribes.[4]

To such a man he would confide the cares of the lord's manors— and they are many. The seneschal must know the size and needs

---

[1] Ault, *Private Jurisdiction*, 145. See also *Cal. Inquis. Misc.* I, 512, no. 1880, for details of the Hastings family, hereditary stewards of the liberty of St Edmunds.

[2] *Inquis. Post Mortem*, Ed. I, III, 443.

[3] For a full account of this, see below, p. 189.

[4] *Fleta*, 159; cf. *Walter of Henley*, 84.

of every manor; how many acres should be ploughed and how much seed will be needed. He must know all his bailiffs and reeves, how they conduct the lord's business and how they treat the peasants. He must know exactly how many halfpenny loaves can be made from a quarter of corn, or how many cattle each pasture should support. He must for ever be on the alert lest any of the lord's franchises lapse or are usurped by others. He must think of his lord's needs, both of money and of kind, and see that they are constantly supplied. In short, he must be as all-knowing as he is all-powerful.

The picture is doubtless an ideal one, but the happy preservation of one thirteenth-century steward's letters is proof that it was not absolutely untrue to actual life. Every steward on taking office swore to preserve his master's interests to the utmost of his ability, and this correspondence certainly shows that at least one steward tried to live up to his oath.[1] Simon of Senlis was his name, and he was steward to the Bishop of Chichester during the second quarter of the thirteenth century. His letters show him to be in correspondence with his master on every kind of business. A handful of examples must suffice: he urges the Bishop to take immediate action against an encroaching neighbour; discusses the advisability of "farming-out" a church, and hints that the price asked is too high; complains of the high-handed action of the bailiffs of the Earl of Arundel; warns his master that the Precentor of Wells intends him some evil; prompts him how to make a hard bargain with a lady whose property is in question; reports the result of a conference at which he has succeeded in getting a rent due from the Bishop reduced. He shows another side of his character when he advises the Bishop to offer hospitality to his Archbishop who is spending a night on one of his Sussex manors, "for", he says, "he will provide for himself out of his own means, and wishes to accept nothing from you...wherefore, if you please, I will pay attention to him so that it shall turn to your advantage and honour". Crops, buildings, mortgages, provisions, the weather —all are discussed in turn. One letter shows him vigorously

[1] For this oath, see *Reg. Pontissara*, 1, 261–2, and for commission given to a steward with jurisdiction over all manors, and a statement of his powers, see *Lit. Cant.* 1, 284.

carrying on assarting and ploughing; building a new ox-shed one hundred feet long; or buying the crops standing on a neighbouring manor. He foresees every need of his master, and lays in lamb's fur for the winter, and 300 ells of cloth from Winchester fair for his poor pensioners; provides plenty of malt for brewing when required; sees that there is ample provision of wood for burning, brewing and baking at the Bishop's London house; gets a new wind-mill fitted up in time for the busy autumn season: these and innumerable other details seem to cause him no difficulty whatsoever and are all in the day's work. He has a good eye for business: the price of live stock at West of England fairs is no mystery to him; he arranges for the purchase of iron and its transport to Gloucester, and then afterwards for its subsequent carriage across England to Winchester at the least expense; he refrains from selling the Bishop's wine at Chichester because there is too much cheap wine on the market; and he suggests to the Bishop that he should think of getting his sheep from the abbey of Valle Dei (Vaudey) in Yorkshire, and of sending them down to his Sussex manors. His knowledge of men seems equally comprehensive. He reports to his master with obvious first-hand information on the notorious vicar of Mundeham who has two wives, or of one of his agents who has become lukewarm in his service. He tells him of the lay-brother from Vaudey who is so excellent with the sheep, and of the *serviens* of one of the manors whom he wishes to promote. He well may write at the end of the harvest, with some complacency: "Know that the crops on your manors are safely gathered, and are in the barns, and that all your other affairs go on well." How could they do otherwise with such a steward to direct them?[1]

Not all stewards were so attentive or so successful, no doubt, and even this indefatigable servant failed to mention one most important duty which devolved on him, namely the holding of the Manor Courts. The steward was the dispenser of justice and presided over the court in the place of his lord. We may easily imagine how important he seemed to the peasant as he saw him ride up to the manor house overnight, with his servants behind him, and, closely following him, his clerk who carried in his saddle-bags the precious Court Rolls on which were written

---

[1] For all the above, see Sussex Arch. Soc. III, 35–76.

many things the peasant would gladly have had forgotten. Every leaf of the parchment roll was covered with entries which concerned him and his fellows, and the clerk and his master, the steward, seemed to have every detail of them at their finger-ends.

So he watched as the little *cortège* rode past him up to the great house, which had been cleaned and prepared for the steward's coming by one of the female serfs, who did this and gathered bundles of rushes to strew in the rooms as part of her services, as on a manor of the Bishop of Chichester.[1] There he and his servants would spend the night, sometimes at the cost of the lord, sometimes at that of the peasants. The customals give us a few details of the latter practice. On a Lincoln manor, for example, the villagers have to find all sufficient necessaries for one entire day and the following night—food, drink, hay, fodder—everything, down to the candles that flickered over the last potations, is mentioned.[2] At Amberley, in Sussex, the tenants had to provide counterpanes and sheeting for guests at the hall, but if guests were quartered out in their houses in the vill, then only house room and beds (*hospicium et lectum*) and no more might be required.[3] When things were not going well between the lord or the steward and the peasantry these obligations seemed particularly onerous, and on the manors of the Prior of Durham the serfs showed great unwillingness to provide beds for the steward's servants as custom demanded,[4] and could not be found when they were wanted to carry his victuals and impedimenta from one manor to another.[5] Generally speaking, however, the costs of the steward's advent were a charge on the manor, and are duly returned in the accounts at the end of the year, when the tallies given by the steward are duly produced by the reeve and checked against the account. For example, on a Norfolk manor in 1342, the tally recorded the consumption of $1\frac{1}{2}$ bushels of wheat; 2 bushels, 1 peck of oats; 1 bushel of barley; 2 bushels of malt; 1 capon; 1 hen; as well as other things costing 1s. $9\frac{3}{4}d$.[6]

---

[1] Sussex Rec. Soc. XXXI, 51.
[2] *Rentals and Surveys*, Roll 403; and compare *Crondal Records*, 128 (1287).
[3] Sussex Rec. Soc. XXXI, 53.
[4] *Durham Halmote Rolls*, I, 72, 101, 140, 146.
[5] *Ibid.* I, 125, 144.
[6] Manor of Hindringham. Information supplied by Mr W. Hudson and Dr H. W. Saunders.

On most manors we may confidently imagine that the steward only came into actual contact with the peasant at the Manor Court or in exceptional circumstances, although his orders and decisions as to the manorial economy must have had a great effect on the lives of everyone in the village. Much closer to the villager—often in daily contact with him we find lesser officials, and of these the bailiff and the reeve are most important. It is necessary to avoid sweeping statements with regard to these two officials, for every manor had its own system. Sometimes we find both bailiff and reeve active on the manor; sometimes the bailiff is in charge of several manors and has to move about frequently to supervise their effective working; sometimes we find no trace of any bailiff at all, for many manors, no doubt, were controlled by the lord in person or by a member of his family, thus obviating the need of a bailiff.[1] Small manors, or manors lying close together and belonging to the same lord, were often overseen by a bailiff who only paid occasional visits. To this end Simon of Senlis writes:

Know also, Lord, that I will, if you please, commit the custody of your manor of Bissopestone to Henry, a serving man (? *serviens*) of Bourne, and chiefly on account of the sheep, because I think Henry will manage in such a business well and competently, and will also be able easily to keep (*custodire*) the manor of Bourne, together with the manor of Bissopestone, and easier than Burne and Bexle on account of the crossing over the water. . .and then some one else will be able to keep Bexle without a horse.[2]

The large number of instances in which we find a bailiff managing more than one manor suggests that this was a very common practice, and that the presence of both reeve and bailiff throughout the whole of the year on any but very large manors was wasteful.[3] These officials who over-saw a number of manors were often given the rank and pay of a sergeant (*serviens*), but there is little to differentiate their duties from those of the ordinary bailiff.[4]

---

[1] Rogers, *Prices*, II, 608 ff.; *Kettering Compotus*, 84.
[2] Sussex Arch. Soc. III, 54.
[3] *Wykeham's, Register*, II, 229, 497, 522; *Min. Acc.* 1143/18; Rogers, *Prices*, I, 13; Davenport, *op. cit.* 50, etc.
[4] Hall, *Winton Pipe Roll*, 13, 15, 16, 34, 50; and especially XVII; *A.A.S.R.* XXIV, 327, 330.

Bailiff or sergeant, whatever his title, the holder stood apart from the other dwellers on the manor. Not only was he a free man, but he was invested with the prestige arising from his position as the mouthpiece of the lord. When he first came on to the manor he brought letters with him from his patron committing the manor into his charge, and commanding all to show him respect and obedience.[1] Sometimes these letters set out his duties at some length, as when the monks of Canterbury appointed a bailiff

for our manor of C. there to cause the land to be ploughed, sown, reaped, manured and cultivated, and all the wagons and ploughs and cattle together with the sheep, lambs, hogs, and all other head of stock there to be managed and tended as shall seem best for our profit, rendering thereof such an account as it behoves bailiffs to render, and receiving, for him and his man, what other bailiffs holding the same office in past time received.[2]

This formal authorisation was necessary, for we find men pretending to be bailiffs for their own ends.[3] The official position of the bailiff was emphasised by the formalities which took place before the steward at the first Manor Court held after a new appointment, at which the bailiff took the oath of fealty, swearing to "behave honestly toward the county, toward rich and poor", and to guard the lord's rights.[4] Not so highly paid as the seneschal, he still could look forward to a stipend far above that of the other manorial servants. For example, the bailiff for Droxford had an annual wage of six pounds, while a ploughman only got eight shillings and a shepherd had to be content with half that amount.[5]

His position was further emphasised by the fact that he dwelt in the manor house at the expense of the lord, residing in "the chamber which the farm-bailiffs are accustomed to have", and from which he could superintend the activities of the whole manor, and could keep a sharp eye on the manorial servants who lived in the outbuildings attached to the manor house. His own

---

[1] See examples of such letters in *Reg. Pontissara*, 465, 589; *Wykeham's Reg.* 270, 427. For appointment, see *Hist. MSS. Com. Bath*, Nos. 707, 742, 749.
[2] *Lit. Cant.* II, 309, and cf. I, 146.
[3] *Cal. Inquis. Misc.* I, 419; *Hales Rolls*, 92; *Wakefield Rolls*, I, 125, 281.
[4] Selden Soc. IV, 77; *Wakefield Rolls*, II, 41.
[5] Levett, *op. cit.* 163. Cf. Davenport, *op. cit.* 22; *Min. Acc.* 1143/18.

responsibilities were many.[1] He carried out the general agricultural policy which had been decided on in consultation with the steward, and had to deal with the intricate details which arose continually on every field and pasture, and to keep a watchful eye lest any services due to his master were evaded or ill-performed. He had to know just what he might demand as laid down by extent and customal, but within these limits his powers were very extensive. We see him directing the work of the peasants, now ordering a ditch to be dug or scoured, now sending them to carry wood for the winter, now setting them to make new wattles for the fold. At his own discretion he determined how various men's work might best be expended. The peasant on the Glastonbury manors, for example, was bound to do whatever handiwork the bailiff should desire,[2] and again and again in the customals the phrase *ad preceptum ballivi* or *quod ballivi voluerint* occurs.

Naturally, with powers such as these he was not the most popular man on the manor, and had to be protected by the lord in the exercise of his duties. Thus we find that if a man assaulted the bailiff of a Berkshire manor he was fined sixpence, whereas his violence to another man would only cost him twopence.[3] Nevertheless, angry or desperate men were not easily put off, and would often attack the bailiff or any other men who tried to hinder them, or to seize their goods, so that we have many examples of savage fights in which the bailiff was involved.[4] Not that all bailiffs were the aggrieved parties. Far from this being so, there is, as we should expect, a continuous outcry against their excesses and harsh behaviour. "The churl like the willow sprouts the better for being cropped", was the belief of some of these men, who earned for themselves the reputation of flayers of rustics (*excoriator rusticorum*). At frequent intervals we hear of bailiffs who compelled men to buy ale from them at double its lawful price, while others extorted illegitimate carrying or harvest services. Sometimes they winked at some infringement of

---

[1] For a very detailed account of the bailiff's activities and responsibilities, see *Fleta*, 161, and *Walter of Henley*, 87.

[2] *Glas. Rentalia*, 102, 146, 205.

[3] *Hist. MSS. Com.* VI, 583.

[4] See, for example, *Thatcham*, II, 272; *Select Coroner's Rolls*, 10; *Ramsey Cart.* I, 428, etc.

manorial custom by a favoured peasant, or were themselves flagrant offenders. In short, there was a wide field for the activities of knavish bailiffs, and many entries in the *Hundred Rolls* and in manorial documents[1] show that such men reaped a rich harvest, and that the popular phrase which spoke of the bailiff as "rough as a boar" had some justification.

While the day of reckoning for such offences was frequently long delayed, the bailiff was well aware that from time to time the coming of the steward gave an opportunity for complaint to be laid against him and also for the steward himself to notice how things were going. While he might hope to escape any serious criticism at the Manor Court—for, after all, his position was so considerably superior to that of the serfs, and he always had the ear of the steward, who would generally support his actions —yet yearly a day of reckoning came. Once a year, soon after Michaelmas, the lord's auditors appeared on the manor, and held a searching inquiry into its financial condition. The bailiff had to face this and give full details of how he had spent the lord's money and with what return. Every smallest detail was investigated. Let us take, as an example, the question of hospitality. As the representative of the lord, the bailiff from time to time gave a night or two's shelter to some passing traveller who claimed to be a friend or dependent of the lord. But the auditors were not satisfied with this. By what authority did he extend such hospitality, and where was the written command from his lord which authorised his action? If he could not produce this, or something that would move these hard-faced men, he found himself surcharged with the amount. Some justification for such scrutiny may be urged, for men found this an easy way of getting a free night's lodging, and it was necessary to take steps to overcome such abuse. So bad, indeed, did it become at times that lords had to refuse all hospitality to strangers, as did the Bishop of Winchester, in 1295, when he issued an order to all his bailiffs commanding them to receive no one except the steward and his clerk.[2]

When at last the day came for the bailiff to leave the manor, he made his final appearance before the auditors, and having given

---

[1] *Rot. Hund. passim; Hales Rolls*, 404; *Vale Royal*, 117, etc.
[2] *Reg. Pontissara*, 529; and see also *Walter of Henley*, 92, 102.

an account of his stewardship, asked for his discharge. But there were often details still awaiting settlement and rents not fully accounted for, and these could lead to infinite trouble for the bailiff in future years. So, if he were wise, he got a chirograph acquittance from the auditors setting forth the state of affairs on his leaving office. Such documents usually set out that on the day the bailiff relinquished office there were on the manor so many horses, so many ploughs, etc. Two copies of this document were written on one piece of parchment which was then divided by cutting it into two by a wavy line. The one part was given to the bailiff: the other was sewn to the account roll for that year, so that in any dispute there it was on record, and could be appealed to, both by lord and by bailiff.[1]

The influence of *Fleta* and *Walter of Henley* on our knowledge of the working arrangements of the manor has already been discussed, and the version they give must be regarded as a Utopian rather than as a realist view. But, whether we are dealing with manors which form part of a vast organisation necessitating steward and bailiff, or with manors which are much more simply managed, one important fact emerges. However elemental the organisation, or however complex, we find universally present one official, and it may be doubted whether sufficient importance has hitherto been attached to this man—the reeve—as an essential unit in the manorial machine. *Et erit prepositus ad voluntatem domini*: these well-known words, which occur in almost every extent, would appear to have misled students into minimising the importance of the reeve's office because of its servile implication. It is perfectly true that to acknowledge liability to serve as reeve usually implied acknowledgement of servile status; but, nevertheless, these serf-ministers were of enormous importance in the effective working of the manor. The bailiff is characterised by Vinogradoff as an "outsider", a man imposed from without on the peasants; the reeve, on the contrary, was one of themselves, a man of the manor, knowing every field in it, and acquainted from boyhood with the eccentricities and habits of every person inhabiting its cots. Therefore, is it not reasonable to suppose that the working of the manor was more effectively aided by the

---

[1] For specimens of chirograph acquittances, see *Min. Acc.* 842/21, 958/26, 1297/23. See also below, p. 192.

detailed and intimate knowledge of the reeve than by the over-bearing exterior pressure exerted by an "outsider" bailiff? This contention is further strengthened when we observe that very frequently it is the reeve, and not the bailiff, who is called on "to account in great detail for everything under his charge". The annual accounts, it is true, may be presented by the bailiff solely, or sometimes by the bailiff and reeve jointly, but quite as often we find them presented by the reeve only. The fact that a serf was so trusted as to be allowed to render on his own authority the most detailed return of every item on the manor, should make us wonder whether he was relatively so insignificant as we have been taught to believe.

Further, when we enquire how long he held his office, the most enlightening evidence is forthcoming. The reeve was generally elected or presented at the Manor Court, usually at Michaelmas, and his term of office was for the ensuing year. It is quite wrong, however, to infer from this that he necessarily held office only for a year. We may remember Chaucer's reeve of Baldeswell who had held office "syn that his lord was twenty yeere of age", and he was not singular in this. Indeed, there is much evidence to show that, if a reeve displayed any aptitude for his office, his lord was only too ready to continue him in the same year after year. The Ministers' Accounts in the Public Record Office furnish valuable evidence on this point, and the present writer has examined all those series which cover a number of years consecutively (and many of those which have breaks in them) and which therefore yield the most exact information obtainable, with the object of finding who presented the accounts and how long they continued in office. The evidence is too bulky to be given here in full, but a few specimens may be quoted. On the manor of the monks of Westminster at Teddington in 1304–5 the reeve is Walter le Notiere. We find this same Walter reeve in every subsequent year for which the accounts are still extant until 1326–7—a period of twenty-two years.[1] At Eastwood in Essex one man is reeve from 1351–2 until 1373–4;[2] at Earnwood in Shropshire Adam atte Halle renders the accounts as reeve in 1379–80, 1384–5, and again, after a break, for the three years 1392–5.[3] In every county in which the accounts can be tested

[1] *Min. Acc.* 918/2–19.   [2] *Ibid.* 840/22–34.   [3] *Ibid.* 967/3–13.

similar results have been obtained; and it is reasonable to infer that, by the fourteenth century at least, the reeve was often as permanent an officer, despite his servile origin, as was the sergeant or bailiff. And when once we have admitted his permanency, it is difficult to resist the conclusion that such a man exercised an enormous influence over the working of the manor. We have seen that the reeve, by reason of his origin, had an initial advantage over the bailiff in his knowledge of his fellows and their holdings; and, if we consider what this meant when enriched by the cumulative experience gained by years of service in office, the claims of the reeve to be considered as the "pivot man" of the manorial administrative system are very great. One last point may be noted. Among the executive officers the reeve alone is always to be found on the manor among the peasantry. Stewards come at fixed times and seasons for the most part; sergeants and bailiffs may, or may not, live *in curia* from year's end to year's end; but the reeve is *adscriptus glebae*, and it is partly this very immobility which gives him his importance.

He is the man who knows his fellows with a thoroughness denied to bailiffs and others. However good the bailiff, however well he conducts the manor from his lord's point of view, he cannot have that understanding of domestic detail and circumstance that the reeve has, an understanding coming from lifelong intimacy in that closest of intimacies—the medieval village. It was the reeve who knew what was John atte Green's weak point, or what was the way to get recalcitrant Wat Hordle to the plough, or where was the place to find the laggardly William Joye. His fixture to the soil gave him all this, and it also gave the lord a pledge that in every manor he had one man at least among the peasantry whom he could hold strictly accountable for all that concerned the manorial economy. Hence, it is not the bailiff but the reeve who generally presents the yearly manorial account, and the reason for this is to be found in the fact that it is the reeve, and not the bailiff, who has watched over the manor all the year, and who now has to account for the detailed working of the manor for each one of its 365 days.

At the outset, then, we can see that the office of reeve was not one lightly to be assumed, and we can easily understand how it became essential in the lord's interest that he should enforce this service from his men. His free tenants were insistent on their exemption from serving as reeve, and rightly, for if a man could be proved to have served as reeve, the lawyers thought themselves well on the way to proving him to be a serf. Self-interest and self-respect were at the back of the free man's claim for exemption, so that the free men of Bisley in Gloucestershire, on being ordered by the steward to elect a reeve, protested that "by ancient custom the reeve must be of villein blood",[1] and that, therefore, they were exempt. This was the general attitude of free men throughout England, but, nevertheless, some lords were insistent enough to force this service from their free men.[2]

This was extremely rare, however, and the luckless serfs had to bear the burden among themselves, even though some of their number were able to escape, for it generally happened that only the larger holders in the village were liable for this duty. This was but natural, for it would not have been easy for the peasant with only his cot and close to have been set above another man who held perhaps 30, perhaps 60 acres, and who probably gave employment to the cottar from time to time. Hence, as Miss Neilson has shown at Sutton in Warwickshire, "the men of the bondage with one virgate were liable to be officers of the King or lord, as was pleasing; but men with half a virgate, or a *nocata*, or a cottage, were liable only to be beadles or tithing-men". She quotes also further examples from various parts of England in confirmation of this.[3]

The reeve was chosen once a year, generally at Michaelmas. An examination of the methods adopted for his election reveals to us such diversity of practice as we should expect. Autocratic selection by the lord; preliminary selection by the peasants and final selection by the lord; democratic election by the peasants: all these methods were in use on various manors and at various times. There seems to have been a general movement from autocratic selection by the lord to democratic election by the peasants, but we must beware of introducing order where all is disorder. Certainly, some of our earliest existing records show the lord exercising his absolute right to elect whomsoever he

---

[1] *V.C.H. Glos.* II, 136.
[2] Gale, *Honour of Richmond*, 66; Davenport, *op. cit.* 51.
[3] *Cust. Rents*, 101, 102.

would to be reeve. This is definitely laid down by the *Battle Abbey Customals*, the only limitation being the obvious one that the man chosen should be one of the larger holders.[1] The same state of affairs is implied by the payment of 6s. 8d. by the men of Staplegrove to the Bishop of Winchester in 1284, in order that they might "elect their own reeve, and have no reeve save by election".[2]

Naturally this crude assertion of rights did not always pass unchallenged. When the steward of Preston, Simon de Pierrepoint, endeavoured to force Hildebrand Reynberd to serve as reeve in 1280, Reynberd was not willing. To convince the steward of this, Reynberd gathered together a band of fifty or more of his fellows who proceeded to the steward's house which they fired in three places. Then they killed his falcon and maltreated his horses. After this, they caught the steward himself, and there and then before his own burning house, threatened him with knives and axes, until he swore not to make exactions against their will in future and not to call them to account for their insubordination.[3] On another occasion the villeins of the monks of Burton were equally recalcitrant. The steward removed the reeve from his office and tried to substitute another in his place, but everyone refused, as the lord had recently seized all their cattle and lands for certain offences on their part. "No land, no reeve", was their cry.[4]

On manors where the powers of the lord were not quite so autocratic we find that the peasants were allowed to make a preliminary selection among themselves, and then the lord or his agent made the final choice. The four men of Brightwaltham mentioned above as the "most competent men of the whole vill" had to appear before the steward, and his choice fell upon Thomas Smith.[5] The most general method, however, was that of election by the peasants themselves. This gave a semblance of power into their hands, and gradually, by purchase or other means, the right to elect their own reeve was obtained by the *villani* on many manors. Yet, even when they had won this

---

[1] *Op. cit.* 66; and see *V.C.H. Middlesex*, II, 68.
[2] Levett, *op. cit.* 14.   [3] *V.C.H. Sussex*, II, 185.
[4] *Burton Cart.* 83, and see p. 305.
[5] Select Pleas of the Crown, 168; cf. *Borough Charters*, II, lxxxvi, for an example of this in a borough; W. Rees, *South Wales*, 183.

privilege from the lord, they found it had its disadvantages. Indeed, some of the manuals distinctly state it to be an advantage to the lord that his serfs should elect their own reeve; for, says the author of *Hosebonderie*: "All those who hold in villeinage on a manor must elect as reeve such an one as they will answer for, for if the lord suffer any loss by the fault of the reeve, and he shall not have of his own goods the wherewithal to make it good, they shall pay for him the surplus which he cannot pay."[1] This was not mere theory, for the manorial injunctions of the monks of Gloucester expressly lay down this communal liability as a corollary of free election, and the same is true on manors in other parts of England.[2]

Once popular election obtained, it was not long before the possibilities of evasion exercised men's minds. Sometimes whole communities paid a lump sum in order that none of their number might be compelled to serve as reeve. Thus the men of Bulverhythe, in 1222, were to pay their lord twenty shillings, for they were all unwilling to serve,[3] while at Inglethorp the twelve villagers there compounded for 6s. 8d. "that they might not be chosen for the reeveship".[4] Individuals also were constantly to be found willing to pay a fine for permission to decline the office, when elected to it, and the fact that they disgorged quite considerable sums indicates the onerous and responsible nature of the office.[5] It may well be that there is some connection between this custom of buying exemption and the fact that on some manors the office devolved solely on the holders of certain lands. Thus at Kirton, in Lincolnshire, an inquisition of 1300 tells us that there were two tofts and four bovates set aside "whose tenants ought to be the lord's reeve".[6] In other parts of the East of England again, somewhat similar conditions obtained, as at Hindolvestone, in Norfolk, where, in 1309, we find that "certain land of William Erl was elected to the office of reeveship".[7]

[1] *Walter of Henley*, 67. It is expressed more briefly by Walter himself on p. 11.

[2] *Glouc. Cart.* III, 221. Cf. *D.S.P.* lxvii.

[3] Gale, *Honour of Richmond*, Appendix, 45.

[4] *Kettering Compotus*, 88; and see *Cust. Rents*, 110.

[5] *Hales Rolls*, 258; *Wakefield Rolls*, II, 14, 54, etc.; Selden Soc. II, 23, 45, 168; cf. *ibid.* IV, 128.

[6] *Inquis. Post Mortem*, Ed. I, III, 470.

[7] *Hist. Teachers' Misc.* I, 157, 180. Cf. Davenport, *op. cit.* 50.

Hence, whoever was holding that particular piece of land was liable for this service. In all such cases the result was that the greater part of the community went free, and the burden of office was thrown upon a mere handful of people. An amusing instance of the way in which men would evade office, if possible, is furnished by the proceedings at a Dulwich Court of 1333. Three of those who should have been present were absent, and as there were three vacant reeveships to be filled, their fellows seized the opportunity to elect them forthwith to these offices; and, in case there should be any doubt in the matter, the Court reaffirmed the election the next time it met.[1]

Whatever method was employed in the election of the reeve, and however many men avoided the office, at last one man was chosen, and there and then was sworn in by the lord or his steward in the presence of the whole Court. Thus there could be no question who was the new reeve, or that everybody knew about it.[2]

We may now turn to consider what were the duties which faced the newly elected reeve, and what powers he had at his disposal. We may put the matter briefly by saying that every item of the manorial economy was his concern. The estate manuals excel themselves in setting out his duties, and their detail runs to many pages. He must, they say, see that the farm servants rise in good time and get to work quickly; he must overlook the ploughing, carting, marling, seeding; he must keep a watch on the threshers so that they neither waste nor steal; he must supervise the livestock and see to their well-being. It is his duty to issue the various food allowances to the servants at stated intervals, and he is expected to hale before the Manor Court all those who fail in their service. The proper upkeep of the manor house, the farm-buildings and all the agricultural implements is his concern—in short there is no end to the variety or the extent of his labours. Nor is he always to be found about the manor, for at times his duties take him to distant parts. The reeve of Cuxham, for example, might have been seen one day in

---

[1] W. Young, *Hist. Dulwich College*, II, 272. Cf. *E.H.R.* XXXIX, 122, where Mr Hilary Jenkinson suspects similar occurrences on East Kent manors. For several reeves on one manor, see Levett, *op. cit.* 37, where it is shown that Waltham had no less than six!

[2] *Durham Halmote Rolls*, 36; *Tatenhill*, II, 48, 66; cf. *Fleta*, 164.

1331 far from his Oxfordshire manor, for he was busy on the wharf at Southwark, whither he had come to inspect and purchase millstones for his lord's mill. We may follow his anxious homeward progress with his five precious stones, for which he had paid the large sum of £15. 16s. 8d. First he took them by water to Henley, and from there he arranged for their transport the rest of the journey in carts hired for the purpose.[1] Similarly many reeves journeyed considerable distances to fairs or markets to buy and sell on their lords' behalf. And from time to time with four of his fellows he was called on to appear at the Hundred Court, there to answer for all things concerning the manor, and at rare intervals he might even have to appear before the dreaded itinerant justices at their Eyre.[2]

The reeve, then, was the chief of the peasants for the time being, and is often found, not peacefully leading his fellows to answer at the King's Courts, but encouraging them to resist authority. Two cases must serve to indicate this phase of his activities. In the first the reeve leads the men of his village of Carleton on an expedition to throw down the dyke which has been erected by the Abbey of Byland at Wyldon,[3] and in the second, after the King's foresters had taken certain beasts as pledges, the animals were rescued by certain men. They were reproved by the bailiff of a local lord, Ralph de Ralegh, whereupon

Robert de Byham, reeve of the said Ralph, ordered all the villeins of his lord and of the Abbess of Pratis, and of the prior of the hospital of St. Bartholomew, London, and all the villeins of Streton to make themselves ready with arms and they made a league (*statutum*) among them and put scouts (*insidiatores*) in a wind-mill and in the church tower to watch when the King's ministers (officials) came to do their office; and when they came all the villeins raised the hue and came together and rescued their beasts and beat and wounded and ill-treated the said bailiffs.[4]

It is clear that the power entrusted to these men was often very great, for frequently they were left in sole charge of the manorial labours for weeks at a time. We have already seen that some bailiffs were unfaithful, and it is not to be wondered at that some

---

[1] Rogers, *Wages*, 113; cf. Cunningham, *op. cit.* 598.
[2] *Statutes of the Realm*, Henry I, cap. 7.
[3] *Cal. Inquis. Misc.* No. 199.   [4] *Ibid.* No. 209.

reeves took advantage of their position, and either deceived and swindled their masters or oppressed and bullied their fellows. Oppression, no doubt, was always possible, and human nature being what it is, we may be sure that even-handed justice was not infallibly administered. It would be hard to believe that bribery did not exist in the circumstances or that favouritism did not flourish. It was so easy to arrange. The reeve frequently had full authority as to how the day's work should be expended, so that it was easy for him to arrange matters to the satisfaction of his friends, and to give this one an easy task, or to let him slip away early. There was obviously a limit to such proceedings: no reeve could afford to fly in the face of the majority of his fellows, and a rough and ready give and take characterised the general relations between reeve and peasants. At times a reeve went too far, and his fellows complained of the matter at the next Manor Court as they had a right to do. It was then for the lord to enquire into the matter, and to determine what was the truth, and this he did generally by means of a manorial jury. It will be seen, therefore, that the reeve had only a limited opportunity for oppression— always provided, however, that his lord was prepared to see justice done and that the peasants who formed the Court were not oppressed and afraid to speak their mind. Thus, in 1278, we have a long complaint before the Court, in which the reeve was accused of discriminating between rich and poor, of taking bribes, and of excusing men from their work for certain payments. Some of the charges were believed to be true by the jury, while others were dismissed, and the case may serve as an admirable example of the way in which the Manor Court acted as a check on any outrageous action by a reeve.[1] In another court, in 1278, a reeve brought a man before the Court, and asserted that he feigned sickness and failed to come to work, while all the time he was hale and at work in his own barn and yard. The manorial jury evidently regarded this as a piece of malice on the reeve's part, and he was not believed, and as a result he was fined for his misbehaviour.[2]

Generally, however, it was not the peasant but the lord who suffered at the hands of the reeve, and when we recall the reeve's position, and the multifarious opportunities he had for taking a

---

[1] Selden Soc. ii, 95.   [2] *Ibid.* 91.

little here and there, we need not be surprised. This side of the reeve's activities was sufficiently common knowledge for Chaucer to comment on it:

> Ful riche he was astored pryvely:
> His lord wel koude he plesen subtilly,
> To yeve and lene hym of his owene good,
> And have a thank, and yet a cote and hood.

Not only this: he was so able to conduct the manorial affairs that he even lent his lord moneys arising from the estate, and did this in so clever a way that the auditors were unable to get the better of him.[1] And this was no easy matter, for, as we have already seen, the annual audit was a very searching enquiry, and whether bailiff or reeve made the return, the proceedings were the same. Everything had to be accounted for, and what wonder if the unfortunate reeve faltered at times, and found himself obliged to invent a reason for the outlay of certain moneys, or the loss of an ox, or the defection of certain rents. So from time to time we stumble across entries which show that something like this has happened: a reeve is fined 6s. 8d. for "many things concealed"[2] in his accounts, or is found guilty of returning certain tenements as empty when in fact they were still occupied,[3] and so on. The whole working of the account will be explained later, and it will be seen what a formidable matter it was for the reeve, and how thankful he must have been once it was over.

Although the lord had the right to require his men to serve as reeves, he was not so harsh as to demand this service gratis. There were emoluments and allowances which compensated in some part for the heavy burdens of office. Nearly always the reeve was given a direct money payment, small indeed when compared with that received by the steward, or even that of the bailiff, but considerably more than was given to any of his fellows who were employed by the lord. It will be found that the reeve's pay is at least double that received by the ploughmen or carters, and usually was paid by the lord.[4] In places, however, as on the Battle Abbey manors, it was exacted from the peasants, and in

---

[1] C.T. Prologue, 587. [2] Rogers, Prices, II, 210.
[3] Levett, op. cit. 150; and see below, p. 191.
[4] See, for example, Winton Pipe Roll, passim.

addition to their rents we find them paying fourpence or eight-pence each *ad stipendium praepositi*.[1] But it was not the money which he received that made up the main part of the reeve's rewards. These he gleaned from three main sources: re-mission of rent, temporary grants of special pieces of meadow or close and relaxation of many services. It is very common to find that the reeve for the time being is excused all, or a part, of his yearly rent. The custom varied, but the general principle was in accord with common sense and justice. The reeve was much occupied with the lord's affairs, and necessarily could give only partial attention to his own strips, and it was not reasonable that he should pay so much for them as in ordinary years. Hence, the Eynsham monks excused their reeve the whole of his rent; on another lord's manor half was relinquished, and on yet another five shillings only was allowed.[2] Each manor had its own custom, and there is no apparent reason for the variations.

From earlier chapters the value of grazing privileges will have been realised, and these formed one of the most highly esteemed perquisites of the reeve's office. At times these took the form of permission to turn out his cattle on the lord's own reserved fields, as at Glastonbury, where the reeve has the right to graze his team of eight oxen with the lord's cattle in the demesne meadows.[3] In other places, the reeve could claim sustenance for his beasts, as on one of the manors of the Dean and Chapter of Wells, where he was entitled to half an acre of meadow to main-tain his draught horse throughout the winter, as well as pasturage for it in summer.[4] On other manors again certain closes were set apart for his use. We have the "Refhammes", consisting of two plots of pasture, allotted to a Glastonbury reeve;[5] or the five *capecia* of meadow allotted to the reeve on one of the Ramsey manors[6] as examples of this. As a further reward he was some-times given a share of the crops on the lord's demesne, as well as what he was able to grow for himself. He is kept severely in his place, however, by the quality of these gifts. The Glastonbury

---

[1] *Battle Customals*, 7, 10, 11, etc. Cf. *Norf. Arch.* xx, 191.
[2] *Eynsham Cart.* II, 137; *Cal. Inquis. Misc.* I, 64; *Castlecombe*, 146.
[3] *Glas. Rentalia*, 243, and cf. 94.
[4] *Hist. MSS. Com. Wells*, I, 343; and cf. *Ramsey Cart.* I, 496.
[5] *Glas. Rentalia*, 140; and cf. 243 "the reevis meadow".
[6] *Ramsey Cart.* I, 433; cf. also *Bleadon*, 194.

reeve was given "1 acre of corn in his lord's third-best field",[1]
while the Battle reeves were forced to be content with one acre of
corn grown on land which had not been manured, and was therefore not likely to yield very highly. Even this was not all, for they
could only take it at the order and discretion of the bailiff, who
could thus give them whatever he wished.[2]

The greatest relief the reeve obtained was undoubtedly from
none of these things, but from a partial or total relaxation of his
customary works. In fact, it would have been wellnigh impossible
for him to act as reeve and also to perform his usual number of
daily works; and most customals realise this and excuse him
completely.[3] Some grudging lords would not assent to this, but
made their reeve pay a fine of half a mark in lieu of the works
their own demands forbade him fulfilling, while others would
excuse the works at the busy harvest season only.[4]

Besides these various privileges, he was on some manors so
identified with the lord that he could demand his food daily with
the lord's other servants at the manor house.[5] On some of the
Ramsey estates this was so, while at Harmondsworth in Middlesex the reeve either dined daily at his lord's table or else received
a weekly allowance of one bushel of wheat. The Harmondsworth
entry concludes "and nothing more save by the lord's grace", as
if to protect the lord from his reeve demanding total and not
partial board. We shall see the importance of this when we come
to discuss the other manorial servants.[6]

A far more frequent custom, however, was to allow the reeve
to eat with the other manorial servants during the harvest period
which extended roughly from the feast of St Peter in Chains
(1 Aug.) to Michaelmas (29 Sept.). This was a period of abnormal
activity, and it was most important that the reeve should be constantly at the head of affairs, and about the manor and the manor
house. So the lord graciously allowed him to feed at the manor

[1] Glas. Rentalia, 243; and cf. 56, 60, 67, 94, etc.
[2] Battle Customals, 66.
[3] See Glas. Rentalia, passim; Ramsey Cart. passim; Eynsham Cart. 10, 61,
137; Rot. Hund. II, 525 a; etc.
[4] Ramsey Cart. I, 52; Castlecombe, 146; but see Davenport, op. cit. lxvi,
where the reeve gets off three works at harvest, and apparently none during
all the rest of the year.
[5] Ramsey Cart. I, 406, 473; cf. D.S.P. lxvii.
[6] V.C.H. Middlesex, II, 68. See below, p. 184.

house throughout that period. In some cases this is defined vaguely as "in autumpno"; other customals state that the reeve may be *ad mensam domini*[1] *a Gula Augusti usque festum S. Michaelis*;[2] others cut the period down to five weeks only,[3] while some emphasise the temporary nature of the arrangement by the emphatic words "from beginning of autumn to the end and no more",[4] or "and afterwards at his own table throughout the rest of the year".[5]

Our examination of the duties and rewards of the reeve, as well as the circumstances of his election, have shown us a multiplicity of local variations governing the general principle, *et erit prepositus ad voluntatem domini*. Custom was strong, here as everywhere on the manor, and no lord could exact more than the course of time had determined as the proper amount, nor could he wisely withhold the customary rewards. The reeve was a valuable servant, and a good reeve was a treasure not lightly to be thrown on one side. Hence it is that we find certain men remaining in office year after year, for it was obviously to everyone's advantage that they should continue to act as reeves. So long as a man could be found willing to undertake the arduous and invidious task, and so long as he did it to the satisfaction of all on the manor, neither lord nor peasants were likely to ask for any change.

But the lord had not finished with his serf once he had served as reeve. There were still several other manorial offices which he might call on him to fill. The chief of these were those of messor (or hayward as he was often called) and that of beadle or constable. Although in many cases it is possible to separate the duties of these two officers, we so often find them exercised by one person that any insistence on a very rigid differentiation would be pedantic. It is a convenience to separate them, but we must beware of making things too clear and of insisting on classifications which the medieval mind did not make. And it is worth our notice in passing to recall that even the idealised systems of *Walter of Henley* and others do not set out in detail

[1] *Battle Customals*, 66; *Wilts Arch. Mag.* XXXII, 326; Clutterbuck, *Hertford*, III, 618.
[2] *Ramsey Cart.* I, 496; *Stapledon's Register*, 347.
[3] Sussex Arch. Soc. *Coll.* LIII, 48, 66, 78.
[4] *Camb. Antiq. Soc. Proc.* XXVII, 169.   [5] *Ramsey Cart.* I, 496.

the duties for both these men on one manor. The beadle is almost always ignored in these treatises, being referred to only in some common-form inclusive way when the general duties of the "provost or beadle or hayward or any other servant of the manor"[1] are in question. We may define the duties of each of these two officers roughly as these: the beadle was the policeman of the village, taking pledges, levying distresses, etc., while the messor was in charge of all those operations connected with the sowing and gathering of the crops. There is little in these two offices that made the holding of them by one man an impossibility, and we therefore need not be surprised to find this is what actually happened on many manors.

At Forncett, for example, the terms *bedelli* and *messores* were used interchangeably in the rolls,[2] and many other examples might be given,[3] while at the Glastonbury manor of Dilcheat we are definitely told that the hayward is also the beadle. With this caution in mind let us see what was the position and duties of the hayward. They are very well defined in *Seneschaucie*:

The hayward ought to be an active and sharp man, for he must, early and late, look after and go round and keep the woods, corn, and meadows and other things belonging to his office, and he ought to make attachments and approvements faithfully, and take delivery by pledge before the reeve, and deliver them to the bailiff to be heard. And he ought to sow the lands, and be over the ploughers and harrowers at the time of each sowing. And he ought to make all [those] who are accustomed to come, do so, to do the work they ought to do. And in hay time he ought to be over the mowers, the making and the carrying (of the hay), and in August assemble the reapers and the boon-tenants and the labourers, and see that the corn be properly and cleanly gathered; and early and late watch so that nothing be stolen or eaten by beasts, or spoilt. And he ought to tally with the reeve all the seed, and boon-work, and customs, and labour which ought to be done on the manor throughout the year.[4]

This account is well substantiated by documentary evidence, and may, therefore, be accepted as substantially accurate. We see the hayward keeping an eye on the pasture, and arresting

---

[1] *Walter of Henley*, 91, 93, 101.

[2] Davenport, *op. cit.* 25.

[3] Clutterbuck, *Hertford*, III, 619; *V.C.H. Middlesex*, II, 68; Selden Soc. IV, 140.

[4] *Walter of Henley*, 103. Cf. *Fleta*, 172 (II, cap. 84).

those who infringe on their customary rights;[1] we meet him in the Manor Courts seeking protection against those who threaten his life and limb, because he executes his office properly.[2] In harvest we see him supervising the work, and measuring the sheaves to see that they are of the right size.[3] Then, after all have gone home for the night, he stays on to see that no one carries off his lord's corn;[4] and, finally, at the end of the year, he tallies with the reeve for all the operations entrusted to him from time to time.[5]

He was elected to his office most probably by one of the methods detailed above in describing the reeve. Our information is not so full, but we have many cases of autocratic selection by the lord, and many in which the hayward is elected by his fellows.[6] The two offices, we may suppose, developed along much the same lines. Similarly, we find that the hayward received emoluments and rewards analogous to those paid to the reeve. His rent is excused or lowered; he gets certain perquisites, such as a measure of seed-corn from time to time, or a piece of meadow (a beadle-mead) for himself, or a number of sheaves at the harvest. He eats with the other manorial officers during harvest, and this is paid for from the lord's purse.[7]

Not only his duties and rewards, but also his conduct of his office bears close resemblance to that of the reeve. Untrustworthy haywards occur as we saw untrustworthy reeves in office. One of these haywards, we are told, used to watch until he found people gleaning without permission. Then he swooped down upon them, wrested away their lawful gains and quietly took them off to the mill to be ground for himself.[8] Another of these men is accused and found guilty of neglecting to guard his lord's fields properly. The jury also found that he took bribes to the

---

[1] *Durham Halmote Rolls*, 55; *V.C.H. Bucks*, II, 43.
[2] *Hales Rolls*, 26.
[3] Hone, *op. cit.* 233.
[4] *Battle Customals*, 67; *V.C.H. Middlesex*, II, 68.
[5] Davenport, *op. cit.* lxx, where the summary of the hayward's accounts gives a good idea of his many activities.
[6] *V.C.H. Bucks*, II, 54; Clutterbuck, *Hertford*, III, 619; *Battle Customals*, 67; and for payment not to serve, see Selden Soc. II, 128.
[7] *Glas. Rentalia*, 64, 243; *Battle Customals*, 82; *Cust. Rents*, 102, and note 5.
[8] Selden Soc. IV, 123.

subversion of justice; kept for himself the fines paid over to him, and generally used the lord's property as if it were his own.[1] There is nothing here for surprise: when we remember the many thousands of men who held this difficult office what is surprising is that we do not get a larger volume of complaint and accusation.

When we turn to the hayward's companion (or other office) we find that while his duties were various, they were mostly associated with the activities of the Manor Court. The following description of the beadle of Stowe in Lincolnshire, in 1283, gives an excellent summary of his duties.

> R. Wale holds 1 bovate of land for which he ought to collect all the moneys of the Bishop [of Lincoln], as well in respect of rents as of other things...and to pay them at the will of the sergeant; and he ought to summon all the work-tenants (*operarii*) and to look after them while they are at work; and he ought to make the summonses for paying hens...and to pay them at the next manors if they ought to be sent there...and he ought to make all summonses and distresses, etc., as often as they should be made....[2]

So on various other manors we find him summoning the tenants to the Court, collecting the fines imposed on them, or evicting them from their holdings by order of the Court.[3] As the harvest season came round he visited all the tenants and warned them of the days they would have to appear to gather in their lord's corn; at other times he would seize their cattle found straying in the lord's meadows or closes, and put them in the village pound until the will of the lord was known concerning them.[4]

Clearly, such an officer was of great practical importance on the manor, and we might extend our list of his duties to any length by recording the innumerable variations of practice throughout England. Much that we should like to know the records do not tell us. Was he a very unpopular man on the manor? Did men hate serving as beadle more than as reeve or hayward? Was he often molested while performing his duty? These and

---

[1] Selden Soc. IV, 140; Davenport, *op. cit.* 75 n. 2. Compare all this passage with the extract quoted above from *Seneschaucie*, and also with *Glouc. Cart.* III, 213 ff.

[2] *A.A.S.R.* XXIV, 332.

[3] Selden Soc. II, 112; *Eynsham Cart.* xiii, xlv; *Hales Rolls*, 36.

[4] *V.C.H. Middlesex*, II, 67; *Hales Rolls*, 26; Davenport, *op. cit.* 25.

many other questions must await a much fuller knowledge of manorial conditions. We may say with confidence, however, that it was not considered so onerous or responsible a task as that of reeve, and we often find men liable for the office who were excluded from the reeveship by the smallness of their holdings.[1]

Besides serving in any of the above offices the peasant could be called on to fill posts such as that of woodward—an officer appointed to safeguard the lord's woods and plantations,[2] or to become a forester and watch over the lord's deer and his rights of chase.[3] Special conditions, again, required special legislation, as in the Fen country, where certain officers were elected to inspect and to report on the protecting dykes. The conditions of election, service and emoluments of all these officers need not detain us, as they are similar, *mutatis mutandis*, to those of their fellow villein officials.

All these men we have been discussing carried out their duties while still keeping their own strips in the common fields in active cultivation, and they were often drawn from the larger holders of villein-tenements. We have seen, however, that there were many men on the manor whose holdings were too small to support them without some other means of livelihood. Some were absorbed by their more prosperous neighbours who were able to offer them work from time to time, but the main source of constant employment was to be found as one of the manorial servants. The lord cultivated a considerable portion of the manor (as we have seen) very largely by the aid he exacted from his villeins, but it is doubtful whether this intermittent aid was ever sufficient in itself. The lord probably always required the help of some of the peasantry to look after his stock, and to perform innumerable daily operations incident to farming, and Sir W. Ashley has conjectured that "some of these, such as the shepherds and oxherds, were probably descended from the slaves of the demesne" of Domesday times.[4] Whether this were so or not, some per-

---

[1] *Cust. Rents*, 101, 102.
[2] See *Political Songs* (Camden Soc.), 149, for mention of "the wodeward waiteth us wo that looketh under rys". Also see *Wilts. Arch. Mag.* XXXII, 322; *V.C.H. Middlesex*, II, 69, for hereditary woodward; *Eynsham Cart.* II, xiii, xlv. Rys=boughs.
[3] *D.S.P.* 75, 98; *Norf. Arch.* XIV, 40.
[4] *Econ. Hist.* I, 1, 32, 61.

manent staff was essential, and this seems to have been provided for in various ways. At first it is probable that men who were chosen to act as ploughmen or shepherds were excused other rents or services, and even sometimes had the use of the lord's team one day a week to plough their own ground, or the right of folding the lord's cattle on their holding at certain intervals. Besides this, they pastured their beasts with those of their lord, and received other privileges in return for their labours.[1] On some manors certain holdings were specially set aside for those who fulfilled the offices of ploughman or swineherd, such as we find on one of the Glastonbury manors, where we are told that "there are small portions of lands which belong to the ploughs called Sulstiche and Goddingchestiche whereof the ploughman ought to have a portion as the others".[2]

From the very inception of the manorial system, however, men were trying to unburden themselves of the constant weekly work the lord imposed upon them. The more successful they were in this, the greater the lord's need for additional help. With the money his peasantry paid for exemption from week-work he was able to hire labourers who would be entirely at his disposition. Hence, by the fourteenth century at latest—and much earlier in many parts—another system was in full working.[3] The lord had a body of servants who had no land of their own—or at the most a few acres, and who were primarily on the manor to cultivate his lands, and to tend his flocks and herds. These men were known as the *famuli*. Their number, of course, varied from manor to manor, but we generally find ploughmen, carters and shepherd or swineherd among them.[4]

On some manors a large staff gradually became the normal thing, and the lord recruited them from his own serfs if possible.

---

[1] *Glas. Rentalia*, 93–5, 122, 138, 204, 217; *Battle Customals*, 66; *Ramsey Cart.* I, 318, 408, 473; *Winton Pipe Roll*, xxii.

[2] *Glas. Rentalia*, 139; cf. 102; Page, *End of Villainage...*, 22; *Worc. Priory Reg.* 66 a; *Cust. Rents*, 102, 103.

[3] Thus at Bray we find (temp. Henry III) the demesne worked by serfs who held land on privileged terms. By the time of Edward I, the work was done by men who received a fixed yearly wage, as well as an allowance of the greater part of the corn grown on the manor. *V.C.H. Berks*, I, 175.

[4] See, for example, *Reg. Roff.* 132–3, where the various types of men, ploughmen, carters, etc. are enumerated for each manor. And compare *Worc. Priory Reg.* 25 a, 119 b.

The *Hundred Rolls* tell us that at Chalgrove, in Oxfordshire, the yardland-holder who had sons old enough to earn a living brought them up to the hall with him at Michaelmas, and there selected one to serve the lord for a year at the usual wages.[1] The peasants on the Gloucester and other manors were evidently liable to be impressed for service, and we find that the lord could even move them about from one manor to another if he found he could employ them more profitably by so doing.[2] The men who were thus chosen were probably from the humbler ranks of the peasants: "the poor cottars who obtain their living by the work of their hands", as the *Inquisitio Nonarum* calls them.[3] They were, in general, lodged *in curia*, that is, in the buildings forming part of what would now be called the "home-farm".[4] Their quarters were much the same as those they found in their own homes, and otherwise they were comparatively well off; for, unlike their fellows, they were not entirely dependent on the seasons for their prosperity. They had payments both in money and in kind. They were given a regular money wage,[5] and if they held any land, their rent was reduced on this.[6] Further, they were entitled to allowances of corn and other farm produce,[7] and during the busy harvest season they shared in the generous rations which were provided at the manor house for the lord's officials at this time.[8]

At Martham (Norfolk) in 1272, for example, we find them consuming quantities of beef (both from the home stock, and from that purchased in Norwich) and washing it down with beer, brewed on the manor from malt there provided. Bread, both of wheat and of rye, plenty of peas-pottage, herrings, cod, cheeses

---

[1] *Rot. Hund.* II, 768.

[2] *Glouc. Cart.* III; Univ. Lib. Camb. MS. Kk. i. i. f. 2216.

[3] *Inquis. Nonarum,* 14, and see *V.C.H. Berks,* II, 175; *Dorset,* II, 223; *Beds,* II, 82.

[4] Davenport, *op. cit.* 24 n. 3. "There is frequent mention of the *domus famulorum* (cf. *E.H.R.* xx, 482) which was situated near the *camera servientis*; and as a maid was kept to prepare pottage for the *famuli,* it seems probable that the ploughmen, carters...were unmarried men, resident in the court." But see Rogers, *Prices,* I, 286–9.

[5] *Min. Acc.* 958/19; *Kettering Compotus,* 33.

[6] Levett, *op. cit.* 20; *Min. Acc.* 958/19; *Crondal Records,* 62.

[7] *Min. Acc.* 751/18, 21 ; 843/31 ; 859/23, 918/17, 998/25 ; *Kettering Compotus,* 47, 53, 57, 65, 67, 69, etc. See above, p. 88.

[8] *Min. Acc.* 918/3; *Kettering Compotus,* 33; Rogers, *Prices,* II, 622, 623.

PLATE IV

The thresher

The swineherd

and an occasional goose[1] made the hard day's work bearable.[2]
Further, they were entitled to a regular issue of corn at intervals
during the year, so that their condition was considerably superior
to that of many of their fellows,[3] whose lot, at its worst, no doubt,
is so movingly related to us in the lines of *Pierce the Ploughman's
Crede*:

And as I wente be the waie wepynge for sorowe,
(I) seigh a sely man me by opon the plow hongen.
His cote was of a cloute that cary was y-called,
His hod was full of holes and his heer oute,
With his knopped schon clouted full thykke;
His ton toteden out as he the londe treddede,
His hosen overhongen his hokschynes on everiche a side,
Al beslombred in fen as he the plow folwede;
Twey myteynes, as mete maad all of cloutes;
The fyngers weren for-werd and ful of fen honged.
This wight waselede in the fen almost to the ancle,
Foure rotheren hym by-forn that feble were worthen;
Men myghte reknen ich a ryb so reufull they weren.
His wiif walked him with, with a longe gode,
In a cutted cote cutted full heyghe,
Wrapped in a wynwe-schete to weren hire fro weders,
Barfote on the bare iis that the blod folwede.
And at the londes ende lay a litell crom-bolle,
And theron lay a litell childe lapped in cloutes,
And tweyne of tweie yeres olde opon a-nother syde,
And alle they songen o songe that sorwe was to heren;
They crieden alle o cry, a carefull note.
The sely man sighede sore, and seide: "children, beth stille!"

As I went by the way, weeping for sorrow, I saw a poor man hanging
on to the plough. His coat was of a coarse stuff which was called cary;
his hood was full of holes and his hair stuck out of it. As he trod the soil
his toes peered out of his worn shoes with their thick soles; his hose
hung about his hocks on all sides, and he was all bedaubed with mud as
he followed the plough. He had two mittens, made scantily of rough

[1] The "rep-goose" appears constantly, as a *bonne bouche* during the
harvest—probably at the end of the work. See e.g. *Cust. Rents*, 56;
Cunningham, *op. cit.* 600; *Kettering Compotus*, 65, etc.
[2] Information kindly supplied by the late W. Hudson and Dr H. W.
Saunders. Cf. *Min. Acc.* 751/18–21, 843/31, 859/23, 918/3–17, etc.
[3] See Rogers, *Prices*, I, 289, or *Six Centuries of Work and Wages*, 170, for
his conclusions as to the "income of a first-rate agricultural labourer", which
he takes to be about £1. 15s. 6d. a year inclusive of money payments and
allowances. Compare also with the evidence above, p. 88, concerning the
incomings of a thirty-acre holder.

stuff, with worn-out fingers and thick with muck. This man bemired himself in the mud almost to the ancle, and drove four heifers before him that had become feeble, so that men might count their every rib so "sorry looking they were".

His wife walked beside him with a long goad in a shortened cote-hardy looped up full high and wrapped in a winnowing-sheet to protect her from the weather. She went barefoot on the ice so that the blood flowed. And at the end of the row lay a little crumb-bowl, and therein a little child covered with rags, and two two-year olds were on the other side, and they all sang one song that was pitiful to hear: they all cried the same cry—a miserable note. The poor man sighed sorely, and said "Children be still!"[1]

With the cry of these children in our ears we may conclude our survey of the manorial servants. They have comparatively little need of our pity: here and there a harsh master may have driven them hard, or fed them with sheep dead from the murrain and hastily salted down for their use,[2] but their lot in general compared very favourably with all but the aristocracy of the manorial peasantry. They had what few men of their class had— comparatively little anxiety as to how they were to live from one year's end to another. The great court of the manor house sheltered them, and the lord's officials provided them with food and drink, and enough spending silver to make them popular at the village ale-house. Medieval life could offer little more to men of villein stock who were "born in the yoke of servitude".

Mention has been made from time to time of the manorial accounts, and these must now be considered. They were generally returned by the reeve and it is possible that no part of his duties caused him more trouble than did the compilation of the annual accounts. The formidable nature of these is apparent as soon as we glance at them, for they usually state in the minutest detail every item of the manorial income and expenditure. It is not easy to explain how the unlettered reeve managed to have all this information available. He relied, no doubt, mainly on tallies and notches on barn-posts, aided by a cultivated memory. There are many living who can recall remarkable instances of the ability of old shepherds and wagoners to account for every detail of the property under their charge, although they relied solely on their memories. I am told that in the early

---

[1] *Pierce the Ploughman's Crede*, ed. Skeat (E.E.T.S.), 17, l. 420.
[2] *Walter of Henley*, 31; *Fleta*, 167.

'eighties of last century, the largest tenant-farmer in Hertfordshire had an entirely illiterate bailiff, who came back every
market evening and dictated to his master, for hours at a time,
the most complicated details of the day's offers and acceptances,
in as orderly a fashion as if he were reading from a book; and the
late Mr William Hudson was good enough to tell me of a
Sussex landowner whose bailiff "could not write, and yet never
made a mistake in accounting for the number of faggots he sold
in a year. He notched them all on a door-post".[1] So it must have
been with the reeves; for, although the Gloucester injunctions
order the reeves to keep careful tallies, and to enter the details
from time to time on rolls provided for the purpose,[2] such
methods were seldom adopted, but rough and ready means
better suited to semi- or wholly illiterate men who were in
charge.

A last survivor of such men is seen in "Ragged Ass Jack" as
described by Mr Ford Madox Ford in his *Return to Yesterday*.
Jack, he tells us, "could do anything (except write, and late in
life he taught himself to read)—patiently and to perfection:
thatcher, wagoner, shepherd, bricklayer, etc. He could keep
tallies and the most complicated accounts on notched sticks,
cutting with a bill-hook I, II, III, IV, etc., as fast as you could
write them with a pen, and adding up quite as fast."[3]

Even if a few of them could have kept rough jottings, such as
are sometimes found sewn to the full account,[4] the actual accounts
would have been utterly beyond them, and we find that these
are the work of trained scribes who made a round of the manors
after Michaelmas for this purpose. One of the commonest
entries on the *compoti* records the scribe's fee for his work, and
often the cost of the parchment.[5] It may well be, of course, that
where a lord had but two or three manors, the account was made
by the parish priest or his clerk.[6] Bishop Pecock, in the early
fifteenth century, advises parish priests to avoid "worldli offices

---

[1] Cf. *Hist. MSS. Com.* v, 444, where the amount of corn in a barn (1480)
was said to be scored on the door-post.
[2] *Glouc. Cart.* III, 213 ff.   [3] *Op. cit.* 153.
[4] *Econ. Hist. Rev.* I, 68.
[5] *Min. Acc.* 987/24–8, 1052/6; Rogers, *Prices*, I, 95; II, 620–1; *Obed.
Rolls S. Swithin* (Hants Rec. Soc.), 238, etc.
[6] Sussex Rec. Soc. XXXI, 51.

and rekenyngis in court or out of court",[1] and we can understand how easy it was for the priest, as the only lettered man in
the village, to be called on to make the account if a professional
scribe were not available. The accounts, in general, followed a
set formula, so that from whatever part of England they come,
they have a strong family likeness, and specimen *compoti*
(accounts) were available for the unskilled.[2] Two qualifications
of their usefulness have to be made: they themselves sometimes
fall into confusion and repetition, thus furnishing no very
infallible guide to an inexperienced man; and they sometimes
quote figures which, though they may have been possible locally,
are very far from being generally applicable.[3]

The general arrangement of the account starts by naming the
manor, the year of the king's reign, and the official who presents
the account, and then gives the several main items; first the
arrears from last year, then the rents of assize, of mills, etc.;
then the sales of corn and stock, the perquisites of the court,
fines, heriots, etc. After this come the details of the expenditure,
and at the foot of the roll the balance is struck. On the back of the
roll the scribe enters an exact account of the produce of the
manor and how it has been consumed, as well as a detailed in-
ventory of the livestock, down to the smallest items. Smyth, in
his *Lives of the Berkeleys* tells us that the accounts of that great
family were kept in such detail that they did not

scorne to discend soe lowe, as to declare, what money was yearly made
by the sale of the locks, belts, and tags of the sheep (as well as of the
fleeces), of the hearbes of the garden, stubble from off the Corne lands,
cropps and setts of withy'es of Osier rods, the Offall wood of old
hedges, of butter, cheese and milk, dung and soile, bran, nuts, wax,
Honey and the like.[4]

In this they only followed what was the common custom throughout the whole country, wherever the lord found it necessary to
keep an account.

The reeve had not finished with the account once the clerk
had completed his task: he had yet to face the auditors. Large

---

[1] *Reule of Crysten Religioun* (E.E.T.S.), 326.
[2] See MS. Ee. i. i. f. 221 and f. 231 *b* in the University Library, Cambridge,
for a specimen *compotus* in great detail. Another in Dd. vii. 6, f. 58 *b*.
[3] This point was made by Prof. A. E. Levett, *Econ. Hist. Rev.* 1, 68.
[4] *Op. cit.* 1, 156.

landholders usually sent their auditors from manor to manor, there to conduct on the spot a searching inquiry into the details of the account. The unknown author of *Seneschaucie* says that the lord ought to "ordain that the accounts be heard every year, but not in one place but on all the manors [separately], for so can one quickly know everything, and understand the profit and loss...and then can the auditors take inquest of the doings which are doubtful".[1]

We may see the steward of the Bishop of Chichester's Sussex manors (*c.* 1225) constantly thus engaged. On one occasion he is unable to fulfil a command because he and another official are making a round of the manors and auditing the accounts.[2] Before Michaelmas he is found writing to his master, and asking for someone to be joined with him "as the feast of Saint Michael is at hand, the season for hearing the accounts".[3] As he gets no answer from the Bishop, he writes again, urging that since "you have directed me to come to you at London within 15 days of Michaelmas, wherefore I should wish most freely to audit the accounts first with some one of your household, so that I might be able reasonably to answer about the proceeds of your diocese".[4]

Walter of Henley and other writers give us considerable information concerning the qualities and duties of a good auditor. He has to be a faithful and prudent man, well versed in his profession, and knowing all the points and details of the accounts, and the many items of rents, outlays, returns, stock, etc. they must contain. He must hear the plaints and wrongs of everybody who complains of any of the lord's officers, and make an enquiry into any doubtful matters and fine those who have been careless with the lord's property.[5]

---

[1] *Walter of Henley*, 105, 107. Cf. with this, however, the practice of the monks of Canterbury, who refuse a plea to examine the accounts *in situ*, since, they say, "We cannot do that without great disparagement of our position, because from old time it has always been our custom that our sergeants from all parts of England should come to Canterbury to our chequer, there to hand in their accounts, and this in the presence of certain of our brethren". *Lit. Cant.* (R.S.), I, 481 (1332).

[2] Sussex Arch. Soc. III, 54.　　　[3] *Ibid.* 65.　　　[4] *Ibid.* 70.

[5] *Op. cit.* 105 ff. The auditors stayed at the manor house (see *Higham Ferrers*, 112, for the "Auditor's Chamber" at the Castle), and the accounts regularly contain items detailing the expenses of their visit. See *Higham Ferrers*, 56, 162; and cf. Davenport, *op. cit.* xxxvi; *Min. Acc.* 843/29, 1078/17, etc.

The auditors were men of considerable standing: rarely the lord himself, but more generally trusted officials; or, in the case of a religious house, the cellarer, accompanied by one or two senior colleagues.[1] They carried with them the rolls of the manor for previous years, and sometimes even the extent or the customal of the manor, as they are advised to do by Walter of Henley,[2] and the reeve must have found them possessed of a seemingly uncanny knowledge of the details of the estate in the past, as they checked his return by reference to previous figures and the details given in the customal.[3] It is very common to find an entry in the neat hand of the scribe struck out and a new set of figures entered in the heavy and less practised hand of the auditor. Again and again the reeve starts his account by admitting that he is twenty shillings in arrears. The auditor consults the balance struck at the foot of the previous roll, and firmly alters it to fifty shillings or eighty shillings as the case may be.[4] The reeve accounts for some 3391 day-works, but the auditors refuse to allow so scanty a return "because the aforesaid total was found false by 382 day-works, as appears by the extent [and therefore] the said total is corrected and made true, namely 3773 day-works".[5]

In the same way every item is closely scrutinised, and the auditors cross-question the reeve concerning every detail which seems unusual, and cause him to deliver up to them his evidences as detailed in the *compotus*.[6] At times the reeves have a melancholy tale to tell of how the lord's property has been taken from them, as when they complain that "the Earl of Lancaster's men as they travelled with the Queen through Gloucestershire, took away from the manors of the lord of Berkeley so many ducks and geese that all their eggs and their broods for the year were lost.

---

[1] *Reg. Roffense*, 65, 66; *Cart. Glouc.* I, xc; *Worc. Priory Reg.* xxxviii; *Reynolds' Register*, 18, 20; Davenport, *op. cit.* xxxvi; *Archaeologia*, lviii, 353, etc.; and see *Lit. Cant.* II, 311, for letter of appointment of auditors. Their office and authority was recognised by the second Statute of Westminster, cap. 11.

[2] *Op. cit.* 7.

[3] See *Min. Acc.* 1004/10, where the auditors refer constantly to the extent in going through the account, and correct it accordingly.

[4] *Min. Acc.* 859/24, 25, 26, etc.; 918/8; 987/21, 26; 1030/5.

[5] *Camb. Antiq. Soc. Proc.* XXVII, 172; cf. *Ely Rolls*, Barton, 21/2 Ed. III.

[6] See *Min. Acc.* 987/24 for a most interesting example of the care with which suspected items were investigated. Cf. *Higham Ferrers*, 60.

They also broke open their barns and took wheat and corn"—
and the reeves ask to be exonerated.[1] Sometimes the reeve paid out
money by authorisation from his superiors, and this authorisation he has to produce before he can avoid being charged with
the debt.[2] Generally, however, he does not produce actual
letters, but hands over his various tallies or his little parchment
"bills", which he has taken care to claim before parting with his
lord's goods to any man.[3] Once he has been foolish enough to
allow grain or stock to go without a written order from a superior
authority, or without first claiming a "bill" or tally from the
purchaser, it will go hard with him before he can persuade the
auditors that he has not made away with his lord's goods.[4]

So the accountants worked through the roll; here adding a few
small items either omitted or sold since the account was drawn
up,[5] there reducing a charge which they consider excessive.[6]
They account for items forgotten in the previous year's account,[7]
and make such allowances as they think justifiable.[8] At last they
come to an end; the balance is struck, and the year's profit or loss
stands revealed. This was an anxious moment for the reeve: if
there were a balance he was called on to produce the money, but
often he had not yet demanded it all, or had failed to collect it
when he applied. On the other hand, a deficit on the year's
working was an unpleasant matter for him and his fellows, since
his lord's livelihood depended on the successful farming of his
manors, and a bad year was liable to lead to increased demands
and a tightening up of conditions in the coming year.

In general, however, there was a balance to the lord's credit,
and the reeve was held strictly accountable for this. The auditors
had discretionary powers, and would, at times, forgive a debt
because of the "weakness and poverty"[9] of the reeve, or as a
matter of special grace of the lord.[10] Most reeves were not so
fortunate, and their debt was firmly fastened upon them, and

[1] *Lives of the Berkeleys*, I, 286.
[2] *Min. Acc.* 936/15; Cunningham, *op. cit.* 600.
[3] *Min. Acc.* 367/1139; 870/9, 10; 1017/14; 1280/5.
[4] Davenport, *op. cit.* 25 n. 3, where a reeve seeks an allowance for payments
made *sine* writ or tally, and also *Reynolds' Register*, 44, 45, 51.
[5] *Min. Acc.* 918/4.   [6] *Ibid.* 913/16.
[7] *Ibid.* 1017/8.   [8] *Crawley*, 273.
[9] *Obed. Rolls S. Swithin*, 150.   [10] *Min. Acc.* 1024/19.

formed the first item (frequently misstated, as we have seen) on the next year's account. Whether it were the same reeve or another, there it appeared on record, and we see it slowly dwindling as, bit by bit, it is accounted for by the debtor. Thus at Stevenage, in Hertfordshire, in 1284, a sometime reeve made two payments—one of 10s. 6¼d. and another of 5s.—being part of the arrears on his *compotus* of the previous year; while during 1285 he paid a further 20s.[1] Sometimes the lord was not so sure of his man, and in such cases he took care to demand adequate sureties. One reeve has to find twenty-five pledges that he will pay up his arrears within the next year *sine ulteriore dilatione*,[2] while another outgoing reeve finds four sureties that he will pay twenty marks of silver (£13. 6s. 8d.) of the arrears due from him on his account within the next nine months.[3] Even more severe measures might be taken, for we read of Roger Losse who was put in the stocks "for arrears of his accounts and not for any other cause",[4] while the auditors of the monks of Canterbury handed over one of their bailiffs to the Sheriff of Kent to be kept in the county gaol.[5]

As we have already seen, on many manors when a manorial officer went out of office he was given a document either acquitting him entirely, or stating what he owed his lord, and setting forth exactly what stock and grain there was left on the manor.[6] A duplicate of this was sewn on the *compotus* for the year, where it might be referred to when necessary.[7] Once the reeve had received this chirograph acquittance he could, if not reappointed, safely retire again into his humble obscurity, from whence he had been drawn to play so important a part in the affairs of his rural community.

[1] *Min. Acc.* 870/9, 10; cf. 859/23, 930/5, 998/25.
[2] *Ibid.* 1070/8; cf. 1120/11.
[3] *Hales Rolls*, 259; *Min. Acc.* 1078/13, where men are given three years in which to pay arrears.
[4] Derby Arch. Soc. XXXI, 122.   [5] *Lit. Cant.* II, 168.
[6] See above, p. 166.   [7] *Min. Acc.* 1030/8, 1070/8, 1297/23.

The Manor Court

CHAPTER VIII

THE MANOR COURT

AND he owes suit of court from three weeks to three weeks. Such is the formula that concludes the list of services owed by many thousands of tenants, and its due fulfilment was often one of the most irksome and difficult of duties. The Manor Court, as its name implies, was held by the lord or one of his officials, and whether his jurisdiction was feudal or manorial in its origin we need not enquire.[1] It was a court with varying powers: on some manors the lord is seen to be dealing solely with his villeins and generally only with matters arising from the economic administration of his manor, while on others not only villeins but free men are in question, and not only economic matters are transacted, but criminal charges are investigated, fines and levies are raised, and the keeping of the King's peace, and other matters which would seem to belong to the Crown are dealt with. By the late thirteenth and the fourteenth century, lawyers were trying to tidy up this confusion of functions: the *Quo Warranto* proceedings investigated the jurisdictions of lords of manors, and the King's lawyers found everywhere that men were exercising rights to which they had no claim whatsoever but ancient seisin, or in plain English—encroachment. Lords in their manorial courts had become possessed of franchises which the lawyers said belonged only to the King: the view of frank-pledge and the right to hold a court leet, for example, were widely claimed, but few could show any document which gave them such rights.

Even greater rights were sometimes claimed. The *Quo Warranto* rolls afford us an immense body of evidence, much of it going to prove that on innumerable manors the King's powers over life and limb, as well as over lesser matters, had been usurped. Some lords, it is true, could produce charters in which "large and general terms" seemed to convey considerable powers to them, but the general tendency from the twelfth century onward

---

[1] See Selden Soc. II, xxxix f. for Maitland's discussion of this point.

was for the royal charter to "except those things which belong
to the King's crown", or to "except murder, treasure trove, rape
and breach of the peace", or to reserve the King's rights by
some terms or other. Wise lords took care to renew their charters
and to get what definition they could into their terms, for the
lawyers were more and more objecting to the vagueness of the
old terminology, and asking for those powers to be extinguished
which were only claimed thereby. By the thirteenth century,
therefore, a position had been reached in which

the prevailing doctrine seems to have been that *sake* and *soke* did
nothing, that *toll* and *team* did nothing, that *infangenethef* and
outfangenethef merely gave the right to hang "hand-having thieves",
"thieves taken with mainour" (*cum manuopere*), while the other old
words could not be trusted to do much, though they might serve to
define, and possibly to increase the ordinary powers of a feudal court.[1]

Doctrine notwithstanding, the powers traditionally attached to
these terms were still being exercised, and the serf on many
thousands of manors was still liable to seizure and punishment
under such quasi-legal rights. Let us take as an example the
question of hanging for theft. What were the rights of any lord
here? Some had, or thought they had, clear rights, in so far that
their charter gave them *infangenethef* and sometimes *outfangenethef*,[2] the one giving them power to hang a thief caught on their
own lands, the other power to hang him, wherever he was taken.
But there was a proviso—the thief must be taken "hand-having"
or "back-bearing", he must be prosecuted by the loser of the
goods, and further the coroner must be present.[3] Thus far the
law; but we have little need for long search in the records to find
that many lords did not bother overmuch about the details: the
man was a thief, and he had been captured—where and how
seemed of small consequence to the non-legal mind.

Thus we find the Abbot of Crowland is accused and convicted
of hanging a man who stole sixteen eggs, although the theft
occurred outside his liberty;[4] the Bishop of Lincoln similarly
arrested five men outside his jurisdiction, and in due course they

---

[1] Pollock and Maitland, *Hist. Eng. Law*, I, 579.
[2] *Outfangenethef* was much less common, however.
[3] Britton, 56, 57; Bracton, 137, 150–154; Holdsworth, *op. cit.* II, 102 and III,
320 for further references.
[4] *P.Q.W.* 519.

were hanged.[1] The brief entry after such trials in the Court Rolls runs, "Let him have a priest", and the marginal note *suspensus est* tells the rest of the tale. But the power to erect a gallows and to hang criminals was essentially a royal prerogative, and the Crown slowly tried to take back into its own hands privileges which had been usurped or claimed by an over-generous interpretation of charter rights and the like. For it must be remembered that the administration of justice was one of the ways of making a profit out of one's possessions: both the land and its holders were subject to the law of the lord. Hence the lawyer's proverb: "Justice is great profit", and hence, to a considerable extent, the desire of all lords to acquire greater privileges which would enable them to exact fines for a wider range of offences and matters, or to take for themselves the goods and chattels of condemned men.[2]

The manorial jurisdiction was checked to some extent by the presence of the royal coroner, for all cases involving death necessitated his presence. Even if the thief were caught in the act he must not be hanged in the absence of the King's coroner, as the Prior of Bodmin found in 1313. The transcript of the proceedings from the Year Book[3] is so instructive that it is given here in some detail. A presentment was made by the tithing-man that in Bodmin a thief had been taken with the chattels on him, and that he had been hanged. Whereupon the justices ordered the suitors of that court to attend and to produce the record relating to those matters. They came and said that on a certain day, etc., there came to Bodmin market-place one John that there found in the possession of Robert a certain horse which had been stolen from his house the previous night. And John raised the hue and cry, and in consequence both were attached (i.e. ordered to appear at the Manor Court). And the Prior of Bodmin, lord of the franchise, straightway caused a court to be summoned, and John accused Robert, and Robert confessed. Whereupon the steward of the court ordered him to be hanged. When the prior came before Justice Spigurnel after some enquiry

---

[1] *P.Q.W.* 43*a*; cf. *V.C.H. Rutland*, I, 172.
[2] *Lit. Cant.* I, 501.
[3] *Y.B. Eyre of Kent*, 6–7 Ed. II (Selden Soc.), 104; cf. *Y.B.* Ed. I (R.S.), 500.

he admitted that he only had the right of *infangenethef*, and that this offence took place outside his territory. Further, when pressed he also admitted that he proceeded to judgment without the presence of the coroner. "Were you entitled to do this in the absence of the Coroner?" asked Spigurnel. "No", was the answer, and the justice ordered the prior to await judgment for so grave an offence, for he had not only hanged a man for an offence which was outside his jurisdiction, but also had done this without sending for the coroner, so that a proper record might have been made of the proceedings.

To overcome difficulties such as this, lords tried to get permission to appoint their own coroners, but this privilege was but sparingly granted.[1] When we consider the difficulty of exercising any supervision over the way in which lords would make use of such a privilege, this is understandable. In general, the King preferred to leave matters in charge of the royal coroners, of whom there were several in each county. Their business was to see that the royal rights were not infringed, and that the goods of felons were not kept by the manorial lords, but duly paid over to the Crown. They were charged to attend all the sessions of the itinerant justices, and to bring with them their records for inspection. Hence, in part, their importance on the manor: their account of the proceedings was held to be authoritative, for their court was "a court of record"[2]—while the manorial court as such could make no such important claim. The manorial courts, however, had often acquired (legally or illegally) prescriptive rights, especially in respect of certain royal franchises, and were not easily supervised and controlled.

By the late thirteenth century there were two main types of manorial jurisdiction in existence. The first of these arose directly from the lord's ownership of the manor—it gave him certain powers to administer his estate and to control his tenants. The lawyers at the end of the sixteenth century made a distinction between the court baron held for the free tenants of the manor, and the court customary or Hallmote held for the unfree tenants, but this distinction does not seem to have existed in actual prac-

---

[1] *P.Q.W.* 24, 92, 121, 125, 148, 241, etc.; *Rot. Parl.* i, 152 and ii, 260; *Rot. Hund.* i, 119 and ii, 169, 280; and see *Statutes of the Realm*, 38 Ed. III, c. 6.
[2] See above and also *Eyre of Kent*, 133; Bracton, ii, 511.

tice during the Middle Ages.[1] Secondly, there was the jurisdiction conferred on the lord by the right to hold the view of frankpledge and to hold a court leet. These two jurisdictions were regalities—that is, they were properly held only by prescriptive grant from the King: otherwise they were only within the competence of royal jurisdiction as at the Hundred Court and the sheriff's tourn. They were originally quite separate things, but in general, and in the course of time, the two things became associated one with another, and the court, at one and the same sitting, held both the view and leet. To add to the confusion the very same court not infrequently dealt with matters strictly belonging to the lord's seigneurial rights, so that the Court Rolls contain entries covering every possible variety of action. Often the two types of jurisdiction were kept separate on the rolls, although this was by no means universal. It was the business of the thirteenth-century lawyer to explain this state of affairs, so that "to whatever quarter we look the law seems to be emerging into clearness out of a confused and contentious past. The courts are drawing a line between franchises and feudal rights, but it is no easy task, and violence must be done to the facts and theories of former times."[2]

But while all this is the legitimate concern of the legal and constitutional historians, it is not strictly our business. The peasant, whether rich or poor, and (with reservations) whether bond or free, was bound to attend the Manor Court, and it was a matter of chance with what powers he found it endowed. In contiguous manors the most unequal conditions could prevail, as we have seen. In the one the lord contented himself with strictly economic matters, and left it to the Hundred Court or the sheriff's tourn to deal with other things which a less scrupulous lord dealt with constantly in his court hard by. We must not hope to find any uniformity of administration in the various manorial courts: we must not indeed say "Such and such a court has such and such a competence", but "So-and-so has such and such powers". A peasant was fortunate or unfortunate in so far as his lot brought him under the control of a mild or a grasping lord, a weak or a strong. So long as we bear this in mind we can

[1] Selden Soc. II, lxiv; and see *Villainage*, 362, 364.
[2] Selden Soc. II. xxiv.

safely proceed to examine the workings of the court as it flourished in the time of the three Edwards.

We have seen that the suitor was bound by ancient formula to attend from three weeks to three weeks, and this has led many writers to assert that the courts were normally held at this brief interval.[1] The records themselves do not substantiate this, but show a bewildering variety of practice; indeed it would not be hard to show that on some manors it was the practice for the court to be held once, or twice or thrice a year; on others there was a court every three weeks—or even more frequently! Undoubtedly local conditions determined the matter, and in many instances the amalgamation of the seigneurial court with the court leet and view of frank-pledge[2] made it convenient and economical to hold but two courts a year. Then again, many manors were held by great lords, or by ecclesiastical corporations, who found it impossible to attend in person, but were represented by their steward who came from time to time to deal with the agricultural and economic state of the manor, as well as to preside over its legal proceedings. Hence, as Maitland notes, "We may follow the Steward as he makes his tour twice a year throughout England, carrying his rolls with him";[3] and there is much to be said for the view that the greater landowners were finding this bi-annual court a perfectly satisfactory compromise.[4] The reason why lords constantly made use of the phrase "from three weeks to three weeks" is quite understandable. So long as this was on record, he could afford to interpret it as leniently as he wished: he knew the lawyers would uphold him if it came to question—as indeed they did.[5]

But whether the court sat frequently or seldom it was essential that the suitors should know exactly when they had to attend,

---

[1] Before 1234 courts were commonly held fortnightly, but an ordinance of that year said they should not be held more frequently than at three-weekly intervals. See *Ann. Dunst.* (R.S.), 139–140. This ordinance was not strictly obeyed, however.

[2] These had to be held twice yearly by the second reissue of the Great Charter of 1217, cap. 42.

[3] Selden Soc. II, 3; and cf. *Collectanea*, Worc. Hist. Soc. 1912, p. 125; *Crondal Records*, 148 n.

[4] But note Vinogradoff's verdict: "Cases like that of the manors of the Abbey of Ramsey, in which the courts are summoned only twice a year, are quite exceptional." *Villainage*, 366.

[5] See Page, *Crowland Estates*, 39, and the authorities quoted there.

and various methods were used to ensure this. On some manors the date of the next court was known before the court then sitting was adjourned:[1] on others it was always held on a definite day, as at Forncett and elsewhere.[2] In such cases no warning appears to have been necessary, unless, as we learn from an early seventeenth-century cartulary, the day of the court was altered. When this was necessary on the manors of the lordship of Gower eight days' warning had to be given.[3] In general, however, there seems to have been a good deal of variation, but here we must again remember that the majority of our records concern the manors of great lords or corporations. It is probable that smaller lords who held their own courts in person found it convenient to hold them on a given day. On the other hand, lords who were forced to use deputies had to consider the most economical way of proceeding, and hence their courts were not held with the same regularity. The best they can do is to give "reasonable summons", or three days' notice,[4] or even only one day or one night's warning.[5] The full harshness of the lord's will is shown on a Gloucester Abbey manor, where the serf is bound to appear on the morrow, even if he is not warned until the middle of the night.[6]

Bond and free were not always treated the same in this respect. The free man was much more difficult to control, and the rule seems to have been that if the lord wanted service of court he had to say so definitely when he granted the land. Bracton lays it down that

in the absence of special stipulation the tenant is bound to attend his Lord's court for what are considered matters of royal concern, but only for those: he is bound to attend when a writ of right is to be tried, when a thief is to be judged, or when there is any business which touches the King's peace....But if the Lord wants more suit than this, if for example he wishes that his tenant should do suit from three weeks to three weeks, he must expressly bargain for it.[7]

The Statute of Marlborough (1267) finally settled the matter:

[1] *Hales Rolls*, 342, 521, 534.
[2] Davenport, *op. cit.* LXIX; *Abbots Langley, passim*; (Clare) *C.R.* 171/45; (Claret) *C.R.* 171/48.
[3] *Gower Surveys*, 184; cf. 172, 300 *op. cit.*
[4] *Ramsey Cart.* III, 62; Blount, *op. cit.* 304.
[5] *Mon. Exon.* 254b; Page, *op. cit.* 9.
[6] *Glouc. Cart.* III, 208.
[7] Selden Soc. II, xlviii, quoting Bracton, f. 35, 35b, 37.

no freeholder is bound to suit at his lord's court unless this was imposed on him by the terms of his charter, or was done before King Henry went to Brittany in the year 1230.[1] It is for this reason that monastic cartularies such as that of Glastonbury or of Gloucester or of Ramsey contain so many entries exacting suit of court of various degrees of severity from the free man. Thus at Glastonbury in the thirteenth century one free man owes suit at all the courts; another comes but twice a year and otherwise is quit; others come to strengthen the court should there be thieves to be tried, or any difficult business to be transacted, while others owe no service, and so forth.[2]

The necessary notice was given in a variety of ways. Sometimes an announcement was made in church,[3] while on some manors notice was given at the tenant's houses by a beadle or bailiff, or sergeant, or even by a peasant whose property was charged with this obligation.[4] On a Sussex manor of the Bishop of Chichester two cottagers are responsible for summoning a larger holder, and he in turn has to summon the whole of the lord's tenants when a court is to be held.[5] In general, no doubt, if there were any uncertainty it was the bailiff or reeve who warned the peasants when he received his orders from the lord or his steward. Thus we have entries of payments to men carrying messages summoning the court, as well as letters sent to the local bailiff giving him such orders.[6] One of these runs thus:

A. of C. the steward of Sir P. to all the bailiffs throughout the honour of Clare. For that we purpose to begin our general circuit on Thursday next, we command you that each of you do cause his court to be summoned for the days named below to meet us. Thou bailiff of A. on Thursday after the feast of S. Hilary. Thou bailiff of B. on the

---

[1] 52 Hen. III, c. 9.

[2] *Glas. Rent.* 56, 115, 128, 134, 144, 152, 159, 190, 191, 225; and cf. the instances from Gloucester and Ramsey given by Maitland in Selden Soc. II, li. Any other cartulary will show a similar state of affairs, and see below, p. 211.

[3] *Anc. Deeds*, A. 13162; *Paston Letters*, ed. Gairdner, No. 823.

[4] *York Inquis.* I. 51; *Gower Surveys*, 184; *Anc. Deeds*, A. 13162. A late-sixteenth-century guide to the keeping of a manor states (p. 18) that "reasonable warning ought to be given to the tenants, not to the person or house of every one of them, but at the church or such other accustomed place", Harl. MS. 6714, published by the Manorial Society in 1909.

[5] Sussex Rec. Soc. XXXI, 120 (Stretham, 1374).

[6] Davenport, *op. cit.* xli, lxv; Camb. Univ. Lib. MSS. Ee. i. i, f. 233 b.

following Saturday. Thou bailiff of C. on the following Monday. Farewell.[1]

While it was generally agreed by law that the court must be held somewhere upon the manor itself, and at a fixed place,[2] local custom determined the exact site. Some were held out of doors, and Sir Laurence Gomme has well emphasised the importance of this fact in his attempt to find in the early village communities the forerunners of the manorial court.[3] At Knyttington, Berks, in the reign of Edward I, the court was held "in a certain green place over against the house of Hugh de Gardin when it was fine, and in wet weather, by leave of the bailiff in the manor house or in that of one of the tenants".[4] In Essex, the Moulsham Hall Manor Court was held outside the manor house under the Court Oak,[5] and in the same county at Little Leigh it was held on Court Hill.[6] "At Eastbourne, the name of Motcombe Lane probably marks the hollow where the moots were held",[7] while the court of the Abbot of St Albans was held "under the ash-tree in the middle court of the abbey".[8] Other usual places were the lord's hall (from which is popularly derived the term Hallmote), or even in the church itself.[9] Myrc, in his *Instructions for Parish Priests*, tells them not to allow the holding of courts in the sanctuary,[10] but despite this it was frequently done.[11] In view of this evidence it is a little difficult to accept Vinogradoff's sweeping assertion: "In the feudal period the right place to hold the court was the manorial hall."[12] The "right place" was clearly the place where long custom had decreed the meeting of the people should be held, and anything else was an assertion of the will of the lord.

When once the court had been summoned it was always necessary for every serf to attend. Unless he had permission to absent himself or sent a sufficient excuse for non-attendance, he was

[1] Selden Soc. iv, 70.   [2] Glanvill, *op. cit.* f. 19.
[3] *The Village Community*, 264.   [4] *Paroch. Antiq.* 474.
[5] *Essex Review*, xx, 100.
[6] *Ibid.* xxv, 4. For other examples see Blount, *op. cit.* 238–9; Hone, *op. cit.* 131; *V.C.H. Durham*, i, 299; *Reg. Malm.* (R.S.), ii, 88, etc.
[7] *Med. Village*, 70.
[8] M. Paris, *Chron. Majora* (R.S.), vi, 438; and *Roy. Hist. Soc. Trans.* 4th series, vii, 52, for Miss Levett's interesting account of this court.
[9] *Wakefield Rolls*, i, 71, 148.
[10] *Op. cit.* p. 11.
[11] This question is discussed at length in S. O. Addy's *Church and Manor*.
[12] *Villainage*, 367.

punished, usually by a fine.[1] He had the consolation on many manors of knowing that his presence there was reckoned as one of the works he was forced to render weekly to his lord, although on some manors he was not allowed to count it as such if the court sat on a holy-day.[2] The attendance of the free man, as we have seen, was another matter. His compulsory appearance was generally a question of the bargain struck between him and his lord when his land was granted to him. But certain considerations other than the strict legal requirements should not be ignored. It must be remembered that the Manor Court frequently exercised both police and criminal jurisdiction as well as private, and to this both serf and free were amenable. Then, again, many free men held villein tenements and were bound to attend to answer any matters touching them. We must also remember that the freeholders were concerned (to some degree) in the stinting of the commons and in the ordinary agricultural arrangements, and these were generally discussed at the meetings of the court. For these reasons, therefore, despite the dangers (perhaps more theoretical than actual) which the free man ran in presenting himself at court, it seems probable that he often did attend, and that by so doing his personal status did not suffer in the eyes either of his lord or of his unfree companions.[3]

As we come closer to the actual working of the Manor Courts we must remember that, while they all conformed to a general pattern, each had its own particularities and customs. The thirteenth-century *How to hold Pleas and Courts* says that "those who plead or have to hold courts...should know the customs of that...court or manor, and the franchises pertaining to the premises, for laws and customs differ in divers places".[4] A number of practical guides to help those whose duty it was to hold courts had appeared in the thirteenth century, and these became particularly notable in the sixteenth century and onwards, when lawyers made further efforts to establish some uniformity

---

[1] See *Durham Halmote* or *Hales Rolls, passim*.

[2] *Ramsey Cart.* I, 464; Suffolk Inst. Arch. III, 237; *V.C.H. Hants*, v, 414; Sussex Rec. Soc. XXXI, 15, 23, 44, etc. See above, p. 114.

[3] For discussion of the view held by Coke and others that the presence of free men was necessary in order to constitute a court, see Selden Soc. II, lxiii, and *Villainage*, 387–9.

[4] Selden Soc. IV, 68.

of practice, and even in the seventeenth and eighteenth centuries the stream did not dry up. Nevertheless, despite all these efforts to achieve a common system, as Professor Hearnshaw writes, "not only is medieval leet jurisdiction extremely nebulous as to its circumference, but also it is uncertain even as to its centre".[1] With this caution in mind let us turn to examine the proceedings of a Manor Court towards the end of the thirteenth century, so far as they were recorded by the scribe on the Court Rolls.

The court was presided over by the lord, or by one of his senior officials, and we have a good deal of evidence to suggest what a stir his coming made in the village.[2] As he took his place on the dais, with his clerk by his side, silence was called for by the usher or beadle, who then with his single "Oyez" if it were only a court for manorial business, or his triple "Oyez", if it were a leet court for graver business, commanded all those whose duty it was to be present to draw near.[3] The proceedings then began, and item by item was taken down by the clerk, and many such documents have survived.[4] If we turn to the roll of the court of the Abbot of Halesowen we find that it opens with the entry: "Essoniatus. Ricardus de Linaker de communi per Johannem filium Johannis"[5]—that is Richard Linaker by means of John excused himself from attendance for common service of court. A message, either verbal or written, had to be produced on behalf of the absentee, and this absence was enrolled by the clerk and protected the man against fine for absence.

It appears that an essoin did not lie or could be objected to for several reasons. If the suitor had two matters before the court, each must be mentioned in the message....At one court the same man is essoined against three separate matters by three separate essoiners.... An essoin must be for some good reason, not sent for mere caprice; two men were fined for being seen in the neighbourhood of the court after they had been essoined....A suitor was allowed three essoins,

[1] *Leet Jurisdiction*, 65. For a list of works on leet jurisdiction, and "How to hold a Court", see pp. 29–42.

[2] Ault, *op. cit.* 145, 146; Holdsworth, *op. cit.* I, 592.

[3] J. Wilkinson, *The Office and Authority of Coroners, etc.* 1651, 161. The triple "Oyez" of the crier, or of the beadle in a Quarter Sessions' Court is a survival of this.

[4] See, for example, the rolls listed on the Public Record Office Calendar, or the British Museum Catalogue of MSS.

[5] *Hales Rolls*, 379 (1297).

after which he must appear or he made default; and the number of his essoins is indicated in the rolls by the figures, j°, ij°, iij°. When he appeared he justified the previous essoins, and all was then in order.[1]

Probably early in the proceedings the jury—or juries—were sworn in: indeed on the Ramsey manors of the thirteenth century this was always the first business. The presence of these juries and the problems they present will demand a great deal of our attention, but nevertheless this must not be allowed to obscure the fact that behind them was the whole body of the court, and that it was to this that they reported, and that it was the court that made the final dooms. We can go a good deal farther in asserting this to-day than Maitland could nearly fifty years ago. Thanks to the publication of some excellent series of Court Rolls of the thirteenth and early fourteenth centuries it has been possible to make much more detailed and extensive investigations than were possible then, and to give chapter and verse for the tentative views Maitland expressed in his often-quoted Introduction to the Selden Society volume of *Select Pleas in Manorial Courts*. There he summed up his conclusions thus:

We may believe that even the customary tenants, even the born villans, were or had been entitled to the judgment, not merely of the lord's steward, but of the manorial *curia*; we even hear a distinct claim of villan tenants to have the judgment of their neighbours.... When, too, we consider that even the king's courts gave the villan an action against all but his lord, and that the freeholders and customary holders of the manor must often have been involved in the same disputes, we shall have some difficulty in believing that the tenants in villanage had no judge in the manor court save the lord's steward.[2]

Maitland was able to show that for freehold tenants, or on ancient demesne, or at the court of a fair, it was not for the lord's steward to make the judgments, but he is forced to add

Elsewhere the position of the *curia* is less clear because it seems to discharge many functions: now it judges, now it presents, now it

---

[1] *Hales Rolls*, Intro. xxvii–ix with full references. It is worth noting that there seems to be some doubt at times as to a serf's essoining, as at Ingoldmells in 1291, when it is said, "the essoin does not lie because A. holds bond land". See p. 2 *Ingoldmells Court Rolls*. The whole law of essoins, however, was very complicated. See *Hales Rolls*, xxviii–ix, and Selden Soc. II, 67, for examples, and Kitchin's *Le Court Leete* (1651 ed.), pp. 187–93, for much information and law.

[2] *Op. cit.* lxx.

serves as a jury of trial. Imitation of the royal courts seems to be transfiguring it; the admission of trial by jury, of presentments by jury, will hardly assort with the maintenance of the old principle that "facere judicia" is the function of the suitors, with the old rule, "Curia domini debet facere judicium et non dominus."[1]

There can be no doubt that Maitland was right in his general conclusions, and that slowly the legal position of the villein was being debased by one means or another. But, at least till the end of the thirteenth century, we have good reason to see him still as the maker of dooms in his Manor Court. The actual terminology of the Court Rolls is often not so clear as we could wish, and we are often forced to interpret what was at best a brief statement only meant to put on record the findings of the court. Much that was common practice in the court is abbreviated or omitted, and we have to reconstruct from very imperfect data. Nevertheless, it is worth making the attempt—incomplete and hazardous though it must be. To begin with, an examination of any thirteenth-century rolls shows the scribes constantly speaking of the decision of the court in such a way that all present are clearly indicated. At Hales, for example, entries such as "per considerationem curie"[2] tell us very little that is definite, but we come a little closer when we read that "*Dicit tota curia* quod Edithia quondam uxor Henrici Trappe fidelis est et immunis ab omni culpa latrocinii *et ideo consideravit tota curia* quod recuperat terram suam post diem et annum."[3] Here it is clear that it is the whole body of the suitors who give what we should call the verdict, and also go on to give judgment, and it is worthy of note that the scribe reporting the proceedings thought so too, for in the margin, against the proceedings, he puts the word "Judicium".

Take another example: "W. de T. venit et petit unam vaccam fuscam que inventa fuit in custodia domini de adventicio et probavit eam suam esse et suum esse catallum sexta manu. Et ideo *per considerationem totius curie et in presentia eiusdem* predicta vacca ei liberata fuit."[4] Here W. de T., by the oaths of six persons, convinced the whole court that the cow was his, and

---

[1] *Op. cit.* lxviii, quoting *Munimenta Gildhallae*, i, 66.
[2] *Hales Rolls*, 41.
[3] *Ibid.* 57; cf. 17, 25, 28, 54, 56, 60, etc.
[4] *Ibid.* 403 (1300).

by their ruling, and in their presence, it was delivered up to him. What, then, is meant by the term *tota curia*? It cannot mean anything but all those present owing suit of court, whether bond or free. When a verdict is wanted from free men they know how to ask for it, and it is enrolled as such. "*Omnes libere tenentes* dicunt per suum sacramentum quod...",[1] or "Ad magnam curiam per sacramentum *liberorum hominum* inquiratur de concelamento villatarum de Oldebure...".[2] On the other hand a verdict of serfs is equally clearly indicated: "*Omnes nativi* dicunt de eorum consuetudine...";[3] here it is a matter of the custom of the manor affecting serf-holdings, and this is not a matter for "tota curia", but for "omnes nativi"—and the record says so.

Tota curia may be expressed in the record in other ways: we find it termed *communitas totius manerii*,[4] or *tota communitas ville*,[5] if it is meant to include everyone on the manor, just as it is limited to *tota villata de Romesle*,[6] or the like, if it is only the inhabitants of one of the townships of the manor that is in question. So strong was the prevailing opinion that the court makes the dooms at Hales and elsewhere in the thirteenth century, that we find decisions postponed if it is thought that the court is not representative enough, or that it is too thinly attended. As an example of the first we may take an entry of 1299: "Omnes homines *tam liberi quam nativi* summoniantur *pro afforciamento* [curiae] pro judicio reddendo de villata de Oldebure que concelavit de tenemento quam W. Thedrich tenuit de domino W. Fokeram."[7] Here we see an attempt on the part of the officials to get every member of the court present to discuss the backsliding of the men of one of the vills. Again, paucity of suitors often led to an adjournment. A good example occurs in 1293 when four men were charged with defaults which they denied, and placed themselves on the judgment of the court. "Et quod [quia ?] *curia tenuis est* judicium ponitur in respectu usque ad proximam curiam. Et ideo *tota curia summoniatur pro afforciamento*." And in the margin "Judicium

---

[1] *Hales Rolls*, 400 (1299).   [2] *Ibid.* 409 (1300); and cf. 500.
[3] *Ibid.* 460 (1302); and cf. 445 where a man puts himself "in veredictum nativorum domini de proximioribus tenentibus".
[4] *Ibid.* 218.   [5] *Ibid.* 14.
[6] *Ibid.* 31, 509.   [7] *Ibid.* 393.

respectuatum".[1] The court was not well enough attended, the case was adjourned, and all the court was to be summoned *pro afforciamento*, that is to afforce, or strengthen it at its next meeting, and finally the scribe notes, "Judgment deferred".

Now that we have seen the important part played by the totality of the suitors, we may turn to consider how far the manorial court had developed the jury system. Let us start with Maitland's view:

So far as we can see, when the lord's interests were not being actively asserted, the serf who sued or was sued in the manorial court got the same justice as that which the free man got; he got in theory the judgment, not of his lord, but of a body of doomsmen who were at least his peers. We say that such a judgment he got in theory: in practice the question became of less and less moment, for trial by jury gradually forced its way into the manorial courts. In strictness of law the lord could not compel his free men to serve as jurors in civil causes; but the lord could force his bondmen to swear, and many a small freeholder would serve rather than quarrel with his lord. At any rate trial by jury made its way into these courts, and it hardly leaves a place for the doomsman; indeed in course of time the cry for a *judicium parium* is (to the great distortion of history) supposed to find its satisfaction in trial by jury.[2]

It is, of course, perfectly true that during the thirteenth century the manorial courts borrowed something from the higher courts, and gradually began to make more and more use of a jury system. This was but natural, since many courts were exercising royal franchises, and especially the view of frank-pledge. Now this involved the empanelling of a jury—not necessarily, or even probably on most manors, a jury of twelve free men—but at least a jury of twelve to enquire into offences against the King's peace. Naturally it did not stop at this. It was likely to make further enquiries on the lord's behalf, and did so, as we may see, by looking at a document of about 1270 from the Gloucester Cartulary. It is headed "Articles of the view of Frank-pledge" and enumerates first some twenty-nine articles which are to be enquired into touching the King's peace and his regalities and franchises. Then it goes on to enumerate eleven items of strictly manorial concern: whether the hallmote is fully summoned;

---

[1] *Hales Rolls*, 241; and see 73, 151, 157; cf. Selden Soc. II, 60, 67, 83.
[2] Pollock and Maitland, *op. cit.* I, 593; and cf. Selden Soc. II, lxv–lxviii.

whether the chief manorial officer and his underlings are satisfactory or no; whether the beasts are well tended and the soil well tilled; whether any have made their sons clerics without leave, or married their daughters without licence, etc.[1]

We have here a hint of the confusion that was arising in the conduct of manorial business. Matters were not kept strictly to their various classes: at one moment the court is dealing with an offence against the manorial economy; at another with an infringement of one of the lord's franchises, but things get muddled one with another in the record—and so are often potential sources of confusion to modern inquirers. The thirteenth-century suitors and the presiding officer, however, were clear enough, and if we look closely we can see they have put various bodies to work in the court. We have first, and most important, the practice of the whole court making its decisions and giving the dooms. Secondly, we have juries of presentment, charged with the business of enquiring into offences against the franchises, or as a Hales entry runs: a jury "ad dicendum veritatem super articulis consuetis";[2] and thirdly we have juries of inquisition, whose business it is to enquire into manorial offences and matters concerning the working of the manor. The work of what we may call these several manifestations of the suitors is not, apparently, recorded in any very ordered way.

It is not easy to see how the jurors were selected, or what determined the number of men thought necessary to form a jury. At the Great Courts or half-yearly courts when the view of frankpledge was made, a jury of twelve seems almost inevitable, and in general we find a jury of this size enrolled as what we have called a jury of presentment. They are generally spoken of as "elected", though we know nothing of how this took place. They seem to have been elected before the actual sitting of the court, for we find men fined for their absence.[3] In some rolls a long list of names is given, and marked "Nomina juratorum",[4] and it may be that these were a panel from which the twelve sworn jurors were chosen.[5]

---

[1] *Glouc. Cart.* III, 221–2. For the Articles in detail see Hearnshaw, *Leet Jurisdiction*, and Selden Soc. II, xxxii, and IV, 93 ff.
[2] *Hales Rolls*, 138. Articulis = the Articles of the View. See above, and cf. Selden Soc. IV, 110.　　　[3] Selden Soc. II, 88.
[4] *Hales Rolls*, 46, 48, 51, 62.　　　[5] *Ibid.* 7 n. 5.

The personal *status* of the jurors is equally difficult to generalise about. Mr Ault's examination of the Ramsey documents leads him to say, "There seems to be no general rule about the status of the members of a jury", and he shows that some Ramsey juries included both free and unfree, although he notes that two men refused to serve on a jury at Elton alleging themselves to be free men, and therefore exempt.[1] No doubt free men were more and more repudiating claims made on them (whether legally or illegally) to serve on all kinds of juries, but it was long before they finally shook off the claims made on them; and, as we have seen, many free men in the thirteenth century and the fourteenth were bound to appear at the Manor Court, and hence were liable to be made part of a jury.[2]

We can, however, discern a growing disinclination to serve on the part of free men—at least to serve on a mixed jury of free and unfree. In the course of time there emerges on some manors a system of two juries—one free, the other unfree. On the manor of Carshalton, in Surrey, we find that after the capital pledges (acting as a jury of presentment) have made their charges, a free jury of twelve is sworn who have to declare that the capital pledges have done everything in order, and have omitted nothing. At Ingoldmells at the end of the fourteenth century we have the two bodies clearly shown. First, in 1391, we hear of the free jurors presenting infractions of the assize of bread and ale, while the "bond tenants" present other offences and elect manorial officers.[3] In 1399, a more exact terminology is used, and we find the free jurors and the bond jurors both mentioned.[4] A little later (1410) each jury seems to deal only with its own peers,[5] and then in 1411 we find (as at Carshalton) that the inquisition of sixteen bond tenants makes presentments, and at the end of the proceedings we read: "The inquisition of (sixteen) free tenants says and affirms that all the presentments above are true, and that they have nothing else to present."[6]

As time went on there is some evidence which leads us to believe that those chosen as jurymen became a select class. Even

---

[1] Ault, *op. cit.* 166, quoting from Selden Soc. II, 94.
[2] *Ingoldmells Rolls*, 107 n. 1.
[3] *Ibid.* 190.
[4] *Ibid.* 194.
[5] *Ibid.* 216.
[6] *Ibid.* 221, 222.

in the late thirteenth century the Hales Rolls show us that the juries of presentment at the Great Courts each half-year were made up on successive occasions of very much the same men. "Of the men in eleven lists of Great Court jurors after 1293, one had served ten times, two on nine occasions and two on eight occasions. In all there are 42 names, and of these 20 served only once, 7 in the last list."[1] Side by side with this we may note that Maitland found a jury at Gidding made up of the chief pledges, and he tells us that "similar entries have been found on other rolls relating to the Ramsey estates".[2] This state of affairs was not confined to Ramsey manors, for Dr Page has found much the same happening a little later on the Crowland estates. There a small group of men formed a "manorial bureaucracy", so much so that an entry of 1368 concerns an order given "to the whole homage, that is to say, the presentors as sworn below".[3] An interesting half-way stage, as it were, is seen at Niddingwirth in 1288, where we have twelve jurors and also eight chief pledges, and all of them present offences of various kinds.[4] After 1294 this practice ceases, and the presentments are henceforth made by a jury of twelve.[5]

The juries of inquisition were much more variable in their size and composition. They were often *ad hoc* bodies, and were more and more used to make sworn inquisitions as to verifiable facts —thus taking the place of the older method of compurgation and appeal to the supernatural. They could consist of any number of jurors—at Hales they range from four or five to twelve members, and once, when a very important investigation had to be made, there were as many as twenty-three.[6] These men were often drawn from the actual vicinity of the matter in question, and are called "the neighbours"; other juries were composed of the men from one or more neighbouring vills; others again were carefully selected, apparently, so as to include representatives from all the vills of the manor.[7]

[1] *Hales Rolls*, xxxi; and cf. *Crowland Estates*, 68.
[2] Selden Soc. II, 87. See also Selden Soc. IV, 110. "Year after year the same names appear, and on comparing these names with those of the chief pledges...it becomes clear that the leet jury was generally, if not always, composed of twelve of the chief pledges." [3] *Crowland Estates*, 67.
[4] *Ramsey Rolls*, 189; and cf. 191, 193, 196, 200. [5] *Ibid.* 202 f.
[6] *Hales Rolls*, 466, 453, 583, 404, etc.; cf. *Ramsey Rolls*, 191, 200.
[7] *Hales Rolls*, 395, 397, 421, 423, 425, 585; cf. *Ramsey Rolls*, 183, 188, 206.

Sometimes they presented their verdict there and then, but frequently they are ordered to present their findings at the next Court, or are told, or they ask to view the site and buildings, or to deliberate as to the lord's rights, etc., before making their decision.[1] If such permission is not granted they are unwilling to give their verdict,[2] just as we find them uneasy about speaking, by reason that several of their more senior members were absent on the King's wars,[3] or because they want the aid of the serfs of a neighbouring manor before they decide.[4] In short the jury of inquisition was a thoroughly practical straightforward way of enquiry into facts, and it was very widely used by the lord and by his tenants.

When any of the tenants wanted to use this means of enquiry he was usually forced to pay for it, and gave the lord sixpence, or a shilling, or even more, up to considerable sums such as 6s. 8d. for the privilege.[5] It was worth their while to do this, for not only did they get a decision, but further it was enrolled on the record of the court, and could be appealed to if necessary at any later date.[6] What does seem strange to our ideas is the fairly common practice of paying at double rates for a satisfactory verdict: A. B. comes and pays the lord for an inquisition concerning... and he will give the lord 4s. if he is successful in his claim, otherwise only 2s.[7]

The duties of such juries were manifold. They had to enquire into all matters of fact, and to declare what was the custom of the manor. When a dispute had to be settled between two parties it was the jurors who deliberated and finally returned their verdict, and upon this the court acted. They made surveys and reported on ancient rights. They were empowered to draw up by-laws for the due regulation of the meadows and common fields, and to make inquisitions, as to the state of various holdings or the condition of houses and barns.[8] They were not always limited in

---

[1] *Hales Rolls*, 42, 56, 65, 198, 219, etc.   [2] *Ibid.* 87.
[3] *Ibid.* 377.   [4] *Ibid.* 500.
[5] Selden Soc. II, 17, 20, 21, 22, 24, 25; *Hales Rolls*, 108, 212, 447, 476, 484, 493, etc.; *Ramsey Rolls*, 267, 280.
[6] *Hales Rolls*, 372, 459, 502, 512; cf. Selden Soc. IV, 112.
[7] *Hales Rolls*, 219; and cf. Selden Soc. II, 17: "J. H.'s son gives 3s. and if he recovers will give 3 marks for having a jury of twelve to inquire...." See also p. 20.
[8] See for example, *Durham Halmote* or *Hales Rolls*, *passim*.

their activities to matters concerning serfs: on some manors they presented free men for offences of every kind, or were called on to declare the age of an heir to the estate, and acted in many ways which seem contrary to strict legal theory.[1]

Not unnaturally, with so much put upon them, we get a mass of complaints as to their incompetence, partiality and slackness. Sometimes, indeed, suitors go so far as to say justice is impossible, since the lord's officers pack the jury,[2] but more generally it is a tardy verdict or a neglect of their orders that is complained of. Sometimes they are fined for concealing the truth of a matter, and frequently subsequent events bring new facts to light and the wretched jury are punished for neglecting to make due search.[3] Their lot in short was unenviable. The lords had long been accustomed to use their courts as a source of profit, and to fine the jurors was one of many ways of making money. Thus we find Wynslow juries fined for concealment of a marriage, of a sale of land, of "waste" on the lord's land, etc., when in all probability the worst that could be said was that they had been careless and inefficient.[4] Again,

uniformity and consistency were strictly enforced upon the sworn men, and the coercion and punishment of a dissentient minority seems to have been frequent. Fines for the contradiction of fellow-jurors were common, and offenders were not merely fined by the lord, but could be impleaded by the parties to the case, who lost prestige through the lack of unanimity in their favour.[5]

The deliberations of the jury were a matter of much interest in the village, and great care had to be taken to keep them secret so as to avoid opportunity for renewed litigation. Again and again the jurors are ordered to keep their deliberations secret under pain of fine,[6] and again and again we learn that this secrecy has been broken.[7] On the other hand their verdicts give rise to violent expressions of opinion: men stood up in court and upbraided the jury; or, as one record runs: "A. B. disturbed the court with his scornful words, and would not be prevailed on by

---

[1] Selden Soc. II, 89, 90, 173; *Ancient Deeds*, V, 495.
[2] Bristol and Glouc. Arch. Soc. IX, 332. [3] *Abbots Langley*, f. 4.
[4] *U.L.C. Wynslowe Rolls*, ff. 4b, 5b, 13b, 63b, etc.; cf. *Durham Halmote*, passim; Selden Soc. II, 90, 97.
[5] *Crowland Estates*, 42.
[6] *Durham Halmote*, 33; *E.H.R.* XLV, 209 n. I.
[7] *Wakefield Rolls*, II, 92; *Crowland Estates*, 42, 43.

the Steward to behave himself reasonably as beseemed him."
Such conduct inevitably resulted in a fine.[1]

So far we have considered only such duties and possibilities as
confronted a serf by reason of his liability to suit of court. We
still have to see what action the court took when he appeared as a
plaintiff or defendant, and not merely as a suitor or juryman.
This may be illustrated by following the adventures of one man
over a series of years and noting his appearances in the Manor
Court, although it must be admitted that he is a particularly
troublesome fellow. His name was Richard Bradwater, and he
lived on the Manor of Tooting Bec, where we first meet him in
December 1394, at the first Court held by the new lord of the
manor, Dom Robert of Windsor, Prior of Merton. Here he
acknowledged that he held from the lord one tenement and
13½ acres of land, paying therefor twelvepence a year as fixed
rent, and for day-works in part commuted two shillings. Also,
he holds 9 acres of land in farm until the coming of age of William
Bradwater, his nephew, paying therefor three shillings a year for
all. Also he holds one cot with curtilage, paying therefor sixpence a year. He was, in fact, one of the largest holders among
the prior's serfs, and he was ordered with his fellows to show his
Copy of Court Roll to prove his holding by the next Court.
Eighteen months later he is again admonished to show his copy.
The following autumn (for there were but two courts—spring
and autumn each year) he is still without his copy and is also in
further trouble, for his pigs have trespassed on the lord's meadow,
and he has held two acres of land without any permission for
two years past and has paid no rent for it. Further, when the
bailiff and the tithing man distrained on him at various times, he
broke the distraint, and assaulted the bailiff who tried to prevent
him. Further, in common with nearly all his neighbours, he has
broken the assize of ale.[2] At the next court (November 1397) we
find him accused of allowing his cattle to stray among a neighbour's green crops to the damage of ten shillings. Bradwater
admits the offence, and asks that the damage may be valued by
the Court. This is done, and found to amount to three shillings,
and it is ordered that this sum be levied and paid to his neigh-

---

[1] *V.C.H. Middlesex*, ii, 82. Cf. *Durham Halmote*, 49; *Abbots Langley*, f. 5;
Wakefield Rolls, i, 97; Selden Soc. iv, 127.   [2] *Tooting Bec Rolls*, 21 f.

bour, and Bradwater is fined twopence for his offence. He is also charged with driving another neighbour's cattle out of the common pasture, but this he denies, and is ordered to make his law with five compurgators. To do this it was necessary for him to appear at the next Court with five friends who would one and all swear with him that to the best of their knowledge he was innocent. When the case comes on again (October 1398) he fails to produce his five compurgators and is adjudged guilty, and ordered to pay the amount claimed and is fined twopence. "And a precept is made to levy the said pence from the goods and chattels of the said Bradwater for the use of the said Nicholas."[1] He is also found guilty of trespassing with his cattle in the lord's grain, and of mowing and lifting the lord's meadow, and is fined. He retaliates by accusing Richard Christmas of depriving him of two acres of land, and Christmas is summoned to answer this at the next Court.[2] The following October (1399) he (Bradwater) fails to prosecute his suit and is fined twopence.[3] Later at the same court he and his wife pay ten shillings in order to take over several plots of ground and cottages from a relative who is leaving the manor and who pays two capons yearly for permission to dwell outside the demesne at the lord's pleasure.[3] The tithing man later presents him for assaulting a neighbour, and also for seizing for his own a stray white hog. For his misbehaviour he is fined eighteenpence, to be levied on his goods.[4] The following May (1400) he is fined for pasturing his beasts and sheep in the lord's meadow; he is accused of assaulting and beating the bailiff, and also of taking away his goods. Part of this he acknowledges and part he decides to clear himself of with five compurgators. He is ordered to bring them at the next Court, and the homage is ordered to assess the damages done to the bailiff by the assault before the next Court.[5]

The following October he produces his five compurgators and they swear to his innocence, and "therefore it is adjudged by the Steward that the said Richard be quit".[6] The homage had not assessed the damage and were threatened with a fine unless they did so in time for the next Court.[6] This they did, and 3s. 4d. was ordered to be levied on his goods to recoup the injured bailiff.[7]

[1] *Tooting Bec Rolls*, 33.   [2] *Op. cit.* 33.   [3] *Op. cit.* 35.
[4] *Op. cit.* 39.   [5] *Op. cit.* 43.   [6] *Op. cit.* 47.   [7] *Op. cit.* 51.

At the next two courts we have no mention of him, but in October 1402 he appears again to answer a number of complaints of much the usual kind, and so it goes on. These details are worth recording at length, not because of Bradwater's many failings, but because they represent the common matter that was constantly before the manorial courts.

We might, perhaps, classify the business possible at a Manor Court possessing the fullest franchises and charters in this way. First, we must distinguish the normal business naturally arising from the economic administration of the manor. This would include such items as the regulation and enforcement of labour-services; the punishment of all types of trespass: the over-crowding of the commons; the too frequent taking of wood or turves, as well as ordinary trespass with cattle on the lord's meadows or in a neighbour's garden. It would also include the transfer of all land held in villeinage, and even of free land if the alienation thereof "would seriously impair the lord's interests".[1] Regulations for the control of the open fields or the commons would also fall within the economic sphere of the Court's activities, and also the control of the serf's personal freedom to marry, to take Orders, to leave the manor would be matters vitally concerning the effective working of the lord's demesne and the manor in general, and therefore matters of which the Court would take cognisance. Similarly, offences against morality concerned the lord: for, if an adulterer was successfully prosecuted in the ecclesiastical court, he was fined and thus in theory lost something which was his lord's. In the same way a woman who lost her virginity was of less value, and was therefore fined for depreciating her lord's property.[2]

Next come what we should now call minor offences against law and order. The lord must obviously be allowed to deal with these, for they affect the smooth working of manorial life, although a strict view might find in this an invasion of the royal franchise. Violence—so long as it was not too violent—was punishable by the Court: attacks on manorial officers, threats and mild assaults of neighbours, brawling, etc. are dealt with, as well as more serious offences such as driving off a neighbour's cattle,

---

[1] Pollock and Maitland, *op. cit.* I, 346.
[2] See below, p. 246.

or the carrying away of other's crops. Then again, civil disputes between tenants were decided at the Court. Both sides were allowed to state their case, and then a verdict was given, either by a jury, or by all the Court. Breach of contract, or failure to fulfil promises and obligations were considered and damages assessed. Personal matters such as slander also came before the Manor Court and wounded pride claimed and sometimes received a monetary solace. Not only the tenant or his family, but even his beasts and crops could be cheapened by unfair criticism, and men were fined for vilifying (*vilipendelant*) a man's pig[1], or for defaming his corn[2], so that he lost the sale of it.

Thirdly we reach the pleas which are strictly matters touching the King's peace and the like, and are fully enumerated in the Articles of the View.[3] Strictly: for they include a number of offences which we have already seen are commonly dealt with by the lord as part of his seigneurial jurisdiction. Besides these, however, the tithing men or sworn jury are asked to make their presentments concerning almost every kind of wrongdoing from brewing against the assize to open murder. Personal injuries, infringements of the highway, the receiving and harbouring of strangers, the use of false weights and measures, the haunting of taverns by night, the snaring of game, the clipping of coins: all are matters the jurors have to consider and report upon to the court so that justice may be done.

Since "justice is great profit" we may well ask, "What was the court worth to a lord?" Apart from the prestige it gave him, and the importance of having some machinery whereby transgressors could be punished, the court had a definite financial side to it, more especially when it included the ordinary business of a leet within its jurisdiction. In general the amerciament (fine) was at the discretion of the lord or his officer. Nelson's *Lex Maneriorum* says: "An amerciament is called *misericordia* in Latin, because it ought to be assessed mercifully, and afterwards to be moderated by the affeerment of the equals of him who committed the offence."[4] This modification is of great import-

---

[1] *Norf. Antiq. Misc.* I, 144.   [2] Selden Soc. IV, 130.
[3] See above, p. 209.
[4] *Op. cit.* 26. There is a distinction made between the amerciaments of the Court Baron and the fines of the Leet Court in the Law Books. A fine was directly imposed by the lord and could not be affeered.

ance: the culprit was not left solely *ad misericordiam domini*, but had both the custom of the manor and the clemency of his fellows to cling to. These helped him, but still left the lord with something, as a glance at the margin of any Court Roll in which the amerciaments are written will show. It has proved quite impossible to work out any figures which would be useful here: on some manors year by year the revenues from this source are trivial, on others they are considerable, but seem to bear little relation to the size of the manor or its annual turnover. In all probability what we require in order that we may get any valuable statistics here is a very detailed enquiry into the whole administration and organisation of each of these manors. On some the lord insisted on money payments for things which were freely allowable on others; many lords took heavy annual payments for leave of absence or permission to marry off the manor, while others made but a token fine sufficient. Yet, by and large, it remains true that the manorial courts were a source of revenue sufficiently valuable to form a separate paragraph in the great annual rendering of account by the reeve's *compotus*.

After looking over many hundreds of Court Rolls before the Great Pestilence certain impressions abide, for what they are worth. First, the courts rapidly developed in technicalities: men soon found that they could avoid a charge by riding off on some point of pleading. At Wakefield, for example, the plaintiff does not name the day or hour on which certain goods were stolen from him and his claim fails accordingly.[1] A. charged B. with assault and carrying off his bow and arrows. B. pleaded that he was not bound to answer, because he was charged with two offences one of which might be true and the other false.[2] Many pleadings of a similar nature will also be found in the books of instruction for young lawyers, published under the title of *The Court Baron*,[3] which illustrate well the complexity of manorial law even by the fourteenth century.

Secondly, we cannot fail to notice how comparatively powerless the Court often was to enforce its own orders. We read in many rolls that such and such a thing is to be done, "as hath been oftentimes commanded", but just as frequently the entry appears

---

[1] *Wakefield Rolls*, I, 104. [2] *Op. cit.* II, 15.
[3] Selden Soc. IV, 24, 41, 48, 67, 76, etc.

again at the next Court. It was not only that men who had fled from the manor could not be brought back, but even when serf-tenants were concerned, the power of the Court seems often to be curiously feeble. Men forget to clear away nuisances, or to replace boundary stones, or to mend their ruinous houses, and the bailiff complacently reports this at the next Court, and once again they are ordered to do so. And so it goes on, till they act— or until the bailiff tires—we do not know which.[1]

Thirdly, the clever man could avoid making any very definite answer for a long time. At the head of most rolls come the essoins such as "Simon Francis [essoins himself] against John of Senholt in a plea of trespass for the third time by Odo of Mursley. Faith pledged".[2] From this entry we see that Simon has managed to absent himself from three courts, and for so long the unfortunate John has had no remedy. At the next court, however, Simon must appear, or his pledge Odo of Mursley will be in trouble. Some men did not even trouble to make essoins, but put off coming from court to court without apparently being judged in default. Certainly the practice varied enormously from manor to manor, but there remains a general impression of dilatory, capricious and uncertain action.

But, whatever weaknesses we may detect, the Manor Court was not entirely useless, nor merely a means whereby the lord could amerce and punish his peasants. It was also a great barrier against violent changes of policy. On its rolls from time to time was entered some new interpretation, or some new item concerning "the custom of the manor", or the findings of the jury as to the liability of the homage to render such and such dues, or their determinations as to the bounds of the lord's acres and their own, etc. True it was not a Court of Record that would be recognised by the King's justices,[3] but it was a true court of record so far as the serf was concerned, and constantly he was ready to pay for a search of the rolls to be made so that the truth or falsity of his claim might be established.[4] When he came into court to take over or to render up some piece of land, not only

[1] H. Barnett, *Glympton* (Oxfordshire Record Society, 1923), 56; Maitland, *Collected Papers*, II, 377; *Banstead*, 139 n. 4; *V.C.H. Middlesex*, II, 80; *V.C.H. Berks*, II, 179.
[2] Selden Soc. II, 6.   [3] *See* above, p. 198.
[4] *Hales Rolls*, 78, 79, 219, 220; *Wynslowe Rolls*, 4a, 5b, 6a, etc.

did the ceremonial exchange "by the verge" take place in court, but the scribe entered the facts on his rolls,[1] and often was asked to give a copy of the entry so that all doubt might be avoided. Again the Manor Court provided a speedy and comparatively inexpensive way of obtaining redress for injury or wrong. While we cannot agree with Vinogradoff's view that "all foreign elements in the shape of advocates or professional pleaders were excluded",[2] it is true that in general the procedure of the courts was simple enough to be followed by most peasants. The old patriarchal system still prevailed sufficiently for a man to be able to go to the court in the reasonable expectation of receiving protection from his lord if wrong had been done him. While the King's Courts were remote and difficult of access, from time to time his lord's court was open to him, and there he could plead redress for almost every kind of wrong, and could claim and could hear the "doom" of the court, which was the verdict of his fellows, before the judgment of the lord was pronounced.

[1] Selden Soc. ii, 28, 35, 40, 46, etc., *Wynslowe Rolls*, 45 u; *Eynsham Cart.* ii, 9, 10, 11, 21, 129, 130. The "verge" was usually a slender rod which was handed from tenant to lord, and symbolised the actual piece of land in question.

[2] *Villainage*, 367. See *Hales Rolls*, 134, 137 where R. de Bosco *per attornatum suum* optulit se versus T. de W. etc., and Selden Soc. iv, 81.

Everyday Life

CHAPTER IX

EVERYDAY LIFE

LITTLE enough is left in England to-day that will give us any impression of the houses of the medieval peasantry. Such structures as the Kentish farm-houses, with their long boarded fronts, and the stone houses of the Cotswolds, the half-timbered houses scattered up and down the countryside are all too grand and too large to be of much help to us. Here and there survivals, such as the old clergy house at Alfriston, or the few remaining old cottages of the Snowdon district, emphasise what we have lost in losing the medieval village home. But to see them, as they were for centuries before the time of Chaucer, and perhaps as late as the sixteenth century, we must go to rural France, or Switzerland, or Austria. There, in village after village, the passage of centuries has scarcely changed the house in which the peasant lives. They are built of various materials, according to the local characteristics. Where good stone is to be had stone houses prevail, while in forest districts wood is used almost entirely, and so on. But they are still in the rudimentary state of development they had reached centuries ago. Two rooms suffice for all their needs: one serving for all purposes of living, eating, cooking, etc., while the other is kept as a bed-room as far as is possible. Only as far as is possible, for in these rudimentary conditions no division can be strictly observed, and chickens and other animals invade the living room, while some members of a family too numerous to find beds elsewhere must perforce couch as best they can amidst the tables and stools and other impedimenta of the living room. At their best such houses afforded a bare shelter, but they easily fell into decay, and patchwork repairs still left them in the condition so graphically described, for example, in a recent picture of rural France:

C'était une cabane bossue et lépreuse, à peine plus haute qu'un homme; on descendait à l'intérieur par deux marches de granit; il y faisait très sombre, car le jour n'entrait que par une lucarne à deux petits carreaux; l'hiver, il y avait de l'eau partout, et cela faisait de la boue qui n'en finissait pas de sécher, sous les lits surtout; il y avait des trous qui empêchaient les tabourets de tenir debout; on les comblait de temps en temps avec de la terre apportée du jardin.[1]

Conditions such as these show how static rural life is in many ways, and how little changed these houses are from that of Chaucer's poor widow, who had but a cottage divided into bower and hall, where she lived a "ful sooty" life with her cows, kine and sheep all about her, while Chauntecleer and his seven wives ran in and out from time to time.

The peasant's house was as simple in its construction as it was rudimentary in its provision for comfort or privacy. One of the most widespread of types—especially it would seem in the area North and West of a line drawn from the Wash to the Bristol Channel—was the house which had for its main timbers curved uprights (crucks) placed opposite to each other with a ridge-pole running the whole length of the house and holding the various pairs of uprights firmly together. The simplest form of this surviving is seen at Scrivelsby, near Horncastle, in Lincolnshire, where a house, popularly known as "Teapot Hall", has for its crucks pairs of perfectly straight principals united by a ridge-tree. The roof runs from ridge-tree to the ground, and the space within the house is severely circumscribed. The type of structure which had curved uprights, however, gave more room than this in the lower part of the house, and from this developed the later form of house in which the lower portion was constructed of heavy timbers which formed the corners and intermediate posts and stood up from the foundations some eight or ten feet—thus giving even more room than did the curved upright form. Upon these posts were erected the principal rafters and crowning these the ridge-tree. Few examples of houses of the fourteenth century still exist, but in remote countryside valleys, such as in the Snowdon area, some still remain. Messrs Hughes and North have examined these carefully and write: "The characteristic of these cottages seems to have been that the roof principals were composed each of two great curved pieces of oak, starting from the floor, against the side walls, and meeting at the ridge.... The

---

[1] E. Pérochon, Les Creux-de-maisons (1921), 14. Cf. H. Bachelin, Le Village, 29; and especially E. Guillaumin, Notes Paysannes, 94. For conditions in the Valais in the mid-nineteenth century, see Ruskin's moving account in Modern Painters, IV, Part V, ch. XIX, §§ 4, 5 and 6.

great curved rafters are each connected by two horizontal ties."[1] Such was the framework of the majority of small houses and cottages, built with the help of the village carpenter and requiring no great skill in setting up. Once the framework was constructed, the walls and roof followed fairly easily. Few instances are recorded of the use of stone for the walls—even in good stone country—but almost everywhere wattle-and-daub, or cob, or earth and mud were the principal materials in use. In the first of these a number of sticks were stuck upright, and twigs were woven in and out between them forming a sort of rude lattice work, and on this was thrown the *dab* until it was of the right thickness. The fragile and easily combustible nature of such buildings needs no emphasising, but may help to explain the constant references in medieval writers to the ruinous condition of the countryside after plague or war.[2]

Other houses, again, were built with mud walls, or of cob as it is called in the Western counties. Mr Addy thus describes the process in Yorkshire:

The walls are built of layers of mud and straw which vary from five to seven inches in thickness, no vertical joints being visible. On the top of each layer is a thin covering of straw, with the ends of the straws pointing outwards, as in a corn stack. The way in which mud walls were built is remembered in the neighbourhood. A quantity of mud was mixed with straw, and the foundation laid with this mixture. Straw was then laid across the top, whilst the mud was wet, and the whole was left to dry and harden in the sun. As soon as the first layer was dry another layer was put on, so that the process was rather a slow one. Finally the roof was thatched, and the projecting ends of straws trimmed off the walls.[3]

The majority of cottages were thatched, although wooden shingles were not unknown. The thatch was nearly always a

[1] H. Hughes and H. L. North, *The Old Cottages of Snowdonia*, 5.
[2] *Hugh, St* (R.S.), 69; *Essex Review*, XIII, 219.
[3] *Evolution of the English House*, 40, 47 and n. 1. *Country Life* (1914), 395. Cf. Thomas Hardy's account: "What was called mud-wall was really a composition of chalk, clay and straw—essentially unbaked brick. This was mixed up into a sort of dough-pudding close to where the cottage was to be built. The mixing was performed by treading and shovelling—women sometimes being called in to tread—and the straw was added to bind the mass together....It was then thrown by pitch-forks on to the wall, where it was trodden down to a thickness of about two feet, till a rise of about three feet had been reached. This was left to settle for a day or two, etc.": *The Times*, March 11, 1927.

straw of some kind: rye straw being the most esteemed as longest and strongest, and after that came wheat straw. The corn was cut close up to the ear so that there was a great deal of stubble for thatching purposes. In certain parts, such as Lincoln and Norfolk, where reeds were plentiful, they were almost invariably used for thatching, and by some were considered the finest thatching material of all. The men of the Ramsey manors, for example, had to cut sedge for thatching the many buildings of the manors, or if they wished to be excused from this duty they had to pay "sedge silver" to the lord.[1] When the thatcher came he was served by his man or often by a woman, and received a comparatively high rate of pay for his skilled work—generally at least twice as much as his assistant.

The ventilation of these houses was non-existent or rudimentary. There was usually no chimney and the smoke from the fire escaped as best it could from the door, windows and crevices in wall and roof, just as it does in Alpine châlets to-day. The fire was made, either on the bare floor, or on an iron plate placed on the floor, and the peasants cooked and lived as best they could in a "ful sooty" atmosphere. Not till the end of the fifteenth century did chimneys become a fairly common feature of any but the greatest houses (the architectural difficulties of making a chimney were considerable), and even as late as 1557 conservatives like Harrison complained of this effeminate innovation.[2]

Nor were the windows of much use in letting out the smoke, for they were few and small. Glass was still far too expensive for the peasant, and he covered his tiny window-opening with a wooden shutter (thus excluding light as well as air) or less often by framed blinds of cloth or canvas termed *fenestralls*.[3] The conditions resulting are vividly described by Langland who pictures the peasant bleary-eyed, or worse, and hoarse with the "smoke and smolder", so that he coughs and curses that God may chastise those whose business it is to bring in dry wood, or at least to blow it until it is blazing.[4]

---

[1] *Ramsey Cart.* I, 308, 431, and see *Cust. Rents,* 57–8.
[2] *Eliz. Engl.* 119. "A room with a chimney" was one of the signs of a decadent age noted by Langland. *Piers Plowman,* B. ll. 94–100.
[3] *Prompt. Parv.* 155.
[4] *Piers Plowman,* B. XVII, 322.

The work necessary to construct buildings such as these was done with a minimum of skilled labour. Every village, of course, had a carpenter (or woodwright) among its inhabitants, and he was undoubtedly one of the essential figures of medieval life; but, save for woodwright and wheelwright, skilled workers were not so easily found, and most medieval building operations of a simple nature were done by the common-sense knowledge and skill of the untrained villagers, assisted where necessary by the carpenter, the thatcher, or the plasterer. "The rougher part was done by customary tenants, who tore down old walls, dug the clay, and fetched water to 'temper' it; pulled off the old thatch and cut and brought stubble for the new."[1] In the same way the tenants of the Bishop of Chichester were forced to aid in the building of new barns under the direction of a master carpenter,[2] and there was little in the everyday run of things that the peasant was not prepared to tackle, both about his own close and at the manor house itself.

This side of medieval domestic life is thus admirably summed up by Lord Ernle:

Women spun and wove wool into coarse cloth, and hemp or nettles into linen; men tanned their own leather. The rough tools required for the cultivation of the soil, and the rude household utensils needed for the comforts of daily life, were made at home. In the long winter evenings, farmers, their sons, and their servants carved the wooden spoons, the platters, and the beechen bowls. They fitted and riveted the bottoms to the horn mugs, or closed, in coarse fashion, the leaks in the leathern jugs. They plaited the osiers and reeds into baskets and into "weeles" for catching fish; they fixed handles to the scythes, rakes, and other tools; cut the flails from holly or thorn, and fastened them with thongs to the staves; shaped the teeth for rakes and harrows from ash or willow, and hardened them in the fire; cut out the wooden shovels for casting the corn in the granary; fashioned ox-yokes and bows, forks, racks, and rack-staves; twisted willows into scythe-cradles, or into traces and other harness-gear. Travelling carpenters, smiths, and tinkers visited detached farmhouses and smaller villages, at rare intervals, to perform those parts of the work which needed their professional skill. Meanwhile the women plaited straw or reed for neck-collars, stitched and stuffed sheep-skin bags for cart-saddles, peeled rushes for wicks and made candles. Thread was often made

---

[1] Davenport, *op. cit.* p. 22.
[2] Sussex Rec. Soc. XXXI, pp. 54, 76.

from nettles. Spinning-wheels, distaffs, and needles were never idle. Home-made cloth and linen supplied all wants. Flaxen linen for board-cloths, sheets, shirts, smocks or shirts, and towels, as the napkins were called, on which, before the introduction of forks, the hands were wiped, was only found in wealthy households and on special occasions. Hemp, in ordinary households, supplied the same necessary articles, and others, such as candle-wicks, in coarser form. Shoe-threads, halters, stirrup-thongs, girths, bridles, and ropes were woven from the "carle" hemp; the finer kind, or "fimble" hemp supplied the coarse linen for domestic use, and "hempen homespun" passed into a proverb for a countryman.[1]

The fragile nature of the houses has already been mentioned, and hence we need feel no surprise at finding constant references to "ruinous and dilapidated cots" in the Court Rolls and elsewhere. It was obviously against the lord's interests that houses should be like this, and therefore tenants were generally ordered to repair their houses within a given time,[2] and sometimes a stake was driven in before their door as a reminder of this.[3] If a cottage was in so "feeble" a condition that it required repair by an incoming tenant, his rent would be reduced for the time being,[4] or he would be allowed timber to help him to put it in order again.[5] Even when in good repair, however, such fragile buildings had their drawbacks, as is brought home to us when we read that thieves broke in indifferently through the walls or the doors; or that a man was killed at his own fireside by a spear thrust in through the side of the house.[6] Once such houses fell into disrepair it only needed a few violent storms and a winter or two to bring them crashing to the ground.[7]

Undoubtedly the greatest incentive to the peasant to keep his house in repair was a generous allowance of timber from the lord's woods and forests, and this was appreciated by many

[1] Lord Ernle, *English Farming, Past and Present* (second ed.), 29. Cf. the account given in *The Countryman*, July 1935, p. 356, of the way the Austrian peasants still live an almost self-supporting life in the villages of the Salzkammergut.
[2] *Abbots Langley*, f. 37 r., 37 v.; *Wilts. Arch. Mag.* v, 74.
[3] *Wilts. Arch. Mag.* xxxii, 294.
[4] *Durham Halmote Rolls*, 21; Thoresby Soc. xv, 157.
[5] Sussex Rec. Soc. xxxi, 83; Davenport, *op. cit.* 32; *Durham Halmote Rolls*, xix.
[6] Selden Soc. i. 3. Cf. *Catholicon*, where "howse breker" is translated "apercularius".
[7] *Wakefield Court Rolls*, i, 274.

lords, although, as Miss Neilson tells us, "the conditions under which he could take wood from the woodland of the manor had to be carefully defined. To cut wood without permission, within the forest or without it, was a very serious offence, included in the Ramsey customal with theft and bloodshed as offences not to be compounded for by *fulstingpound*".[1] Other lords, less harsh, fined culprits who took wood without leave.[2] Other manors again had curious customs, such as obtained on the royal demesne of Pickering in Yorkshire, where the tenants could take all dry wood lying on the ground, as well as any wood they could knock down with hooks (by hook or by crook).[3] This custom is also found as late as the sixteenth century on the lands of William, first Earl of Pembroke, whose tenants had also the privilege on Holy Thursday of felling and carrying away on a cart drawn by men, a load of young oak trees, wherewith they decorated the village church and their own dwellings.[4] Such accounts as these are sufficient to indicate the strict control the lord usually kept over timber rights on the manor, and the Court Rolls constantly show us men being fined because they have cut down trees without leave.

This same survey, late though it is, may be used to emphasise what has been said above, for the scribe has not only given a detailed account of the various holdings and villages, but has added delightful bird's-eye drawings of two of them—Wilton and Paignton. Here we may see the thatched, single-story mud and wattle houses with their small windows and comparatively few chimneys. Each house stands in its own little curtilage (or enclosed piece of ground) and this is laid out by the villager as his own private garden where he can cultivate what he pleases quite apart from his strips in the common fields where he was only able to act in concert with his fellows.[5]

What he could cultivate was not very much according to our modern notions, but was perhaps more than is commonly

---

[1] *Cust. Rents*, p. 52.

[2] *Abbots Langley*, f. 36 v.; *Tatenhill*, II, p. 21 ff.; *Wilts. Arch. Mag.* v, 76; and for surviving rights in the seventeenth century see XLI, 174.

[3] *Cal. Inquis. Misc.* I, p. 40. Cf. p. 41 where they are free to take whatever they can get without tools of any kind.

[4] *Pembroke Survey*, lxx.

[5] *Op. cit.* I, 182, Plate VII; II, 388, Plate IX.

believed.[1] Fruit trees of various kinds were widespread: apples, pears and cherries being quite common. Plums, quinces and medlars were also grown by many, and walnuts, chestnuts and filberts were very popular. These were grown in what is sometimes called the *hortus* in surveys and terriers, and it has been suggested that we ought to distinguish between this and the *gardinum*, where a few flowers were grown and such vegetables and herbs as were available.[2] So far as the ordinary peasant was concerned we need not bother about this minute sub-division (which seems, in any case, to be of doubtful validity), but may imagine him growing whatever he could in a fine confusion: a few apple and pear trees, and vegetables, such as cabbages, leeks, onions, garlic, mustard, peas and beans, together with pot herbs—parsley and "herbys to make both sauce and stewe". Piers Plowman, for instance, speaks of the harvest in his croft that will give him beans and peas, leeks, parsley and shallots, "chiboles and chervils and cherries, half-red".[3]

When we turn to view the interior of the peasant's house we find that it had little to commend it. The floor was usually of earth, trodden or beaten as hard as was possible, but liable to become wet and messy with constant coming and going in wet weather. Straw was freely used, both for warmth and cleanliness, however.[4] The fire was made on an iron plate or a hob of clay, and about it clustered the cooking utensils—pots and pans of earthenware (or perhaps brass or latten[5]), with ladles and forks of metal of some kind; while bowls and basins of wood, and forks and spoons, and many other odds and ends of use to the cook, were carved and hollowed out by the master and his sons during the long winter evenings from rough pieces of beech or oak. Add

---

[1] Medieval gardening was fairly fully treated in 1862 by T. Wright in his *Hist. Domestic Manners and Sentiments*, 293–303. The most authoritative modern work on this subject, however, is by A. M. Amherst, *Hist. of Gardening*. Sir F. Crisp's *Medieval Gardens* has admirable illustrations of rich men's gardens, but does not help us to know much about those of the lower classes. See e.g. *Rent. and Cust. (M. de Ambresbury)*, Somerset Rec. Soc. v, *passim*; *Ramsey Cart.* s.v. gardens.

[2] *The Athenæum*, Aug. 7, 1909, p. 146.

[3] *Piers Plowman*, B. ll. 288–96. *Chiboles* = small onions; *chervils* = pot-herbs, O.F. cerfeuil.

[4] Selden Soc. VII, 52, 91; and cf. Myrk, *Festial* (E.E.T.S.), p. 39, l. 22.

[5] Latten was a mixed metal of yellow colour, either identical with, or closely resembling brass.

a few stools and a trestle-table on which the meal could be spread, with a chest to hold the best clothes, and we have almost exhausted the furnishing of the medieval cottage. Beds we know little of: occasionally a feather-bed is mentioned in a will, and is evidently a precious thing; but in general bags of straw or flock had to serve, either thrown on the floor, or resting on rudely constructed frames placed by the walls of the house. Indeed, even in 1557, Harrison writes contemptuously of beds, and though he exaggerates, he is evidence of a still existing conservatism:

Our fathers and we ourselves have lyen full ofte upon straw pallettes, covered only with a sheet, under coverlets made of dogswain or hopharlots (I use, says he, the very words of the old men from whom I received the accounts) and a good round logge under their heades, insteade of a boulster. If it were so that our fathers or the good man of the house had...a matteres or flock bed and thereto a sacke of chafe to rest hys heade upon, he thought himself to be as well loged as the lorde of the towne, so well were they contented. Pillowes, they sayde, were thoughte mete only for women in childbed. As for servants, if they had any sheete above them, it was well, for seldome had they any under their bodies, to keepe them from the pricking straws, that ranne oft thorow the canvas, and rased their hardened hides.[1]

Few inventories of peasant's goods have survived, and even these are not very helpful. One dated 1293 enumerates the chattels of a man who died worth only thirty-three shillings and eightpence. His "household stuff" consisted of a bolster, a rug, two sheets, a brass dish and a trivet.[2] Nearly a century later the *Durham Halmote Rolls* record the "goods and chattels" of two serfs, but in neither instance are any domestic effects mentioned.[3] Again, a jury of Tatenhill, about 1380, assessed Richard Holland's goods at £5. 3s., and here the household goods were comparatively small in value. Among them we read of bedding (sheets, blankets, counterpanes) as well as of kitchen utensils (pans, cresset, tripod, skillet, five spoons of silver, colanders and a board-cloth), the whole being worth less than £2.[4] Lastly, the jury of Easington, in 1409, assessed the "domestic utensils" of Richard Watson at 6s. 8d., out of an estate worth £8. 17s. 2d.[5]

---

[1] *Eliz. Eng.* 119.
[2] *Arch. Journ.* III, 65.
[3] *Op. cit.* 151, 168.
[4] *Tatenhill*, II, 55.
[5] *V.C.H. Durham*, II, 199. Cf. *D.S.P.* xcvii.

With this we may compare the contents of a hall as given in an early fifteenth-century book of vocabularies. They are: a board, trestle, banquere (a piece of tapestry to throw over a bench), a dorser (hanging), table dormant (standing table, as opposed to the easily movable trestle-table), basin, laver, fire, hearth, brand, logs, andirons, long settle, chairs, benches, tongs, stools, bellows, "screne".[1] Few peasants had such costly things as tapestries or hangings or even chairs, and a "dormant" table would have been a great nuisance in the restricted floor space of a medieval cottage; but otherwise the list is a fair indication of the kind of furniture and fixtures to be found in the ordinary village home.

Thorold Rogers, in his well-known book *Six Centuries of Work and Wages*, filled many pages in detailing "evidence as to the condition of the English peasantry, in order, if possible, once for all to show how untenable the opinion is which doubts that, as far as the mere means of life were concerned, the Englishman of the middle ages lived in ordinary times in coarse plenty".[2] Yet, despite his efforts, obstinate doubts still assail us. We cannot easily forget Chaucer's poor widow in the *Nun's Priest's Tale*, who lived in her little two-roomed house on a diet of "milk and brown bread, singed bacon, with sometimes an egg or two"; or the still more poignant pictures drawn by Langland of the peasants of his day. No chickens, geese, pork or bacon come their way, but two green (new) cheeses, curds and cream, and a cake of oats. This, together with bread of pease or beans for their children, is all the food they can look forward to until harvest comes.[3] Langland sees the poor, "charged with children and chief lord's rent", spending their small wages in milk and meal to make porridge "to glut the maws" of their children that cry after food. "Also in winter they suffer much hunger and woe. ... It would be a charity to help them: bread and penny-ale are a luxury; cold flesh and cold fish is to them like baked venison; on Fridays and fasting-days, a farthing's worth of mussels or so many cockles were a feast for such folk." Such pictures as these,

[1] *A Volume of Vocabularies*, ed. T. Wright, 197.   [2] *Op. cit.* 63.
[3] *Op. cit.* C. IX, 304. Cf. also 331. Cf. Gower's *Mirour*, ll. 26, 437 ff., where labourers of old ate beans or coarser corn washed down by water. Milk and cheese were a feast to them, and they rarely ate other dainties.
[4] *Op. cit.* C. X, 71.

PLATE V

Domestic scenes
Folding linen. Dividing the carcase. Kitchen scene. Outdoor cookery.
The rope wheel

together with other contemporary and earlier testimony,[1] cannot be ignored. Doubtless the aristocracy of the peasants "lived in ordinary times in coarse plenty"; but, as we have already seen, there were many others besides these people on the manor, and their lot was much as Langland has pictured it.

When we turn to the documents themselves, we find how very limited was the range of foodstuffs available. Our best evidence, perhaps, comes from the lists of food provided by the lord for his serfs engaged in the hard work of harvesting and the like. We may summarise many hundreds of such lists by saying that the serf was given bread, ale or cider, a mess of pottage, followed by a dish of fish or flesh and perhaps a lump of cheese. The researches of Sir W. Ashley have suggested that in general the bread was of rye, or at best, of a mixture of rye and wheat (*maslin*).[2] If otherwise, this was plainly stated in the customal or elsewhere.[3] The size of the loaf handed over to the workers varied, and sometimes no ale but only water was given. The pottage was "a grewell without flesh boiled in it",[4] and often made with peas or beans.[5] Herrings or dried fish were commonly supplied for the harvesters on fast days, while "a dish of meat" formed the *pièce de résistance* on other days.[6] Meat was expensive for the serf, and only seldom came his way, except as a feast or when he fed at his lord's costs. We can get a little nearer the day's rations by noting the practice on some of the Abbot of Battle's manors where the workers get two or three meals during the day: at Craumarey in Oxfordshire at *nonam* (noon) they got wheaten bread, ale and cheese, and at vespers, bread, ale, pottage, flesh or herrings and cheese.[7] On other manors something of the same is found: the carters of Ferring in 1289 got a morning meal of rye bread, with beer and cheese; at noon they had bread and beer, with pottage and the usual dish of fish or flesh, and in the evening a drink before leaving the manor hall.[8]

---

[1] *Med. Village*, 311–20, summarises the English and foreign evidence.
[2] *The Bread of our Forefathers*, passim; Econ. Journ. XXXI, 285.
[3] Sussex Rec. Soc. XXXI, 72, 89, 107; cf. pp. 34, 43, 81.
[4] Dugdale, *Warwick*, p. 177a.   [5] *V.C.H. Middlesex*, II, 67.
[6] Sussex Rec. Soc. XXXI, *passim*; Camb. Univ. Lib. MS. Kk. v. 29, ff. 26b, 32b, 103, 104; *Battle Customals*, 5, 20, 87, 89. *Min. Accounts*, 1030/3–6; 998/21.
[7] *Battle Customals*, 87, 89.   [8] Camb. Univ. Lib. MS. Kk. v. 29, f. 104.

The above rations, however, must not be looked on as normal, but as something superior to the ordinary daily meals which most men were able to afford themselves. On special occasions, no doubt, poultry or a hare or rabbit found its way to the pot, or even a piece of salted beef, or perhaps a cut of tainted mutton (dead of the plague) was passed off by an unscrupulous master to his serfs. As an earlier chapter has shown, rabbits were very plentiful, and at times even game preserves, or the sacred forests themselves, were raided. Poaching was common, and one of the most spirited pieces of medieval literature tells of a poacher's adventures in quest of his quarry; while the manorial courts were constantly called on to repress such adventurers.[1]

We have little evidence to guide us as to the number or the times of medieval meals for the humbler folk. In default of anything certain, it may be hazarded that most of them had a hunk of bread and a mug of ale in the morning; and a lump of cheese and bread, with perhaps an onion or two to flavour it, and more ale for their midday meal. At the end of the day (as is still common among Continental peasants) the main meal was served. It was not very varied, nor very palatable to modern ways of thinking. A thick soup or pottage was the main dish, and bread and cheese followed to complete the meal, on most occasions. Rarely a dish of meat was forthcoming, and the poultry, which ran in and out of the medieval home, also served to garnish some special occasion when the villager put his best on the table. Drink was equally monotonous: ale was the most usual drink for all humble folk (although cider took its place in some parts), and even this was a thin and not very heady liquid. The "moist and corny ale" only came on rare evenings when the lord entertained his men, or some very exceptional village celebration demanded such an unusual extravagance.

Hence, when all has been said, despite his occasional feasts and the short seasons of harvest and abundance, the lot of the medieval peasant, as M. Henri Sée concludes from his study of French conditions, was "assez misérable".[2] He draws attention to the limited number of things the peasant could grow, and to

[1] See above, p. 218, and for the poem, see below, p. 271.
[2] *Op. cit.* p. 547.

the lack of any widespread knowledge of methods of re-fertilising the soil. Further, he notes that agricultural instruments were still comparatively undeveloped, and difficulties of communication encouraged attempts to grow things in climates and soils quite unsuited for them.[1] Add to this the hazards attendant on weather, and it is not difficult to realise that the peasant was frequently near to starvation,[2] and, perforce, eked out a difficult existence as best he could, especially through the long winter months.

With so much else in medieval times the details of married life escape us. The fortunate survival of *The Paston Letters* and *The Stonor Letters*, or the indiscreet memoirs of a Pepys, allow us to glean innumerable facts concerning the relations between husbands, wives and children in the fifteenth and the seventeenth centuries. No such aid is forthcoming for the historian of thirteenth- or fourteenth-century peasant life. The earliest manuals of behaviour, and rules for the upbringing of children do not date before the fifteenth century; and, even if they did, would be of little help, for they are concerned with the behaviour of people and of children of considerably higher status than the peasant. Documents, again, will not help us, for they are almost invariably concerned only with the peasant's relation to his lord. His personal concerns are of little interest to the lord, save where, as in his choice of a wife, they are liable to affect the lord's interests. But his home life, and his daily routine therein matter nothing to the lord, and as a result these figure nowhere in any records which have come down to us. Our ignorance of these conditions remains profound.

The nearest we can now hope to get to such conditions, perhaps, is when we have a few minutes inside the dwelling of a peasant family, not in England, for things have changed so radically here, but in some tiny French or Swiss hamlet, where

---

[1] *Op. cit.* p. 540.
[2] Conditions do not seem to have been so severe in England as in France. A. Luchaire, in his *Social France at the time of Philip Augustus*, asserts that in the twelfth century "men died of hunger, on an average, one year in every four" (and adds that 48 famine years are recorded in the eleventh century (p. 7)). In England we have no evidence of such appalling conditions: indeed Thorold Rogers asserts that he knows "of only one distinct period of famine in the whole economic history of England", i.e. 1315-21 (*Work and Wages*, 62; cf. 217).

medieval ways and customs are only of yesterday. One such glimpse remains clear in my memory. Caught by a heavy rainstorm high up in the mountains of Aubrac, in the department of the Cantal in France, I was forced to shelter in a wayside shed; and, after a few minutes, was seen from the house, and invited to enter. It was a meagre room, some fourteen feet square, and so little light entered from a small window that it was difficult at first to see clearly. The floor was of earth, and on a rude stone hearth an old woman tended a wood fire and, from time to time, stirred the soup. Two dark wooden cupboards filled up some of the little space, and a home-made table of chestnut, a few chairs and a couple of stools were all the other furniture, save for a cradle rudely fashioned from a log of wood. The baby, swaddled in medieval fashion, and but a few days old, lay in it; on its crying, the mother (who had already risen from childbed) got up from where she sat on the other side of the fire and hastened to suckle it. She did not remove the child from the cot, but lifted the cot itself, with the child in it, to her breast. She and her mother talked to me while she did so, and explained how they lived in this remote spot: their little garden grew much of their food, and the strips of meadow and pasture round about but barely provided for their cattle on which they depended. From time to time the son-in-law went down the mountains to the fair at Marjevols or Espalion, and from the sale of a cow was able to purchase those necessaries which they were unable to grow or fashion for themselves at home. It would be useless to press the likeness to medieval conditions very far; but, at least, nobody could fail to realise that here life was going on as it had done in many particulars for countless generations. So too, in the narrow village street at Salers, or at Besse-en-Chandesse in the Auvergne, or pushing our way through the market at Mauriac, and hearing the raucous cries of the peasants as they bartered and sold, or the clack of the old wives chattering and gossiping while still endeavouring to get rid of chickens or vegetables—in such places medieval daily life is once again before our eyes and imagination.

Readers of *The Nun's Priest's Tale* will easily recognise how similar were the conditions in which Chaucer's "poor widow" lived to those of the Cantal peasants of 1930:

A poure wydwe, somdeel stape in age,
Was whilom dwellyng in a narwe cotage,
Biside a grove, stondynge in a dale.
This wydwe, of which I telle yow my tale,
Syn thilke day that she was last a wyf,
In pacience ladde a ful symple lyf,
For litel was hir catel and hir rente.
By housbondrie of swich as God hire sente
She foond hirself and eek hir doghtren two.
Thre large sowes hadde she, and namo,
Three keen, and eek a sheep that highte Malle.
Ful sooty was hire bour and eek hir halle,
In which she eet ful many a sklendre meel.
Of poynaunt sauce her neded niver a deel.
No deyntee morsel passed thurgh hir throte....
No wyn ne drank she, neither whit ne reed;
Hir bord was served moost with whit and blak,
Milk and broun breed, in which she foond no lak,
Seynd bacoun, and sometyme an ey or tweye;
For she was, as it were, a maner deye.
    A yeerde she hadde, enclosed al aboute
With stikkes, and a drye dych withoute.[1]

Amidst such material conditions the peasant lived, and did his best to rear his family. The frightful wastage of medieval life, even omitting the toll taken by war, is not easily comprehended in these softer days. Many of the things we think most necessary to health were lacking. The normal modern safeguards against infection were unknown; the proper care of the sick was in a rudimentary state; the dangers of childbirth were immense, and the years of infancy a constant battle against plague and fevers which were endemic in medieval England. To all these must be added the limited variety of foodstuffs, as well as the desperately scanty rations which at times were all that were available.

As a result of these conditions the increase in population from the Conquest to the time of the Great Plague of 1349 was very slow. If we take the figure commonly accepted, the population in 1066 was some 2½ millions, and the most optimistic estimate of that of 1349 does not exceed 5 millions. This means that the growth of population per annum over this period was only

[1] *Nun's Priest's Tale*, B. ll. 4011–28.

0·147 per cent. Now if we imagine the average English village to have been about 300 souls in number (i.e. some 60 families) the rate of increase in the whole village was only 0·441 each year. In other words the loss by death was so severe that it took over two years to add one new individual to such a village community.

From this it is easy to see how static conditions were in the village, and what a limited number of young people there were in any of them at any given time, and how limited the potential list of marriageable men and women must have been. This was by no means the only difficulty which faced the serf. The words of Justice Belknap, in 1342, may serve to remind us of the condition in which the vast majority of peasants found themselves at this time and for some centuries earlier. "There is no service in the world", he said, "which so quickly proves a man to be a villain as making a fine for marriage."[1] This fine went by the name of "merchet", and Vinogradoff and others—notably L. O. Pike—have discussed fully the origin of the term and the widespread incidence of this service.[2] We need not labour this further, but may usefully note how very unevenly and with what differing conditions "merchet" was enforced on various manors. The serf being (in legal theory) a possession of the lord it followed that all he possessed was also his lord's, and his offspring, in common with the offspring of his horses and cattle, were both designated by the one word (*sequela*), and were looked on as possessions. Hence they were all of some value to the lord, and he often refused to allow man or woman (especially the latter) to make any important decisions which might remove them from his power without first obtaining (by payment in general) his sanction.

As a preliminary we may usefully bear in mind that the sale of marriage rights came to cover many possibilities in the course of time. *Merchet*, strictly speaking, was a fine paid by a serf for the marriage of a daughter within the manor. It was rapidly made to cover the fine paid for such a marriage, either within or without the manor, and also frequently was so stretched as to include sons as well as daughters.

[1] *Y.B.* 15 Ed. III (R.S.), xiii.
[2] *Villainage*, 153–6; *Y.B.* 15 Ed. III, xiv–xliii.

The question of marriage upon the manor presents small difficulty. The serfs, in general, found themselves subjected to little control. Unlike other people—the nobles, the great land-holders, the wards or the rich merchants—no one had much interest in their marriages among themselves and upon the same manor. This still left both parties in the hands of the lord; and they, and any future progeny, remained at his will and disposal. At worst, and as a sign of ownership, a small fine was exacted: "they must buy their blood."[1] At best, they were allowed to marry freely one with another, and they found it worth while to see that such a privilege was recorded when the custom of their manor was written down. This we see on the manors of the monks of Glastonbury, or on those of the canons of St Paul's.[2] Needless to say, if there was any special reason, e.g. if the girl would her-self inherit her parent's holding in due course, the lord's consent to her marriage was necessary,[3] since her husband would have to discharge the duties which went with the holding.

The real difficulties began when marriage outside the manor was contemplated, or when marriage with one of free birth either in or out of the manor was in question. Marriage off the manor involved an entirely different set of considerations, unless both manors belonged to the same lord. If they did not, the marriage meant the loss of property to one of the lords, and he, not un-reasonably, expected compensation. This compensation (some-times called *redemptio* or *forismaritagium*) was fixed at various prices, but does not seem at any time to have been nearly so heavy in England as it was in France until the end of the twelfth century.[4] It is rare to find a payment of more than a few shillings entered in the rolls: the most unsatisfactory conditions were those obtaining on some estates which left the amount of the fine to be settled by the serf with his lord on the best terms he could get. Even here, as on the Ramsey manors, custom had

---

[1] *Cust. Roff.* 12, cf. 33; *Hist. MSS. Com. Wells*, I, 327; *Crondal Records*, 64, 150; Selden Soc. II, 27; Camb. Antiq. Soc. XXVII, 164, etc.
[2] *Glas. Rent.* 83, 92; *D.S.P.* cxxv.
[3] *Cust. Roff.* 12.
[4] Cf. Bloch, *Liberté et servitude personnelles au moyen-âge*, 15 n. 23. "Les amendes étaient certainement très fortes: allant, en droit, jusqu'à la con-fiscation des biens, selon une charte de 1070....Il y avait de tels abus qu'en 1385 le Parlement crut devoir se substituer au chapitre de Laon pour fixer le taux d'une amende." See also, Luchaire, *Les Institutions populaires*, 302.

come to his aid, and it is generally stated that the amount of the fine was not to exceed five shillings.[1] In order to protect themselves serfs bought the right of marriage when they took over their father's land on succeeding,[2] or bargained with their lord for the privilege of marrying "wheresoever they would", or "whenever they chose", without hindrance from any manorial authority.[3] And they went further: they paid to have such special exemptions written down in the manor rolls to which they might appeal if the memory of steward or bailiff ever proved defective on this matter.[4]

A further difficulty sometimes arose over the children of such a marriage. To which lord did they belong? In France there were endless disputes and claims upon this matter, and highly complicated systems were invented to deal with the problems of a single child or of an unequal number of children. In England we have little evidence to guide us; but we may first note that Glanvill laid it down that the children were *proportionaliter* divided between the two lords.[5] That this was no mere theory is borne out by a quit claim to the monks of Chester (*c.* 1216–40) by John Fitzalan, whereby if any of his villeins takes a wife from those of Ince, or vice versa, a division of the children should be made between him and the abbot, according to the custom of the country.[6] This seems to argue that there was a perfectly well-known custom, at any rate in this part of England, in the first half of the thirteenth century; while three instances of about 1285 from the east of England[7] encourage the belief that the custom was found on a number of manors, and over a considerable area, until at least the end of this century.

Despite a multiplicity of local differences, so far it has not been difficult to trace the guiding principle underlying the marriage of serfs—they must "buy their blood" as the phrase goes. When we come to the vexed question of mixed marriages—of marriages,

---

[1] *Ramsey Cart.* I, 384, 395, 472, 490. At Chatteris, however, they were entirely at the will of their lord (I, 432, and cf. 416).
[2] *Abbots Langley*, f. 1; *U.L.C. Wynslowe*, ff. 17a, 20a, 22a.
[3] *V.C.H. Warwick*, II, 143; *Hales Rolls*, 420.
[4] *Wynslowe*, 34a, 45a, 56a; *Abbots Langley*, 20b, 21b.
[5] Glanvill, *op. cit.* lib. 5, cap. 6.
[6] *Chester Chart.* 210, No. 313.
[7] *Norf. Arch.* XVII, 319.

that is, between free and bond—the subject becomes very complicated and gave the medieval lawyers many a happy hour. The *Leges Henrici*, Britton, Glanvill and Bracton all lay down rules and counter-rules in bewildering variety; but

ultimately, "the better opinion of our books" was that marriage of a female serf with a free man, other than her lord, did not absolutely enfranchise her, but merely made her free during the marriage.... In the converse case in which a bondman marries a free woman, he of course is not enfranchised though Bracton's doctrine would make the children free if born in her free tenement,

but doubtfully so if born in his unfree tenement.[1]

Apart from personal status, mixed marriages between free and unfree raised difficult points of inheritance and the like. In a lawsuit of 1277 on the manor of Hales concerning a freeholding, it was shown that one of the parties interested had married a bondman. Her claim, thereafter, was quietly dropped, as by so marrying her rights (for the time being at any rate) had lapsed.[2] The prevailing custom is clearly stated about the same time (1275) in a Northampton manor court at Wedon Beck, when "the full court declares that in case any woman shall have altogether quitted the Lord's domain and shall marry a free man, she may return and recover what right and claim she has in any land: but if she has married a serf then she cannot do this during the lifetime of the serf, but after his death she may".[3] From this we can see that to be of free condition in itself is not a thing that can be lost altogether, though it may become inoperative in such circumstances as these, and if the will of the lord is sufficiently strong, or manorial custom sufficiently undeveloped, it may be hard to reassert one's status after a lapse of years.

The widow, who had inherited her husband's property, or some dowry therefrom, was subjected to considerable control by her lord. In general she was not allowed to re-marry without permission,[4] and the lord looked with some anxiety as to where

---

[1] Pollock and Maitland, *op. cit.* I, 423. See full discussion there and in *Villainage*, 61–3.

[2] *Hales Rolls*, 87–8. Cf. *Lit. Cant.* I, 520.

[3] Selden Soc. II, 24; *E.H.R.* XX, 480. But note *Abbots Langley*, 36b, where the tenement reverts to the lord on marriage to a free man.

[4] *Glouc. Cart.* III, 208, 210; Sussex Rec. Soc. XXXI, 102; *Durham Halmote Rolls*, II.

her choice would fall. If, as often happened, she wished to withdraw from his manor altogether he was faced with a serious loss, not only of the revenues arising from personal dues and fines, but also of the services or their equivalents due from her holding. We find women, therefore, forced to pay for leave to re-marry, or to withdraw from the manor.[1] Conversely, a man wishing to enter a manor, having married a woman holding land therein, finds himself forced to pay for such a privilege.[2] Otherwise, as on a manor of the monks of Canterbury, the land could be taken into the hands of the lord. The prior wrote to his official at Risborough to enquire which would be most to his advantage: to accept a fine of five marks or to seize the land![3]

Worse than these payments was the fact that at times the lord forced his serfs to marry when it suited his interests. We see this in a number of cases, especially on the manor of Hales, where the Abbot again and again attempted to force men into marriages they had no wish for. In 1274, "John of Romsley and Nicholas Sewal are given till next court to decide as to the widows offered them". At that court, three weeks later, "Nicholas Sewal is given to next Sunday to decide as to the widow offered to him in the presence of the cellarer" who held the court.[4] Nothing more is heard of either John or Nicholas, so probably they submitted. A few years later (11 Dec. 1279) Thomas Robins of Oldbury was ordered to take Agatha of Halesowen to wife. He said he would rather be fined; and, because he could find no guarantors, it was ordered that he should be distrained. On 7 January 1280, he is again distrained to take a wife as ordered, and on 23 January he paid a fine of three shillings, and so the matter ended.[5] Similar cases occurred on the manors of the monks of St Albans and elsewhere,[6] while an instance on the manor of Brightwaltham in 1335 will help to explain why the lord was often anxious to bring about some marriage, and so provide a widow or heiress

---

[1] *Wakefield Rolls*, I, 256; II, 49.
[2] *Hales Rolls*, 415; *Wakefield Rolls*, II, 192.
[3] *Lit. Cant.* I, 501. Cf. the case at Wisbech, where a holding is seized by the Bishop of Ely till he is satisfied by a fine. *C.R. Wisbech*, 33 Ed. I.
[4] *Hales Rolls*, 55, 57.
[5] *Op. cit.* 119, 121, 124. Cf. the case of R. Ridyacre who also refused and apparently succeeded in neither taking a wife or paying a fine, 121, 124, 126.
[6] *Abbots Langley* 13, 25; *Tatenhill*, II, 2.

with a husband, and himself with the certainty of labour-services, dues, and perhaps a future inheritor. At Brightwaltham no less than six widows, who had come into possession of their husbands' holdings without being able to render the labour that was due, were ordered, if they wished to retain their land, "to provide themselves with husbands".[1] A late piece of evidence comes from the Petition of the Commons to the King in 1394, when it was asserted that the religious houses caused their serfs to marry free women with inheritances, so that the religious could thereby claim the estates.[2]

The lord's concern to restrict marriages within the limits of the manor no doubt seriously limited the choice of the young, but what was still more important it brought them into difficulties with the Church. "Before 1215 Canon Law forbade all marriages of kinsfolk to the seventh degree; that is, between all who had a common great-great-great-great-great-grandfather. Innocent III, in the great Lateran Council, reduced these prohibitions, 'because they cannot now be kept without grievous harm'; thenceforth, the prohibition extended only to the fourth degree, but this must be kept with inviolable strictness".[3] It is easy to see how impossible it was on innumerable small medieval manors to keep this rule strictly. Either a man had to remain unmarried, or pay the increased fine for taking a wife from outside, or break the law of the Church. "Even when Innocent had softened the law", writes Dr Coulton, "at least half the bondmen in a normal village had probably some common great-great-grandfather with any prospective bridegroom or bride".[4] We have only to look at the earliest parish registers to see how intermarried village communities became, and the same thing has continued, to a lesser degree, even down to our own day.[5] Any small village cemetery in France or Switzerland bears instant confirmation of this fact, and it was also noted as a characteristic of village life in the English enquiry concerning rural conditions in Germany in 1870.[6]

Closely associated with the fine for marriage was that imposed

---

[1] Page, op. cit. 36 n. 2.   [2] Walsingham, 258.
[3] Quoted from Med. Village, Appendix 16.
[4] Op. cit. 472.
[5] V.C.H. Survey, IV, 413 n. 31.   [6] Land Tenure Reports, 387.

for incontinency—*Leyrwite*, or *lecherwite*, as it was called. As it is put in a Glastonbury record, the lord must have his fine "whenever one of the bondswomen is unchaste of her body, whereby my lord loseth the sale of her".[1] Since in strict law the serf was the absolute property of her master, anything she did to depreciate her value was to his loss. Hence the lord felt he had every right to be interested; and, as Maitland puts it, "to exercise a paternal control in the interests of morality". We may perhaps doubt how far morality was an urgent consideration: here was another opportunity to make a profit out of his serfs—and the lord took it! The Court Rolls—such as those of Halesowen, for example—illustrate the constant vigilance that the lord and his agents exerted: cases of immorality occur as a constant item of business and the offender is fined.[2] To make doubly sure, the onus of reporting such cases was a communal responsibility, and we find manorial jurors fined for neglecting to present offenders at the earliest possible moment.[3]

At the same time, it must be remembered, that incontinency was primarily an offence which came under the jurisdiction of the Church: the lord, therefore, was not only concerned because his property was depreciated, but also because the Church exacted fines from the serf (which theoretically were fines from him). Hence the rule that stewards should make enquiry in the manor court "whether any bondman's unmarried daughter hath committed fornication and been convened in chapter, and what she hath given to the [rural] dean for her correction".[4] Two cases from the Abbot of Ramsey's manors will illustrate the lord's point of view: "Richard Dyer a married man was convicted in the chapter [court] of adultery with a certain woman...*and so lost the chattels of the Lord*. Therefore he is in mercy. The amercement is forgiven."[5] The words in italics show the *gravamen* of the charge: in this case the lord was merciful, but his rights were put on record and thus safeguarded.

An even more interesting case is reported from the same manor

---

[1] *Villainage*, 154.
[2] *Op. cit.* 107, 120, 124, 161, 221, 230, etc. The Cartularies (e.g. *Ramsey*, I, 309, 314, 317, 339, etc.) constantly assert the lord's right to *leyrwyte*.
[3] *Op. cit.* 310; *Abbots Langley*, 26 b; *Wroxall Records*, 29.
[4] Selden Soc. IV, 102.
[5] *Ibid.* II, 97.

(Gedding) during the reign of Edward II. The chief pledges report that

John Monk still continues his lechery with Sarah Hewen, wife of Simon Hewen, and is constantly attending divers chapter courts *where frequently he loses the Lord's goods* by reason of his adultery with Sarah, as has often been presented before now; nor will he be chastened. Therefore let him be put in the stocks. And afterwards he made fine with one mark.[1]

Attendance at archidiaconal or ruridecanal courts and the fear of being summoned thither was always present in the wrong-doer's mind. Sometimes, of course, a rascally summoner, such as Chaucer depicts, would allow him a year's wantoning with his concubine for a quart of ale,[2] and even higher officials were capable of accepting bribes. "Purs is the erchdecknes helle", is more than a disreputable flourish: Gower only says what professed moralists were saying, when he cries out against the ecclesiastical courts, and declares "in all countries men may nowadays buy off their sins of the flesh... without repentance... thus our Dean covets sin rather than honesty; for he finds the prostitute more profitable than the nun".[3] Nevertheless, not all were able to avoid an actual appearance, as we may see from the records of the ruridecanal courts of Wych in the diocese of Worcester. These present an interesting account of the actual proceedings which were held in different parish churches of the deanery at three-weekly intervals.[4] Not only fines, but actual corporal punishment was inflicted, and the disgraced culprit was forced to do public penance.

At one court, for example, we read that Thomas of Bradley confessed his misbehaviour with Agnes, daughter of Gilbert the smith. Thomas was flogged, while Agnes was suspended for contumacy and then excommunicated. This frightened her, and she afterwards was reconciled, confessed and was flogged. Another couple, Henry of Frankley and Matilda Honderwode,

---

[1] *Ibid.* ii, 98.   [2] *C.T. Prologue*, 649.
[3] *Mirour de l'Omme*, v, 20,089 ff. Cf. Gascoigne, *Loci e Libro Veritatum*, 123 ff.
[4] Worc. Hist. Soc. *Collectanea* (1912). The medieval deanery of Wych included the two modern deaneries of Droitwich and Bromsgrove. Four sessions of the court are recorded, which dealt with 20, 22, 10 and 3 cases respectively.

were brought before the court for fornication. The woman confessed and abjured her sin, and was flogged once through the market place. The man was obdurate and was excommunicated. So the tale of offenders runs on.[1] The Hereford visitation also shows how prevalent immorality was in the parishes, and how the culprits were formally named to the ecclesiastical authorities at intervals.[2] Little, however, that was effective was, or could be done to prevent such a state of affairs. It was, and has remained, an inseparable part of village life, both in England and abroad, right down the ages. The Normandy village custom, whereby a marriage did not take place until it was evident that children would be born, has a long history behind it.

When the peasant felt his end approaching, what rights had he in the bestowal of his own personal goods? The right of the unfree man to make a will was for long disputed. It opened up difficult and dangerous questions, and many lords were strongly opposed to it. Yet, as the serf found his little personal possessions growing in number and value, the question of what would happen to them after his death became a matter of interest to him. No man wished to die intestate "for, unless death was so sudden that there was no opportunity for confession, to die intestate was probably to die unconfessed; and of the future state of a person who had thus died there could be no sure and certain hope. Thus there arose a feeling that intestacy, except in case of sudden death, was disgraceful".[3] Furthermore, the Church taught that a man's last hours were of supreme importance, and encouraged and exhorted him to "make a good end". Among other ways of accomplishing this was the comparatively simple one of leaving a gift to the Church, so that prayers and masses might be offered up on behalf of himself, of his family and of all Christian souls. From this it was a simple step to make provision also for the living so far as he was able. The law forbade him to leave his land to others than his heirs (and indeed, for the serf, there could be no question of this, for he only held the land from his lord),

---

[1] The Editor points out that other rolls exist dealing with the working of the ruridecanal courts: one belonging to Lincoln of 1337, and another in the British Museum, dated 1436 (Add. MSS. 11,821).

[2] See below, pp. 332ff.

[3] Holdsworth, op. cit. III, 535; and cf. Pollock and Maitland, op. cit. II, 354-7.

but his personal property he could dispose of as he would. In his last moments, therefore, the priest having come, his confession made, and at peace with God, he could turn to make provision for those who would survive him. There and then, in the presence of witnesses, he made known his *ultima voluntas*— and we may readily understand that there was little need to write down the few simple bequests of his personal property which were all he could make. Nor was it necessary according to law. The nuncupative, i.e. spoken, will only required the presence of two witnesses (and there is even some doubt whether either of these need have been a priest).[1] How simple, then, in circumstances such as these, for men to forget or to ignore the fact that what they were giving away was not in strict legal theory theirs to dispose of. However the Church may have viewed the matter, many lay lords (and many ecclesiastics in their temporal capacity as holders of manors) saw much danger in such practices. What was this "personal property" which the peasant was bequeathing to his friends? It was, according to the law, the property of the lord—had not the Abbot of Burton told his serfs that they owned nothing but their bellies—and to admit that a man had the right to bequeath any property was tantamount to relinquishing any rights in it. The lawyers finally got round the difficulty by saying that the lord undoubtedly had the right of seizure, but if he did not exercise it, the serf's will was valid. The lord, however, could step in and take the chattels at any time before probate of the will had been obtained.[2]

The Church, in the thirteenth century, came out boldly on the side of the serf. As early as 1261, Boniface, Archbishop of Canterbury, had declared that the serf had the right to make a will,[3] and this was reiterated at the Synod of Exeter in 1287.[4] Evidently opposition to this was encountered throughout the country, for in 1292 this right was included in the list of *gravamina* presented to the King by some of the Bishops.[5] Again, in 1295, Archbishop Winchelsey, when complaining to the Pope of subterfuges adopted by the Secular Courts to usurp juris-

---

[1] Wilkins, *Concilia*, II, 155, and Pollock and Maitland, *op. cit.* II, 337 n. 5; cf. Holdsworth, *op. cit.* III, 539.

[2] Swinburne, *Testaments*, 47, 48.   [3] Lyndwood, *Provinciale*, 171.

[4] Wilkins, *Concilia*, II, 155.   [5] *Reg. Pontissara*, 775.

diction which by right belonged to Ecclesiastics, mentions that
"testamenta laicorum defunctorum liberorum et aliorum qui
servilis conditionis reputantur per dominos Feudorum im-
pediuntur".[1] Lastly, at the Synod of Winchester, in 1308, and
at Canterbury in 1328 and 1342, the Church repeated its claims
on behalf of the serf.[2] This continuous agitation was finally met
by a petition to the King from Parliament, which asked him to
disallow any testamentary rights to the serf, since this "is against
reason". The royal answer, "The King wills that law and reason
be done",[3] shows that the Crown realised the thorny nature of
the matter, and that it were better left with only an oracular
answer.

We must not, of course, fall into the error of supposing that,
because the ecclesiastical hierarchy saw one side of this problem,
and endeavoured by threats of excommunication to enforce their
views, the whole Church throughout England was of their
opinion. It is to the credit of the Church that she took up this
attitude (the more so inasmuch as ecclesiastical holdings of land
were very large) but not every cleric was prepared to obey these
constitutions. As landowners, and therefore the lords of innumerable serfs and their property, many ecclesiastics (especially
corporations, such as abbeys or monasteries) were loth to assent
to a rule which definitely weakened their control over their own
peasants. Thus the monks of Vale Royal in Cheshire, in the
fourteenth century, were still asserting that their bondmen
"could not make a will, nor dispose of anything, nor have or
give any thing of all their goods, but all their goods shall remain
wholly to the lord except a penny, which is called Masspenny,
and a 'principal' to the parish church".[4] The importance, as it
seems to the monks, of maintaining such a claim is clear when
we read the rubric at the head of the document: "These are the
conditions by reason of which the abbot and convent of Vale
Royal say that the people of Over are their bondmen (neiffez)."[5]
Another document, however, suggests that the monks were pre-

[1] *Reg. Pontissara*, 203.
[2] Wilkins, *op. cit.* II, 293, 553, 705.
[3] *Rot. Parl.* II, 149b, 150a.
[4] *Vale Royal Ledger Book*, 121. Principal=mortuary, see p. 144.
[5] *Ibid.* 120.

pared to allow the making of a will so long as it was done with the licence of the lord abbot.[1]

It may well be that many lords protected themselves as did the Abbot of Ramsey on one of his manors. There a will was only valid if made in the presence of the reeve or bailiff[2]—possibly as a reminder of the lord's rights and to safeguard his interests. On other Ramsey manors the serf was more generously treated, and allowed to make his will without either bailiff or reeve being present.[3] Similarly, on the St Albans' manors the peasants could make wills (presumably unfettered by the presence of the lord's representative) which were proved before the cellarer. Those of free men were dealt with by the superior court at St Albans itself.[4]

Even with these limitations, however, the fact that wills were encouraged by the Church, and allowed by more liberal lords, is of considerable importance, and marked a definite stage in the struggle for emancipation. The right to leave their personal goods to whomsoever they would was not compatible with the legalist's doctrines, but must have made for happiness and a sense of security on all those manors where it flourished.

The death of the head of the family saw his wife and children deprived of some of their goods, which were taken as "heriot" or "mortuary", and it also left them to face the problem of succession to his unfree holdings. In theory the land belonged to the lord and reverted to him on death, when he could re-allocate it as he would. In very rare cases he allowed a different family to take the holding and evicted the old tenants, but in general he left the same family in possession, ceremonially admitting them at the Manor Court, after due payment of *gersuma* and the swearing of loyalty had been performed. Then, and only then, could they feel safe as they saw the scribe making his entry of the whole transaction in the Court Roll to which they could, and did, appeal if their rights were challenged. In most manors the widow seems to have enjoyed the privilege of holding the tenement during her lifetime. This was called "Freebench", and she was entitled to hold it unmolested so long as she remained

---

[1] *Vale Royal Ledger Book*, 119.   [2] *Ramsey Cart.* I, 477.
[3] *Ibid.* I, 384, 411.
[4] *Wynslowe Rolls*, 53 b. Cf. Seebohm, *op. cit.* 30.

unmarried and chaste. It was considered to be a sign of villein tenure that the whole of the tenement went to the widow, rather than only a third or a half as would be the case in a free holding, or if the property were held at a fixed money rent.[1]

Such was the general practice, but it is worth noting a few examples of the ways in which men sought to protect themselves against vagaries of their lord or the uncertainty of local custom. At times, for instance, men would make a fictitious surrender of their holding during their lifetime, and would receive it back again, after payment of a fine, with the express provision, enrolled in the court, that son or daughter were to succeed.[2] Or again, a man obtained leave to make over half his holding to his wife, to last for the term of her life,[3] thus making sure that she would be provided for in any circumstance. A long series of customs, said to date from 1343, show us in detail the arrangements on the manors of the Abbess of Shaftesbury; and, in their complicated ingenuity, they are evidence of the many possibilities that were available there, and probably on many other manors.[4] The *jus viduae* was well enough established throughout England to be regarded as a right on which the widow could reckon, and with which she could make bargains or demise at her convenience.

The widow who found herself left with her husband's holding was not *ipso facto* in an enviable position. Everything depended on the circumstances. If she had a large holding, and no able-bodied sons to cultivate it and to render her necessary obligations on the lord's demesne, she at once found herself in difficulties. The lord could not countenance his land being allowed to deteriorate through lack of cultivation, nor could he do without the work she (or her deputies) were liable to perform on his own lands. Consequently, if the widow was unable to carry out these liabilities, she was forced to surrender her holding or to make arrangements (with the lord's sanction) for the proper performance of her duties. If she surrendered them outright she

---

[1] Pollock and Maitland, *op. cit.* II, 418–26. References to the widow's right will be found widespread; e.g. *E.H.R.* April 1928, 219; *Durham Halmote Rolls*, 9, 18, 85; Suff. Inst. Arch. II, 232; Som. Arch. Soc. xxx, 77; Selden Soc. IV, 121, etc.
[2] Page, Camb. Hist. Soc. III, 127; cf. *Crowland Estates*, 109 ff.
[3] *Hales Rolls*, 108.
[4] *Wilts Arch. Mag.* V, 7 ff.; cf. XLI, 174.

had nothing to live upon and must needs seek the charity of a relative or neighbour. More frequently she made an agreement with her relatives or some other person whereby she handed over her land in return for an adequate home and proper provision for her food and clothing. On some manors, at least, this matter was not left as a private affair, which could be easily repudiated, but constituted a definite binding agreement, which was enrolled at the Manor Court and received the lord's assent. We may take as a good example a case at Hales, in 1281, wherein a son and his mother came to an agreement whereby Agnes, widow of Thomas Brid, surrendered to Thomas her elder son

all the land she held in the vill or in other places, on condition that he will, so long as she lives, honourably and fully provide for her as follows. At Michaelmas next she shall receive from him a quarter of wheat, a quarter of oats, and a bushel of peas. On All Saints' Day (1 Nov.) she shall have five cart-loads of sea-coal. Eight days before Christmas she is to have a quarter of wheat, a quarter of oats and a bushel of peas; on Good Friday a quarter of wheat and a quarter of oats; at Pentecost 5s. of good money; and at Midsummer half a quarter of wheat and a quarter of oats. Also Thomas engages to build at his own expense a suitable house for Agnes to live in, 30 feet in length and 14 feet in width within the walls, of timber with three new doors and two windows. And the aforesaid shall be carried out fully from year to year so long as Agnes shall live. Thomas shall bring the things to her door, or send them by one of his family. And Thomas will answer to the lord for all customs and services known to belong to the land. If Thomas has not the grain ready at the time, he must pay her its value according to the price of the better grain in the market, outside seed corn. And if it should happen that the terms of this agreement are not carried out Thomas binds himself to pay half a mark to the Pittancer of the Convent, so often as Agnes, with the testimony of two lawful men, shall find it necessary to appeal to the Abbot and the Convent. If this should be the case Agnes can forthwith resume possession of the land and deal with it as she pleases in spite of the agreement. And to ensure the perpetual force and memory of the agreement, before it was recited word for word in the full court, it was written down in the rental of the Abbey by the wish of both parties, Nicholas then being Abbot, and brother Geoffrey the Cellarer.[1]

Here we see that Agnes is to have a house, money and corn at stated intervals, while other entries in these same rolls show that

[1] *Hales Rolls,* 166.

such arrangements were not uncommon. Sometimes a father makes over his holding to his son,[1] or a brother to a brother,[2] or more rarely an old man makes an arrangement with the lord.[3] Sometimes elderly people make arrangements which they hope will make their declining years easier, and hand over half their tenement at once, and the whole upon their death, on condition that the recipients serve them as long as they live.[4] All this is peculiar to the manor of Hales, only in so far as it is more fully stated there than in most other places. The *Durham Halmote Rolls*, for instance, meant much the same as is fully expressed in the arrangement between Agnes and Thomas Brid, when they said that William takes his father John's holding and promises to sustain him "honorifice pro posse suo".[5] On another Durham manor the father is to be lodged and given 3 rods of land, i.e. one in each field, for his own,[6] and Dr F. M. Page has shown how a similar practice obtained on the Cambridgeshire manors of the monks of Crowland. There she finds that

the share varied in amount and detail, but preserved the same essential characteristics. There was a "camera" or "receptaculum" (defined in 1345 as one-third of a messuage) and usually a curtilage, a toft or garden, and one strip of land "in croft" went with it. In addition, a number of strips in the common-field were given—varying from one to six, but the allowance was nearly always divided between the three fields.[7]

Widows then, like the old and feeble, were not uncared for under the manorial regime, and the death of the head of the family saw the rule pass into the hands of his widow and not into those of one of his sons. So long as she remained unmarried and chaste her rights remained intact. Thus, at High Bicklington, in Devon, a widow is stated to have retained a life-interest in the whole of the lands held by her husband (unless she had

---

[1] *Hales Rolls*, 152, III, 53; cf. Bed. Hist. Rec. Soc. x, 471.
[2] *Op. cit.* 316.
[3] *Op. cit.* 336; cf. Bed. Hist. Rec. Soc. XIII, 338*k*, where a widow surrenders a tenement to the Abbot of Wardon who gives her "in regard of charity" a messuage and two pair of shoes at Christmas.
[4] *Op. cit.* III, 38; cf. III, 55, 93.
[5] *Durham Halmote Rolls*, 9; cf. *Manor of Manydown* (Hants Rec. Soc.), 130, where the son promises to sustain his father *bene et competenter*.
[6] *Op. cit.* 10; cf. 85, 115.
[7] *Camb. Hist. Journ.* III, 130; and cf. *Crowland Estates*, 109 ff.

previously relinquished it) and this interest could only be forfeited by some act of her own, such as re-marriage without
permission or unchastity. Her re-marriage was obviously a
matter of consequence, both to her lord and to her family, for it
put a new man in virtual charge of the family holding for the
time being. He might prove to be a good or a bad husbandman,
and this would seriously affect them all. He seems to have had
no more than a temporary right to the holding, however, for,
according to the few cases that came before the Manor Courts, the
rights of the children of the first marriage to the holding seem
always to be protected at the expense of the husband and any
children of the second marriage, unless the woman had been
allowed to surrender her right and seisin, and it had been
granted in court to her new husband.[1] Such an act meant that
any children of her first marriage were forever barred from her
holding, and we may well believe that this did not often happen,
but that, in general, a second husband was only allowed to enter
on his wife's holding on sufferance, and for the term of her life—
and often only during the minority of her children. In himself
he had no rights, and on the death of his wife was forced to give
up the holding.[2]

The other reason liable to cause the widow's holding to be
forfeited was unchastity, for the lord had an interest in her re-
marriage, and objected to any action on her part which would
make that less possible or which would tend to cheapen her in
the eyes of possible suitors. A West Country custom, reported
on several manors, says that the widow could recover her holding
if she rode into court on a ram, repeating the jingle:

> Here I am,
> Riding upon a black ram
> Like a whore, as I am...
> Therefore, I pray you, Mr Steward,
> Let me have my land again.[3]

On the death of the widow the holding went *in toto* to one of
the children. The division of the holding was repugnant to
medieval law, and in some places the elder, in some the younger,

---

[1] Selden Soc. II, 29.
[2] *Ancient Deeds*, IV, 175; *Cal. Inquis. Misc.* II, 76 (No. 299).
[3] *Law Mag.* New Series, XIII, 33, and cf. references there.

son inherited. No convincing reasons have been given for this curious state of affairs, and its history is still obscure. "Borough English", as it came to be called by an accident—the succession of the youngest son—was widespread, but not universal,[1] except in Kent, where all conditions of land-holding were peculiar.

[1] For full discussion and references, see Pollock and Maitland, *op. cit.* II, 279. A useful article in Suff. Inst. Arch. II, 227 ff., notes and analyses the variations of this custom, and says that Borough English was law on 84 Suffolk manors, 28 Surrey manors and 135 Sussex manors.

" Merrie England"

CHAPTER X

"MERRIE ENGLAND"

THE picture which has slowly been building itself up in these pages has shown the medieval peasant in his home and in his fields, at church and at the Manor Court, and has occupied itself with many of his activities. But what, it may be asked, of his leisure? Where is the "Merrie England" which for long has been associated with this age? The questions demand an answer, both because so much absurdity has been written about a past which never existed in reality, and also because it would be a patently untrue picture of any society which omitted all account of its lighter moments.

Yet, as a preliminary, let us take one more rapid survey of the peasant's daily life, superficial and imperfect though it must inevitably be. We cannot too constantly remember that much that to us is picturesque or even amusing, bore a different aspect to the men of the thirteenth century, and we must ever be on our guard lest we impute our feelings and ideas to those remote times. When Dr Dryasdust of York, as Sir Walter Scott remarks,

is placed in his own snug parlour, and surrounded by all the comforts of an Englishman's fireside, he is not half so much inclined to believe that his own ancestors led a very different life from himself—that the shattered tower, which now forms a vista from his window, held a baron who would have hung him up at his own door without any form of trial—that the hinds, by whom his little pet farm is managed, would, a few centuries ago, have been his slaves.

We shall be making a rough guess at the medieval peasant's condition if we observe the present circumstances of the small peasant-proprietor in France, Germany or Austria. Tens of thousands of French "small-holders" are facing the daily struggle now that their forbears endured many generations ago. They are freed of week-works and boon-works, they no longer are subject to certain "customs of the country" which exact tallage or chevage, or the like, nor are they forced to grind here nor sell there. But the land is always there: harsh, exacting, insatiate, and rapidly overcoming the puny efforts man can put into it unless he is constantly fighting. And the fight is unending—the harvest is but the signal for the autumn ploughing; and the autumn ploughing for the sowing, and so on. Season follows season: the rhythmic passage of the year drags in its wake the rural society. And this society, now as then, is a unit, a little world of its own. Necessarily the great world affects it, and the fair once a year or the weekly markets take the villager some miles out of his own fields just as they did in the Middle Ages. But otherwise, the village is the unit, and there in the main life goes on as it always has and (seemingly, to the peasant at least) always will. There are a few days or hours of happiness, but on the morrow the old routine reasserts itself. Always, as the day wears on to evening, in the falling dusk the horses and oxen are put into their stalls for the night. The cows are milked and bedded down. Lights move about the farm outbuildings as the tired men assure themselves that everything is well for the night. Meanwhile, the housewife, busied at her fire, tends the soup and makes all ready for the men's return. When at last they come and gather round the table, set out with its rude and meagre cutlery and platters, the evening meal begins—bread, soup, cheese, beer—the same meal eaten by peasants since the beginning of time as it seems. There they talk or jest or argue as the occasion serves; and, after the meal, perhaps sit awhile by the dying embers before fatigue calls them to sleep, only in order to begin yet another day.

That is the background: and in that endless routine most of their life is spent, and so it was with their ancestors six centuries ago. There are, however, a few days now and then given over to festivity, and a few hours snatched from this grim travail with the soil. It is to these that we must now turn, in order to see yet another side of medieval peasant life.

We may well start with John Stow's translation of the famous account by Fitzstephen of the manner in which the Londoner of the twelfth century refreshed himself when work was put on one side.

Every yeare also at Shrovetuesday, (that we may begin with childrens sports, seeing we al have beene children,) the schoole boyes do bring Cockes of the game to their Master, and all the forenoone delight themselves in Cockfighting: after dinner all the youthes go into the fields to play at bal. The schollers of every schoole have their ball, or [staff], in their hands: the auncient and wealthy men of the Citie come foorth on horse-backe to see the sport of the yong men, and to take part of the pleasure in beholding their agilitie. Every Friday in Lent a fresh company of young men comes into the field on horse-backe, and the best horsman conducteth the rest. Then march forth the citizens sons, and other yong men with disarmed launces and shields, and there practise feates of warre.... In Easter holy dayes they fight battailes on the water. A shield is hanged on a pole, fixed in the midst of the stream; a boat is prepared without oares to bee caried by the violence of the water, and in the fore part thereof standeth a yong man readie to give charge upon the shield with his launce; if so be hee breaketh his launce against the shield, and doth not fall, he is thought to have performed a worthy deed. If so be without breaking his launce he runneth strongly against the shield, downe he falleth into the water, for the boat is violently forced with the tide; but on each side stand great numbers to see, and laugh therat. In the holy dayes all the Somer the youths are exercised in leaping, dancing, shooting, wrastling, casting the stone, and practising their shields: the Maidens trip in their Timbrels, and daunce as long as they can well see. In Winter, every holy day before dinner, the Boares prepared for brawne are set to fight, or else Buls and Beares are bayted.

When the great fenne or Moore, which watreth the wals of the Citie on the Northside, is frozen, many yong men play upon the yce; some, striding as wide as they may, do slide swiftly...some tie bones to their feete, and under their heeles, and shoving themselves by a little picked staffe, doe slide as swiftly as a bird flieth in the ayre, or an arrow out of a Crossebow...thus farre Fitzstephen of Sportes. [Stow continues] Now for sportes and pastimes yearely used. First, in the feaste of Christmas,...every mans house, as also their parish churches, were decked with holme, Ivie, Bayes, and whatsoever the season of the yeare afforded to be greene.... In the moneth of May, namely on May day in the morning, every man, except impediment, would walke into the sweete meadows and greene woods, there to rejoyce their spirites with the beauty and savour of sweete flowers, and with the harmony of birds praysing God in their kind.[1]

We must discount something for the romantic glow cast over the past by Stow's eager imagination, and make other necessary allowances, but when all is done, does not this passage suggest to us innumerable happy hours spent on water or in the fields, not only by the Londoners, but by the peasants of the days

---

[1] *A Survey of London*, 1603, 92. Holme=holly.

of Fitzstephen and for centuries afterwards? In the countryside, even if the opportunities for merriment were more limited, the great Church festivals of Christmas and Easter, or the more popular festivals associated with the harvests, gave considerable opportunities for enjoyment. At Christmas, for example, work ceased altogether for some fourteen or fifteen days, and often a feast was provided for the peasantry by the lord.[1] Thus in 1314 the customal of Northcory in the diocese of Wells tells us of one William Brygge, a villein who had the right of "*gestum* and medale...but he must bring with him to the *gestum* his own cloth, cup and trencher, and take away all that is left on his cloth, and he shall have for himself and his neighbours one wastel [loaf] cut in three, for the ancient Christmas game to be played with the said wastel".[2]

What exactly took place at the "Christmas game" is a matter of some dispute, and we need not stay to argue it, but from frequent references to "the Christmas play", or to expenses during the Christmas season, we may infer that the manor house saw much conviviality and mirth during the period brought to a close by Twelfth Night. On one of the manors of St Paul's, for example, a peasant was appointed to watch all night and to keep up a good fire in the hall,[3] while on many Glastonbury manors there was a feast at the manor hall. The tenants cut and carried the logs for the Yule fire: each brought his faggot of brushwood, lest the cook should serve his portion raw, and each had his own dish and mug, and a napkin of some kind, "if he wanted to eat off a cloth". There was plenty of bread and broth and beer, with two kinds of meat. At East Pennard the serfs had the right to four places at the Yule feast and each man was entitled to have a fine white loaf, and a good helping of meat, and to sit drinking after dinner in the manor hall.[4]

To while away the long winter nights popular amusements were everywhere to be found. They were essentially of the folk, although they had been much affected by Christian elements, so that it was a strange mixture of pagan and Christian that had

[1] *Law Mag.* N.S. xiv, 351. Cf. Tusser, ed. Hartley, 122; Sussex Rec. Soc. xxxi, 15, 18, 23, 42, etc.
[2] *Hist. MSS. Com. Wells*, i, 335.
[3] *D.S.P.* xxxiv.
[4] *Glas. Rentalia*, 244. For details, see 97, 126, 127.

evolved by the twelfth and thirteenth centuries. All this is admirably dealt with in Sir E. K. Chambers' fascinating volume, *The Medieval Stage*, where the development of the various elements which went to the making of the medieval play are analysed and discussed. To the lord and his dependents, however, the strange history behind the Christmas festivities or the setting of the Midsummer watch were mysteries of which they knew or suspected nothing. Christmas, to them, was a brief respite in the yearly cycle of events, bringing its central and heavenly message, but also bringing much that was of the earth earthy. The villager, gaping admiringly at the pranks and buffoonery of the mummers' play, or joining in the choruses of the songs, or taking part in the dispute between the holly and the ivy, in which the young men and women of the village all took sides, forgot for a while the fatigues of the autumn and the ardours of the coming spring.

The spirit of the festival is well caught by a carol:

> *Make we merry both more and less,*
> *For now is the time of Christmas!*

Let no man come into this hall,
Groom, page, nor yet marshall,
But that some sport he bring withal!
> *For now is the time of Christmas!*

If that he say he can not sing,
Some other sport then let him bring!
That it may please at this feasting
> *For now is the time of Christmas!*

If he say he can nought do,
Then for my love ask him no mo!
But to the stocks then let him go!
> *For now is the time of Christmas!*[1]

So from time to time throughout the year the great religious festivals gave the peasant a few hours of pleasure making: the ceremonies connected with Easter would enthral him with such dramatic incidents as crawling to the Cross on the Good Friday, or the rending of the veil which had hidden the sanctuary throughout Lent; or perhaps, if he were near some great Abbey

---

[1] A. W. Pollard, *Fifteenth Century Prose and Verse*, 86. More and less = rich and poor. See also Chambers and Sidgwick, *Early English Lyrics*, 232 ff. and R. L. Greene, *The Early English Carols*, 4 ff. for other examples.

church, he might behold the elaborate miming which portrayed to the congregation the rising of Christ and His absence from the tomb. Then again at the Corpus Christi feast he would take part in the processions, and enjoy such rough dramatic representations of the events of the Scriptures as the wandering players, or the nearby town gilds could perform. Less closely associated with the Church were the great popular festivals of May Day, or of Midsummer Day, when the whole village gave itself up to mirth and dance. "From a very early period in England the summer festivals were celebrated elaborately with dance and song and games, and there are many references to them in the fourteenth century",[1] and these references make no suggestion that the games are new. On the contrary they tacitly assume their antiquity, and "somour games" may be looked on as one of the oldest elements of English social life.

As well as these ceremonies which were part of the communal life of the whole village we must also notice the way in which the great occasions of life in the individual families were celebrated. Birth, marriage and death were all eagerly seized upon by the peasant as a welcome relaxation from his daily cares. Marriage, indeed, was so scandalously made an occasion of immoderate mirth that we have a constant series of episcopal pronouncements against the lax behaviour of those attending the marriage ceremony. Bishop Poore, about 1223, ordered that marriages "be celebrated reverently and with honour, not with laughter or sport, or in taverns or at public potations or feasts".[2] A number of similar injunctions during the next hundred years show how difficult it was to keep these "bride ales" (as they were often called) within reasonable limits.[3] After the church ceremony the party would adjourn to a private house, or to the village alehouse, and there drink heavily of the ale which had been brewed for the occasion, and the profits of which went to the new bride.[4] These "bride ales" attracted such characters as Perkin, the prentice of *The Cokes Tale*, and the Wife of Bath herself.[5]

---

[1] Baskervill, *Studies in Philology*, XVII, 51 ff. and references there.
[2] *Charters and Docs. of Salisbury* (R.S.), 154; cf. Wilkins, *op. cit.* I, 581.
[3] See Wilkins, *op. cit.* I, 595; II, 135, 513. *E.H.R.* XXXI, 294–5.
[4] *Piers Plowman*, B. II, 54; C. III, 56; and for much information of later conditions, see Brand's *Popular Antiquities*, ed. Ellis (1841), II, 90 ff.
[5] *C.T. Cokes Tale*, l. 11; *Wife of Bath's Prologue*, l. 558.

Funeral ceremonies were also the occasion of much rude merriment. The vigil or wake had its serious moments, but it also had much about it that caused moralists to link "wakes" and taverns together as leading to sin. In 1342, a church council denounced wakes as giving opportunities for fornication and theft,[1] while a century earlier bishops had prohibited singing, games and choruses during the time the dead person still lay in the house.[2] Although we have little direct evidence for our period the constant series of prohibitions from Anglo-Saxon times onwards against pastimes at vigils for the dead, together with the abundant evidence from the sixteenth century onwards, makes us certain that throughout the Middle Ages elaborate meals and drinkings, accompanied by boisterous behaviour, were an inseparable part of funeral ceremonies. The rich, as we should expect, made much of these occasions, and rich and poor were summoned to pay their last respects to the dead, and were lavishly entertained during and after the ceremonies. The death of Maurice, the fourth Lord Berkeley, on 8 June 1368, was the signal for the reeve on his manor of Hinton to start fatting up one hundred geese for his funeral, "and divers other Reeves of other Manors the like, in geese, duckes, and other pultry".[3] These were but a small part of what was provided, as may be seen from more detailed accounts of some fifteenth-century funeral arrangements.[4] And there, it will be noticed, the presence of "poor men" is constantly mentioned, and we may feel sure that the funeral of the lord of the manor, no less than the funeral of a neighbour, was a day of mixed sorrowing and feasting for the medieval peasant. Sidney's famous phrase "Hornpipes and funerals" is but another way of indicating the frame of mind which was capable of turning "the house of mourning and prayer into a house of laughter and excess".

Mention of the "bride ales" and "wake ales" recalls one of the most popular forms of medieval festivity. Scot ale, church ale, play ale, lamb ale, Whitsun ale, hock ale, and the like: we

---

[1] Wilkins, *op. cit.* II, 707.
[2] *Ibid.* I, 600, 625, 675; cf. III, 61, 68.
[3] *Lives of Berkeleys*, I, 378.
[4] See my *The Pastons and their England*, 197–9. Cf. the arrangements for a clerk's funeral, *Arch. Journ.* XVIII, 72.

are constantly meeting with such terms in medieval documents.[1] Each of these ales was the excuse for much heavy drinking, together with dance and games. They were frowned upon by the Church (as we have seen in speaking of the "bride ales" and "wake ales") and with good reason, for they undoubtedly encouraged licence. Yet, all the efforts of the Church could not suppress them, and little by little we find the Church forced to recognise the church ales in an endeavour to exercise some control over their more extravagant phases.[2]

But even though the church ales gradually came under ecclesiastical control, many other ales remained. The main function of many of these was undoubtedly to provide money for the lord or his bailiff or the forester who held them, and in consequence they were not always welcomed by those who were invited. They were, in fact, a kind of bazaar, which all had to attend and at which all had to buy. The Glastonbury tenants, for example, were forced to appear thrice a year at ales held by their lord: the married and young men on Saturday after dinner and to drink "as at Cunninghale", and to have three draughts (*ter ad potandum*). On the Sunday and Monday each husband and wife were bound to bring 1*d*., the young men on Sunday their ½*d*., but on Monday they might drink without fee (*libere*), if not found sitting above the settle (*scamnum*), but if found above that boundary to pay as the others. The *plena scotalla* lasted three days, and the peasant was summoned to attend three such ales: one before Michaelmas to which he went with his wife and gave 3*d*., and two after Michaelmas, at which he gave 2½*d*.[3] Many other entries tell us of oppressive sums being exacted at the ales,[4] and of some officials using their power to force men to attend.[5]

The village ale-house must have its place in any account of village life. It is true that many families brewed their own ale, but there was room for some houses (perhaps a little larger than most villagers' cots) where "bride ales", or convivial meetings

---

[1] For much information, see *Statutes of the Realm*, I, 120, 234, 321; *Cust. Rents*, 150–4 and further references given there.
[2] The subject of church ales may be studied in *Arch. Journ.* XL, 1 ff.; Coulton, *Medieval Studies*, 153, 161, and Wilkins, I, 474, 530, 574, 600, 624, 642, 672, etc.
[3] *Glas. Rentalia*, 103, 143.
[4] *Select Pleas of Forest*, Selden Soc. XIII, 126; *Cust. Rents*, 150.
[5] *D.S.P.* cvii.

could be held. We have only to turn the pages of the preachers and didactic writers to see what an evil reputation they had. "The devil's chapel" was well known to the medieval moralist, and Dr Owst in his learned *Literature and Pulpit in Medieval England* devotes several pages[1] to the outbursts of Bromyard, Rypon and other English preachers, who season their discourses with "details of the scene, such as the rude pot-house songs, snatches of lewd conversation from the bench of cronies, the low tricks played amongst this fellowship of Satan".[2] Apart from this (and indeed before Dr Owst's untiring researches brought such a wealth of confirmatory material together) such writers as Langland and Skelton had given us vivid pictures of the medieval tavern and its intimates. There are few passages in all medieval literature which present a more graphic re-creation of the medieval scene than that recounting Glutton's adventures in the tavern which welcomes him on his way to church:

> But Breton the brewster bad him good morrow,
> And asked him with that whither he was going:
> "To holy church", said he, "to hear the service,
> And so I will be shriven and sin no longer."
> "I have good ale, gossip: Glutton, will you try it?"
> "What have you?" he asked—"any hot spices?"
> "I have pepper and peonies", she said, "and a pound of garlic,
> And a farthing worth of fennel seed for fasting seasons."
> Then Gluttony goes in with a great crowd after,

and so the debauch begins, and continues with wagers and good cheer.

> Then there was laughing and lowering and "let the cup go it",
> And sitting till evensong and singing catches,
> Till Glutton had gulped a gallon and a gill.
>
> .   .   .   .
>
> He could neither step nor stand till a staff held him,
> And then began to go like a gleeman's bitch,
> Sometimes aside and sometimes backwards,
> Like one who lays lures to lime wild-fowl.
> And he drew to the door all dimmed before him,
> He stumbled on the threshold and was thrown forwards.[3]

[1] *Op. cit.* 425 ff. and see Index, *Taverns.*
[2] *Ibid.* 438.
[3] *Piers Plowman,* v, 422 ff., as modernised in the excellent version of H. W. Wells, 1935.

Literature tells us of many of these tavern-haunters: Glutton, or the good wife and her gossips who frequent the tavern since "Whatsoever many man thynk, we com for nowght but for good drynk"; or that other roisterer who sang so lustily:

> Back and side, go bare, go bare,
> Both hand and foot go cold,
> But belly, God send thee good ale enough,
> Whether it be new or old![1]

Documents, on the other hand, do not help us so much. After all, the ale-house was outside the manorial scheme (save for a tax on ale brewed and a general supervision of its quality), and unless strife and bloodshed arose there, the lord cared little how his men spent their time lounging on the tavern-bench, and drinking and merrymaking "till the stars 'gan to appear".[2]

We must not exaggerate the number of such ales and drinking bouts, and we must also take account of the convivial meetings which marked various stages of the agricultural year. The Abbot of Ramsey, for example, on the day that the men on various of his manors completed the mowing of "the Haycroft", gave them 8*d*. or 12*d*. from his purse for a drinking festivity called Scythale.[3]

The conclusion of the hay-cutting seems to have been the occasion for a widespread custom by which the lord released into the field a sheep or ram, and it was the business of the peasants to catch it before it could escape from them. If they were successful in this it formed a major part in the feast they held to celebrate the end of their labours, and evidently the whole affair was an enjoyable bit of rough hurly-burly, once the last load of hay had been taken from the field.[4] Again, on St John's Eve, we hear of a ram being given to the villagers for their feast, as at East Monkton, where a procession round the corn was made, the men carrying brands of fire in their hands.[5] Agricultural opera-

---

[1] Chambers and Sidgwick, *Early English Lyrics*, 229; cf. 222–8.

[2] *Cust. Rents*, 37; *Wynslowe Rolls, passim*; *Hales Rolls, passim*. See Selden Soc. I, 27, for false measure; *Wakefield Rolls*, II, 3, 4, 6, 45, etc. for weak beer; *Hales Rolls*, XXXIV, 128, 149, 372 for ale-tasters.

[3] *Ramsey Cart.* I, 49, 286, 301, 311; II, 18, 45; III, 61; *Worc. Priory Reg.* 14*b*, 34*a*, 43*a*, 65*b*.

[4] *Ramsey Cart.* I, 298, 307, 476; *Glouc. Cart.* III, 64.

[5] *Law Mag.* N.S. XIV, 350, and other references given there; *Paroch. Antiq.* II, 137; *Inquis. Post Mortem*, Ed. I, vol. II, 313; *Cust. Rents*, 56.

tions, as was natural from their importance, gave rise to a variety of similar festivals (Plough Monday, Hock Day, Midsummer Eve, Martinmas), culminating in the elaborate celebrations at the end of the corn harvest—virtually the end of the agricultural year.

The ale-house, again, was frequently attacked because it was there that folk indulged in dancing, and although we do not hear much in England concerning that most common of medieval amusements, yet from the frequency and violence with which it was attacked by the medieval moralists we may realise something of its prevalence.[1] It kept men and women from church and was said to be provocative of sin. Bromyard, the great Dominican preacher of Chaucer's day, constantly rebukes those who go to dances, especially women, decked in their bewitching finery, who entice men from their prayers.[2] His is but one voice among many of those who decry the dance. Yet "dance, and Provençal song, and sun-burnt mirth" had a way of breaking in, and who will wish to deny the medieval peasant those hours of pleasure on village green or even at the tavern, despite the undoubted fact that "unclene kyssynges, clippynges and other unhonest handelynges" were often part of the proceedings?

Not unnaturally, however, the open countryside all about him provided the peasant with some of his happiest hours, when, despite all rules and penalties, he hunted and snared in his lord's woods and preserves. Poaching, we have seen, was one of the most common of medieval offences, and was indulged in by all the villagers from the parson downwards. Laws were enacted against the keeping of hunting dogs or implements; and, in the areas of the royal forests, savage penalties were inflicted on those found within the precincts. But all in vain: the temptation was too great, and whether it was a royal stag, or only a miserable coney, the excitement of the chase, and at times it must be admitted sheer poverty, drove men to break the law, and to run the risks consequent upon being caught red-handed.

---

[1] The whole subject of the medieval dance has been treated at great length by Dr Coulton in his *Med. Village*, 255, 275, 425, 558, and *Five Centuries of Religion*, I, Appendix, 23, and references are given there to other writings. See also G. R. Owst, *Holborn Review* (1926), 32, and *Literature and Pulpit*, *passim*.

[2] S.v. *Bellum*. See *Literature and Pulpit*, 393-5, to which I owe the reference.

A glance at a set of precedents for use in a manorial court shows us that cases of poaching were expected to occur in the normal course of business. In one specimen case we are told of a man and his servant taken with two greyhounds within the lord's park. The defendant pleads that he had taken no beast of any kind, and adds:

Not but that I will confess that my two greyhounds escaped from the hand of my small boy by reason of his weakness, or that I followed them to the park and entered thereby a breach that I found already used, and pursued my hounds and retook them, so that no damage was done to any manner of wild beast on that occasion.[1]

Unfortunately the steward adjourned the case till the next court "to speak of the amends", so that we do not know what effect this specious plea had upon him.

Or take again one of the most vivid pictures we have of rustic life which is contained in another specimen plea from the same manuscript. It reads:

Sir, for God's sake do not take it ill of me if I tell thee the truth, how I went the other evening along the bank of this pond and looked at the fish which were playing in the water, so beautiful and so bright, and for the great desire I had for a tench I laid me down on the bank and just with my hands quite simply, and without any other device, I caught that tench and carried it off; and now I will tell thee the cause of my covetousness and my desire. My dear wife had lain abed a right full month, as my neighbours who are here know, and she could never eat or drink anything to her liking, and for the great desire she had to eat a tench I went to the bank of the pond to take just one tench; and that never other fish from the pond did I take.[2]

One last glimpse of this side of the peasant's life comes from the fourteenth-century poem *The Parlement of the Thre Ages*,[3] with its magnificent account of a night in the woods. It is difficult to believe that the writer of this poem was not speaking with an intimate knowledge of what had happened in many an English woodland of his time:

---

[1] Selden Soc. IV, 53; cf. 34, "Of chasing or taking beasts in the Lord's park".

[2] Selden Soc. IV, 55; cf. other precedents, 37, 75. For actual cases, see pp. 122, 124, 128, 131; cf. *Durham Halmote Rolls*, 91, 131, 144, 178. Davenport, *op. cit.* 75.

[3] Edited by Sir I. Gollancz, 1915.

In the monethe of Maye when mirthes bene fele,
And the sesone of somere when softe bene the wedres,
Als I went to the wodde my werdes to dreghe,
In-to þe schawes my-selfe a schotte me to gete
5 At ane hert or ane hynde, happen as it myghte:
And as Dryghtyn the day droue from þe heuen,
Als I habade one a banke be a bryme syde,
There the gryse was grene growen with floures—
The primrose, the pervynke, and piliole þe riche—
10 The dewe appon dayses donkede full faire,
Burgons & blossoms & braunches full swete,
And the mery mystes full myldely gane falle:
The cukkowe, the cowschote, kene were þay bothen,
And the throstills full throly threpen in the bankes,
15 And iche foule in that frythe faynere þan oþer
That the derke was done & the daye lightenede:
Hertys and hyndes one hillys þay gouen,
The foxe and the filmarte þay flede to þe erthe,
The hare hurkles by hawes, & harde thedir dryves,
20 And ferkes faste to hir fourme & fatills hir to sitt.
Als I stode in that stede one stalkynge I thoghte;
Bothe my body and my bowe I buskede with leues;
And turnede to-wardes a tree & tariede there a while;
And als I lokede to a launde a littill me be-syde,
25 I seghe ane herte with ane hede, ane heghe for the nones;
Alle vnburneschede was þe beme, full borely þe mydle,

1 In May, when there are many things to enjoy, and in the summer season when airs are soft, I went to the wood to take my luck, and
5 in among the shaws to get a shot at hart or hind, as it should happen. And, as the Lord drove the day through the heavens, I stayed on a bank beside a brook where the grass was green and starred with flowers—primroses, periwinkles and the rich penny-
10 royal. The dew dappled the daisies most beautifully, and also the buds, blossoms and branches, while around me the soft mists began to fall. Both the cuckoo and pigeon were singing loudly, and the
15 throstles in the bank-sides eagerly poured out their songs, and every bird in the wood seemed more delighted than his neighbour that darkness was done and the daylight returned.

Harts and hinds betake themselves to the hills; the fox and pole-cat seek their earths; the hare squats by the hedges, hurries and
20 hastens thither to her forme and prepares to lurk there. As I stood in that place the idea of stalking came to me, so I covered both body and bow with leaves, turned in behind a tree and waited there
25 awhile. And as I gazed in the glade near by me I saw a hart with tall antlers: the main stem was unburnished and in the middle very strong. And he was full grown and adorned with horns of

And he assommet and sett of vi. and of fyve,
And þer-to borely and brode and of body grete,
And a coloppe for a kynge, cache hym who myghte.
30 Bot there sewet hym a sorwe þat seruet hym full ȝerne,
That woke & warned hym when the wynde faylede,
That none so sleghe in his slepe with sleghte scholde hym dere,
And went the wayes hym by-fore when any wothe tyde.
My lyame than full lightly lete I doun falle,
35 And to the bole of a birche my berselett I cowchide;
I waitted wisely the wynde by waggynge of leues,
Stalkede full stilly no stikkes to breke,
And crepite to a crabtre and couerede me ther-undere:
Then I bende vp my bowe and bownede me to schote,
40 Tighte vp my tylere and taysede at the hert:
Bot the sowre þat hym sewet sett vp the nese,
And wayttede wittyly abowte & wyndide full ȝerne.
Then I moste stonde als I stode, and stirre no fote ferrere,
For had I myntid or mouede or made any synys,
45 Alle my layke hade bene loste þat I hade longe wayttede.
Bot gnattes gretely me greuede and gnewen myn eghne;
And he stotayde and stelkett and starede full brode,
Bot at the laste he loutted doun & laughte till his mete
And I hallede to the hokes and the herte smote,
50 And happenyd that I hitt hym be-hynde þe lefte scholdire

six and five tines, and was large, broad and big of body: whoever
30 might catch him, he was a dish for a king. But there followed him a
fourth-year buck that most eagerly attended him, and aroused and
warned him when the wind failed, so that no one should be sly
enough to harm him in his sleep by stealth. He went in front of
him when any danger was to be feared.

I let the leash fall to the ground quietly, and settled down my
35 hound by the bole of a birch tree, and took careful note of the
wind from the fluttering of the leaves. I stalked on very quietly so
as to break no twigs, and crept to a crab-apple tree and hid underneath it.

40 Then I wound up my bow and prepared to shoot, drew up the
tiller and aimed at the hart, but the buck who attended the hart
lifted up his nose, looked cautiously around, and eagerly snuffed
about. Then, perforce, I had to stand without moving, and to stir
no foot, although gnats grievously troubled me and bit my eyes,
45 for if I had tried to move, or made any sign, all my sport, that I
had so long awaited, would have been lost. The hart paused, went
on cautiously, staring here and there, but at last he bent down and
began on his feed. Then I hauled to the hook (i.e. the trigger of the
50 cross-bow) and smote the hart. It so happened that I hit him

Þat þe blode braste owte appon bothe the sydes:
And he balkede and brayed and bruschede thrugh þe greues,
And alle had hurlede one ane hepe þat in the holte longede;
And sone the sowre þat hym sewet resorte to his feris,
55 And þay, for frayede of his fare, to þe fellys þay hyen;
And I hyede to my hounde and hent hym vp sone,
And louset my lyame and let hym vmbycaste;
The breris and the brakans were blody by-ronnen;
And he assentis to þat sewte and seches hym aftire,
60 There he was crepyde in-to a krage and crouschede to þe erthe;
Dede as a dore-nayle doun was he fallen.

behind the left shoulder and the blood streamed out on both sides.
He stopped: brayed and then brushed through the thickets, as if
everything in the wood had crashed down at the same moment.
55 Soon the attending buck went off to his mates, but they were
terrified by his manner, and took to the fells. I went to my hound,
and quickly grasped him and untied his leash, and let him cast
about. The briars and the bracken were smeared with blood, and
the hound picked up the scent and pursued the hart to where he
60 was, for he had crept into a cave, and, crouched to the earth, had
fallen down—dead as a door-nail.

So from time to time throughout the year the peasant had a
few hours of pleasure making: the great ecclesiastical celebrations at Easter, Whitsun and Corpus Christi, or the summer
festivals of May Day and Midsummer may serve to remind us of
such opportunities, and the records show how eagerly they were
seized. Robert Manning of Brunne, in his *Handlyng Synne*,
1303, declaims against the prevalence of these popular amusements which took people from Holy Church:

> Karolles, wrastlynges, or somour games,
> Who so ever haunteþ any swyche shames
> Yn cherche, oþer yn chercheȝerde,
> Of sacrylage he may be a ferde;
> Or entyrludes, or syngynge,
> Or tabure bete, or oþer pypynge,
> Alle swyche þyng forboden es,
> Whyle þe prest stondeþ at messe.[1]

---

[1] *Op. cit.* ll. 8989 ff. Cf. Owst, *Literature and Pulpit*, 362, quoting MS.
Harl. 45, fol. 58, where the common people are accused of enjoying "ydel
pleyes and japes, carolinges, makynge of fool contynaunces, to geve gifts to
iogelours...for to her ydel tales and japes, smytyng, snarlynge, ffyndyng
and usynge of novelryes...in wrastlynge, in other deedes of strength
doynge".

As we look back, however, across the centuries, we do not feel so censorious, and like to think of these peasants at the end of the day carolling their dissonant but joyous snatches on the alehouse bench; or watching stout carls like Chaucer's miller winning his ram or wrestling successfully against all comers; or following with rapt admiration Nicholas, that merry clerk, as he acted his part so well in the village pageant. These and like pleasures gave but few enough happy moments in lives which otherwise were so bare.

The Road to Freedom

CHAPTER XI

THE ROAD TO FREEDOM

IT is a commonplace of historians that the greater half of the people of England were unfree during the three centuries before the Peasants' Revolt of 1381. Yet any picture of medieval England would be false which failed to take account of the constant efforts to obtain freedom which were being made throughout this period. Everywhere men were at work seeking to break the bonds which tied them to the land, although unfortunately the evidence of their efforts is curiously thin and sporadic. Even in the fifteenth and sixteenth centuries it is difficult to produce a *catena* of unimpeachable documents to support what we know to have happened: that the year 1350 saw England with more than half its population serfs, while the year 1600 saw England without a single serf left in the realm. We can see several large-scale causes for this—the scarcity of labour after 1349; the new system of stock and land leases: the compelling attraction of the towns: the growing belief that money rents were more advantageous to the lord than the ancient feudal services— but the documentary evidence surviving and available so far is comparatively small. And in the earlier centuries it is even smaller, but it is sufficient to encourage us to examine this weak spot in the great structure of the manorial system. What were the possibilities before a determined man of the thirteenth or fourteenth century who wished to free himself of the ties holding him to the soil where he was born? Before we discuss this we must emphasise the one tremendous fact which must ever have been in the mind of the would-be runaway, and must have kept thousands on the manors. To leave "the villein nest" meant adventuring into the unknown without more than he could carry on his back.

For the majority of them livelihood and training were inextricably linked up with their fields, their flocks, and the little cot and close about it which they called home. None of these could they take with them: a single man might think the risk worth while—the married man was forced to hesitate, and often to draw back. So that the possibilities of freedom limit themselves as soon as the serf begins to think out their consequences. But besides absolute freedom there were states of comparative freedom which also held their attractions, and some of these were more easily within his reach. At the moment we may comprehensively group together all the various alleviations of his condition that the serf might obtain—commutation of works and personal services for money rents, freedom from the payments of such servile dues as tallage and merchet, and so on—and say that the serf moved a step towards a freer condition by getting quit of these, although he still remained a serf. To become a free man was more difficult: the safe and straightforward way was to win a manumission from his servile state from his lord. Then (more adventurous) was the temptation to run to the nearest town, hoping to win shelter within its walls; and, if fortune were kind, complete freedom would follow in due course. Lastly, there was the bold, hazardous, adventure of flight without definite objective, and with only a hope of better things to sustain him. In all these various ways the serf was attempting to gain his freedom. It will be our object in the following pages to see how this all worked out in practice; and, more difficult, to see how it all appeared to the serf.

We have already seen that by the thirteenth century a great many lords felt it necessary to have prepared elaborate extents or surveys of their lands and of their tenants, and from then onwards such documents give us invaluable evidence of the relation between lord and tenant. And among other things they allow us to watch the first efforts on the part of the unfree to shake off their servile obligations—be they of recent creation or of long standing—obligations which were now part of their daily being. Naturally, among the earliest ways of alleviating matters, men conceived the idea of flight. What this involved will be considered later.

At the moment all that is necessary is to make clear the manifold temptations which the serf saw attracting him in the haze of distance. We are not now concerned with what actually awaited him in the world, so much as with trying to ascertain how he was lured away to it. To a proportion of the workers on the manor any change seemed good; and it is natural enough that some were for drastic and others for mild methods of relief. But, as I have said, to leave the manor altogether without the lord's leave was too drastic for the majority, since it involved leaving wellnigh everything. Yet, in spite of this risk, every manor in England knew of so and so who had gone and was now living a free man in the nearby town, or farming his own acres as a free man in some distant manor. Every manor could recall how such and such ran away to marry outside the manor and refused every order from the Manor Court demanding his return. Every manor knew how difficult it was to lay hands on one of their number once he had got a few miles away. All these things must have been constantly brought forcibly to the notice of manorial lords, and the majority of them bowed to the necessity of coming to terms with their natives.[1] And, as the serf gathered more and more control over his own affairs, so the movement gathered momentum, and the fifteenth century saw its rapid consummation. Two points in particular may be stressed as having contributed most strongly to the desire for emancipation: the dislike of fixed services and works to be rendered to the lord, and a hatred of exactions such as tallage or the fine on marriage—in short a hatred of all charges which were characteristic of serfdom.

The dislike of fixed works and services is easily understandable: as we have seen on many manors they were a heavy burden, and often made vexatious and inconvenient demands on the serfs at moments when their own crops most needed their attention. At the same time it was often the lord who wished to make a change: "customary servants neglect their work, and it is necessary to guard against their fraud", says Walter of Henley.[2] Many lords saw that the forced work system was injurious to husbandry in the long run, and that they could do better with hired labour than with forced. The serfs naturally tried to buy off their more vexatious services, and relief from week-work with its ploughings, carryings and sowings was bargained for; and, on many manors, there came a day when all the various kinds of work were valued in money. This was advantageous to both parties: the lord knew what the works were worth and could take cash when it suited his purpose, while the serf knew the penalty

---

[1] For all this see below p. 291. [2] *Op. cit.* 11.

for each work left undone. In general it was the week-works which were most easily commuted, since they went on throughout the year and the lord could plan to hire labour to cover any defaults. Harvest-works—the boon-works—were not so easily redeemed, as it was so very advantageous to the lord to have his labour on the spot, and available at any moment that should seem propitious for gathering his crops.

But we must beware of introducing system and uniformity where neither in fact ever existed. The question of commutation has been discussed by scholars at some length during the past half century, and there is still much dispute and much to be done before any valuable generalisations can be made.[1] Nevertheless, all investigators are agreed that commutation was a very uncertain thing: it depended on a mass of conditions to which we have lost the key: it varied from manor to manor; it changed from year to year. On some manors its progress was steady, on others it was irregular. Miss Levett has pointed out that William of Wykeham's need of ready money with which to maintain New College had a far greater effect on commutation in his manors than had "that traditional parent of all economic development, the Black Death";[2] and we may suspect that the progress of commutation on every manor was conditioned more by local and personal causes than by any wide-reaching economic forces. Be this as it may, all we are concerned with is the fact that as a result of such causes, the serfs gradually won a measure of freedom. True they were still bound to the soil, but that uncertainty, which Bracton noted as characteristic of serfdom, is to some extent lessened; and, for the greater part of their time, they could carry on their own work unvexed by constant seigneurial demands.

---

[1] The whole problem of commutation may be profitably studied in the following: T. W. Page, *The End of Villainage in England*; H. L. Gray, "The Commutation of Villein Services in England before the Black Death" in *E.H.R.* xxix; A. E. Levett, *The Black Death on the Estates of the See of Winchester*; E. E. Power, *The Effects of the Black Death on Rural Organisation in England* in *History*, iii, and E. Lipson, *Economic History*, cap. iii. The last two volumes give an admirable survey of the problem and of the controversies, which I have very rapidly sketched above. There remains much work to be done in this field, but it is a full-time occupation for a whole band of students. A valuable contribution has been made by E. A. Kosminsky in his "Services and Money Rents in the Thirteenth Century", *Econ. Hist. Rev.* Vol. v, No. 2, pp. 24 ff.

[2] Levett, *op. cit.* 160.

Perhaps even deeper than their dislike of services was the serf's hatred of all those fines and charges which the lord could make, and which were so marked an indication of servile status. The nature and burden of such a fine as tallage has already been discussed,[1] and besides this there were a number of other fines which emphasised the gulf between free and serf. When the serf wished to marry his daughter, or sell or exchange his colts or steers, both were equally matters in which the lord interested himself, and in which he exacted a money payment before he would allow the peasant to do what he wished.[2] And this really states the whole matter in a sentence: to the lord the sale or alienation of a serf's daughter, or the sale of a serf's colt were much the same thing. Both were begotten on his manor by creatures of his, and before either could be disposed of he had a right to be consulted. What wonder if the serf hated conditions such as these, and tried his utmost to gain his liberty and freedom from these degrading obligations! He realised from an early hour that such servile dues were incompatible with any real notion of freedom, and they became an early object of attack. As well as this, once the peasant had succeeded in persuading his lord to accept a money rent in lieu of services, the road to freedom was enormously widened and the way to full emancipation in sight. In sight only, for the promised land was not easily won, and the serf, desirous of emancipation, had many difficulties before him which we must examine.

Since Church and State were in such close relation throughout the Middle Ages we may begin by asking what attitude the Church took to this question of serfdom and freedom. The answer is clear: there can be no question that the Church recognised serfdom as reasonable and necessary. St Thomas Aquinas defends servitude as economically expedient, and it was recognised and enforced by Canon Law.[3] Indeed the Church could do little else, for by the acquisition of property the great religious orders had become important landowners, and a very great number of

---

[1] See above, p. 138.　　　　　　　　[2] See above, p. 240.

[3] *Summa Theol.* 1 a, 2 ae, quaest. 94, art. 5. iii; Gratian, *Decretum*, Causa x, Quaest. ii, c. 3, and Causa xii, Quaest. ii, c. 39. In this latter case bishops are severely condemned for freeing serfs of the Church. The whole question of the attitude of the Church to serfdom is discussed by Dr Coulton in his *Medieval Village*, chapters xii–xiv.

serfs were contributing daily to their wealth and sustenance. To have denied serfdom would have been wellnigh an impossibility for them in practice, but at least we might have expected from them some theoretical expression of a higher view. Yet, as Pollock and Maitland write: "It is to the professed in religion that we may look for a high theory of justice; and when we find that it is against them that the peasants make their loudest complaints, we may be pretty sure that the religion of the time saw nothing very wrong in the proceedings of a lord who without any cruelty tried to get the most he could out of his villein tenements".[1] Certainly the Church saw nothing very wrong with it, for it was her own practice, and the manumission of any serf represented a loss of property, and of present and future service to the Church, and was, therefore, strictly forbidden by Canon Law, unless there was a definite reason for the manumission.[2] It was the hope of a definite return that doubtless allowed the Bishop of Worcester to manumit a serf of his who had done good service as a bailiff. In the charter of manumission the Bishop says that he has acted thus so that the man "may with the more spirit devote himself to her [the Church of Worcester's] rights and business; and that others, in hope of the like reward, may with the more vigour and fidelity discharge the duties entrusted to them".[3]

Naturally, from time to time both ecclesiastical and lay lords found it to their own interests to free some serf. Then it is that the fine-sounding phrases are rolled forth: it is pious and meritorious to restore men to that state of natural freedom which originally belonged to all human beings; it is an act of charity and piety, acceptable to God and delightful to men and so on. But these are, in general, but "common form" phrases, copied mechanically by one scribe from another, and their effect is considerably lessened when we observe that the lord often extracts a handsome monetary payment for the enfranchisement he confers.

[1] *Op. cit.* I, 378. For the Anglo-Saxon period see Vinogradoff, *Growth of the Manor*, 332, where he says, "Manumissions of this period are best explained by the operation of economic and social considerations. Not philanthropy or influence of Christianity have reduced slavery to the modest dimensions of Domesday."

[2] See above, and cf. *Cal. Papal Regs. Papal Letters*, I, 505; IV, 398; V, 71; *Hist. MSS. Com. Bath*, II, 36.

[3] *Worc. Liber Albus*, ed. J. M. Wilson, 223.

Both lay and ecclesiastical lords made the best of both worlds: their charters were embellished with the words of God, but their account rolls noted with exactitude the "eight marks of silver", or the £10 "legalis monete Anglie" which went with them.[1]

But seldom do we find the lord's motives so candidly expressed as they are in a charter of 1355 whereby Grandisson (one of our greatest bishops) freed one of his serfs. He writes:

Whereas thou, being now come to thy fifty years, hast no longer any wife or offspring lawfully begotten of thy body, and art so insufficient in worldly goods that thou must needs live from thine own labour, and knowest no art but that of a boatman, having learned none other from thy youth upward, therefore we cannot hold it unprofitable to us or to Our Church of Exeter to restore thee to thy natural liberty. Wherefore, in order that thou mayest be able to labour more freely and seek thy daily food and clothing by boatmanship, in consideration of the aforesaid facts and moved by pity, We do hereby, insofar as pertaineth to Ourselves, manumit thee and restore to natural liberty both thyself and all goods and chattels whatsoever, occupied or possessed by thee in any manner, specially reserving for Ourselves and Our successors and Our Church the patronage of thyself, and all thine offspring if perchance thou do beget any such.[2]

Without wife or children, and growing old with straining at the oar, he was no doubt of little use to the Bishop (although it will be noted that a "patronage"[3] of him is reserved), but what future had this serf, and what kind of piety was it that liberated him?

The fact that the majority of manumissions of which we have record are accompanied by an entry of the price paid for such freedom is one of great significance. Economic pressure in various directions rather than humanitarian sentiments were the dissolving agents employed. "Ah! Freedom is a noble thing!" cried the poet Barbour (although, in passing, it may be noted that he himself was an owner of serfs and a seller of serfs). But noble things are not to be had merely for the asking, and so the peasant

---

[1] A fair number of these charters have survived, but in general our information comes from the *compoti* and entries in court rolls and business documents. For the former, e.g. see *Manydown*, 102; *Crondal*, 34; *Eynsham Cart.* I, 267; *V.C.H. Durham*, II, 207, etc. For entries in *compoti*, etc., see *Winton Pipe Roll*, 28, 74; *Vale Royal Ledger*, 28, 29; Selden Soc. II, 175; Blomfield, *Bicester*, 145; *Glouc. Cart.* III, 190; *Hales Rolls*, 421, etc.

[2] *Reg. Grand.* 1159.

[3] By this the Bishop probably reserved his right of a heriot, etc. See p. 143.

found when he approached his lord. Indeed, but for the need of money and the changing conditions in England as the centuries wore on, the serf might long have continued to desire freedom without more than a few of his number ever gaining it. But the growing luxury of the aristocracy and their retainers, the Royal exactions for personal and general purposes, the wars at home and overseas, and the constant difficulty of all medieval landlords in finding ready money all helped the serf. We frequently find lords entering into agreements with their serfs which relieve them of all their servile duties for an annual cash payment. By this means villages won for themselves what practically amounted to emancipation; for, although the lord sometimes reserved certain services, as at South Biddock in 1183, where the serfs have to find 160 men to reap in autumn and 36 carts to carry the corn to Houghton, yet otherwise they are their own masters, when once the yearly rent is paid.[1] In the same way, the register of the Priory of St Mary Worcester shows that by the mid-thirteenth century the serfs on many of the manors had bought off a great deal of their services and payments by contributing a lump sum annually.[2] At Carthorpe in Yorkshire an inquisition of 1245 tells us that the villeins did no work but had farmed the manor from the lord for a fixed rent.[3] Again a document of about 1270 says there are no serfs on the lands of John FitzWarin because the heir's father sold to them all his villein rights,[4] and so on.[5] No doubt it was of mutual advantage to the parties to make such arrangements as these, and we cannot but believe that these changes encouraged men on neighbouring manors to strive for like privileges as they observed what freedom or quasi-freedom others had won. Occasionally it so happened that a body of serfs would be given their freedom outright, as in the mid-thirteenth century, when Herbert de Chaury freed fifteen men and women, for which they paid one mark of silver and submitted to an annual increase of fourteen pence in their rents, and promised to plough at three fixed seasons for one day, so long as they had plough teams

---

[1] *Boldon Book* (Surtees Soc.), 47.
[2] *Worc. Priory Reg.* XXIII and *passim.* Cf. *Glouc. Cart.* III, 37.
[3] *Yorks Inquis.* I, 3; and cf. *Cal. Inquis. Misc.* I, Nos. 43, 60, 846.
[4] *Cal. Inquis. Misc.* I, No. 416.
[5] For other examples, see *Reg. T. de Cantilupe*, 22; *E.H.R.* xv, 35; *Yorks Inquis.* I, 216; *Cal. Pat. Rolls*, 6 Ed. III, 2; *Econ. Docs.* (Tawney), 81-2.

and the lord fed them.[1] Sometimes men were given their freedom only to suit the lord's convenience, and at the price of abandoning their holdings altogether. When the Earl of Lincoln wished to found Revesby Abbey, in 1142, he offered all the men of the three villages involved in his new foundation either fresh land in exchange for their holdings, or leave to "go and dwell where they will". Six accepted land (and the charter sets out their holdings and services), but 31 left the Earl's lands to seek new habitations.[2] Again, when Henry II was founding the Carthusian Priory of Witham in Somersetshire, he cleared the villeins off the land, but gave each of them the choice of freedom or a tenement on any royal manor that he might choose.[3]

Generally, however, freedom came by direct action on the part of the serf himself. Bit by bit, we may imagine him saving enough to offer to his lord as a fair sum for his charter of manumission. Medieval records, as noted above, are full of such entries, and we need not be surprised to find that the sums paid to the lord vary very considerably. All that is recorded is the sum paid: the willingness or unwillingness of the lord or the reasons for the release are seldom apparent; and, as we have seen, even if reasons are given, they are not always to be taken at their face value.

Even when the lord consented to free a man he was not always willing to give away all his rights. The Prior of Bath manumits a serf, but only on condition that he serves the priory all his life in his office of plumber and glazier;[4] the Chapter of Canterbury confirm a manumission by the Archbishop of a bondman and his sons, with the reservation that his youngest son is to remain a serf and stay on the manor with the family fixtures and livestock.[5] The Bishop of Winchester grants a charter to J. de Wamblesworth and his children, but does not include John's tenants, nor does he excuse John and his heirs from certain duties such as suit of court, and payment of pannage and heriots on their death.[6] And so the list might be continued endlessly;

---

[1] Bed. Hist. Rec. Soc. II, 239–40.
[2] Northants. Record Soc. 1930, 4; and cf. *Monasticon Anglicanum*, ed. Caley and Ellis, v, 454; and see for Kirkstall, v, 530.
[3] *Hugh, St* (R.S.), 68.
[4] *Hist. MSS. Com. Bath*, II, 164.
[5] *Lit. Cant.* II, 411.   [6] *Reg. Pontissara*, 274.

everywhere we find the lord only willing to allow just so much as suits his purpose. The serf's aspirations mean little or nothing to him.

While all this was going on the lawyers were far from certain about their law. Glanvill (c. 1187) lays down his view in some detail.[1] He says that a serf is unable to buy his freedom, since he has nothing but what belongs eventually to his lord. "Hence, if the latter liberates him in consideration of a sum of money then a difficulty arises; this is met by the intermediation of a third person who purchases the serf nominally with his own, though really with the serf's money".[2] Glanvill seems to imagine that a lord can manumit his serf so as to make him free as regards himself, while he remains still a serf as regards all other men. The whole conception is puzzling, and neither Vinogradoff nor Pollock and Maitland have been able to clear up the involved law as stated by Glanvill.[3] By Bracton's time (c. 1250), how-ever, things had changed, and he reports cases of serfs buying their freedom with their own money,[4] although the older prac-tice was still known. The law on the subject was still fluid; and, as Vinogradoff has pointed out, "Everything seems in a state of vacillation and fermentation during the thirteenth century".[5]

Besides difficulties arising from these straightforward types of manumission medieval lawyers wrangled a great deal over certain actions which, as some held, carried with them a recognition of free status. Of these the most important was whether by entering into an agreement with a serf his lord confers freedom on him: by treating him as a free man does he make him free? Vino-gradoff points out that "the line between covenant and enfran-chisement was so easily passed, and an incautious step would have such unpleasant consequences for landlords, that they kept as clear as possible of any deeds which might destroy their claims as to the persons of their villeins".[6] Nevertheless, instances can

---

[1] *Op. cit.* Bk. v, 5.
[2] Pollock and Maitland, *op. cit.* I, 427, 428 n. I. For examples of manumission through a third person, see Salzman, *Charters Sele Priory*, No. 118; *Hist. MSS. Com. Wells*, I, 62, 138; *Derby Arch. Soc. Journ.* XVI, 166.
[3] Pollock and Maitland, *op. cit.* I, 427–9; *Villainage*, 86–8.
[4] *B.N.B.* Nos. 31, 343.
[5] *Op. cit.* 128.
[6] *Op. cit.* 73.

be shown where such agreements have been made;[1] and, what is more to the point, we have instances which reveal that some lords were aware of the risk and acted accordingly. Thus, when the Chapter of Wells made a grant in 1247 to a villein who held 2½ acres of their demesne, they added a clause which stated that, "nevertheless he and his heirs should not be free men by means of the said grant but perform rents and services as before".[2] The risks the unwary lord ran are well illustrated by the case in *Bracton's Note Book* where a certain Roger de Sufford gave a piece of land to one of his villeins, William Tailor, to hold freely by free services, and when Roger died, his son and heir William de Sufford confirmed the lease. The lord afterwards ejected the tenant who brought an action against him and recovered possession.[3] Here, it is clear that the lawyers considered the serf had acquired the freehold by reason of the free services attached to it, and therefore they decided that, before the law, he was a free man.

By Britton's time (c. 1291) a great many things were taken by the lawyers to imply constructive manumission:[4]

A villain may recover his freedom several ways, as if his Lord enfeoff him of any tenement to him and his heirs, whether he receive his homage or not.... A bondman also becomes free if he marries his Lady, as well as a bondwoman when her Lord marries her.... When any bondman or bondwoman once becomes free, or is enfranchised by the free bed of his Lord or of any other, we ordain in favour of freedom and of matrimony that they and their issue shall for ever be held free.... A bondman may be enfranchised by the recognisance of his Lord, as if his Lord has acknowledged him to be free in a court of record.... Likewise by writing of his Lord as if his Lord has for himself and for his heirs quitclaimed to the bondman and his heirs all manner of right... by reason of the bondage of his blood.... So also where the bondman can prove by record of our court that the Lord has knowingly suffered him to be upon juries and inquests in our courts as a freeman.

The above passage may serve as a comprehensive statement of the law concerning such manumissions, and undoubtedly it aided a number of men to win their freedom. But the law of the King's Courts was not a thing easily comprehended by the

---

[1] Pollock and Maitland, *op. cit.* I, 418; *Cal. Inquis. Misc.* II, 473.

[2] *Hist. MSS. Com. Wells*, I, 72. In 1327 another grant makes similar reservations; I, 216.

[3] *B.N.B.* No. 184.

[4] *Op. cit.* I, 198–209 *passim.*

majority of peasants, who were only aware in the vaguest way that, afar off in London, or may be at some distant city, the King's justices dealt with problems arising from the plaints of men so insignificant as themselves.

No very explicit grounds for desiring freedom are generally given in manumission charters, and none are necessary, for it is obvious that all men knew what a difference there was between the free and the servile state in innumerable ways. Most freed men had no desire to leave their village: they remained peasants, and continued to work on their fields, but no longer burdened with rents and services as before. They longed to call their cots their own, and to do what they would in their own way, and especially no longer to hear the hated epithet "rustic" or "serf", hurled at them from time to time. A few exceptions to this general rule must be noted, however, in which an external motive encouraged a man to seek his freedom. No medieval family was so ignorant as not to realise the power and prestige of the Church, and few did not know at first hand that the Church offered a safe honourable career to those who were her servants. Even the poorest village priest was high above his peasant parishioners in status; and, in general, on level terms with the best of them in worldly goods. Hence the Church and its service were constantly absorbing recruits from the villages; and, as the centuries wore on, the call became more and more insistent. But both Canon Law and civil law demanded that all who would take orders should be free of any defect of birth, and hence it was necessary for serfs who wished their sons to become clerics to gain their freedom.[1] "The villain redeems his son from the Lord, and on each side covetousness fights and wins when freedom is confirmed on freedom's foe", writes Walter Map bitterly as he observes this going on about him,[2] and finds it matter for complaint that serfs were trying to educate their "ignoble and degenerate offspring". But he was powerless to stop this movement which continued to the end of the Middle Ages. Langland, nearly two centuries later than Map, voices the same grievance:

---

[1] Gratian, *Decretum*, pars i, distinctio liv; Const. of Clarendon, § 16; and see below.
[2] *De Nugis Curialium* (ed. M. R. James), 7.

For shold no clerk be crouned bote yf he ycome were
Of franklens and freemen and of folke yweddede.
Bondmen and bastardes and beggers children,
Thuse by-longeth to labour and lordes kyn to seruen
Both god and good men as here degree asketh;

. . . .

But sith bondemenne barnes han be mad bisshopes,
And barnes bastardes han ben archidekenes,
And sowters and here sones for seluer han be knyghtes,
And lordene sones here labores and leid here rentes to wedde

. . . .

Lyfe-holynesse and loue han ben longe hennes,
And wole, til hit be wered out or otherwise ychaunged.[1]

The whole opposition to these upstarts thrusting their way into
the Church and thence into high places came to a head in the
famous petition to Richard II, asking him to forbid villeins to
send their sons to school "to learn clergee".[1] This plea was refused, and in 1406 an enactment in Parliament secured the right
"of every man or woman, of what state or condition he be,...to
set their son or daughter to take learning at any school that
pleaseth them within the realm".[2]

Before this statute every serf wishing to leave the manor for
this purpose, or wishing to get leave for his son to do so had to
plead for, and usually to buy, his freedom from his lord. The
accounts and Court Rolls are full of these happenings. Thus in
1295, Walter, son of Reginald the carpenter, presented by the
manorial jury of Hemingford Abbots, Hunts, for being ordained without leave, appeared before the lord, the Abbot of
Ramsey, and by special grace was licensed to attend school and
take all orders, without being reclaimed as a serf. For this he was
to recite the whole of the psalms ten times for the soul of the late
Abbot William and also to pay a fine of ten shillings.[3] When we
remember that the yearly wages of a first-class agricultural
labourer at that time (exclusive of his keep) were seldom more
than half this sum we can realise the importance the lord attached

[1] *Piers Plowman*, C. VI, 63–81. There was a good deal of truth in this
statement. Cutts (*op. cit.* 133) tells us that of Archbishops of Canterbury,
Winchelsey was probably of humble birth; Reynolds, the son of a Windsor
baker and Chichele, a shepherd boy.
[2] 7 Henry IV, cap. 17.
[3] Leach, *Schools Medieval England*, 206, and cf. 236.

to this permission. On the Halesowen manor two men are distrained because their sons have gone *ad scholas clericales* without first getting leave,[1] and year by year the Court at Ingoldmells ordered a certain Peter, son of Reginald Saffron, to be attached because he was ordained without license of the lord.[2] In 1330 the Archbishop of Canterbury directs his bailiff to take security for the payment of a fine from two bondmen who had caused their sons to receive Holy Orders; and a few years later he warns his Chancellor that it is unlawful to ordain men of servile condition without the consent of their lords.[3] These instances from a crowd of similar records will serve sufficiently to show the importance attached to this method of gaining freedom. The lawyers, however, insisted that, in order to retain this freedom the recipient must continue to live as a cleric: if he relapsed into secular life his serfdom revived.[4] But this was little more than an expression of legal opinion, and must have happened extremely rarely.

So too with knighthood. There was nothing to prevent a serf becoming a knight according to the lawyer's theory, however rare it was in practice; but, should he be degraded, he at once reverted to his servile state. When we remember, however, the disdain with which the chivalric romances look down upon the peasant, it is hard to believe that many rose from the ranks of the serfs to become knights. It is a pleasing fancy: *The Squire of Low Degree* and the romance of *Guy of Warwick* remind us of its attractiveness as legend; but, even here, are we dealing with anything more degraded than impoverished gentlemen, or at very least with free men? No doubt a generation or two made all the difference; Sir William Paston, one of the King's justices in the early fifteenth century, was accused by the "unfriendly hand"

---

[1] *Hales Rolls*, 193, 205. "Scholas clericales", i.e. a grammar School, at lowest, with its tonsure. No doubt, if there were a parish school, it was not prohibited.

[2] *Ingoldmells Rolls*, 34, 35, 40.

[3] *Lit. Cant.* (R.S.), III, 389; I, 307. Similarly we have records of arrangements being entered into by religious houses not to receive recruits without the lord's leave; and, if this should be done unwittingly, they agree to expel the postulant so long as his period of probation is not yet ended. See Bed. Hist. Rec. Soc. XIII, No. 240.

[4] Bracton, ff. 5, 190 *b*; Britton, I, 200, 208; *Fleta*, III; Pollock and Maitland, I, 429.

of being but one generation from servile stock; and we may well believe that it took something like this to shake off one's servile origins.[1]

Our enquiry, up to this point, therefore, shows us that although medieval England saw a large part of its population of servile condition, this state of affairs was not willingly assented to by the serfs themselves, and unceasing attempts were made by them to alleviate their condition. They took whatever opportunity arose of buying themselves free from various services and obligations; individuals and sometimes whole villages bought themselves complete freedom, and in various other ways the yoke of servitude was shaken off. These were not the only means of obtaining freedom, however, and we must now pass on to consider how far the towns, so seemingly secure and desirable within their walls, and dowered with privileges, acted as magnets to untold numbers of men.

The long struggle which the serfs had to wage before they became free men was materially influenced by the freedom possessed by dwellers in boroughs, and we shall find it difficult to overestimate the part played by the towns in aiding the steady emancipation of the peasants. From the earliest times we find the burghers setting an example. Living as they did, with their houses oftentimes clustered round some episcopal palace, or lying in the shadow of the fortress of their feudal lord, they had ample opportunity of realising the ever-present burdens these great ones imposed on them; for we find them subject to services, to tallages, or to heriots, as were their brothers of the fields. But, unlike their brothers, they realised at an earlier stage that these conditions were not inevitable, and that means could be found of overcoming seigneurial exploitation. As towns became more and more attractive, by reason of their natural and other advantages, so they drew within their walls some of the richest,

---

[1] Luchaire (*Social France at the time of Philip Augustus*), 271, says: "In the chansons de geste villeins who had succeeded in emerging from their status, entering the military class and reaching knighthood are sometimes mentioned; but in such a case, the poet never fails to put strong protests in the mouths of his noble characters. It is true that in real life this transformation did occur, especially in southern France, where the gulf between the classes was narrower; but, on the whole, the occurrence was rare." See also p. 346, where an account is given from *Garin le Lorrain* of the knighting of a serf, but it is made ridiculous.

most intelligent and most enterprising men of the nation. At the same time, these men came into contact with traders and others from foreign countries, and so gleaned from them new and disturbing ideas of the steps taken by men of such towns as Rouen, or of Laon, to win free from the control of feudal lords. Gradually arose the imperious need to be masters in their own town, and they agitated for their freedom.

But, as we have seen, freedom was not gained merely for the asking. A multiplicity of reasons actuated the holders of the franchises; but, generally speaking, no liberty was won except at the expense of much effort and much gold. Nevertheless, we must remember that some lords realised it would be to their own advantage to establish a free borough, well knowing that the development of such a borough with its accruing profits from fairs, markets, tolls, etc., would more than compensate them for the loss of the services of their sometime serfs. At times a lord would find that the granting of a charter of burgess rights was the most fruitful method of restoring a dwindling revenue, or a dwindling population, as William FitzAlan found about 1190, when he granted a charter undertaking to protect his burgesses of Oswestry who took messuages from his bailiff "ad emendationem mercati mei".[1] Everywhere such local conditions had their effect; yet, it is true that, in the majority of cases, the towns bought their franchises from impoverished and needy overlords.

The process was gradual, going on step by step, faster here, and more slowly there, according as circumstances favoured the towns, and the chances of buying their own freedom occurred; the needs of the nobles who were setting out for the East gave the opportunity of bargaining for grants of privilege; and similarly the towns were able to secure many immunities from royal interference at times when Richard I started for the Holy Land, and when it was necessary to raise money for his ransom.[2]

Even when necessity or expediency dictated the abdication of some of his powers, the lord did not part with his franchises at a blow. Only bit by bit, in many cases, could the burgesses win completely free. We may see this struggle for freedom taking place all over the country. It was long, for example, before either Sheffield or Manchester gained complete freedom; the men of

---

[1] *E.H.R.* xv, 522.   [2] Cunningham, *op. cit.* 211, 212.

Wells were continuously at variance with their overlord; while in countless cases the lord reserved certain rights over his men. At Morpeth, in Northumberland, Roger de Merlai gave to his free burgesses "all liberties and all free customs to be held and had to them and their heirs of me and my heirs for ever, honourably and freely and completely, as the charter of my Lord the King defines".[1] Nevertheless, from subsequent agreements made with his heirs, we find that the men of Morpeth lacked many of the essentials of complete freedom although they were paying £10 yearly in rent for their franchises. For years after this charter the lord held a common bakehouse, a mill at which the burgesses were forced to grind the corn grown on the lord's lands, and a stall where meat and fish were sold till noon to the exclusion of their rights. Besides this, the lord received a fine for every gallon of ale they brewed, and another for every one of their cattle straying in the fields.[2]

Such incidents of servage still remained in many other boroughs: we find the burgesses must ride with the lord when summoned for an expedition; they must give tallage when required; they are forced to render the old-time ploughings or reapings, or to do suit of mill and oven. But even so, the situation of the burgesses is most favourable compared with that of the villagers, for their charter gives them great privileges—they are no longer at the will of the lord and their services and payments are fixed and regulated. Mr Ballard thus sums up the advantages of the burghers' situation:

In the first place, their burgage tenure enabled the burgesses to dispose of their houses in the borough almost as easily as their chattels, and freed them from death duties in the shapes of heriots and reliefs. Then, by having a court of their own...they were tried by their fellow townsmen. Then, there was often some limitation of the amount of fines that could be levied in the borough court, for instance, in the boroughs that received the law of Breteuil, whereas there was no such [definitely legal] limitation on the fines imposed by the manorial court. In many cases the burgesses were free of toll, not only in the market of the borough, but also throughout the possessions of their lord.[3]

---

[1] Hodgson, *Hist. Northumberland*, II, 2, 480–8.
[2] Ballard, *op. cit.* I, 89, 91, 94, 96; II, 114–15, 116 ff., 121, 122 ff.
[3] *Op. cit.* I, xciv.

The possession of these advantages by the towns must constantly be borne in mind when we are considering the various agencies which slowly brought about the emancipation of the English countryside. Every one of these towns, with its charters and privileges, was a constant challenge: to the serf, they reminded him of the difference between his manorial tenure and that of his more fortunate brother of the borough; to the lord, they were an ever-present threat to his autocracy. Therefore, in order to retain his peasants on the manor, he was often obliged to allow their conditions to approximate to those of the nearby borough.

But when we have discussed the long struggle waged by most boroughs for their freedom, and their attraction to the serfs, as places of refuge, once they had gained this freedom, we are only at the outset of our task. It is obvious that this slow winning of self-government represents, in effect, the gradual acquisition of personal freedom for the burgesses. Men who owe merchet, and are forced to render agricultural services, or to give heriots, are clearly sprung from the unfree population of the villages. But we may go further than this, and say that in many cases these burgesses of the thirteenth century were the villeins of the twelfth. Maitland has taught us that the medieval burgher was a "rustic", and that the investigators of the early history of towns "will have fields and pastures on their hands". And so conversely. If we have any doubt of this we may see the serf transformed into a freeholding burgess by a stroke of the pen. On St Gregory's Day, in 1251, the Earl of Derby founded his borough of Higham Ferrers. No less than 92 men, whose names are all recited in the charter, therefore rose in the morning as serfs, and by evening were free men, "so that from them and their families (*sequela*), with all their lands and tenements and chattels, the Earl and his heirs could not from henceforth have or exact any servitude from them or from their issue".[1] Many of the boroughs founded in the late twelfth and thirteenth centuries (especially

---

[1] Ballard, *op. cit.* II, 47, 142; cf. Latin text in *E.H.R.* VII, 290, and *inspeximus* of charter in *Cal. Charter Rolls*, I, 372. The Rev. W. J. H. Kerr, who has an intimate knowledge of the H.F. documents, tells me that there were 92 names in the original and that "it is obvious from the small aggregate of land held by them that they were the very lowest type of bondmen". By 1314 there were 101 burgages and they held in all only 30½ acres.

the seigneurial boroughs) have a similar history behind them, and are therefore of great importance to our study of the methods by which the villein won his freedom. When we read, for example, that the Knutsford burgages were measured in selions and ridges, do we not at once see the little borough arising from the midst of an agricultural community?[1] and when we read that the burgesses of Leicester were freed from their reaping services, or their fellows of Lancaster from their ploughing and other servile customs, it is clear enough that the village community has but recently become the town community.[2]

The serf, then, always had the chance that his lord, for one reason or another, might enfranchise the village, and make it a borough. But, in the nature of things, this chance was slight, and even slighter than may appear at first sight, since a large number of medieval boroughs only kept their municipal status for a time, and then relapsed again into villages as conditions changed.[3] But it is not only the actual borough itself we have to consider, for its influence was not confined within its walls. First, as we have seen, the presence of this highly privileged locality was both an attraction to fugitive and restless serfs, and also an exemplar to them of privileges to be won. And even more important was its effect on the immediately surrounding countryside. The common fields of the town marched side by side with those of innumerable surrounding manors. How could the manorial peasant be prevented from grumbling when he found himself with innumerable burdens, while his neighbour of the next field went free? How often must he have yielded to the temptation to pass across the narrow strip which would give him the safe shelter, and ofttimes the welcome, of the town? The records of our towns show clearly enough how they were constantly receiving an influx of "foreigners". At Norwich, for example, from an examination of the list of citizens at the end of the thirteenth century,

---

[1] Ballard, op. cit. II, 52.
[2] Ibid. I, 94, 95. We might also note the importance attached in the charters to the abolition of *merchet* and *suit of mill or oven*.
[3] For instance Prof. Tait tells us that "of the 23 boroughs created in the poor and backward county of Lancaster between 1066 and 1372, with burgesses ranging in number from six up to one hundred and fifty or so, only four retained an established borough status at the end of the Middle Ages". *Proc. Brit. Acad.* vol. X. So also at Halesowen, where the borough never appears to have enjoyed any vitality. *V.C.H. Worc.* III, 139 ff.

Mr W. Hudson was able to tell us that they are drawn from more than 450 localities in Norfolk and Suffolk.[1] The other side of the picture is made clear enough by looking over the Court Rolls of any manor situated near to a town: again and again men are reported as being fugitives, and dwelling in the neighbouring town; and, although order is given that they be brought back, the town continued to shelter them, and generally their names drop out of the Rolls after these ineffective commands have been made for several years.[2]

From their side the burgesses frequently helped the unfree, for once they were secure themselves, it was not long before prosperity caused them to find their borough too small, and they cast envious eyes on some manor whose fields were contiguous to their own. A few examples will make this clear. In the year 1256 the men of Scarborough found themselves cramped, and got a charter from the King allowing them "for the increase of their borough", to absorb the King's own manor of Wallesgrave [Palsgrave] with all its appurtenances and 60 acres in the fields of Scarborough".[3] Now, although the men of Scarborough absorbed this manor for their own ends, so far as the dwellers on that manor were concerned they became, *ipso facto*, men of Scarborough, and entitled to its privileges and rights. We find similar things happening all over the country. The Abbot of Burton-on-Trent founded the borough there before 1213, granting burgess tenure to all who took burgages in the street extending from the great bridge of Burton to the new street of Horningclawe. By 1273 he was obliged to enfranchise another part of the little town, and yet again, in 1286, he enlarged the confines of the borough.[4] In similar fashion the new lands and burgages at Berry Pomeroy were added to the town of Bridgetown Pomeroy by a confirmation and extension of the original charter of 1268.[5] Lastly, let us examine the very instructive proceedings at Newcastle-on-Tyne. Here the foundation charter dates from the time of Henry I; but, by 1298, the town was ready for expansion, and so it got a grant from the King of all the lands in Pampadene [Pandon] in Byker, adjoining the said town

---

[1] *Norf. Arch.* XII, 46. [2] *Hales Rolls, passim* and below, 308, 309.
[3] *Cal. Charter Rolls*, III, 190. [4] *Hist. MSS. Com.* xv, part vii, 134–5.
[5] *Arch. Journ.* VII, 422 ff.

of Newcastle, with all the rents and services of all the tenants there,
...to be held by the said burgesses and good men of Newcastle and
their heirs from the King for the same sums, which they render to the
King from the town of Newcastle, with all the appurtenances, to be
united with and included in the said town for the bettering and se-
curing thereof. And the said burgesses shall have in Pampadene a free
borough as in Newcastle; and the said lands and tenements shall be
free burgages and held in free burgage; and they shall have in Pampadene all the liberties and customs as in Newcastle, and Newcastle and
Pampadene shall be one borough.[1]

As an outward and visible sign of this unity, when the citizens
built their new wall a few years later, it made a considerable
detour in order to enclose the newly enfranchised portion.[2]
Henceforth the sometime rustics could sleep safely: all danger of
their reverting to their former servile status was past.

It was not only the enfranchisement of townships and the
absorption of the neighbouring manors that offered opportunities to the serf. For some time, especially during the reign
of Edward I, there was the constantly recurring opportunity
offered by the creation of entirely new towns. Hitherto we have
seen the serfs of a certain village transformed into burgesses by
the formation of a borough from the village; yet, important as
this was in many ways, its initial advantage was obviously
limited to those happy few who had the fortune to reside there
at that moment. With new boroughs it was different. Here a
town was deliberately created on a spot where, hitherto, nothing
but waste, or, at the most, a few wretched huts had stood. It was,
therefore, essential to bring settlers to such places, and so all
were welcomed. The King (for they are mainly royal creations)
offered land and burgage rights to every one who would come
and take up residence in the new borough. Thus, in 1286, the
King appointed two men

to lay out, with sufficient streets and lanes, and adequate sites for a
market and church, and plots for merchants and others, a new town
with a harbour in a place called Gotowre-super-mare [co. Dorset]...
which was formerly of R. de Muchgros, and contiguous to the said
place, the lands and tenements of the which said town the King is

[1] *Cal. Close Rolls*, II, 474.
[2] R. Welford, *History of Newcastle*, I, x.

prepared to commit to merchants and others willing to take them, and to enfeoff them thereof for building and dwelling purposes.[1]

A further example is to be found in the Welsh border, where the harassed countryside was to be repopulated, and "all who wish to become feoffees or farmers" are ordered to appear before the King's officers at Hereford or Shrewsbury, while those wishing for the further security of the town might apply to the Justice of Chester and his fellow, who had power "to assign places in Rhuddlan to all who desire to receive and hold the same from the King".[2] So also at Chard, at Kingston-on-Hull, and at other places, we see the opportunity offered to the adventurous; and, so far as the documents go, there is nothing to make us believe that the serf was barred.[3]

It is clear from our survey that the towns offered great opportunities and had great advantages, but we have still to investigate these opportunities and advantages in so far as they concerned the serf. It was not sufficient for him merely to pass through the town gate to win his freedom: during the first four days of his absence from the manor the lord might pursue him, and bring him back from wherever he found him. After that it was another matter, for by then he was *in possessione libertatis*, and the lord would have to seek the aid of the courts to get possession of him.[4] Therefore, the serf was not really free: his seisin of liberty must be clearly distinguished from the full and lawful liberty he desires, and it is here that the towns played so great a part, for by dwelling within the walls of a chartered town or royal demesne for a year and a day, a serf acquired a certain freedom. But here we must go warily: it is by no means clear that simple residence in a borough or city gave a serf the privileges which some writers have assigned to him. Pollock and Maitland, as we should expect, put it guardedly: "The serf

---

[1] *Cal. Pat. Rolls*, 14 Ed. I, m. 24, and cf. *Cal. Chart. Rolls*, II, 337. For the fate of this borough see Tait, *Proc. Brit. Acad.* x, 6.

[2] *Op. cit.* 8 Ed. I, m. 21 (p. 366); cf. Sée, *op. cit.* p. 298, n. 2: "dans les bastides se réfugier un grand nombre de serfs."

[3] Indeed, the Chard document expressly states the Bishop's offer is to *all persons*. *Cal. Pat. Rolls*, 14 Ed. I, m. 24 (p. 216).

[4] Bracton, *op. cit.* f. 6 b. It should be noticed, however, that Britton, *op. cit.* I. 201, says that the fugitive may be pursued and brought back within a year and a day. For an account of how his lord regained possession of his serf, see below, p. 309.

who dwells in [the borough] for a year and a day, at all events if
he has become a burgess or a member of the merchant guild,
becomes free, or at least cannot be claimed by his Lord so long
as he remains within the borough."[1]

This guarded statement is necessary, for the actual position is
uncertain, and it may well be that for a considerable time it was
constantly changing. Not every city or borough was a chartered
town or royal demesne, and without such a status the town could
afford the serf but little protection. The widest claim is to be
found in the laws called *Willelmi Articuli Retractati*, where it is
stated, "If slaves (*servi*) have remained a year and a day without
being claimed, in our cities or in our walled boroughs or in our
castles, from that day they shall become free men and shall
remain for ever free from the yoke of slavery".[2] These laws,
however, do not date in their present form from the time of the
Conqueror, although no doubt they are expanded from some
earlier enactments. As we now have them they appear to be
written after 1200,[3] but before that date we have much evidence
which modifies their force. Glanvill, in a well-known passage,
says that the serf who dwells in a privileged town without
challenge for a year and a day, "so that he shall have been received like a citizen into their common gild, he will be liberated
from serfdom by that very fact".[4] It will be noted that it is not
mere residence, but reception in the gild that is the essence of this
case. And this insistence on something more than residence is
to be noticed in the charters which the towns were acquiring
from the twelfth century onward. Thus at Newcastle, the town
charter, which dates before 1135, insists that the serf (*rusticus*)
must stay his year and a day, as a burgess (*sicut burgensis*); or, as
another charter at Lincoln (1157) has it, "he is free if he dwells a
year and a day and pays the customs of the city". At Northampton, in 1190, the custom was shown to require the would-be
citizen to be resident and at hearth and home and lot and scot
with the citizens for a year and a day, and similar laws obtained
at Dunwich and Hereford in 1215. Furthermore, a careful ex-

[1] Pollock and Maitland, *op. cit.* I, 648.
[2] A. J. Robertson, *Laws of Kings of England from Edmund to Henry I*, cap. 16.
[3] Liebermann, *Gesetze der Angelsachsen*, III, 278.
[4] Glanvill, *op. cit.* Bk. V, cap. 5.

amination of the Charter Rolls shows that only very occasionally (as at Pembroke, Nottingham and Derby) did the charter allow simple residence as a sufficient reason. The qualifying phrases vary, but all have the implication that the citizens are ready to receive the outsider who has shown a willingness to accept communal burdens, and who wishes to be part of the borough and not a mere parasite upon it. The lawyers do not go quite as far as this: Bracton says that freedom is acquired by dwelling for a year and a day in any privileged town, or on the royal demesne; and Britton and the author of *Fleta* at the end of the thirteenth century say much the same.[1] But the citizens and the lawyers are not dealing with quite the same matter, though the two things have become hopelessly entangled in subsequent discussion. Mere residence in the borough undoubtedly gave the serf a seisin of liberty, so long as he remained there, and it is this that the lawyers are concerned with. If he wished to be more than this—a *freeman* not merely a free man—then it was necessary for him to associate himself very closely with the townsfolk.

And this was not always a simple matter. Sometimes there would be a limiting clause in the town charter which refused any such privileges to the serf. Thus at Plympton, in 1242, Baldwin, Earl of Devon, in giving a charter to the borough definitely excluded from its terms "our born serfs, who if they happen to remain or sojourn in the aforesaid borough, cannot claim or usurp any liberty by reason of the aforesaid liberty granted to our aforesaid burgesses, without our consent".[2] Similar instances may be seen at Weymouth in 1252, and at Bridgetown Pomeroy in 1268.[3] Even if there were no such clause in the charter there was a great gulf between the citizen and the serf—a gulf which often could not be crossed, and which, in any case, required a deal of negotiating. At London, for example, it was comparatively easy to obtain personal freedom, for the section of the *Willelmi Articuli Retractati* quoted above was there regarded as authoritative and often pleaded in the courts.[4] But such freedom was

---

[1] Bracton, *op. cit.* f. 190 *b*; Britton, *op. cit.* I, 200, 209; *Fleta*, III, 235.
[2] Devon. Assoc. XIX, 561; Ballard, *op. cit.* II, 141, 143; Eyton, *Shropshire*, X, 133. Cf. Luchaire, *Communes Françaises*, 58.
[3] Ballard, *op. cit.* II, 142, 143.   [4] *Letter Books*, A 170: K 90.

restricted: it gave no right of entry to the gilds or of protection without the city. Freedom, indeed, was an essential condition of membership of a gild, and the gilds were autocratic institutions, and exercised a rigorous scrutiny over candidates for admission. By the fourteenth century this had gone so far that villein origin was regarded as tainting the blood. In an ordinance of 1387 it is laid down that no "foreigner" should be enrolled as an apprentice unless he first swore that he was a free man and not a serf, and later on a serf is defined as the son of a man who was a serf at the time of the boy's birth. From this it would seem that if a villein became free by residence in the city, his sons born after this would be eligible for membership of a gild, but those born earlier were of servile origin and were excluded. We may understand the reason for this decision by recalling the well-known case of Simon de Paris, mercer, alderman and sheriff of London. Simon had been a freeman of the City since 1288; but, in 1306, while visiting his home at Necton in Norfolk, he was seized by the lord's bailiff who ordered him to serve as reeve, arrested him on his refusal, and kept him in prison from tierce to vespers. Simon brought an action against his lord, pleading that he was a free citizen of London. His lord pleaded that he was a villein, taken in his "villein nest", and therefore liable for service. Justice Bereford here interposed: "I have heard tell that a man was taken in a brothel and hanged, and if he had stayed at home no ill would have befallen him. So here. If he was a free citizen why did he not stay in the City?" The jury, however, refused to entertain the view of Simon's opponent; and, no doubt, jealous for the liberties of the City, found for him, and declared that he was a free man, and had suffered damage by his few hours' imprisonment to the sum of £100.[1] No wonder the gilds were chary of accepting any one whose blood was not completely free, when a few days spent without the walls might lose them the services of apprentice or journeyman.

Much the same conditions prevailed elsewhere: at York, at Andover, at Lynn, for example, no one of servile birth could gain entrance to the gild—their birth was an absolute bar.[2] At

---

[1] Y.B. 1 Ed. II (Selden Soc.), 11 ff.
[2] Hist. MSS. Report, I, 109 a; Gross, op. cit. II, 164, 317; T. Jones, Hist. Brecknock, II, 786.

Norwich, it was not an impossibility, but the citizens required the serf to produce his lord's licence before they would admit him to their number,[1] and in the fifteenth century free condition was made an essential for entry to the gilds.[2] An early poem, dealing with the mason's craft, may perhaps be taken as summarising the general view:

> The fowrthe artycul thys moste be,
> That the mayster hym wel be-se
> That he no bondemon prentys make,
> Ny for no covetyse do hym take;
> For the lord that he ys bonde to,
> May fache the prentys wheresever he go.[3]

To sum up: the towns, on the whole, certainly gave a considerable measure of protection to the serf, so long as he exercised due caution in leaving the town. In general, however, their beneficent activities stopped here. The advancement of the serf was not particularly dear to the citizens' hearts: indeed I think we shall not be far wrong if we look at it in quite another light. To the majority of townsmen the landless serf was like the casual labourer is to the contractor to-day. He assumes little responsibility for him, but uses him as and when and where required, and then turns him adrift. In the medieval town there was great demand for casual labour; and the more highly organised the gilds became, the more they found it beneath their dignity to carry out the many necessary functions of day-to-day town life. This is where the fugitive found his opportunity. We may imagine him employed on sporadic scavenging; on digging the foundations for buildings and doing navvy's work on the City walls; acting as porter and carrying heavy loads from river to warehouse; hanging about the inns and assisting carriers and ostlers; doing the rough work incident on the housing and feeding of a master's apprentices and journeymen. There was no end to the work constantly to be done, and many serfs found they had but exchanged the service of their manorial lord for that of a burgher.

---

[1] *Norf. Arch.* xii, 78.
[2] *Norwich Records*, ed. Hudson and Tingey, ii, 291.
[3] J. O. Halliwell, *Early History of Freemasonry*, 16 (quoting from MS. Reg. 17 A, f. 3). Knoop and Jones, *The Mediaeval Mason*, 107, 168. Fache = bring back.

Here we may conveniently pause to examine the results of these changes we have been discussing. When Higham Ferrers was made a borough, the 92 burgesses of the new borough became free men and a self-governing commonalty. They retained all their lands and had in them the possibilities of a livelihood, but in addition their charter gave them their own tithings, their own three-weekly court for small pleas and transfer of burgage tenements and a half-yearly view of frankpledge for their own men. In short, they were completely their own masters, while around them on all sides they saw others still subject to the manorial lord's courts and services. So too in the New Boroughs established by the King's command: the new citizens had the full enjoyment of all the privileges given to them by their new charter. At Kingston-on-Hull, for example, the inhabitants of the newly created borough were to have all the liberties pertaining to a free borough, with two markets a week and a yearly fair. The burgesses had the right to make wills, to have their own coroner, to plead in their own borough court only, to have the return of royal writs, etc.[1] Again when the burghers of Newcastle enlarged their borough boundaries so as to include the former manor of Pandon, their charter explicitly stated that "they should have in Pandon all the liberties and customs as in Newcastle; and Newcastle and Pandon should be one borough".

Thus far, then, it is clear that any serfs fortunate enough to be on the spot at the birth of boroughs such as these were in an enviable condition as compared with that of their fathers. They were free in the eyes of the law, masters of their own property and holdings, and able to participate in all the communal activities of their new town. In short, their opportunities were what they made of them, and many might have cried "Bliss was it in that dawn to be alive, But to be young was very heaven". When we turn to the serf who came into an already existing town, we see that his condition was by no means so blissful; and, unfortunately for him, it was to the existing towns that he and his fellows fled for the most part. True by such flight and residence within the town they acquired a seisin of liberty, and in due time became free men—at least in the eyes of the law. But what freedom had they in actual fact? Had they done much more than

---

[1] *Cal. Pat. Rolls* (1299), 475; and compare pp. 216, 296, 366.

escape from one evil to others that they knew not of? Instead of the certain dues and services to be rendered to the manorial lord they had to face the uncertainties of the changing economic conditions, and the whims and fancies of their new master in the town. Their work was sporadic, seasonal, at the will of their employer—it is difficult to see how many of the peasants found the exchange worth while. And we must remember that the peculiar organisation of town life did not help them. Around them they saw the great ones of the town: the merchant gild, which in many places had assumed control of the town-government, and the craft gilds, which controlled almost every worthwhile trade in the borough. "If ordinary inhabitants were allowed to buy and sell food or the bare necessities of life, all profitable business was reserved as the monopoly of the full citizen." And, beside the full citizen, various privileged classes may be discerned in the towns: the tenants and dependents of bishop, or abbot, or of a lord, who lived within the liberties of the borough and had limited trading rights; the "foreigners" who lived without the walls, but who were allowed within it for trade "according to the town's discretion and convenience". And so on down by subtle gradations till we reach our men from the countryside—the non-burgesses—without rights, without champions, without traditions. Yet, though many of them must often have longed for their fields and the comfort which comes from "use and wont", and often, at the end of a long arduous day spent at wretched and unremunerative toil, must have wondered what the end of it all was to be: even so, it was a necessary phase in the history of emancipation. Though John-atte-Grene himself was little better off as a free man in the town of Leicester than his father had been as a serf of the Earl, yet a generation or two hence saw John Green an alderman of the city and one of the controllers of his craft. His father, like a multitude of other fugitives in the towns, may indeed have "bought his blood" at a heavy price, but future generations were to bless him for it.

Little wonder then that when all other methods failed him the peasant's thoughts turned to the possibilities of flight. Indeed, in some ways, the prospects in a nearby town or at a distance often must have seemed so rosy that we must ask ourselves: "What, then, kept the majority of the peasant population fixed to the soil?" Many things, no doubt; but one was of overwhelming importance: a sense of fair play and an ability to compromise. We have seen that changing conditions were forcing men to view things in a new light: little by little even the most grasping lords were relinquishing some of their immemorial rights. Here and there up and down the countryside, week-works were dying out as the lord and his serfs found their interests marching side by side in exchanging a service rent for one of money. Again, we have seen the constant challenge of the towns: privileged, comparatively safe, seemingly luxurious—they were throughout these centuries a magnet which attracted a percentage of those peasants living around them—how large a percentage we cannot tell. But there they were; and, as we have seen, the lord with average foresight knew he must deal with them. Once let the opinion gain ground that the manorial conditions were unfairly exacting, and flight became a subject of discussion within the village ale-house, and in the moments of rest in the fields and at the plough. The Abbot of Burton may have won the applause of lawyers when he told his serfs that they had nothing of their own save their bellies (*nihil praeter ventrem*), but he was a foolish fellow nevertheless.[1] Again, the story of Bury St Edmunds shows clearly enough what difficulties landlords created for themselves by a resolute refusal to see how the times were changing.[2] In general, however, lord and peasant found it mutually convenient to compromise—the well-known phrase of the customals "and he shall serve *ad voluntatem domini et secundum consuetudinem manerii*" shows how custom had taken its place in manorial life, and that "the will of the lord" had been softened by the passage of time, so that it had now to be interpreted by the custom of the manor.[3] The majority of peasants were kept on the manor by a reluctance to leave home, and a general belief that their lot was not unduly hard but approximated to that of their neighbours.[4]

[1] Wm. Salt Soc. v, 82.

[2] See *Jocelin of Brakelond, passim*, and compare conditions at Dunstable in 1229 (*Ann. Dunst.* R.S. 122), or at Darnall and Over in 1326 and 1336 (*Vale Royal Ledger Book*, 37 ff. and 117 ff.).

[3] See above, p. 100.

[4] Compare *V.C.H. Herts*, IV, 186, where it says that flight was rare in the thirteenth century, for as commutation increased there was less necessity to bind tenants to the soil.

Notwithstanding this, when once the serf made up his mind to run away it was difficult to restrain him. Once the four days had elapsed in which the lord could pursue his serf and take him wherever he found him, henceforth he had power of arrest only in his own manor. The serf, therefore, had only to get outside the manor—which in many cases simply meant crossing a road and walking a mile to the town—and in a few days he had sufficient preliminary protection to keep his lord at bay. Henceforward, if the lord wanted him, he must take due legal action to get him, and in the meanwhile he might disappear again.[1]

Naturally the lord did what he could to insist on the immobility of his peasantry. Every serf was a potential source of income, and was not lightly to be allowed to escape from his obligations. Hence it is that in such comprehensive instructions as we find the Abbot of Gloucester issuing to his officials, he includes clauses which prohibit the practice of leaving the manor without leave,[2] while the Prior of Worcester in his inquiry into the state of his manors demands an account of those who have left them and by what authority.[3] But such instructions, in the nature of things, were more academic than practical. No doubt the officials did their best, and the steward at the Manor Court often explained that the whole duty of man was to stay where he was put, yet something more than words was needed on many occasions. It frequently happened that the lord got to know that a man was uneasy and threatened to desert,[4] so that he was able to take precautionary measures. In general these took the form of requiring the suspect to produce pledges for his good behaviour: John Boneffant, in 1275, was forced to find two pledges that he would not withdraw himself from the lord's land, and that he would be prompt to obey the lord's summons.[5] On some manors sureties had to be found to answer that the man would not remove his goods and chattels from the lord's manor,[6] or in others his cattle are seized into the lord's hands in the hope of keeping him from flight.[7] A man's relatives are at times held

---

[1] For all this see below, p. 309, and compare *V.C.H. Sussex*, II, 178, n. 63, on the difficulty of recovering a fugitive serf.

[2] *Glouc. Cart.* III, 218, and compare 176.   [3] *Worc. Priory Reg.* 25 b.

[4] Page, *op. cit.*   [5] Selden Soc. II, 22.

[6] *Wakefield Rolls*, I, 252, 257; II, xix; and cf. *Econ. Documents* (Tawney), 69.

[7] *Hales Rolls*, 120, 121, 124, 125, 169, etc.

responsible for him, as at Cuddington in 1331 where five villeins had fled. The Manor Court ordered their return, and added that if they were not present at the next court their relatives were to be distrained in all their lands and tenements.[1] Such measures as these were everywhere in operation, but even so, migration still went on. Very occasionally we hear of severe repressive measures being taken, such as confinement to the stocks, or even the use of chains to hold an unwilling serf; but, in general, if milder measures failed and the serf absconded, the lord had to make the best of it, or pursue his man with the aid of the courts.[2]

In early times, at least, the King's aid could be prayed, and about 1160 the Abbot and monks of Colchester got a charter from Henry II ordering the delivery to them of their fugitives with all their goods *ubicunque inventi fuerint* upon threat of a fine of no less than £10.[3] A similar writ in 1271 to the Prior of Tynemouth suggests that this method of regaining recalcitrant serfs may have been used to some considerable extent,[4] the more so as we have a charter of Earl Hugh II of Chester giving to the Abbot of St Werburgh exactly the same rights within his lands.[5] It may be that lords acted together in a common interest and allowed access to their lands in order that fugitives might be arrested;[6] but, for the most part, it is clear that a writ from the courts was necessary. It is for such a writ that the Bishop of Chichester's steward writes to him on more than one occasion.[7] But this was a slow business, and as the steward well knew, involved expense, risk and often disaster.[8]

Often, therefore, the lord felt it wisest to bow to the inevitable, and to give leave of absence where he could scarce withhold it, and to retain some appearance of authority and control. This he did by exacting an annual payment, which was called chevage, from all those who wished to live outside the manor. In general the sum exacted was quite small—a few pence or a couple of capons at Christmas, etc., but sometimes the lord added a clause to the effect that the villein should come when required, or that he should attend the half-yearly Leet Courts. These permissions

[1] Page, *op. cit.* 36 n. 1. Cf. *Hales Rolls*, 562, 565, 569, 577.
[2] *Jacob's Well* (E.E.T.S.), 186; Selden Soc. 1, 2.
[3] *Col. Cart.* 40.   [4] *Cal. Charter Rolls*, II, 172.
[5] *Chester Cart.* 73.
[6] H. Barnett, *Glympton* (Oxfordshire Record Society, 1923), 10, 11.
[7] Sussex Arch. Soc. III, 51, 68.   [8] See below, p. 309.

to leave the manor were granted at the Manor Court, and enrolled in the Court Rolls; first, in order that no question might arise as to the legality of the serf's absence, and secondly to impress on his fellows that there was a right and a wrong way of doing these things.[1]

Nevertheless, despite all the efforts on the part of the manorial authorities to check the exodus, men constantly fled from the manor. So long as they were unnecessary to the manorial economy, their lords may have relinquished them, more or less reluctantly, at any rate feeling they were not worth the expense and bother of fetching back. At the same time it was a more serious matter when one who held land and a cot took to his heels *cum omni sequela sua.* Then the manorial machinery was put in motion against him: he was proclaimed as a fugitive in the court and ordered to return, and any goods left behind were sequestrated. But, despite all the steward's admonitions to the homage, when once a man's name appeared as a wanderer it was seldom removed by his return. At meeting after meeting the court orders his return "as many times before", his neighbours are ordered to produce him at the next court, but the years pass by, and he does not return, until after some ten or twelve years hope finally dies, and these useless commands to the peasants are allowed to lapse.[2] The ineffectiveness of these courts, especially after the Black Death, is well shown on the manors of the monks of Eynsham. To take one example:

At a court held on 30 April 1382, it was presented that several *nativi* had withdrawn from [the manor]; and an order is made in one case to the father, in other cases to the homage as a whole, to see that the culprits are brought back. Similar presentments are made at every Court down to 1462; but from 1469 onwards the matter is not mentioned. Although injunctions were always given to the next of kin, or the homage, to bring back those who had escaped, and sometimes a fine of 6s. 8d. or even 20s. was threatened, yet nothing was done either by the lord, or the homage; the fines were not inflicted, nor were the *nativi* produced. At the court held in 1437 when it was presented that

---

[1] These licences are everywhere to be seen in Court Rolls. See e.g. *Hales Rolls,* 58, 361, 485; Selden Soc. II, 24; *Tooting Bec,* 239; *Winton Pipe,* 17; *Kettering Compotus,* 13; Levett, *op. cit.* 29, 135; *V.C.H. Berks,* I, 187; *Durham Halmote Rolls,* XVII, 185, etc.

[2] See *Econ. Documents* (Tawney), 73; *Hales Rolls,* 116, 117, 501; *Durham Halmote Rolls,* 21.

John Rogers, a *nativus* who had not resided [on the manor] for more than 30 years, was living at "Hongrynge Aston", the homage was commanded to bring him back "or to answer for his 'chevage' henceforth", but no "chevage" was paid in this or in any other case. Not that there was any difficulty in finding these *nativi*.[1] They were living in neighbouring villages whither they had removed, probably to obtain better land.... The Abbot's remedy would have been to procure the King's writ to recover his villeins, and on many occasions the entry runs "the Lord's Council should be consulted concerning a writ", but it does not appear that this step was taken.[2]

Why this step was not taken will appear clearly enough when we turn to the King's courts, and the attitude of the law towards the runaway villein.

"In the beginning, every man in the world was free, and the law is so favourable to liberty that he who is once found free and of free estate in a court of record, shall be holden free for ever, unless it be that some later act of his own makes him villein."[3] These words, spoken in 1309 by a great medieval lawyer, Justice Herle, indicate clearly the difficulties besetting a lord who craved the aid of the courts to recover his fugitive serf. He had, as we have seen, four days for "self aid"—days during which he need evoke no other power than his own forces. But once these were elapsed the serf had a seisin of liberty, and his lord must turn to the courts for aid.[4] His first step was to sue out a writ *de nativo habendo*. By this writ the Sheriff of the county was ordered to deliver the villein up to his lord—but only if he admitted he was a villein. If he asserted he was a free man the Sheriff could not seize him, and the lord was forced to sue forth a *pone* to remove the plea before the justices of the Common Bench, either in London or on circuit. The other course open to

---

[1] Cf. the numerous records which state the dwelling places of absentees: *Tooting Bec Rolls*, 235; *Hales Rolls*, 230; *Ramsey Cart.* III, 252, 257; *Ingoldmells Rolls*, 38, 104; *Cal. Inquis. Misc.* II, 34, 473; *Econ. Documents* (Tawney), 72 and *Banstead*, 149, where a serf tells of his four sons and two daughters. "John who is a carpenter, and is engaged, and his fiancée dwells at Southwark: the second is called John, and is a butcher, and dwells at Bletchingly; the third is called William, and he knows not where he dwells; the fourth is called Richard and dwells at Handon in Hedenhall and sells timber boards. Joan is married to G. Taylor and dwells at Claydon, and the other daughter, Emma, is married to R. Halcote and dwells in Bletchingly." But they are all out of the control of their lord.
[2] *Eynsham Cart.* II, xxvi–xxvii.   [3] *Y.B.* 3 Ed. II, 94 (Selden Soc).
[4] Bracton, *op. cit.* f. 191; Britton, *op. cit.* I, 201.

the villein, and a most valuable protection, if he had fallen into his lord's hands, was to bring a writ of *de homine replegiando*. Such a writ ordered the Sheriff to set free the villein from whomsoever had custody of him, or failing his surrender, to seize the person holding the villein, until he produced him.[1] Upon the serf giving security that he would appear to answer the charge of villeinage brought against him, the Sheriff would free him for the time being.

An even more powerful weapon was available to the serf in the shape of the writ *de libertate probanda*. This was the writ used by the man who feared his status was in question and was determined to clear the matter up, once for all, in a court of record; and it was also the writ used by the man who, rightly or wrongly, was accused of being a serf, but who believed the lord had insufficient evidence to prove him so.[2] Such a writ stayed all proceedings against him until the next coming of the itinerant justices. When the case came to trial the lord was under serious disabilities, because of the growing belief that "judgment must be given in favour of liberty".[3] The onus was upon him to prove his case, and

the defendant was not called on to plead to the claim of villeinage unless the Lord at the time of declaring on his title brought his witnesses with him into court, and they acknowledged themselves villeins, and swore to their consanguinity with the defendant; and if the plaintiff failed in producing such evidence, the judgment of the court was that the defendant should be free for ever, and the plaintiff was amerced for his false claim.[4]

Further, it was imperative that the kinsfolk produced should not be less than two in number, and also they must be males, for women were too frail to stand as witnesses in such a matter.[5] Again, the defence was allowed to set up two or three pleas

---

[1] Prof. W. S. Holdsworth says: "As early as the reign of Henry III the group relating to personal freedom followed the writs connected with waste. This group naturally attracted others to it. The replevin of a prisoner connects itself with the replevin of cattle. The writs connected with villein status were also allied." *Op. cit.* II, 434, and cf. I, 95.

[2] This writ was taken away from the serf by 25 Ed. III, cap. 18, but the writ *de homine replegiando* remained to him. See *Rot. Parl.* II, 242 *a*.

[3] Bracton, *op. cit.* ff. 191 *b*, 193.

[4] Sommersett's Case, fol. 20, *State Trials*, 43. The pleading of Hargrave in this case is of great interest and embodies the fullest presentation of the law and the cases on it that we have.   [5] Britton, I, 207.

against their opponents, despite the rule forbidding duplicity in pleading. This leaning in favour of liberty also declared that a bastard was a *filius nullius*, and that therefore it could not be presumed that he was of villein stock.[1] The law also assumed that a stranger settling on the land was a free man, and the courts declined to construe any uncertainty of condition against him.[2] Again, the justices were willing to allow the defence to take full advantage of any slip in pleading or any technical error. These and other difficulties[3] which beset the lord will become clearer if we examine some actual cases.

It is not likely, I think, that the large majority of serfs who appeared in the courts can be thought of as representing the average of their class. It required both brains, courage and money to set in motion the machinery of the medieval lawyers, and only a few would dare attempt it. It meant the delay until the itinerant justices should come: it meant the employment of an attorney and the production of the necessary witnesses, etc. Small wonder that comparatively few serfs cared to enter the courts of law and those that did so deserved all the protection that a tolerant judge could give them. But although the law was favourable, it never denied the rights of the master over his serf. When, in 1302, A. acknowledged himself to be R.'s villein, Justice Brumpton said to R.: "Take him by the neck as your villein, him and his issue for ever."[4] Often it would seem that a lord would take a recalcitrant serf into the courts so as to make clear for ever his condition. There are numerous cases which show that the wretched serf put up little or no fight once in the presence of the overwhelming majesty of the judges and their ceremonial. Again and again the records, *mutatis mutandis*, say that "H. Pilcher was attached to answer W. le Waleys in a plea of naifty. H. could not deny his naifty and so W. had him".[5] Or

---

[1] See *Y.B.* 5 Ed. II (Selden Soc.), 113.

[2] *Villainage*, and 19 Ed. III (R.S.), 110.

[3] The Statute of Merton (20 Henry III) limited the time within which a writ *de nat. hab.* could be brought, and henceforth it was not to exceed "the last return of King John into England" (i.e. 1210). By 38 Henry VIII, cap. 2, the period was limited to sixty years. Also this writ could only be used by a lord who had inherited a villein, and not by one who had an interest for a term of years, etc. See Bracton, f. 195 b.   [4] *Y.B.* 30 Ed. I (R.S.), 200.

[5] *Chester Rolls*, 73; cf. *Lanc. Assize Rolls*, 19, 40, 43; *North. Assize Rolls*, 34, 146, 225. Wm. Salt Soc. VI, 71. Naifty = the state of being a serf.

again: "A. B. sues for his serf C. D. who takes a writ of *de libertate probanda*, and they come to the Assize. There, C. D. acknowledges himself the serf of A. B. Therefore it is ordered that A. B. shall receive C. D. as his villein with all his cattle and children, and C. D. is liberated to him in full court. At the same time C. D. and his pledges are fined because he has not prosecuted his writ".[1]

In these, as in many other cases, it is obvious that the serf has no case, and is forced to acknowledge his condition. This is final: for an acknowledgement thus made in a court of record can always be appealed to, and once the serf has admitted his status his hopes are for ever gone.[2] Indeed, to make doubly sure, his lord may even insist on his repeating the scene at home in his own manorial court, as we see happened, in 1239, when the Abbot of Ramsey forced Gilbert Harding to acknowledge himself a villein and subject to all servile dues levied in his manor of Brancaster, although Gilbert had previously admitted all this at an Assize at Norwich.[3]

For men like this, who were forced to admit their status, the law could do little, although it is worth remarking that the judges refused to allow villeinage to be confessed "except by the party himself in court in *propria persona*".[4] Apart from this, however, the law was powerless, unless the man himself put up some show of defence. Then, at once, as we have seen, everything that could be used in his favour was used. The lord's word was insufficient, and he had to produce his witnesses from the defendant's own kin. Hence, when a man was claimed before the justices at Chester on a writ of *de nativo habendo*, he said he was not bound to appear, because no serf of his kin was brought forward to prove his servitude.[5] Some years later in the same court the defendant made a similar plea. The plaintiff said that production of kin was not necessary until it had been demanded by the other side, but the judges were against him and the defendant was set free.[6]

The plaintiff came into court with his witnesses and opened his case by pleading:

[1] *North. Assize Rolls* (1280), 225.   [2] See Bracton, *op. cit. passim*.
[3] *Ramsey Cart.* I, 423.   [4] *Y.B.* 7 Ed. II (Selden Soc.), 172, n. 1.
[5] *Chester Rolls*, 14.   [6] *Ibid.* 44.

John who is here declareth this to you, that Peter who is there wrongfully fled from him, and herein wrongfully, that he is our villein who fled from his land within the term etc.,[1] and of whom he was seized as of his villein until such a year when he fled from him, and if he denies this, he denies it wrongfully, for the plaintiff hath good suit and sufficient.[2]

Then, says Britton,

immediately let the suit be examined, not only by taking their acknowledgements whether they are villeins to the plaintiff, but whether he against whom the plaint is prosecuted was ever upon the land of the plaintiff, and in what manner the plaintiff was seized of him. And if the suit be found to disagree, in so much it is bad and defective, and the plaint shall be lost.[2]

The plaintiff may well have hesitated, for the production of kin was a risky business. They could evidently be driven into court, but once there, it was by no means certain what they would say. A man produced in court to prove the unfree condition of his brother, on being questioned says he is a free man and no villein, and the lord's case promptly collapses.[3] And so with many cases: the men are not of close enough kin, or indeed turn out not to be kinsmen at all. A plaintiff brings forward two men whom he says are serfs of his, and kinsmen of the defendant, but the defendant says he never had a grandfather bearing either of their names, and he goes free.[4] Again, in an interesting case in Northumberland, in 1280, there are produced as witnesses a man's sister as well as two of his more distant relatives—a William Rudd and Cristina his sister. The defendant at once takes exception to these on the score that women ought not to be admitted in such a suit, being of a more fragile nature than are males, and the court decided that the plaintiff was wrong to bring such feeble witnesses, and inferred that he could find no satisfactory male evidence, and declared for the liberty of the defendant.[5] Cases such as this show that a clever attorney could often take full advantage of the many opportunities the law offered him.

But we must not imagine that such suits were, in general,

---

[1] The term allowable by the statute. See above, p. 311, n. 3.
[2] Britton, I, 204.
[3] Fitzherbert, *Abridgement*, Villeinage, § 39; and cf. *B.N.B.* No. 1812.
[4] *Chester Rolls*, 86.
[5] *North. Assize Rolls*, 274; and see Britton, I, 207; *Villainage*, 84.

unsuccessful. It is not possible to give any precise figures, but a general impression after looking over a great many of these cases leads me to believe that the lord was the victor roughly three times out of four. It is clear that many lords took great care in getting their evidence together and were able to present a very strong case to the court. Vinogradoff says (with perhaps some exaggeration) that "villeins born had their pedigrees as well as the most noble among the peers. They were drawn up to prevent any fraudulent assertion as to freedom, and to guide the lord if he wanted to use the native's kin in prosecution of an action *de nativo habendo*".[1] How useful such a document would be, can be seen from what has already been said, and from such a case as that reported in 1312.[2] In this case William of Cressy claimed William, son of Siward, as his serf. Further he produced no less than six of his kin against him, all of whom acknowledged themselves to be serfs. To meet this formidable array, the attorney of the defendant pleaded that for various reasons they ought not to be admitted. The case illustrates so well the intricacy and possibilities of a medieval action of this kind that I give the rest in full from the record.

And the aforesaid William, son of Siward, cometh and doth deny the right of William of Cressy and all naifty...and he saith that he is a free man and of free estate. For he saith that the aforesaid Harry, Richard, William, Nigel, Gregory and Robert, whom William bringeth into his proof to show that he, William, son of Siward, must answer to this writ ought not to be admitted in such proof. And as to Richard, son of Robert that is brother of the aforesaid Siward, of whom the aforesaid Roger, father of the claimant, was seized, he doth answer and say that he ought not to be admitted into the claimant's proof, because Robert, his father, is alive and not present; and while his father is alive, not being present, he himself cannot make answer. And as to William, son of William, son of Hugh, brother of the aforesaid Siward, whom he produceth in proof, he ought not to be admitted,

---

[1] *Villainage*, 143; and see Appendix x for one such elaborate pedigree. Compare also *V.C.H. Lincs*, ii, 300, where such a pedigree is successfully sustained in court by the lord, and *The Times*, Jan. 23, 1933, where Miss H. M. Cam is quoted as saying that "she had been surprised at the precision with which family trees were produced and cited in the lowest levels of society in the twelfth and thirteenth centuries. Not only a serf but his Lord could trace the serf's descent and collateral relationship back for 4 generations."

[2] The editor of the *Year Book* thinks, however, that it was really heard *temp*. Ed. I.

because William, his father, was not born in lawful wedlock, but during the widowhood of his mother. And if William his father, son of Hugh, were alive, he would not be admissible in proof, because he was a bastard. And the said William, his son, cannot be in a better condition than William, his father. And he asketh judgment if he ought to be admitted, etc. And as to the aforesaid, Nigel, Gregory and Robert, sons of Denise, sister of the said Siward, whom the claimant bringeth in proof, etc., they ought not to be received, because Denise, their mother, was espoused to a certain free man of W.; and he saith that the aforesaid Nigel, Gregory and Robert were born in lawful wedlock, and ought, therefore, to follow their father and not their mother, and he asketh judgment whether they are receivable to prove that any man of the issue of their mother must answer a writ of naifty. And as to Harry, son of Robert, son of Siward, he saith that he is not receivable in proof, because he is alone, and the testimony of a single person is as the testimony of no one. And he saith further that if the Court shall rule that the aforesaid men whom the claimant offereth in proof are admissable, the aforesaid reasons and challenges notwithstanding, then he saith as before that he is a man of free estate, and he saith that the aforesaid Harry, Richard, William, Nigel, Gregory and Robert are free men, unless in the King's Court they confess that they be villeins. And he saith that one Otes, father of the aforesaid Siward, is and was a free man, and came as an *adventif*[1] from the neighbourhood of Northfield and took [land] in villeinage from the ancestors of the aforesaid William of Cressy to have and to hold at their will, and he is ready to aver this in such a way as the Court of the lord King shall award....And the said William of Cressy saith that the aforesaid Otes, father of the aforesaid Siward, was a villein through his grandfather and his great-grandfather, and was born on his land; and he asketh that this be inquired of by the neighbourhood. And William the son of Siward asketh the like. So the Sheriff is commanded, etc.[2]

[1] An *adventif* is one who comes onto the manor from outside, and is always presumed to be a free man (see above, p. 311).

[2] *Y.B.* 5 Ed. II, 121–3. The relations between the various parties will be easily seen from the following:

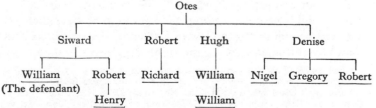

The underlined names are those of the kinsmen present in court.

Unfortunately we do not know how this action was concluded, and can only admire the resourcefulness of the attorney's pleading and the skilful way in which he tried to dispose of his opponents. Generally the records do not give us so detailed an account as this, but merely say that the kinsmen were produced against the man and he was found to be of servile condition.[1] But the brevity of the record must often hide pleas as elaborate as the one set out above; we have only to look at Bracton's treatise to see this, where on turning to Book IV, chapter 23, we may read of the difficulties of pleading when villein status was in question, and from which it is obvious a clever attorney could put up a bewildering variety of defences. In his earlier account Britton says that the defendant shall "aid himself with exceptions to the judge, and then to the person of the plaintiff, and afterwards to his own person; and next by exception to the writ if there is any defect or error; and afterwards to the declaration, if there is any defect, omission, or variance in it; and lastly to the action".[2] He then gives an example of how to except against the kinsmen, which evidently was in the mind of the attorney who defended William, son of Siward, and goes on to an elaborate exposition of other defences which could be urged.

One more point may be noted. We have extant a considerable number of cases in which the lord failed to prosecute when it came to the day of the Assize.[3] They are not sufficient, perhaps, to afford good grounds for any argument, but the comparative frequency of these defaults encourages the belief that the writ was sometimes used *ad terrorem*, in the hope that the serf would not face the dangers, anxiety and expense of an assize. The default of the lord automatically ended his claim, and he was at once subjected to a fine for false plea, and the Sheriff instructed to see that he ceased to aggrieve the defendant in the future.[4]

Here our enquiry may well end. The courts of the fourteenth century and later were making it more and more clear that serfdom was repugnant to the law of England, whatever precedents drawn from Roman Law, or the subtle arguments of theologians

---

[1] See e.g. *B.N.B.* No. 1005; *Curia Regis Rolls*, I, 22, 45, 67, 187, 263.
[2] Britton, I, 206. For a good example see *North. Assize Rolls*, 195.
[3] For such cases see, e.g., *B.N.B.* No. 1934; *Linc. Assize Rolls*, 32, 35; *Lanc. Assize Rolls*, 28, 34; *North. Assize Rolls*, 25, 38, 61, 156, 170, 172, 177.
[4] Britton, I, 202; cf. *B.N.B.* No. 1934.

and schoolmen might declare. There was indubitably a general movement towards freedom, although we may find it difficult to see clearly how an incident here, or a manumission there, could do much to aid its forward march. So, at times, we look at a mountain stream a few miles from its source and marvel at its impetuous volume, but our wonder would be lessened by a better knowledge of the hills through which it has passed, and of the innumerable freshlets which have each contributed their store of waters, gathered in their turn from vast areas of forest or snow-field. Our knowledge of the medieval world is much less than our knowledge of the mountain stream. All we can do is to assemble our little groups of facts from wherever we can find them, and try to see how they fit together. The slow march of the peasant towards freedom is one to which many circumstances contributed: the harshness of overbearing lords, the attraction of the towns, the growing realisation that forced labour was not so profitable in the long run as hired labour, the pressure of events when war, famine or pestilence depleted the manorial population and thus left the lord with holdings on his hands which he was glad to let at a money and not a servile rent—all these, and many others, were so many contributory causes which finally brought the manorial system to an end—and with it came the end of personal subjection and all its humiliating consequences.

The Church

CHAPTER XII

THE CHURCH

IN my first chapter I stressed the importance of the Church and of religion to medieval man, and now that we have seen many other sides of his activity, it is time to return to consider the part played by religion in the lives of the peasants. Of all our investigations this is perhaps the most difficult, for here we are dealing with something that was so much a part of everyday life that many of its most common details have left but little trace. What it was everyone's business to observe it was no one's business to record. Who should trouble to note down the multitudinous details concerning matters which were part of everyday life—nay more, were part of the whole surrounding scheme of things and of the very air men breathed? Most medieval peasants, if questioned about their beliefs, would have been unable to answer any more explicitly than can their present-day brothers in any mountain village of Catholic France or Switzerland. They do what has always been done. The services, the ceremonial, the offerings, the obligations—all are part of the scheme of things, not to be questioned, save by the wicked, and even they, *in articulo mortis*, are often not so sure.

Obviously, the peasant's attitude to religion is not a matter we can dogmatise about, any more than we have found we can dogmatise about his status, obligations or privileges. His religion, to be sure, was not so much a matter of geography: the devout believer was much the same everywhere, while the doubter and blasphemer were animated by like prejudices wherever they were to be found. In speaking of the peasant's religion, therefore, we may assume that the majority were believers, although the fervour and sincerity of their belief is much more difficult to estimate. The heretic, declared, was rare, and not to be envied. He was an outcast from the great body of the faithful, and was made to feel his exile. Most men feared the isolation of such a position, and were liable to suffer more than loneliness once the Church took active steps against them. If we leave them on one side and concentrate on the faithful, we shall be considering the great body of medieval peasantry.

Let us start with the village church and the services which the peasant was accustomed to attend there. The building itself was symbolic of security, although it was rarely in England that it became literally the one place of safety, as so often in Germany and Switzerland, when people sheltered themselves behind its walls and doors, and the passage of the enemy left of their frail houses only wreckage and smouldering ruins. Besides giving a sense of security, the comparative magnificence of many village churches must have made a deep impression on the simple mind. The lofty tower, the spacious nave, together with the tracery of the windows and the carvings on capital and portal, gave men a sense of "other-worldliness", while the comparison between the peace and dignity of God's house and the squalor and turmoil of their own hovels made its constant appeal—not very consciously, perhaps—but inevitably and as part of the whole *ethos* of the religious world.

There the church stood, and the peasant could not but be aware of it, as he passed it on his way to his fields, or as he heard the Mass bell sounding as he worked in the meadows or on some distant forest clearing. How often he entered it is another matter. We have already seen conclusive evidence that on some manors the lord was unwilling that his work should cease because a holy-day strictly required his serf's attendance at the church; and we may well conclude that any theory that the majority of men and women spent their holy-days, as well as Sundays, at church has no foundation in actual fact. Even writers such as Myrc do not seem to contemplate any very serious attempt by ordinary folk to attend all such services.[1] We shall probably be near the truth if we think of the peasant as attending Mass on Sunday, and on a few great festivals, such as Christmas and Easter, on the name-day of the patron saint of the church, and on days when some special local ceremony, such as carrying the Virgin from the church to a little chapel on the edge of the parish, was performed. Otherwise, church-going was much as it is now —a matter of daily refreshment and happy duty for some, and only a matter of "use and wont" for many, for whom the Sunday and other special services sufficed.

Such attendance, however, had more importance than we are

[1] Manning, *op. cit.* 5.

at first inclined to attribute to it, for medieval religion centred mainly in the building itself. No doubt a limited amount of simple instruction was given by parents in answer to childish questions. The crossing at prayers or thanksgiving; the holy wells and the use of holy water; the sight of the priest carrying the sacred oils to the house of the sick—these and many other daily events necessarily provoked enquiry, but it was mainly, if not solely, in the church itself that instruction was given. "What mean ye by this service?" would have been a hard question for the peasant to answer, and he would rightly have said that it was a matter for the priest and not for him. Indeed, his knowledge and understanding of what went on in church was not very profound. He was ignorant, unlettered, without other means of instruction than that which could be imparted to him by his village clergy, or by a passing friar. More he only got by his attention to the details of the service, and to the ideas and stories embodied in sculpture and painting within and without the church. These could do something to help educate the peasant; but, for most of them, their religion was less a matter of thought than a matter of habit. In common with all their neighbours they held certain beliefs, did certain things and made certain donations because, as far as they knew, people had always thus behaved. The services, themselves, were mysterious to them for the most part, since the vast majority of medieval congregations were unable to follow one word of the Latin in which they were said. The priest rehearsed the words and performed various actions, while they repeated such prayers and devotions as they knew. Not that these were many: the *Pater Noster* and the *Ave* were generally known, but even this minimum could not be assumed; and, although the Apostles' Creed was looked on as the layman's creed, many were ignorant of this. The most that could be expected from the earnest peasant was the Creed, *Pater* and *Ave*, with, perhaps, the Commandments, and the devout recital of these was expected to occupy him during the saying of the Mass. He was thus thrown on his own spiritual resources to a considerable extent, but this was no real solution and for the majority some more practical help was necessary.

To meet this need the Church had strained every resource. Music, painting, miming, imagery—all played their part. The central service of the Church—the Mass—was one great mimetic rite, and in the ceremonial of the Mass there was set forth every detail and every aspect of the atonement of mankind. Not a dogma was omitted, not the minutest event in Christ's passion but was commemorated there. From an art symbolism had been transformed into a science. Every faculty of man, every property of nature had been captured and subdued for that supreme drama of worship. Music and silence, colour and distance, light and darkness, imagery and gesture, all contributed to the final result. The church itself, even the humblest, was the poor man's service book....All helped to make real the unseen things that are eternal. Earth was "crammed with heaven and every common bush afire with God".[1]

We must not stress unduly the statement that the church was "the poor man's service book", for the church could only show a limited number of Biblical episodes, and many important aspects of the teaching of Christ were not easily conveyed in paint. Nevertheless, the wavering and credulous mind was much impressed by the wall paintings which showed in crude colours some of the major events of Biblical history, often depicted with such a realism that our softer age rapidly covers them up when they are now disclosed at a cleaning or restoration of a church. The horrors of hell, or the anguish of the Crucifixion, came home to the peasant, either soon or late, as week by week his wandering gaze fell upon them, and half-remembered snatches of sermons reminded him of that "fearful place and a dyrke wher-in appered a fornace all brennyng within; and that fyr had not elles to brenne bot fendes and quyke sowlys".[2] Such scenes as these, or that of the Last Judgment, could not but have their effect, and men felt about them the presence of an unseen yet all-pervading deity, attended by his cohorts of angels, and ever at war with the powers of darkness.

Further help was less general and less certain in its effect. Symbolism was much used in medieval ceremonial, but most of it had no very clear interpretation, especially for the peasant, so that its force was dissipated and it became the occasion for the most absurd deductions. In any case very little of it appeared in the humble village churches—certainly not sufficient to be as

---

[1] Manning, *op. cit.* 12.
[2] *Revelations of S. Birgitta* (E.E.T.S.), 44.

PLATE VI

The Last Judgement

effective as half-a-dozen straightforward sermons from a wise village priest would have been.

Here we begin to come to grips with the root weakness of the medieval Church. Wherever we are able to examine the relation between clergy and parishioners we are forced to the conclusion that most of the ordinary parish clergy were inefficient, ill-educated, undistinguished men. It is unwise to indict a whole class, but it seems clear that much that was weakest in the medieval religious system was primarily due to the ill-trained, ill-educated parish clergy. This, certainly, was the view of some of the greatest prelates from the thirteenth to the sixteenth century. The unworthy clergy of Archbishop Stephen Langton's day were still sufficiently prevalent in Wolsey's time for him to be forced to take action against their ignorance and slack behaviour. Indeed it is evident from the reiterated exhortations of Archbishops and Bishops that they were painfully aware that all was not well with the clergy. Throughout the four centuries preceding the Reformation there was a growing feeling that the condition of the Church would never be improved until the quality of her clergy was improved. From the thirteenth century onward we have a series of pronouncements from Church synods and convocations. Archbishop Peckham's well-known constitution of 1281 runs: "The ignorance of the priests casteth the people into the ditch of error; and the folly or unlearning of the clergy, who are bidden to instruct the faithful in the Catholic faith, sometimes tendeth rather to error than to sound doctrine." This had been preceded by Langton's description of some of the clergy as "dumb dogs", whose ability to read the Canon of the Mass he casts in doubt; and so the plaint goes on down the ages to the time of Wolsey, who in 1518 tells the synod of York that he republishes the time-worn constitutions because they had been ignored in the past, and for emphasis repeats Peckham's words. This matter is so important to a proper understanding of village life that a brief account of the parish priest and his education must be given here.

The crux of the whole matter was put into one of F. W. Maitland's revealing statements, when he spoke of the clergy as belonging to the manorial aristocracy—perhaps at the head of that aristocracy—but essentially of it. We have evidence in plenty of the way in which the clergy of the thirteenth and fourteenth centuries were recruited from the peasant class, and fourteenth-century writers draw attention to beggar's brats who have risen even to the rank of bishops, and of men, like Chaucer's parson, whose brothers were ploughmen. Few of them, indeed, could hope for much advancement or for rich livings, but they were glad to serve in more humble positions as vicars and drudges for richer and more influential men who were seldom seen in their parishes. Langland's seemingly autobiographical references in *Piers Plowman* picture one such type of man—of peasant stock, roaming from place to place and "singing for silver" at funerals or other ceremonies, or striving to "pierce heaven with a pater-noster", and making a bare living "in London and on London both".

If we imagine how such men became priests it seems probable that many of them found themselves being slowly drawn into the ecclesiastical machine without any very active efforts on their own part. Perhaps a boy started, to the delight of a pious mother, as server to the village priest. He would receive the first tonsure, and afterwards, if still willing to continue, was gradually (or at times *en bloc*) promoted through the four minor orders of clergy. A kindly and lettered priest might teach a promising boy the elements of Latin, so that he could follow the service and join in the responses. Sometimes, again, such a boy was made "holy-water clerk", and thus got a small income which enabled him to remain a servant of the Church; and, where it was possible, to gain a little learning from a private teacher or at a local grammar school. Learning, however, was not very easily come by for such men, and those who had the advantage of the formal training at the grammar school or even at a university found themselves at the end of it all with what we should consider a very narrow education. Latin and cognate subjects occupied their studies, and such things as mathematics, science, history or geography did not come their way. Nor was there any training peculiarly fitted to instruct them in their pastoral office. At best, a man returned from the university a competent Latinist, able to dispute with some readiness, and the imperfect master of such fragments of the schoolmen, and of the Fathers and such ancient authors as his course had set before him. But for the majority not even this was possible: a moderate ability to read and construe the Latin of the service books, and a knowledge of the Church services, gained by years of experience, was all their stock in trade.

With a limited training such as this, it was the fortune of many to find themselves serving first as deacons, and then as priests in the smaller rectories and the vicarages in town and country. The value of many rectories made them a close preserve of the rich or influential, but there were a large number of vicarages for which an absentee rector required a deputy, and there were also the subordinate positions, such as that of the stipendiary chaplain or the assistant priest to be filled. Thus there were plenty of opportunities for those men, from whom not over much would be expected, and who could not look forward to a very generous stipend or allowances. Mr H. G. Richardson puts it clearly:

Vicars probably had a higher average annual income than the mere stipendiary chaplains and assistant priests. A great many vicars, however, received but five or six marks and even less a year, and though rectorial incomes ruled higher, yet there were some who must have been very badly off, particularly if they endeavoured to dispense any measure of hospitality in addition to meeting the various claims that fell on an incumbent in respect of the maintenance of the church and its services.... We cannot go far wrong if we consider the stipendiary chaplains and assistant priests as forming the lowest-paid grade of the body of priests and beneficed clergy. Below them come the unbeneficed minor clergy, a little above them the perpetual vicars and poorest rectors, and on an altogether different economic and social plane the rectors of the really valuable churches. If, further, we suppose the average chaplain to have had from all sources before the Black Death an income of six or seven marks (say 90 shillings), and accept forty-eight shillings as a moderate estimate of the income of a first-class agricultural labourer, such as a ploughman or carter, at the same period, we have some indication of whereabouts in the social scale to place the great mass of poorly paid parish clergy.[1]

It is evident then that neither birth, training nor emoluments was peculiarly favourable to the production of a priesthood of outstanding merit, and the records, both historical and literary, bear damning witness of their shortcomings. Such records as survive of official enquiries into the intellectual state of the village clergy are staggering. We have, for example, the visitation

[1] "The Parish Clergy of the Thirteenth and Fourteenth Centuries," *Trans. Roy. Hist. Soc.* Third Series, vol. VI, 1912.

by the Dean of Sarum, in 1222, of the clergy of Sonning and the neighbourhood, in which he found that five of the clergy serving some seventeen parishes were unable to construe the central portion of the service of the Mass. The curate of Sonning, who had been a priest for four years, was unable to understand the gospel for the First Sunday in Lent, and could not construe the first words of the Canon of the Mass, nor could he tell the difference between one antiphon and another. Another curate, who had been priested four years previously, was reported as knowing nothing of reading or singing. Another could give no answer to simple questions; and the next examined is reported as knowing nothing.[1]

It was to men such as these that the peasant turned, perforce, in his time of need. Sometimes he was lucky, and found a man as humane and clear as to his pastoral duties as was Chaucer's parson; sometimes he was unlucky, and had a man as weak and idle as those pilloried in the visitations, or in Langland or Gower. But, good or bad, their help was limited, for they had had no systematic training in theology or pastoral duties, and could offer little more than sympathy and an imperfect exposition of the mysteries of the Faith. Even the simple eloquence of many a latter-day preacher in his weekly sermon was not theirs, for sermons were far from frequent, and the ordinary priest but little skilled in preaching. He was, indeed, ordered to deliver four sermons a year by Archbishop Peckham, and in the thirteenth century we find frequent sermons advocated. But sermon making was an art beyond the ordinary priest: he left that to those trained rhetoricians—the friars; and, for his own part, endeavoured to explain the tenets of the Faith, and to give elementary instruction to his parishioners. This was, however, all very elementary, and his own limited intelligence and reading were reflected in his teaching. The best he could do was to administer the sacraments and to conduct the services in an orderly and decent manner.

The fact that he, himself, was frequently of peasant stock made him the more capable of understanding his parishioner's point of view. What would have been sheer heresy or gross superstition to a better informed man was frequently part of his

[1] *Reg. S. Osmund* (R.S.), 1, 304 ff.

own intellectual make-up, and he therefore kept a closer contact with his flock than a more erudite but less sympathetic mind would have done. It is of the greatest importance that we should emphasise this identity of interests: indeed, it has remained a strength (despite its many drawbacks) of the Catholic Church until to-day. The ample priest, with his soiled soutane and heavy boots, who clambers into the local French autobus, and after greeting most of the passengers settles down in happy converse with them *en route* to their village, is the modern descendant of most medieval parish priests. No one can view such a group without realising that there is some close relation between such people which the parson of the average English country parish, drawn as he is from a different social status and educated at the university and clergy school, will not easily achieve.

Were there no more to be said, we might be inclined to feel that on balance the peasant-priest was the right man in the right place. But, unfortunately, there is more in it than this; the priest must live, and, as we have seen, his stipend was not a princely one. Certainly it put him on a level with the largest holders in the fields, but often no more than this, and it must be remembered that his salary had to support not only himself, but sometimes one or more clerics who assisted him, as well as a "hearth-mate"—a frequent inhabitant of clerical homes, even though Canon Law and Church discipline refused her the title of wife. In consequence, many incumbents found it impossible to exist solely on their ecclesiastical income, and were therefore forced to participate in worldly matters, which in general meant agriculture.

Indeed, practically all had a certain amount of land, called glebe, assigned to them in the manor by virtue of their office. This glebe land was at times scattered over the common fields, and at other times was consolidated in blocks or closes, and the parson cultivated it himself, or let it out to others. These "Church furlongs" or "parson's closes" forced the clerics to take part in the agricultural life of the village, and many, for economic reasons, were obliged to go further than this, and to engage in the common agricultural routine and organisation of the open-field system. In stepping down in this way into the area of everyday affairs they lost something by way of prestige, and were drawn into economic and petty quarrels of a most undesirable nature. For example, they were forced to enter into open competition for the sale of surplus stock and crops, and to indulge in buying and selling, although this was against Church law, which a long series of admonitions tried in vain to enforce. And with all this went other scandals. Priests found themselves haled before Manor Courts; accused of various manorial offences; fined, admonished, and treated in many ways like their peasant flock to the detriment of their position. Not only this, the priest constantly found his worldly ends conflicting with those of his parishioners, who were his rivals at a fair, or were his competitors for some piece of assart, or favoured close, which each wished to control. The claims of strict business and those of true religion marched ill together, and hot blood engendered in the market-place was not easily cooled elsewhere, so that the priest and a number of his flock were liable to find themselves at loggerheads, almost despite themselves, as a consequence of the system which controlled them both.

In addition to the difficulties which arose in these ways, there was the ever-present difficulty of tithe. Then, as now, men paid tithes very reluctantly, and with many a curse against the Church (and sometimes its agents) which extracted them. Tithe seemed unreasonable to many, since to their way of thinking it took part of their small property and bestowed it upon a man, certainly no worse off than themselves for the most part, and frequently a man who was comparatively well-to-do. The Church, moreover, did not help matters by the severity with which she had laid down what things were tithable, and by the rigour with which she insisted on their due payment. In addition to the great tithes, which were principally taken on corn, there were the lesser tithes, and these were wellnigh all-embracing.

The tithes constituted a land tax, income tax and death duty far more onerous than any known in modern times, and proportionately unpopular. The farmers [were] bound to render a strict tenth of all their produce—theoretically, at least, down to the very pot-herbs of their gardens.... Moreover, the law was pitiless to the peasant. Tithes of wool were held to include even the down of his geese; the very grass he cut by the road side was to pay its due toll; the farmer who deducted working expenses before tithing his crops damned himself thereby to hell.... We need scarcely wonder that the laity, thus situated, excogitated many subterfuges of "excessive malice...to the manifest prejudice of ecclesiastical rights and liberties, and to the grievous harm of their own souls" which may be found set out at length in Stratford's constitutions and elsewhere.[1]

The multiplicity of things tithable suggests how important a source of income tithes represented to the Church, and it is, therefore, not surprising to find that they were exacted with considerable pressure where this was necessary. "Full loath were him to cursen for his tithes", says Chaucer of his model parish priest, and few of his contemporaries would have failed to recognise how rare a man this made him. The fiercest curses of the Church were stored up for those who were recalcitrant, and the priest was instructed to pronounce their excommunication with book, bell and candle.

It is without question that these demands for tithe, continuously asserted and enforced as they were, led to frequent difficulties, and tended to estrange the priest from his flock. Men could not see why they should make these payments to a man, whom, although a priest, they knew to be drawn from their own ranks, and whose parents and brethren, nay, often himself, still worked side by side with them in their unending struggle to win a living from the soil.

The priest, then, needed to be a man of unusual character to overcome these many difficulties, and we must always bear this in mind before we condemn him for the innumerable lapses that undoubtedly occurred. Throughout these centuries we need not doubt that many priests tried, and did their utmost —so far as their birth, education and the system would allow— to be true shepherds to their flocks. Medieval England would have been immeasurably the poorer without them: their presence in the parish gave a natural leader to those forces and aspirations making for good, even amidst the dangerous passions of a half-civilised world. Whether from love or fear, many peasants were kept within bounds by the occasional rebuke or the kindly remonstrance of their village priest, and their influence in this way was undoubtedly considerable.

Yet, it still remains true that, wherever we can glimpse the actual life of the medieval clergy, it falls far short of what would seem desirable, even at a moderate estimate. The opportunity

[1] G. G. Coulton, *Ten Medieval Studies*, 124.

was much greater than the fulfilment. From time to time (though, unfortunately, not often within the period mainly dealt with here) a "close-up" of religious life in the parish is given by means of an episcopal or archidiaconal visitation. On such occasions, as is well known, the worst side of affairs is presented: it is as though we had to judge the morality and conduct of a town or country solely by its police-court records. Nevertheless, the damning facts remain: the evil is there, however much it may be set off by the good, and when the evil in a parish finds its focus in the clergy, and within his house, do what we will, we cannot but admit that this is peculiarly potent. The clergy may well be considered as the salt of the earth, but what if the salt hath lost its savour, or, as Chaucer put it, "If gold ruste, what shal iren do?" The visitation documents, it must be admitted, show a very tarnished gold in many parishes. The Hereford visitation of 1397 is the fullest we have left, and even when we make every allowance for it being a border diocese, and for the influence of "Wild Wales", the total effect of the evidence is so startling as to be almost incredible to modern readers.[1] The condition of affairs in 281 parishes is surveyed, and in 44 of these the jury report that all is well. In some of the remaining parishes the main offenders are the laity, but with surprising frequency the clergy also are involved. Their offences come under many heads: gravest of all is the constant charge of immorality. There are more than sixty cases mentioned of clerical offenders—rectors, vicars, chaplains—all are again and again denounced as fornicators and adulterers, and as keeping women from their husbands. When we notice the monotonous regularity with which men and women in almost every parish are accused of this same offence, it is impossible to ignore the part played by this evil clerical example. Complaints against the clergy are distressingly frequent: John Pole, the chantry priest at Weston, absents himself for weeks at a time from his church, and his Mass is not said; the vicar of Werley similarly neglects his cure; the rector of Monesley does not reside as he should and the divine services go unsaid, for neither here, nor at Cowarne Parva, is any deputy provided by the absent rector. With this neglect to provide a deputy go other wrongs: here at Cowarne the chancel of the

Complaints [margin annotation]

[1] *E.H.R.* xliv, 279–89, 444–53; xlv, 92–101; 444–63.

church is dilapidated, with broken windows, and leaky roof, and the rectory house is falling to pieces for want of repair. At Peterchurch, the rector refuses to provide the necessary service-books, or to mend a breach in the churchyard wall, or to repair the chancel. At Werley, the rector is accused of threshing his corn in the churchyard, and is ordered not to do so again; but an accusation that the vicar pastures his horses, cows and ducks therein is expressly denied. Parish after parish presents similar pictures: the vicar or the chaplains are absentees or irregular; the services are neglected or hurriedly said: at Garwy, where Welsh and English both were spoken, the parson could not understand many of his congregation who spoke only Welsh. Some parsons were ill-famed of tavern-haunting and drunkenness; others were common traders, "buying and selling various goods and taking money therefor"; others, again, refused to bury the dead, or to baptise, or to administer the last sacrament without giving sufficient reason. The chaplain of Colwall is accused of forging a will, and naming himself as executor; while the vicar of Yazore, and the vicar of Erdesley are both known as common usurers.

So we might go on with this wearisome list. If we turn to look at the individual parishes in detail some astounding complaints come to light. To take one or two examples, almost at random. The parishioners complain that the rector of Wentnor does not efficiently conduct the Mass and other services, that he has allowed his manse to fall into disrepair, and that he frequents taverns by day and night to the scandal of religion. This, however, he denies. They also assert that he does not provide the vestments as he is bound to do, and that he had "put his benefice to hire" to John Bent, a dishonest and uncapable chaplain, who still retains some of the church ornaments, and who is ill-famed with a certain Meveddus. The affairs of another parish (North Lydbury), which were dealt with the same day, showed that the chancel needed repair, and the necessary vestments were lacking, both by the rector's neglect. The deacon neglected the bell-ringing, and the vicar absented himself from Michaelmas onwards, but drew his salary all the time. The deacon was accused of having lost a chalice, while the vicar was said to have committed adultery with Johanna Staltoghe. The same day, the parishioners of Clun said that their parish chaplain provoked quarrels and strife in the parish; he refused to take the sacrament to a dying man, who therefore died unshriven; while another was buried without the funeral Mass and prayers by his neglect. He also absented himself on Corpus Christi Day, and was incontinent with a married woman, and actually baptised his own child by her, and afterwards had by her another infant.

These two pages must suffice. They are neither better nor worse than the average presented by this visitation, and even when we have made all allowances for village gossip, malice and ignorance, what a picture they present! In a few parishes all is well; but the others unroll a continuous story of indifference, neglect and worse. The parson of Eardisley, at war with his parishioners, served by his two maid servants at Mass, and gravely suspect of his relations with them, is pictured for us as he buries a parishioner, and shouts at the corpse, "Lie you there, excommunicate". John, the chaplain of Kilpeck, is another strange cleric who, the villagers say, "seemeth to them by no means firm in the faith, for he hath oftentimes conjured by night with familiar spirits" (*fecit pompam suam tempore nocturno cum spiritis fantasticis*). Richard Sterre, although he has been convicted of adultery and excommunicated by the bishop, still continues to celebrate in the church at Scheldesley, and is accused of continuing his luxury with the woman, even within the church itself, and is also ill-famed of her sister. He and his fellow chaplain go about armed by night, chattering and frightening the parishioners. The shortcomings of these Hereford clerics would be unbelievable, were they not recorded item by item as a result of this official enquiry.[1]

"As the shepherd, so are the sheep." These same documents show us the low state of morality and of devotion to the Church in the villages of this diocese. Adultery and immorality are widespread; men and women refuse to come to church, and go about their work on holy-days and Sundays; they neglect to provide the necessary lights for the church, or to repair the nave and churchyard wall when necessary. Mortuaries and tithes are evaded, and the *panis benedictus* is not presented by some in their

[1] A detailed examination and commentary on this visitation will be found in G. G. Coulton, *Old England*, Chapter 14.

due turn. Superstition is an integral part of life, and some are even accused of witchcraft. These things required a strong good clergy to control them, for men will listen to those whom they know to have convictions—even though they are inclined to dispute them: but many a priest was obviously a by-word in these parishes, just as Sloth the Parson was in his parish, and men could attach but little credence or respect to anything they said.

Let us leave them on one side, and take a man as capable and sincere as Chaucer's "poure parson of a towne", and try to imagine what was his influence in his parish. In the first place, he stood for something outside the daily round of toil and bartering, and only reluctantly entered the arena if forced to do so by stubborn or hostile parishioners who denied him his dues or privileges. These, undoubtedly, he was forced to stand up for; but, given a man such as Chaucer's parson, we may well imagine that he got what was his without undue friction. Secondly, small though his learning was, he was frequently the only "clerk" in the village. His superior knowledge and reputed wisdom settled many disputes, both at the formal "love-days", and at other times when occasion offered. He could make the rough account for the reeve, and the preliminary survey called for by the lord's steward. But, above all, his sacred calling gave him an authority and a special place which were generally un-challenged. The Church and its ministers, as we have seen, stood for much in medieval life, and most villagers went without ques-tion to their parish church week by week, as well as in moments of exaltation or of despair. The priest consoled, advised, ad-monished, encouraged: he was with them at the great moments of life and death, and for good or ill he was emphatically the parson—that is *the person* of the village. Hence we may well regard him as a focus of all those forces making for good in the parish, and a constant warrior against evil and superstition. Evil and superstition, as we have seen, were ever present in the medieval village; but the Church standing in the centre of things was a constant reminder to the peasant of that great un-seen cloud of saints and believers who had gone before, and whose witness encouraged him to believe in the omnipotence of God and of His Holy Angels, and in the salvation only to be found in the Church, "the Mother of us all". These beliefs were part of his life, only counterbalanced to some degree by his fear of the Devil and his agents, and by his credulous anxiety to do what he could to avert the evil eye or the machinations of some malign spirit. Whether his parish was served by a good or a bad parson, and whether his own faith was strong or otherwise, he could not resist the constantly recurring thought that he was living in a world in which these clashing forces of good and evil were ever at war—a war in which his own soul and eternal future was the stake. Few men, if pressed, would have denied this; and, as it coloured the whole of their thought, so we, in our turn, must try to see the medieval peasant living under its dominating shadow.

GLOSSARY

affeer. To settle the amount of an amercement, to assess.

assart. A piece of forest or waste, converted into arable by grubbing up the trees and brushwood.

assize of bread and ale. The statutory regulation or settling of the price of bread and of ale, with reference to that of grain, in accordance with the ordinance of 51 Henry III.

balk. A ridge left between two furrows, or a strip of ground left unploughed as a boundary line between two ploughed portions.

boon-work. A day's work, given gratuitously to a lord by his men on a special occasion.

"Borough English." The name of a form of land-tenure whereby a man's property descended to his youngest son.

bovates. An ox-gang, or as much land as an ox could plough in a year; varying in amount from 10 to 18 acres according to the system of tillage.

chevage. An annual payment made to a lord by each of his unfree tenants.

court-leet. A court held periodically in a lordship or manor, before the lord or his steward, having jurisdiction over petty offences and the civil affairs of the district.

croft. A piece of enclosed ground, generally adjacent to a house, used for tillage or pasture.

curtilage. A small court, yard, or piece of ground attached to a dwelling-house, and forming one enclosure with it.

customal. A written collection or abstract of the customs of a manor.

dooms. Judgments or decisions made formally by the suitors or the jury of the Manor Court.

essoin. The allegation of an excuse for non-attendance at a court at the appointed time.

extents. The formal recitation and valuation of the various lands of a manor, and also of the services, rents, profits, etc. of the same.

eyre. The circuit court held by the justices in eyre (Lat. *in itinere*, on a journey).

fire-bote. The wood granted to the tenants by a lord for the purpose of fuel.

frank-pledge. The system whereby every member of a tithing (q.v.) was answerable for the good conduct of, or the damage done by, any one of the other members.

— *view of.* A court held periodically for the production of the members of a tithing, later of a hundred or manor.

gavelkind. The name of a form of land-tenure whereby a man's property was divisible among his sons.

gersuma. A fine paid to the lord on entering upon a holding.

gestum. A guest's portion: an allowance of meat and drink.

Gules of August. The first day of August.

haye-bote. The right to take wood or thorns for the repair of fences granted to the peasant by the lord.

hayward. A manorial officer having charge of the enclosures, especially in haymaking or harvest times.

heriot. The surrender of the best live beast or dead chattel of a deceased tenant due by custom to the lord of whom he held.

Hock Day. The second Tuesday after Easter Sunday; in former times an important term-day, on which rents were paid, Hock-day and Michaelmas dividing the rural year into its summer and winter halves.

homage. A body of persons owning allegiance, and attending a manorial court.

hous-bote. The right of a tenant to take wood from his lord's estate for the repair of his house.

infangenethef. Jurisdiction over a thief apprehended within the lord's manor; the right of a lord to try and amerce a thief caught within his manor.

medale. A drinking festivity after the lord's meadows had been mowed.

medkniche. A haymaker's fee, viz. as much hay as the hayward can lift with his middle finger to his knees.

merchet. A fine paid by a servile tenant to his lord for liberty to give his daughter in marriage.

messor. An official appointed to oversee the manorial reapers or mowers.

messuage. A portion of land occupied as a site for a dwelling-house and its appurtenances.

mortuary. A customary gift (usually the second best animal) paid to the parish priest from the estate of a deceased parishioner.

naifty. The state of being born in bondage or serfdom.

nativi. Persons of servile birth.

outfangenethef. The lord's right to pursue a thief outside his own jurisdiction, bring him back to his own court for trial, and keep his forfeited chattels on conviction.

pannage. The payment made to the lord for the privilege of feeding beasts in the woods about the village.

pinfold. A place for confining stray or impounded cattle, horses, etc.; a pound.

pittancer. An officer of a religious house who had the duty of distributing charitable gifts or allowances of food.

pone. A writ, whereby an action could be removed from the county court into the royal court.

pytel. A small field or enclosure; a close.

rebeck. A musical instrument, having three strings, and played with a bow; an early form of the fiddle.

reeve. A manorial official, usually of servile status, appointed to oversee the general working of the manor.

sake and *soke.* A right of jurisdiction claimed by some manorial lords.

seisin. Possession.

selions. A ridge or narrow strip lying between two furrows formed in dividing an open field.

sheriff's tourn. The turn or circuit made by the sheriff of a county twice a year, in which he presided at the hundred-court in each hundred of the county.

stinting. Limiting, especially the rights of pasture.

suit of mill. The obligation of tenants to resort to a special mill (usually that of their lord) to have their corn ground.

tallage. A tax levied by a manorial lord upon his unfree tenants.

tally. A notched stick, which was split in two, one half being kept by the seller and the other half by the receiver.

tithing. A company (originally) of ten householders in the system of frank-pledge.

tithingman. The chief man of a tithing.

toft. The site of a house and its outbuildings.

virgate. A measure of land, varying greatly in extent, but very frequently averaging 30 acres.

week-work. Work done for the lord by his bond-tenants so many days a week.

ABBREVIATIONS AND AUTHORITIES

ABBREVIATIONS

E.E.T.S. Early English Text Society.
E.H.R. English Historical Review.
R.S. Rolls Series, Chronicles and Memorials.
V.C.H. Victoria County Histories.

AUTHORITIES

This list makes no pretence to bibliographical completeness, but endeavours to record the principal authorities consulted and quoted in this volume.

Manuscript materials

Abbots Langley. Halimota tenta apud Langele (28 Hen. III–51 Ed. III). Sidney Sussex College, Cambridge. MS. Δ. 1. 1.

C.R. Court Rolls preserved in the Public Record Office.

Ely Rolls. Rentals, Accounts, etc. preserved in the Muniment room of the Bishop of Ely. (Ely Diocesan Registry.)

Min. Acc. Ministers' Accounts, preserved in the Public Record Office.

Rentals and Surveys. Rentals and Surveys, preserved in the Public Record Office.

U.L.C. University Library, Cambridge, Manuscripts in.

Printed materials

A.A.S.R. Associated Architectural Societies' Reports and Papers. Lincoln, 1867– .

Addy. S. O. Addy. *The Evolution of the English House.* (Social England Series.) 1898.

Alphabet of Tales. An Alphabet of Tales in Northern English, from the Latin. Ed. Mary M. Banks. (E.E.T.S. Original Series, 126, 127.) 1905.

Ambresbury Cust. Rentalia et custumaria Michaelis de Ambresbury, 1235–52, et Rogeri de Fora, 1252–61. Ed. T. S. Holmes. (Somerset Record Society.) 1891.

Ancient Deeds. Ancient Deeds in the Public Record Office, Descriptive Catalogue of, 1890–1900.

Ann. Dunst. Annales prioratus de Dunstaplia. Ed. H. R. Luard. (Rolls Series.) 1866.

Arch. Journ. Journal of the British Archaeological Association. 1845– .

Ashley, *Bread.* Sir W. J. Ashley. *The Bread of our Forefathers, an inquiry in Economic History.* Oxford, 1928.

Ashley, *Econ. Hist.* Sir W. J. Ashley. *Introduction to English Economic History and Theory,* vol. I. (Ninth impression.) 1913.

Ault. W. O. Ault. *Private Jurisdiction in England.* (Yale Historical Publications.) New Haven, 1923.

B.N.B. Bracton's Note Book. Ed. F. W. Maitland. 1887.

Ballard. *British Borough Charters,* 1042–1216. Ed. A. Ballard. Cambridge, 1913.

Banstead. H. C. M. Lambert. *History of Banstead.* 1912.

Baskervill. C. R. Baskervill. *Dramatic Aspects of Medieval Folk Festivals in England.* (Studies in Philology, Vol. XVII.) 1920.

Battle Cust. Battle Abbey, Customals of. Ed. S. R. Scargill-Bird. (Camden Society.) 1887.

Bed. Hist. Rec. Soc. Bedfordshire Historical Record Society. Aspley Guise, 1913– .

Benham, *Red Book. The Red Paper Book of Colchester.* Transcribed and translated by W. G. Benham. Colchester, 1902.

Bensington. M. T. Pearman. *History of the Manor of Bensington.* 1896.

Bilsington Cart. The Cartulary and Terrier of the Priory of Bilsington, Kent. Ed. N. Neilson. (Records of the Social and Economic History of England and Wales, vol. VII.) Oxford, 1928.

Black Book Aug. The Register of St Augustine's Abbey, Canterbury, commonly called the Black Book. Ed. G. J. Turner and Rev. H. E. Salter. (Records of the Social and Economic History of England and Wales, vol. II.) Oxford, 1916.

Bleadon. The customal of Bleadon.... Ed. E. Smirke. (Royal Archaeological Institute of Great Britain.) 1851.

Bloch. M. Bloch. *Les Caractères originaux de l'histoire rurale française.* (Instituttet for sammenlignende Kulturforskning, Serie B. XIX.) Oslo, 1931.

Blount. T. Blount. *Tenures of Land and Customs of Manors.* New edition by W. C. Hazlitt. London, 1874.

Bracton. *De legibus et consuetudinibus Angliae libri quinque.* Ed. Sir Travers Twiss. (Rolls Series.) 1878–83.

Bridges, *Northants. The history and antiquities of Northamptonshire.* Compiled from the manuscript collections of...J. Bridges by P. Whalley. Oxford, 1791.

Bristol and Glouc. Arch. Soc. *Trans.* Bristol and Gloucester Archaeological Society. *Transactions.* Bristol, 1876– .

Britton. *Britton: the French text...with translation.* Ed. F. M. Nichols. 1865.

Burton Cart. Abstract of the contents of the Burton Chartulary. Ed. G. Wrottesley. (Wm Salt Archaeological Society, Collections V, part 1.) 1884.

Cal. Charter Rolls. Calendar of the Charter Rolls, preserved in the Public Record Office, Henry III– . 1903– .

Cal. Close Rolls. Calendar of the Close Rolls, preserved in the Public Record Office, Edward I– . 1892– .

Cal. Inquis. Misc. Calendar of Inquisitions Miscellaneous (Chancery) preserved in the Public Record Office, 1219– . 1916– .

Cal. Pat. Rolls. Calendar of Patent Rolls preserved in the Public Record Office, Henry III– . 1891– .

Camb. Antiq. Soc. Proc. Cambridge Antiquarian Society. *Proceedings.* Cambridge, 1859– .

Camb. Hist. Journ. The Cambridge Historical Journal. Cambridge, 1923– .

Castlecombe. G. P. Scrope. *History of the Manor and Ancient Barony of Castlecombe.* 1852.

Catholicon. Catholicon Anglicum: An Early English Dictionary, 1483. Ed. S. J. Herrtage. (E.E.T.S. Original Series, 75.) 1881.

Charters Salis. Charters and documents...of cathedral, city and diocese of Salisbury. Ed. W. D. Macray. (Rolls Series.) 1891.

Chester Chartulary. The Chartulary or Register of the Abbey of S. Werburgh, Chester. Ed. J. Tait. (Chetham Society, vol. LXXIX, N.S.) Manchester, 1920.

Chester Rolls. Calendar of County Court, City Court and Eyre Rolls of Chester, 1259–1297. Ed. R. Stewart-Brown. (Chetham Society, Vol. LXXXIV, N.S.) Manchester, 1925.

Clare. G. A. Thornton. *A History of Clare, Suffolk.* Cambridge, 1928.

Clutterbuck. R. Clutterbuck. *The history and antiquities of Hertford.* 1815–27.

Col. Cart. Cartularium monasterii S. Johannis Baptiste de Colecestria. Ed. S. A. Moore. (Roxburghe Club.) 1897.

Corn Milling. R. Bennett and J. Elton. *History of Corn Milling.* 1898–1904.

Coventry Leet Book. The Coventry Leet Book. Ed. M. Dormer Harris. (E.E.T.S. Original Series, 134, 135, 138.) 1907–9.

Crawley. The Economic and Social History of an English Village (Crawley, Hampshire). N. S. B. Gras and E. C. Gras. (Harvard Economic Studies, XXXIV.) Cambridge, Mass. 1930.

Crondal Records. Records and documents relating to the hundred and manor of Crondal. Ed. F. J. Baigent. (Hampshire Record Society.) 1891.

Crowland Estates. The Estates of Crowland Abbey. A Study in Manorial Administration. F. M. Page. Cambridge, 1934.

Cumb. and West. Arch. Soc. Trans. Cumberland and Westmorland Antiquarian and Archaeological Society. *Transactions.* Kendal, 1874– .

Cunningham. W. Cunningham. *The Growth of English Industry and Commerce during the Early and Middle Ages.* 4th edition. Cambridge, 1905.

Cur. Regis Rolls. *Curia Regis Rolls, preserved in the Public Record Office,* Richard I– . 1923– .

Cust. Rents. N. Neilson. *Customary Rents.* (Oxford Studies in Social and Legal History, ii.) Oxford, 1910.

Cust. Roff. J. Thorpe. *Custumale Roffense.* 1788.

Cutts. E. L. Cutts. *Parish Priests and their People in the Middle Ages in England.* 1898.

D.S.P. The Domesday of St Paul's of the year 1222. Ed. W. H. H. Hale. (Camden Society.) 1858.

Dart. Pres. Assoc. S. A. Moore, *Rights of Common upon the Forest of Dartmoor and the Commons of Devon.* (Dartmoor Preservation Association Publications, i.) 1890.

Davenport. F. G. Davenport. *The Economic Development of a Norfolk Manor,* 1086–1565. Cambridge, 1906.

Delisle. L. Delisle. *Études sur la condition de la classe agricole...en Normandie au moyen-âge.* Évreux, 1851. Repr. Paris, 1903.

Denton. W. Denton. *England in the Fifteenth Century.* 1888.

Derby Arch. Soc. Derbyshire Archaeological and Natural History Society. *Journal.* London and Derby, 1879– .

Devon Assoc. Devonshire Association for the Advancement of Science, Literature and Art. *Transactions.* Plymouth, 1863– .

Dives and Pauper. Anonymous dialogue, probably by a friar of about 1400, printed by W. de Worde in 1496. It is not paginated, but divided into *commandments* and *chapters.*

Dugdale, *Warwick.* W. Dugdale. *The antiquities of Warwickshire, illustrated.* Coventry, 1765.

Dulwich. W. Young. *The History of Dulwich College.* 1889.

Dunstable Cartulary. *A digest of the Charters preserved in the Cartulary of the Priory of Dunstable.* Ed. G. H. Fowler. (Bedfordshire Historical Record Society, vol. x.) 1926.

Dur. Halmote Rolls. *Halmota Prioratus Dunelmensis,* 1296–1384. Ed. W. H. D. Longstaffe and J. Booth. (Surtees Society.) Durham, 1889.

Econ. Documents (Tawney). *English Economic history: select documents.* Compiled and edited by A. E. Bland, P. A. Brown and R. H. Tawney. 1914.

Econ. Hist. Supplement to the Economic Journal. 1926– .

Econ. Hist. Rev. Economic History Review. 1927– .

Econ. Journ. The Economic Journal. 1891– .

Eliz. Eng. Elizabethan England: from "A Description of England" by *W. Harrison.* Ed. L. Withington. N.D.

Eng. Farming. R. E. Prothero (Lord Ernle). *English Farming Past and Present.* 1912.

Essex Review. The Essex Review. 1892– .

Evolution Eng. Farm. M. E. Seebohm. *The Evolution of the English Farm.* 1927.

Eynsham Cart. Eynsham Cartulary. Ed. H. E. Salter. (Oxford Historical Society, 49, 51.) Oxford, 1907–8.

Eyre Kent (Seld. Soc.). *The Eyre of Kent,* 6–7 Edward II. Ed. W. C. Bolland. (Selden Society, 24.) 1910.

Eyton, *Shrops.* R. W. Eyton. *Antiquities of Shropshire.* 1854–60.

Festial. J. Myrk. *Mirk's Festial.* Ed. T. Erbe. (E.E.T.S. Extra Series, XCVI.) 1905.

Feudal Docs. Feudal Documents from the Abbey of Bury St Edmunds. Ed. D. C. Douglas. (Records of the Social and Economic History of England and Wales, vol. VIII.) Oxford, 1932.

Field Systems. H. L. Gray. *English Field Systems.* (Harvard Historical Studies, XXII.) Cambridge, Mass. 1915.

Fitzherbert. *The Book of Husbandry.* (English Dialect Society.) 1882.

Fitzherbert, *Abridgement.* A. Fitzherbert. *La Graunde Abridgement,* 1514.

Fleta. Ed. J. Selden. 1647.

Frideswide's, St. Cart. The Cartulary of the Monastery of St Frideswide at Oxford. Ed. S. R. Wigram. (Oxford Historical Society, 28, 31.) Oxford, 1895–6.

Gale, *Richmond. Registrum honoris de Richmond.* Ed. R. Gale. 1722.

Gascoigne. *Gascoigne's Theological Dictionary*...1403–1458. Ed. J. E. T. Rogers. 1881.

Glanvill. R. de Glanvill. *Tractatus de legibus et consuetudinibus regni Angliae.* 1673 edition.

Glas. Rent. Rentalia et Custumaria Monasterii beatae Mariae Glastioniae. (Somerset Record Society.) 1891.

Glouc. Cart. Historia et Cartularium Monasterii Sancti Petri Gloucestriae. (Rolls Series.) 1863–7.

Godstow Cart. The English Register of Godstow Nunnery. Ed. A. Clarke. (E.E.T.S. Original Series, 129, 130.) 1905–6.

Gomme. G. L. Gomme. *The Village Community.* 1890.

Gower, *Mirour. The Complete Works of John Gower,* vol. 1. Ed. G. C. Macaulay. Oxford, 1899.

Gower Surveys. Surveys of Gower and Kilvey. Ed. C. Baker and G. G. Francis. (Cambrian Archaeological Association.) N.D.

Gross. C. Gross. *The Gild Merchant.* Oxford, 1890.

Growth of Manor. P. Vinogradoff. *The growth of the Manor.* Oxford, 1911.

Guisborough Cart. *Cartularium prioratus de Gyseburne.* Ed. W. Brown. (Surtees Society.) Durham, 1889–94.

Hales Rolls. *Court Rolls of the Manor of Hales*, 1272–1307. Ed. J. Amphlett, etc. (Worcester Historical Society.) 1910–33.

Handlyng Synne. *Robert [Mannyng] of Brunne's Handlyng Synne* (1303). Ed. F. J. Furnivall. (E.E.T.S. Original Series, 119, 123.) 1901–3.

Hatfield's Survey. *Hatfield's Survey, A Record of the Possessions of the See of Durham.* Ed. W. Greenwell. (Surtees Society.) Durham, 1857.

Helmbrecht. *Peasant Life in old German Epics: Meier Helmbrecht and Der Arme Heinrich.* Trans. by C. H. Bell. New York, Columbia University Press, 1931.

Higham Ferrers. W. J. B. Ker. *Higham Ferrers and its...Castle and Park.* Northampton, 1925.

Hist. MSS. Com. *Historical Manuscripts Commission, Reports.* 1874– .

Hist. Teachers' Misc. *The History Teachers' Miscellany.* Ed. H. W. Saunders. Cambridge, 1922– .

Hodgson. J. Hodgson. *A History of Northumberland.* 1820–58.

Holdsworth. W. S. Holdsworth. *A History of English Law.* 3rd edition. 1922– .

Hone. N. J. Hone. *The Manor and Manorial Records.* (Antiquary's Books.) 1906.

Hugh, St. *Magna vita S. Hugonis episcopi Lincolniensis.* Ed. J. F. Dimock. (Rolls Series.) 1864.

Icklingham Papers. H. Prigg. *Icklingham Papers.* Ed. V. B. Redstone. Woodbridge, 1901.

Ingoldmells Rolls. *Court Rolls of the Manor of Ingoldmells*, 1291–1569. Ed. W. O. Massingberd. 1902.

Inquis. Non. *Nonarum Inquisitiones.* (Record Commission.) 1807.

Inquis. Post Mort. *Calendar of Inquisitions Post Mortem and other analogous Documents preserved in the Public Record Office*, Henry III– . 1904.

Jacob. G. Jacob. *New Law Dictionary.* 1761.

Jocelin of Brakelond. *The Chronicle of Jocelin of Brakelond.* Trans. Sir E. Clarke. 1907.

Kettering Comp. *Compotus of the Manor of Kettering*, 1292. Ed. C. Wise. 1899.

Kitchin. J. Kitchin. *Le Court Leete et Court Baron.* 1587 and 1651.

Kosminsky. E. A. Kosminsky. "The Hundred Rolls of 1279–80." (*Economic History Review*, vol. III, No. 1.)

— "Services and Money Rents in the Thirteenth Century." (*Economic History Review*, vol. V, No. 2.)

Lanc. Assize Rolls. *A Calendar of the Lancashire Assize Rolls.* Ed. J. Parker. (Lancashire and Cheshire Record Society, vols. XLVII, XLIX.) 1904.

Land Tenure Reports. *Reports from H.M. Representatives respecting the tenure of land in...Europe.* 1870.

Law Mag. *The Law Magazine and Review.* 1830– .

Leet Jurisdiction. F. J. C. Hearnshaw. *Leet Jurisdiction in England....* (Southampton Record Society, vol. v.) Southampton, 1908.

Letter Books. *Calendar of Letter Books of the City of London.* Ed. R. R. Sharpe. 1899– .

Levett. A. E. Levett. *The Black Death on the Estates of the See of Winchester.* (Oxford Studies in Social and Legal History, v.) Oxford, 1916.

Linc. Assize Rolls. *The earliest Lincolnshire Assize Rolls, 1202–1209.* Ed. Doris M. Stenton. (Lincoln Record Society.) Lincoln, 1926.

Lipson. E. Lipson. *The Economic History of England.* 5th edition, 1929.

Lit. Cant. *Literae Cantuarienses: the letter-books of the monastery of Christ Church, Canterbury.* Ed. J. B. Sheppard. (Rolls Series.) 1887–9.

Lives of Berkeleys. J. Smyth. *The Lives of the Berkeleys.* Ed. Sir J. Maclean. (Bristol and Gloucestershire Archaeological Society.) Gloucester, 1883–5.

London Plea Rolls. *Calendar of Plea and Memoranda Rolls...of the City of London, 1364–1381.* Ed. A. H. Thomas. Cambridge, 1929.

Luttrell Psalter. *The Luttrell Psalter,* with introduction by E. G. Millar. 1932.

Lyndwood. W. Lyndwood. *Provinciale.* Oxford, 1679.

Maitland, *Coll. Papers.* F. W. Maitland. *The Collected Papers of F. W. Maitland.* Cambridge, 1911.

Mamecestre. *Mamecestre: chapters in the early history of...Manchester.* Ed. J. Harland. (Chetham Society.) Manchester, 1861–2.

Manning. B. L. Manning. *The People's Faith in the time of Wyclif.* Cambridge, 1919.

Manydown. *The Manor of Manydown.* Ed. W. G. Kitchin. (Hampshire Record Society.) 1895.

Med. Cheshire. H. J. Hewitt. *Mediaeval Cheshire. An Economic and Social History of Cheshire in the Reigns of the three Edwards.* Manchester, 1929.

Med. East Anglia. D. C. Douglas. *The Social Structure of Medieval East Anglia.* (Oxford Studies in Social and Legal History, IX.) Oxford, 1927.

Med. Lore. *Medieval Lore from Bartholomew Anglicus.* R. Steele. (King's Classics.) 1905.

Med. Village. G. G. Coulton. *The Medieval Village.* Cambridge, 1925.

Melsa Chron. *Chronica monasterii de Melsa.* Ed. E. A. Bond. (Rolls Series.) 1866–8.

Mon. Exon. G. Oliver. *Monasticon dioecesis Exoniensis.* Exeter, 1846.

Morris. J. E. Morris. *The Welsh Wars of Edward I.* Oxford, 1901.

Myrc. J. Myrc. *Instructions for Parish Priests.* Ed. E. Peacock. (E.E.T.S. Original Series, 31.) 1868.

Neilson, *Ramsey.* N. Neilson. *Economic Conditions of the manors of Ramsey Abbey.* Philadelphia, 1898.

Norf. Antiq. Misc. *The Norfolk Antiquarian Miscellany.* Ed. W. Rye. Norwich, 1873–87.

Norf. Arch. *Norfolk and Norwich Archaeological Society. Journal of.* Norwich, 1847– .

North. Assize. *Assize Rolls for the County of Northumberland.* Ed. W. Page. (Surtees Society.) Durham, 1891.

Northants. Rec. Soc. Northamptonshire Record Society. *Publications.* Kettering, 1926– .

Norwich Records. *Records of the City of Norwich.* Ed. W. Hudson and J. C. Tingey. 1906.

Obed. Rolls S. Swithin. *Compotus Rolls of the Obedientiaries of S. Swithun's Priory, Winchester.* Ed. G. W. Kitchin. (Hants Record Society.) 1892.

Old Wardon: Cartulary of the Abbey of Old Wardon. Ed. G. H. Fowler. (Bedfordshire Historical Record Society, vol. XIII.) 1930.

Owst. G. R. Owst. *Literature and Pulpit in Medieval England.* Cambridge, 1933.

Oxford Hist. Soc. Oxford Historical Society. *Publications.* Oxford, 1885– .

P.Q.W. *Placita de Quo Warranto.* Ed. W. Illingworth. (Record Commission.) 1818.

Page. T. W. Page. *The End of Villainage in England.* (Publications of the American Economic Association, Third Series, vol. I, No. 2.) New York, 1900.

Paroch. Antiq. W. Kennett. *Parochial Antiquities attempted in the history of Ambrosden, Burcester* (Bicester), *etc.* Oxford, 1818.

Pecock's Reule. R. Pecock. *The Reule of Crysten Religioun.* Ed. W. C. Greet. (E.E.T.S. Original Series, 171.) 1927.

Pemb. Survey. *Survey of the Lands of William, First Earl of Pembroke.* Ed. C. R. Straton. (Roxburghe Club.) Oxford, 1909.

Piers Plowman. W. Langland. *The Vision of William concerning Piers the Plowman.* Ed. W. W. Skeat. Oxford, 1886.

Pollock and Maitland. Sir F. Pollock and F. W. Maitland. *The History of English Law before the time of Edward I.* 2nd edition, Cambridge, 1898.

Powell. E. Powell. *The Rising in East Anglia in 1381.* Cambridge, 1896.

Prompt. Parv. Promptorium Parvulorum sive Clericorum. Ed. A. Way. (Camden Society.) 1865.

Ramsey Cart. Cartularium Monasterii de Rameseia. Ed. W. H. Hart and P. A. Lyons. (Rolls Series.) 1884–93.

Ramsey Rolls. Court Rolls of the Abbey of Ramsey and of the Honor of Clare. Ed. W. O. Ault. (Yale Historical Publications, 9.) New Haven, 1928.

Reg. Grand. The Register of John de Grandisson, 1327–69. Ed. F. C. Hingeston-Randolph. London and Exeter, 1894–9.

Reg. Malm. Registrum Malmesburiense. Ed. J. S. Brewer. (Rolls Series.) 1879–80.

Reg. Pontissara. Registrum Johannis de Pontissara (Diocesis Wyntoniensis). Ed. C. Deedes. (Canterbury and York Society.) Oxford, 1913–24.

Reg. Roff. Registrum Roffense . . . illustrating the history of the diocese and cathedral of Rochester. Ed. J. Thorpe. 1769.

Reynolds' Reg. The Register of Walter Reynolds, Bishop of Worcester, 1308–1313. Ed. R. A. Wilson. (Dugdale Society, IX.) Oxford, 1928.

Rogers, *Prices.* J. E. T. Rogers. *History of Agriculture and Prices in England,* 1259–1400. 1866.

— *Wages.* J. E. T. Rogers. *Six Centuries of Work and Wages.* 1890.

Rossendale. G. H. Tupling. *An Economic History of Rossendale.* 1927.

Rotherfield. Catherine Pullein. *Rotherfield, the story of some Wealden Manors.* Tunbridge Wells, 1928.

Rot. Hund. Hundredorum Rotuli (Temp. Henry III and Edward I). (Record Commission.) 1812–18.

Rot. Parl. Rotuli Parliamentorum, 1278–1503. (Record Commission.) 1767– .

Savine. A. Savine. *English Monasteries on the Eve of the Dissolution.* (Oxford Studies in Social and Legal History, I.) Oxford, 1909.

Sée. H. Sée. *Les Classes Rurales et le Régime Domanial en France au Moyen Age.* Paris, 1901.

Seebohm. F. Seebohm. *The English Village Community.* 1890.

Selden Society. *Select Pleas in Manorial Courts.* Ed. F. W. Maitland. Vol. II.

The Court Baron. Ed. F. W. Maitland. Vol. IV.

Select Coroner's Rolls. Ed. C. Gross. Vol. IX.

Select Pleas of the Forest. Ed. G. J. Turner. Vol. XIII.

Som. Arch. Soc. Somersetshire Archaeological and Natural History Society. *Proceedings*. Taunton, 1851– .

Som. Rec. Soc. Somerset Record Society. *Publications*. 1887– .

South Wales. W. Rees. *South Wales and the March*, 1284–1415. Oxford, 1924.

Stapledon's Reg. The Register of Walter de Stapledon, Bishop of Exeter, 1307–1326. Ed. F. C. Hingeston-Randolph. London and Exeter, 1892.

State Trials. State Trials. 1809–28.

Statutes of the Realm. Statutes of the Realm, vol. I. (Record Commission.) 1810.

Stenton. F. M. Stenton. *Documents illustrative of the Social and Economic History of the Danelaw*. (Records of the Social and Economic History of England and Wales, vol. v.) Oxford, 1920.

Suff. Inst. Arch. Suffolk Institute of Archaeology and Natural History. *Proceedings*. Lowestoft, 1849– .

Suss. Arch. Soc. Sussex Archaeological Society. 1848– .

Suss. Rec. Soc. Sussex Record Society. *Publications*. 1902– .

Swinburne. H. Swinburne. *A briefe treatise of Testaments and Last Wills*. 1640.

Tatenhill. History of Parish of Tatenhill, Stafford. Ed. R. A. Hardy. 1907–8.

Templars Records. Records of the Templars in England in the Twelfth Century. Ed. B. A. Lees. (Records of the Social and Economic History of England and Wales, vol. IX.) Oxford, 1935.

Terrier of Fleet. A Terrier of Fleet, Lincolnshire. Ed. N. Neilson. (Records of the Social and Economic History of England and Wales, vol. IV.) Oxford, 1920.

Thatcham. S. Barfield. *Thatcham, Berks, and its Manors*. 1901.

Thoresby Soc. Thoresby Society. *Publications*. Leeds, 1889– .

Tooting Bec Rolls. Court Rolls of Tooting Bec Manor. Ed. G. L. Gomme. 1909.

Towneley Plays. The Towneley Plays. Ed. G. England and A. W. Pollard. (E.E.T.S. Extra Series, LXXI.) 1897.

Trigg Minor. J. Maclean. *The parochial and family history of the deanery of Trigg Minor*. 1873–79.

Tusser. Thomas Tusser. *His Farming in East Anglia*. Ed. D. Hartley. 1931.

Vale Royal. The Ledger-Book of Vale Royal Abbey. Ed. J. Brownhill. (Lancashire and Cheshire Record Society, vol. LXVIII.) 1914.

Villainage. P. Vinogradoff. *Villainage in England*. Oxford, 1891.

Wakefield Rolls. Court Rolls of the Manor of Wakefield, 1274– . Ed. W. P. Baildon, etc. (Yorkshire Archaeological Society Record Series, XXIX, XXXVI, LVII, LXXVIII.) 1901– .

Walter of Henley. Walter of Henley's Husbandry, together with an anonymous Husbandry, Seneschaucie, etc. Ed. E. Lamond. (Royal Historical Society.) 1890.

Whitaker, *Whalley*. T. D. Whitaker. *The history of the parish of Whalley.* 1872–6.

Whitby Cart. Cartularium abbathiae de Whitby. (Surtees Society.) Durham, 1879–81.

Wilkins, *Concilia*. D. Wilkins. *Concilia Magnae Britanniae et Hiberniae.* 1737.

Wilts Arch. Mag. The Wiltshire Archaeological and Natural History Magazine. Devizes, 1854– .

Winton Pipe Roll. Winchester, Pipe Roll of the Exchequer of the See of, 1208–9. Ed. H. Hall. (Studies in Economics and Political Science.) 1903.

Wm. Salt Soc. The William Salt Archaeological Society. *Publications.* Birmingham, 1880– .

Worc. Hist. Soc. Worcestershire Historical Society. *Publications.* 1893– .

Worc. Priory Reg. Registrum...prioratus beatae Mariae Wigorniensis. Ed. W. H. Hale. (Camden Society.) 1865.

Wroxall Records. Records of Wroxall Abbey. Ed. J. W. Ryland. 1903.

Wykeham's Reg. Wykeham's Register (1366–1404). Ed. T. F. Kirby. (Hampshire Record Society.) 1896–9.

Yeatman. J. P. Yeatman. *The feudal history of the county of Derby.* 1880.

Yorks Inquis. Yorkshire Inquisitions of the reigns of Henry III and Edward I. Ed. W. Brown. 1892.

INDEX

No attempt has been made to index the names of individuals or of separate manors, unless of considerable importance.

Christmas game, the, 262
Chroniclers, the, 34
Church, the medieval, Ch. I, *passim*,
Ch. XII, *passim*; attitude towards
death, 9, 31, 248, 321; desire for
Holy Orders by peasant and, 288,
289; heretics and, 321; holy-days
and, 6, 13, 106, 114 ff.; immorality
and, 246 ff.; mortuary claims by,
144; serfdom and, 281, 282; tithe
and, 330, 331; wills and, 248 ff.
Church furlongs, the, 329
Church services, "Ales" and the,
265, 266; "Crawling to the
Cross", 263; games and, 273;
going to, in Langland, 267; holy-
days and, 6 ff., 322; in Latin, 9,
323; irreverence during, 10, 11;
peasant's ignorance of, 9, 10, 323;
peasant's participation in, 11;
talking during, 11; Vespers, 13,
115
Churches (medieval), Ch. I, *passim*,
Ch. XII, *passim*; comparative
safety of, 322; impression made
by, 30, 322; instruction mainly
given in, 323; paintings in, 9, 32,
323, 324; rich and poor in, 8;
seating in, 8, 10; size and beauty
of, 4, 30, 322
Church-scot, 31
Churchyards, desecrated by animals,
7, 333
Cider, 108, 235, 236
Cirencester, Abbot of, seizure of
horse and corn by, 131; seizure of
millstones by, 132
Clearings, *see* Assarts
Clergy (parish), as agriculturalists,
33, 329, 330; education and
training of, 33, 326, 327; income
of, 16, 327; inefficiency of, 33, 325,
328, 332 ff.; immorality of, 160,
332 ff.; important part played by,
331, 335; instruction given by, 10,
33, 323; lowly origin of many, 9,
10, 288, 325, 326; poaching by, 93;
preaching by, 10, 33, 328; "worldly
offices" and, 187, 188, 329, 330,
333
Clerks, the lord's, 21, 65, 160, 187 ff.
"Close", the, 44, 51, 82, 95
"Close, the parson's", 329
Cloth, 160
Clothes, the peasant's, 185, 186

Cob buildings, 227
Cod, 184
Colchester, Red Paper Book of, 135
Commissioners of array, the King's,
120 ff.
"Common, right of", 56 ff., 89
Common appurtenant, 57
"Common fields", the, Ch. II,
passim, 43, 44, 66, 70, 79, 84, 217;
by-laws for, 49, 89, 213; composition of, 55; conditions on, 49, 51;
consolidation of holdings in, 49 ff.;
co-operation in, 44 ff., 80; diffi-
culties in working, 46 ff.; privileges
of holders in the, 52, 57; sub-
division of, 46; *and see* Selions
Commons, the, 31, 56 ff., 213, 217;
and see Inter-commoning
Community rights, 55, 56
Commutation of works and services,
68, 72, 103, 105, 183, 278 ff.,
280 n. 1; partial nature of, 284,
285; uncertain progress of, 280
Compoti, *see* Accounts
Compurgation, 212, 216
Conquest, the Norman, 72, 100, 239
Conscription of peasants, *see* Military
service
Cooking utensils, 232 ff.
Co-operation among peasants, 44 ff.,
51, 70, 80
Corn, defamed, 218
Coroner, 7, 197, 198, 205 n. 3, 303
Corpus Christi, festival of, 264, 273
Cottages, *see* Houses
Cottars, 63, 64 n. 1, 184
Coulton, G. G., *Social Britain*,
34 n. 2; *Ten Medieval Studies*,
330, 331; *The Medieval Village*,
43, 45, 139, 245, 269 n. 1, 281 n. 3
Counterpanes, 161
Court baron, 198, 219
— customary, 198
— Leet, 21, 195, 199, 200, 205, 307
— Rolls, 21 ff., 132, 149, 156, 160,
199, 220, 308; copy of, 221; num-
bers of, 205; published, 206;
record change of holdings, 251;
record exemptions, 242, 252, 253;
record names of fugitives, 296;
and see Manor Court
"Court of record", 198, 220, 310,
312
Courts, *see* King's Courts, Leet Court,
Manorial Court